Dynamics of Clipper ™

Dynamics of Clipper™

A Library for Software Development

Arthur Fuller

BUSINESS ONE IRWIN Homewood, Illinois 60430

Sponsoring editor: Susan Glinert Stevens, Ph.D.
Project editor: Jean Roberts
Production manager: Ann Cassady
Cover designer: Michael Finkelman
Printer: R. R. Donnelley & Sons Company

Library of Congress Cataloging-in-Publication Data

Fuller, Arthur.
Dynamics of Clipper.™

1. Clipper (Computer program language) 2. Computer software—Development. I. Title.
QA76.73.C23F85 1989 005.74 88–25654
ISBN 1–55623–131–8 (pbk.)

Printed in the United States of America

7 8 9 0 DO 6 5 4 3 2 1 0

Dedication

This book is dedicated to Ustad Zakir Hussain, tabla virtuoso and inspiration.

Acknowledgements

Without the help, encouragement and friendship of Peter Brawley, this book would not have been possible.

Others helped in important ways. I'd like to thank my brother David Fuller for bringing his design skills to the project; John Cardiff for his splendid copy-editing; Roger Clay, who read the first few chapters and told me it was worth finishing; and Ray Love, who helped in numerous ways.

I also owe a large debt to the technical support team at Nantucket Corporation, who spent considerable time, intellect and money keeping me supplied with beta versions, anomaly reports and knowledge. Finally, I owe a monumental debt to Dennis Dias, creator of DBU and an inspiration in Clipper programming. Several times now, Denny's code has sunk me into my chairback in awe. Thanks, Denny.

Software Trademarks

Clipper is a trademark of Nantucket Corporation.

dBASE is a trademark of Ashton-Tate Corporation.

Turbo C, SideKick Plus and TLINK are trademarks of Borland International.

Microsoft C and Microsoft Quick C are trademarks of Microsoft Corporation.

SNAP is a trademark of Walter J. Kennamer.

Genifer is a trademark of Bytel Corporation.

The UI Programmer and The Documentor are trademarks of Wallsoft, Inc.

SayWhat!? is a trademark of The Research Group.

Tom Rettig's Library is a trademark of Tom Rettig Associates.

Data-Based Advisor is a trademark of Data-Based Solutions, Inc.

NETLIB is a trademark of Communication Horizons.

BREEZE.LIB is a trademark of Logitek.

WordPerfect is a trademark of WordPerfect Corporation.

Brief and dBrief are trademarks of Solution Systems.

Table of Contents

Introduction and Overview

Professionals approach software development much differently than hackers, crackers, weekend hobbyists and most nine-to-fivers in corporate information centers and MIS departments. They know that with the right tools, application development can be a piece of cake. Therefore professionals write or buy the tools required to do the job — not just a particular application, but *all* applications.

Professional Clipper is more about the art of programming than it is about Clipper. You'll learn a lot about Clipper in the course of this book, but more important, you'll learn how to develop powerful software very quickly. We'll push Clipper, and probably your notions about database management, to the limit.

The Concept

In the course of this book we'll construct a powerful library for software development, which will become the center of your programming efforts in Clipper.

Before we can create it, however, we need to know what belongs in it. To determine our target, we'll foray into the world of application development, looking for similarities among the programs we write. Wherever we can, we'll generalize the tasks we must perform at the highest level possible. We're after the *highest* common denominator, not the lowest.

For some of you, this book is going to be a tour through a foreign land, so best you take a road map along. Map in hand, you are free to tour as your fancy strikes you.

Assumptions

Any writer on programming must make certain assumptions about the reader. The ones I made are outlined below.

You

You are familiar enough with dBASE to have grown dissatisfied with it. Either you are already using Clipper, or you're looking at this book to help you decide whether to begin.

You may work in an Information Centre or even manage one. You may work for a smaller firm as an applications programmer. You may be a consultant on your own who has turned a talent for dBASE programming into a Clipper-based livelihood. You may be a student in a dBASE course.

Even an expert Clipper programmer may find many useful things in *Professional Clipper*. The pressures of crisis can prevent even professionals from achieving the detachment necessary to devise an overall application scheme, then write the program modules necessary for a comprehensive development library.

The reader who will have most fun with this book, I suspect, is the dBASE user new to Clipper. To say the least, for such a person this book will be an eye-opener. More than that, the library of routines included here will provide a very quick start in accessing the full range of Clipper's powers.

I hope this book will prove a valuable investment to you, no matter which stage of Clipper programming you're at.

Hardware

First, I assume you have a hard disk and 640 KB of RAM. If not, close this book at once, run to your favorite hardware dealer and correct this gaping hole in your environment. Borrow from your parents if you must, but do it at once. You cannot program like a professional without a hard disk — it's that simple.

If there's money available, I strongly recommend an investment in lots of extra RAM. There are dozens of good boards available and I make no specific recommendation. Whichever board you choose, a couple of megabytes of RAM disk can significantly improve your turnaround time, to say nothing of your computing pleasure. As we step into the gigabyte-sized nineties, you can rest assured of at least one truth: no matter how much memory you buy, you'll soon want more.

Software

If you are a seasoned Clipper user, you are already well aware that it is only one of the suite of software tools you need in order to do your job effectively. For newcomers, I'll discuss how these tools help you, along with some of the capabilities of such tools. Depending on your style of programming, some tools are more useful than others. Given that this book advances an approach to programming, I'll mention some products which have proven useful to me.

Some of what I'll say is narrowed by the supporting software I happened to choose, and my remarks are not meant as a criticism of other similar tools. In other cases, I'll tell you flat out that if you don't buy this software, you need to be debugged. A RAM-resident editor, for example, cuts development time by at least 30 percent, while any of several excellent screen/code generators can save you almost as much time again.

A Top-Down Book

Of the books I have seen which attempt to present a library of routines to the user, most have taken an approach opposite to that taken here. Typically, they begin with the "atoms" of their library, then move on to show how these atoms combine to form molecules, and the molecules combine to form complete programs.

The irony of this approach is that most of its proponents also preach the philosophy of top-down structured programming. In an attempt to practise what I preach, I present a top-down book.

Professional Clipper begins with a (hopefully not too) theoretical discussion of the business of programming in Clipper. We arrive at several conclusions, then present a few atoms to show the style of programming. Almost immediately, we jump into applications.

Following a discussion of the purpose of each application, we examine its code in a top-down fashion, beginning with the application program itself, then its main branches, and finally to some of the key atoms comprising it.

This means that many of the most primitive and commonly-used functions are not presented until the end of the book, in the section appropriate to them. There are sections on string, date, numeric and logical functions, as well as on menus, file manipulation, memo fields, creating reports, and finally, on user and hardware interface.

Thus the book adheres to one of its own central tenets — that details should be hidden from view so the programmer can think about the problem at hand, at the level appropriate to it. Each block of code is as transparent as I could make it: you can go through it at any level you like, without losing the thread.

The down side to this approach is that to get any of the code presented here — your future library — running, you may have to do a lot of typing — much more than is apparent at first glance. The given application will call a function which may call two or three more, which may call others in turn.

The publisher and I discussed this problem as we set out on this project. Somewhat naively, I wanted to include floppy disks in the book. The publisher responded with a long list of reasons why booksellers hate such packages: bar-code readers, theft, damaged disks, re-mailing and more. In short, there are no disks in the book for excellent reasons which have nothing at all to do with programming.

Stealing from the Best

In computer programming, originality is extremely difficult to define. Many thousands of computer programs owe their sorting algorithms to the efforts of half a dozen men. Every relational database owes a large debt to Professor Codd, the original theorist of relational database management. Magazines such as *Data-Based Advisor*, books such as this, and a wealth of other sources of code and algorithms are available.

More than once, I have been reading a book on *Turbo Pascal* or C and realized that a given algorithm could easily be applied to Clipper programming. As you work through this book, you'll see that extensive use is made of arrays, and the techniques for processing arrays have often been lifted from works on other languages.

There's another level to this, the most superficial but perhaps the most important. This is the look and feel of the software. What should a program look like? What should its commands and their presentation be?

I point all this out simply to say that I make no claims to complete originality for the code in this book. Precisely the opposite, in fact. This code was written under the influence of some great software.

Pull-down menus, for example, have proven not only useful but valuable instructional tools. New users simply have to pull the menus down to get a bird's eye view of your program. This style of learning a program is increasingly popular. For this reason, I have used pull-down menus quite freely.

If you're going to steal, steal from the best. Take the pieces and solve problems with them. As for the routines in this book, nothing would please me more than seeing them in widespread use.

A Word on Coding Style

In the code presented here keywords are in upper case, field names are in mixed case, and everything else is in lower case. The code is blocked with an indent of three characters. Since blank space is irrelevant to Clipper and useful to us in terms of legibility, there is plenty of it. Finally, I admit to an occasional wisp of black humor in the naming of variables and functions.

If your standards differ, excellent, I'm not here to convert you. Go through all the source with your text-editor and change those things that offend you. On the other hand, if you have no standards, you need some. You might as well begin with these.

Coming Soon to a Monitor Near You

Basic Toolkit

We begin our excursion by developing several basic tools for software development. These include routines to open files and indexes, display messages, obtain input, draw boxes and so on.

Meta-Functions

Meta-functions, as their name implies, exist on a higher level than the functions in the basic toolkit. Chances are they exist on a higher level than *any* functions you've seen. These meta-functions include DO_IT() and PD_MENU(), a light-bar and pull-down menu system respectively. Both are independent of the menus they present, which means we can rely on them to perform *all* our menuing tasks. We simply decide whether a given program will rely on one or the other scheme, or both. Both routines more than display menus — they administer your entire program.

Two more meta-functions are THE_USUAL() and BROWSER(). Each addresses an entire style of program. These functions are programmed on the assumption that whatever you *always* have to do, you should *never* have to do. Because of their careful design, they are flexible enough to accommodate even highly complex and sophisticated demands.

In part, their power depends on a handful of conventions or rules. These rules limit you only in the most trivial sense — you must create certain variables; here and there you must name some functions in accordance with a pattern. What these variables contain and what the functions actually do are left to you.

At almost every point, THE_USUAL() and BROWSER() respond intelligently when information is missing. This allows you to do very little programming, yet still tap the resources in the library and create professional-looking applications. The default behavior of these functions is carefully considered, so that often they alone are enough to meet the requirements of an application. On the other hand the functions are flexible enough to permit, in fact to invite, customization to suit specific needs.

To call THE_USUAL() and BROWSER() successfully, you must do a little preparation first. Once we've cut our way through the jungle of generalities, we'll address these underlying assumptions, developing a master program template which you can use as the basis for future application development.

Whenever you use either of the meta-functions, a suite of powerful program modules comes into play automatically, providing the scaffolding for your program. On this structure you hang the particulars of the program you're writing. The structure bends and shapes itself to accommodate the specifics, retaining its overall control of events, no matter what the events.

Next we examine the resources underlying THE_USUAL() and BROWSER(). A typical function on this level is SEARCH(), which manages all your searching requirements — no matter how complex. This function also calls several more basic functions, one of which is ASK_FOR(), a completely generalized module capable of getting user input of any type and satisfying any conditions you care to supply. ASK_FOR() also calls several functions , one of which is SHADOWBOX(), which draws a box with a shadow behind it.

So it goes, and so we go, descending into the library level by level. You are free to delve into the code as far as your interest takes you. You may decide to put the library to work immediately, reading the code only as some particular function awakens your interest.

On the other hand, some people are sufficiently disturbed that they actually enjoy reading code, and you may be one of those. If so, you'll love Section 4, the complete function library. Its eight chapters present functions by category, with chapters devoted to arrays, strings, numeric, logical, date and time functions; and to the more general questions of interface, file-management and system-related tasks.

An Offer You Shouldn't Refuse

The code presented here comprises about 10,000 lines, in over 150 functions. Besides these, there are several example programs of varying complexity. In short, even touch typists have a formidable task ahead of them.

To all the usual problems in writing error-free code, we add the difficulties in translating it into a set of instructions for typesetting. Even if I could be absolutely confident that no bugs entered the typesetter, I could not be certain that typesetting did not introduce bugs or discrepancies of its own.

In other words, you can save yourself a couple of weeks of typing and hours of frustration, while also being sure of obtaining the most recent bug fixes, by sending directly to me for the code. The disks include all the source code in the book, both library functions and applications, and a .LIB file so you don't even have to compile the library code. Data files containing sample records are also included, so you can get the example programs running immediately. Just include the library in your link command, and all its resources are available at once.

The disks cost $29.95. Contact me at this address:

Dynamics of Clipper Library
Artful Applications
2 Bloor Street West
Suite 100-512
Toronto, Ontario
M4W 3E2

The source code presented here is a subset of the code available in ARTFUL.LIB, a Clipper library which includes source code to all the functions. This library is available for $99 from the same address.

Finally, I also run a bulletin board dedicated to Clipper programming, called eBBS. Membership on the board is $25 per year for individual programmers. The telephone number is (416) 538-3107. Purchasers of the *Dynamics of Clipper* source disks can obtain the latest updates and bug fixes directly by modem.

Want to Load and Go?

If you want to put the library to work with as little effort as possible, send for the source code diskettes. While you wait for the postperson, read the first few chapters, perhaps more than once. When the disks arrive, compile and link the programs BBS.PRG, SOFTWARE.PRG and MAGS.PRG, then take them out for a spin. You'll see the library in action, and glimpse the variety of situations it can gracefully address.

As you test-drive the applications, glance through the source code for each program. I think you'll be pleasantly surprised at how small each program is. The code is brief because the library does all the work: you just have to tell it what work to do.

Next, try your hand at an application based on THE_USUAL(). You could copy one of those presented, substituting new information (data files and screens) in the appropriate places. Alternatively, you could work from the templates supplied. Compile and link your program, then try to run it. If you have problems, you may have to browse the section on THE_USUAL() to locate the source of your difficulty. Since you only have to write four functions to call THE_USUAL() successfully, you should have no trouble locating any errors.

With the three example programs based on THE_USUAL(), you can observe how the function bends to accommodate the areas of difference between the applications. You'll also see that as soon as you understand how one of them works, you know how they all work.

Next, compile and link dCAT.PRG, which introduces window-based programming. Besides showing you how to do pannable, scrollable windows, this program illustrates the concept of a system or configuration file to shape the run-time behavior of your application.

Finally, compile and link O.PRG and its related source files (O*.PRG). O.EXE is an order-entry program based on the concept of smart windows. The code is quite short, but it relies on a fairly complex memory map of the data structures, so it may take you a while to grasp how it works. To write a smart-windows application, you probably have no choice but to read the section on DBEDIT() in entirety.

Want to Learn Clipper Inside Out?

Read the book in the order presented. Don't rush into writing any programs with it. Take your time. Consider some of the larger questions addressed in the first part of the book. Kick them around. Take issue with them if you like. Read the early chapters more than once.

Then compile and link the example programs BBS, SOFTWARE and MAGS. Play with them long enough to get a feel for the way the library functions work. Where you go from there, and in what order, is up to you.

If you want to look at the components of THE_USUAL(), dig into the next section. If you prefer to pause with the book while you knock together a program or two of your own, excellent. Alternatively, you may want to delve into the next section, on window-based programming, at once.

This is complex material, and although I have presented it as clearly and simply as I can, you may find it a steep climb. If so, compile and link the programs dCAT and O, then play with them. Try out all their commands, experiment with illegal entries, add some records of your own. Once you're familiar with their design, the code will make a lot more sense.

The last section of the book presents the source code to all the functions in the library, in groups according to purpose. You can exploit the full power of the library without ever reading through this code. If you prefer to know all the details of how the machine works, it's all there for you to study or modify to suit your needs.

The Library — A Brief Survey

Let's scan some of the major functions in the library. For convenience, they are arranged in groups according to data type or functionality. First, we have the *meta-functions* already mentioned.

Meta-Functions

- BROWSER — the foundation of the smart-windows style of program.
- DO_IT — a light-bar menu system which administers a program or sub-program, working from up to 3 arrays.
- PD_MENU — administers an entire program using a pull-down menu scheme. It remembers the last selections, executes the appropriate functions and regains control afterwards.

- THE_USUAL — a powerful file-maintenance routine capable of handling any number of tables in any relationship, multiple indexes, memo fields, custom functions and more.

Validation Functions

- EXIST — checks input for existence in a file, optionally executing a separate routine on success or failure of the search.
- FETCH — looks up a variable in a file and returns either a field or the result of a user-defined function.
- HELPFILL — checks input against a file. On invalid entry (including an empty field), it pops up a scrolling window displaying any field or expression, and returning any desired field. That is, you can display the company names while returning the account code. You can even apply a condition to the lookup table.
- LOOKUP — like FETCH but designed for use with VALID, so it returns a logical.
- MENU_REC — turns a table into a menu.
- NEXT — increments the key of the last record in a table, e.g. NEXT(Invoice_no).
- UNIQUE — ensures that input does not exist in a table.
- GET_RANGE — gets a range (lower and upper value) based on the current controlling index.

Array Functions

- ABLANK — fills an array with blanks mirroring the fields in a table.
- ACOUNT — returns the number of occurrences of a variable in an array.
- AFULL — returns the number of the first undeclared element of an array.
- AGET — GETs an array element at the specified row and column.

- AINDEX — fills an array with the active indexes.
- ALENGTH — returns the total length of an array of strings.
- ARRAY_DIR — creates a sorted array of filenames.
- AVALID — checks user input via an array of conditions.
- AEXIST — checks the existence of a variable in a file.
- ASAY — displays an array element at the specified row and column.
- ASEEK — searches an array for a value, then returns the corresponding value from a second array.

Date and Time Functions

- BOM — beginning of month.
- BOW — beginning of week.
- BOY — beginning of year.
- DATE_KEY — sets specified function key to system date.
- EOM — end of month.
- EOW — end of week.
- EOY — end of year.
- IS_LEAP — true if the specified year is a leap year.
- LDATE — returns long string date, e.g. "Monday, May 3, 1989".
- SAY_TIME — displays time (cursor off) at specified location.
- TDIFF — difference between two times.
- TIMER — times the execution of another function (optimizing aid).

- TNUM — returns a time expressed as a number of seconds.
- TSTRING — turns a number of seconds into a time string.

File-Oriented Functions

- BLANK — returns a blank of the field name passed.
- DB_OPEN — file-handler, opens all files/indexes in a program.
- CHK_DICT — combines DB_OPEN() with a file dictionary.
- DUST_1 — deletes/recalls the current record, on confirmation.
- DUST_EM — packs the current file.
- GET_FILE — creates a pop-up menu of filenames, returns selected name.
- GO_BOT — goes to the bottom of the current file.
- GO_TOP — goes to the top of the current file.
- GET_STD — a powerful, generalized add/update routine which executes intelligent defaults or any custom validations or behavior you may require.
- GET_DBF — a specialized version of GET_FILE.
- NEXT_REC — moves to the next record in a table.
- PREV_REC — moves to the previous record in a table.
- QUERY — allows the user to find virtually anything in a database.
- RPL — automates replacing fields with memory variables.
- SELE_SCR — allows the user to select among several screens.
- STAT_LINE — provides status information on line 24.
- XBROWSER — provides default functionality to routines based on BROWSER.

- TRANSFER — transfers data from one table to another, creating the target if necessary.

Interface Functions

- ASK_FOR — gets input from the user in a pop-up window sized automatically, displaying any message, receiving any data type, checking it against any desired conditions.
- BLINK — displays a message followed by 3 blinking dots, right-justifed, on line 24.
- BASIC_BOX — draws a box for use in BROWSER-based programs.
- CLEAR_GETS — clears pending GETs; a procedure to assign to a key.
- DRAW_BOX — draws every box of every type in every program.
- GEN_PIC — generates a picture statement according to an intelligent system of defaults.
- HEADER — centers the specified string in a box on lines 1 to 3.
- MSG — displays a message right-justified on line 24, with or without waiting, with or without blinking dots afterward, with or without an additional "press any key".
- POP_MSG — pops a message onto the screen, waits for a keystroke, restores the screen. The message may be one or several lines long.
- READ_IT — performs all READs in all programs.
- SHADOWBOX — draws a box with a shadow behind it, optionally displaying a header.
- SIGN_OFF — closes the files, displays your logo and says goodnight.
- SIGN_ON — clears the screen, displays your logo.
- SEARCH — administers all searching requirements in all applications, no matter how complex.

- WAIT — a procedure which waits for a keystroke (called by some other functions).

Logical Functions

- AND — returns true if all conditions or functions stored in an array return true.
- CASE_OF — translates input into one of a series of outputs. Equivalent to a DO CASE, but works as a function.
- IS_ARRAY — returns true if the parameter passed is an array.
- IS_BTW — determines if an input is between two boundaries.
- IS_CHAR — returns true if the parameter passed is character.
- IS_DATE — returns true if the parameter passed is a date.
- IS_DEF — returns true if the parameter passed has been defined.
- IS_DATA — returns true if the character input is alpha or numeric.
- IS_EVEN — returns true if a number is even.
- IS_FIELD — returns true if the parameter passed is the name of a field.
- IS_IN — returns true if a variable is "in" another. This function works with strings or arrays.
- IS_INT — returns true if the parameter passed is an integer.
- IS_KEY — returns true if the expression passed is an active index key.
- IS_LOGIC — returns true if the parameter passed is a logical.
- IS_MEMO — returns true if the parameter passed is memo.
- IS_NUM — returns true if the parameter passed is numeric.

- IS_OP — returns true if the string passed is open is a relational operator, e.g. is one of =, !=, <>,>, <, >=, <=, $, or !$. This routine is useful when parsing strings to separate operators from data.

- IS_OPEN — returns true if the file passed is open.

- IS_PHONE — returns true if the parameter passed is a valid phone number.

- IS_TIME — returns true if the string passed is a valid time.

- IS_TYPE — compares two inputs, returning true if they are the same data type.

- IS_VIRTUAL — returns true if the expression passed in is not a field. Protects against attempting to edit a virtual field (e.g. "qty*price").

- NOR — checks an array of conditions, returning true if any condition is false. Equivalent to Not Or

- OR — checks an array of conditions, returning true if any condition is true.

- UN_DEF — returns true if the parameter passed has not been defined.

- VERIFY — pops up any message with OK and Cancel buttons, returning true if OK is selected.

Memo Functions

- MEMO_POS — returns the field number of the next memo field, defaulting the starting position at 1.

- READER — reads a text file into a memo field, presenting a menu of filenames if none is passed.

- READ_MEMO — displays/edits a memo field in a pop-up window of the specified dimensions, defaulting if none are passed

- WRITER — writes a memo field to a disk file, prompting for the filename if none is passed.

- NOTEPAD — administers a generalized notepad, allowing the user to store information about anything yet search by subject etc..

Menu Functions

- CHOOSE — presents an on-the-spot menu of strings, returning the corresponding character from a string of characters. Useful for instantly translating user input in a data-entry routine.
- L_MENU — turns one or two arrays into a light-bar menu, using the second array (if passed) as messages. The display defaults to rows 0 and 2 with a graphic line between, unless row(s) are specified.
- MENU_ORD — presents a menu of the possible orders in which the current file may be viewed (based on the active indexes as well as record number order).
- V_MENU — presents a pop-up vertical menu in a box at the location specified, executing the appropriate function.

Numeric Functions

- COUNT_EM — counts the records in the current table, modifying its behavior slightly if a filter is in effect.
- KCOUNT — searches a child-file for records belonging to the current parent, returning the count. You may specify a further condition as well.
- LONGEST — returns the length of the longest element in an array of strings.
- MCOUNT — returns the number of memo fields in a table.
- XCOUNT — returns the number of active indexes in the current work area.

String Functions

- ALLTRIM — returns a string shorn of leading and trailing blanks.
- CENTRE — returns the column number at which to begin displaying a string.

- CHK_MARK — displays a check mark in place of true for a logical field.
- CRLF — returns CHR(13) + CHR(10). Useful for multi-line headers in reports.
- ENCODE — encrypts a string.
- EXPAND — double-spaces a string.
- FILLOUT — "fills out" a single-character into a string.
- LANG — a version of FILLOUT, oriented to language.
- LCHAR — returns the last character of a string.
- LPAD — pads a string with leading blanks to the specified length.
- LTOC — turns a logical into a character.
- MIDDLE — centers a string in the specified width, filling it out with blanks on either side.
- MAKE_STR — turns any input into a string.
- PAD — pads out a string with trailing blanks to the specified length.
- PROPER — forces proper case on input string.
- PASSWORD — asks for a password, checks it against legitimate entries.
- SEX — turns M/F into Male/Female.
- SIN — formats input according to Social Insurance Number convention (Canadian).
- SSN — formats input according to Social Security Number convention (American).
- STRINT — returns a trimmed string version of the input number.

System-related functions

- BELL — rings the bell.
- DOS — opens a DOS window, or runs the program whose name is passed.
- SET_PRN — handles printer control, using a data table to store codes.
- SET_SYS — sets various system flags such as CONFIRM.
- SYSCOLOR — handles all color-control tasks.
- TUBE — draws a show-biz series of boxes on the screen. You might like it for your sign-on.

Readers, Start Your Engines

Now you have an idea of the ground we're going to cover. Chances are, the tools you'll develop here will transform your approach to programming in Clipper, even if you've been at it a while. The routines themselves, while very useful, are the least this book has to offer. The approach, the pattern of analysis, is the real subject here, and once you've got it under your belt, you'll be able to tackle even the most difficult Clipper programming assignments.

Ready?

Chapter 1

Invisible Software

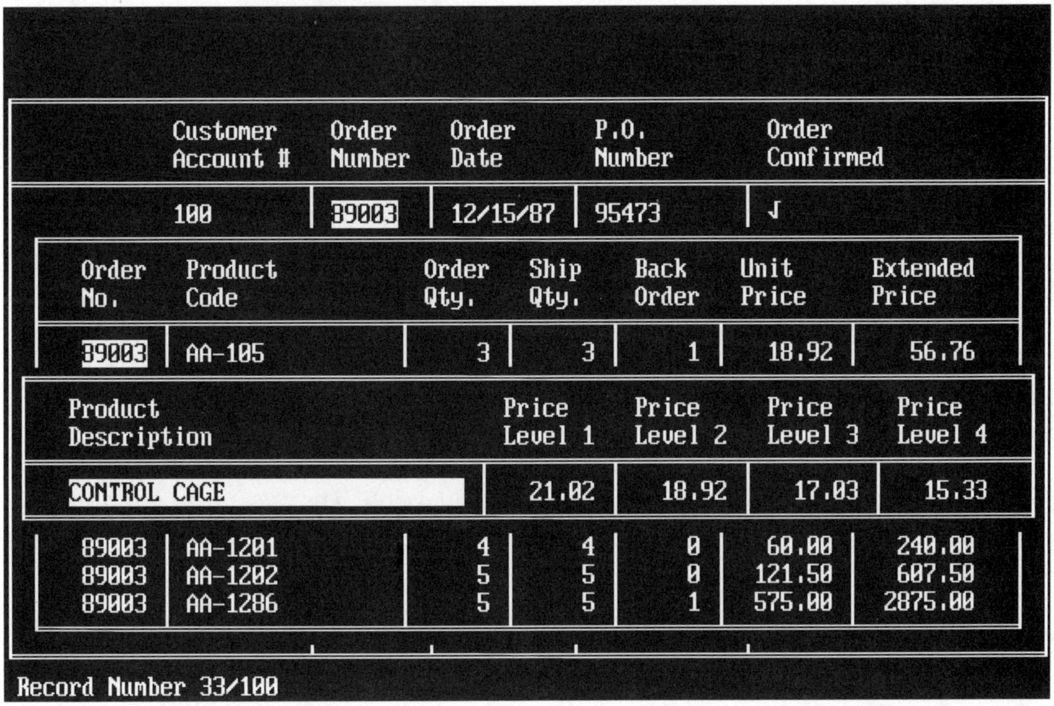

Invisible Software — the goal is to give the user an information window. Present information, not data, not menus, not limits.

The Death of Structured Programming

This chapter advances the notion (aesthetic might be a better word) of *invisible software*. It describes a philosophy and approach to software development that will transform the way you build applications.

Structured programming has been the guiding principle behind software development for a couple of decades now, and it is now painfully clear that it does not work. The classic method assumes that software can be planned down to its tiniest detail before writing a line of code. Life is not like that. Business is not like that. Why should software be like that?

The traditional answer is that without careful planning, a programmer can only flounder. True, as far as it goes; unfortunately, the evidence clearly shows that a programmer can flounder equally well *with* careful planning.

One fundamental difference between the micro arena and the mainframe world is the user. Very few people who use a microcomputer can write a batch file, but it does not follow that they are fools, any more than you were before you could write batch files. There is no excuse for contemptuous software.

Think back to your own first days on the box. The learning curve is astounding — every few days you double your knowledge base. As novices grow accustomed to software, their horizons expand profoundly. They see new areas in which software might help them. Our job is provide it.

In the business world, software evolves: we deliver software; users test it, returning with bug and enhancement lists; we deliver a new version. The cycle may continue for a long time. In the traditional view, this situation might be regarded as failure. In our view, this is success.

We need new design principles, more organic in conception than the rigid traditional scheme. It's as if we must design a house on the assumption that a new room might be added at any moment. *We must build in the certainty of change.* In the face of this formidable requirement, the old approaches are irrelevant. We need a new style of programming and new tools to assist us. This book describes the new style, and provides some of the tools for it.

A Philosophy of Programming

Input is a necessary evil — people buy systems for their output. The first task of database software is to provide speedy retrieval of any piece of information in the database, with a minimum of fuss.

Besides single facts, we often want reports of some kind. Some of them are automatic (i.e. the same from run to run, with only the contents varying); over other reports, we may want control of format (special headings, summary or detailed, etc.) and contents (sales staff from Chicago).

We also have to get the data into the files, of course. The routines to do this should either prevent the entry of bad data, or — arguably a better idea — permit it but flag the record as bad, so it can easily be found later for correction.

All good systems accomplish these tasks. The ideal system just performs them better. Ideally, the user of a system should have the ability to do anything at any time — to move from anywhere to anywhere in a keystroke or two, to undo any decision at the last moment, and even to control the way the software performs.

The Information Window

In a word, software should be *invisible*. From sign-on to sign-off, the user should have the feeling that there is no software there at all, no commands to learn, no menus to step through to get to where you want to go, not even data — only information. Information leads to other information — *not* to other commands or menus. Only a programmer would even argue the point.

The user's relationship with a computer should be similar to his or her relationship with a musical instrument — so intimate and automatic that it seems to both player and audience that the two are one.

As creators of software, our job is to bring about this relationship between our user and the computer. We have to make the computer invisible.

Our user should perceive *information*, not software. Several techniques can help us create this illusion: the speed of our program, its intuitive command syntax, our consistent use of screen areas, our placement of menus, and the obviousness of the choices we present. This book illustrates a number of these techniques, but fundamentally this is a decision, not a technique: you have to decide that software should be invisible, that it's worth the effort to provide an information window.

Software for Power Users

Power users *like* invisible software. In this lies an important lesson — it's time to recognize that idiot- friendly programs treat their users like idiots, and though they may not realize right away that they're being insulted, they soon enough will, and hate the software.

Data entry routines, for example, should be designed for speed, even if the actual traffic doesn't warrant it. If your program is designed to allow extremely rapid data entry, your users will soon catch up to you, never fear. You might, for example, include a routine which allows the user to assign strings of text to the function keys, saving the definitions in the system file. That way the user can decide what needs automating, and change his or her mind later.

If your design can guide a novice and also support the demanding expectations of the most skilled and knowledgeable user, the others can grow into it at their own pace, encouraged to do so by the software itself. Rather than insulting the users, your software will make them look good.

Sloth as a Design Principle

Our task is to deliver seamless and instantaneous information retrieval, flexible enough to accommodate varying user requirments. Our method is to create a system in which we send messages to objects, whose behavior changes depending on the messages.

We achieve this in several ways. One of the most important is through *granularity*, or the progressive reduction of a task to smaller and smaller components, until each component does only one thing.

Among the most important benefits of granularity is hidden detail. By hiding the details of each step in a process, you make each block of code more readable, to yourself or anyone else. This allows you to create at a higher level.

A second technique employed throughout the library is that of *indirection*. We strive to eliminate the literal — references to actual things (fields, memory variables, arrays, files) — from our code. Wherever possible, we pass parameters to functions, so the functions can "nickname" their objects, with private names for them known only to themselves.

A third technique is *separation.* A genuinely useful program atom is intelligent enough to check what kind of data was passed in before taking action. In a word, such a function is robust — it frees you to use it in a wide variety of situations, this time with a string, this time with an array.

Many of the functions presented in this book adapt as a result of their inputs. The required bulletproofing is built into the functions themselves, freeing you to use them in widely disparate situations, in complete confidence that they will work as expected.

All you have to do is remember what will result with different combinations of data. The functions are designed to let you pass only as much information as you wish. Intelligent defaults are built in where typically required, patterned on the assumption that you'll do less rather than more. The defaults are a product of the applications I have written, and may not fulfill your needs exactly — all the source code is here for you to revise as you wish.

The Birth of Re-Structured Programming

We want to retain all that is good about structured programming, yet center our efforts on events rather than data. The difference lies in the level at which the principles are applied. We'll design very flexible structures which combine into high-level event managers which work with almost no reference to the actual situation. Thus we'll be able to use them everywhere, without regard for file structures, indexes, screens and other trivialities.

When the time comes to enhance our programs, we'll be able to do it with almost no rewriting. Using this approach, we can develop powerful software *very* quickly — software built to handle the evolving requirements of business. For a change, you'll be able to make money in this game, instead of wondering why you didn't.

Chapter 2

The Clipper Compiler

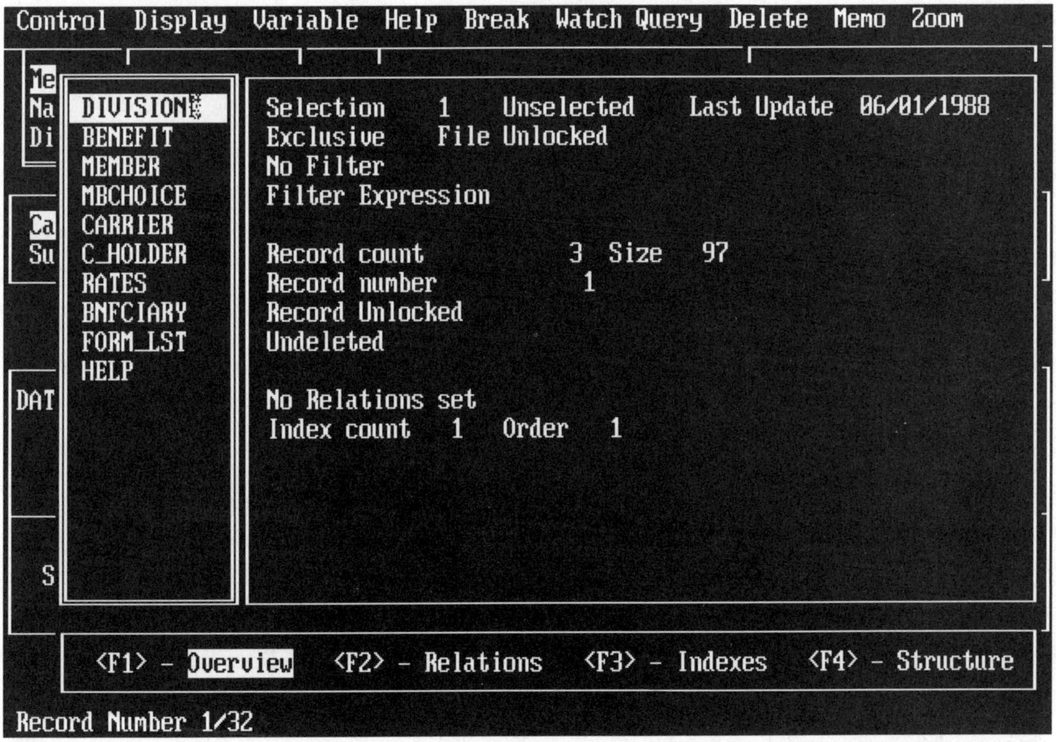

The Clipper debugging environment, with the *Display Database* window opened and the errant program underneath. Note the number of open tables. Thanks to HANDLES.OBJ, this program runs in versions of DOS prior to 3.3.

A Bit of History

In October, 1979, the first advertisement for Vulcan appeared in Byte magazine. Written by Wayne Ratliff, Vulcan was based on the mainframe language JPL/DIS but ran in the 64 K environment offered by CP/M. Shortly afterwards, Ratliff and George Tate struck a marketing agreement for the product, renamed to dBASE II after Harris Computing, which marketed an operating system called Vulcan, objected to Ratliff's use of the name.

One of the fundamental rules of marketing software was proved during these early days: win the power users and you win the market. Thanks to its simplified concept of database management and its built-in language, dBASE won the power users of CP/M. dBASE was within the grasp of serious but untutored micro users. On the strength of the power users' recommendations, dBASE became the standard database package for microcomputers.

dBASE II became dBASE III, III Plus and IV, Ashton-Tate swelled into one of the largest software development firms in America, and dBASE became the de facto business language for microcomputers — one of the most successful programs in software history. Millions of people use dBASE, and the most adventurous among them write programs in its language.

Somewhere along the way, however, Ashton-Tate lost its driving force. It was not the first firm to walk away with the market, then grow smug, and finally lose significant segments to upstart competitors; nor will it be the last.

After the initial release of dBASE III Plus, years passed without an update. Meanwhile, out in the trenches of corporate America, data files grew from thousands of records to hundreds of thousands — they grew almost as quickly as the expectations of their users. A new market arose: the high end of the dBASE market, chafing at the bit, itching for power to match their ambitions.

At the heart of dBASE's success lay its programming language — an interpreted language with a command-line mode. You could write programs in dBASE, but you could also issue commands right from the dot prompt. It seemed to be the best possible combination: you could experiment, trying commands one at a time until you got the flavor of the dialect; as you became familiar with the steps required to accomplish a task, you could write them all down and turn them into a program.

The greatest strength of the dBASE language turned out to be its greatest limitation. As it runs a program, dBASE reads in a line, scans it for syntax errors, then attempts to execute it. Once a program is bug-free, most of this work is redundant as well as time-consuming.

It was only logical, then, to think in terms of compiled dBASE. Unlike an interpreter, a compiler does not (usually) offer an interpretive mode: you write your program and feed it to the compiler; if there are no syntax errors, the compiler turns your source code into object code.

Object code is a kind of interim, not quite executable code since it lacks all the memory addresses it would contain as a program. The next step in the sequence is the link, which reads in all your object code, constructs a table and resolves all the addresses, writing your finished executable program to disk. Using a linker such as *PLINK86 Plus* (supplied with Clipper), *LINK* (supplied with DOS) or *TLINK* (supplied with *Turbo C*), you combine one or more object files with the library of Clipper functions.

Features

Clipper is a compiler. You can't try commands out one at a time with Clipper, as you can with dBASE. You must write a program, then compile it, then link it, and then (if you're anything like this author) debug it. At the end of the tunnel, you have a sparkling new program which runs many times faster than the equivalent program in dBASE. Clipper programs run so quickly that many observers mistake them for programs written in C and even in assembly language.

Brian Russell, creator and principal author of Clipper, wanted to write something more than a dBASE compiler. He began with a brilliant question: why not allow the user to write functions just as s/he could in a "real" language such as C or Pascal? The result is the *udf*, Clipper jargon for *user-defined function*. Brian did not stop there, however: he also included the Clipper Extend system, a bridge out of Clipper into C and assembler. Thanks to this access, numerous developers have marketed Clipper libraries written in C and assembler.

When you write in Clipper, therefore, you write in perhaps the richest application development language available for microcomputers. You are free to take Clipper in any direction you like, limited only by your imagination. Even if you cannot write in C or assembler, you can use the libraries to get you where you want to go. You say you want to write a BBS program? Several companies offer communications libraries. You want windows? Take your pick of libraries. You want complex scientific and statistical functions? Choose from a half-dozen packages. Networking? The NETLIB library lets you exploit networks to the maximum.

Even without the numerous third-party packages, however, Clipper remains a splendidly rich language. Particular areas of strength include file-handling, array processing, control over memo fields and above all, speed. Clipper delivers wonderfully fast application programs. Best of all, anything you can imagine, you can write a user-defined function to do.

Weaknesses

Clipper is also weak in several areas, most significantly in its huge RAM requirement. A Clipper program of any consequence demands at least 200 Kbytes of free RAM. This sticks in the craw of the programmer who arrives at Clipper by way of Pascal or C, whose programs often require only a tenth that much RAM. Clipper programs are large primarily due to a design decision made by Clipper's creators. They decided that any Clipper program would support the entire Clipper language. Therefore even a "hello world" program contains all the code for all the native functions and commands. To prove this, compile a simple "hello world" program and link the debugger into it. Call up the debugger and enter this expression:

```
SQRT(LEN(TRIM("HELLO WORLD    ")))
```

Your program can answer the question because SQRT(), LEN(), and TRIM() are included in its code, even though you didn't use those functions in your program.

Another area of significant weakness lies in Clipper's reporting "capability". Here and in other areas, Clipper's origins in the dBASE language work against it, and striving to preserve compatibility with dBASE has meant emulating that program's weaknesses. The dBASE label and report generators are laughable, and Clipper inherited them intact.

The serious Clipper programmer is well advised, therefore, to purchase a powerful report writer to go along with Clipper itself. The one I use is *Relational Report Writer*, a truly remarkable piece of software, and I recommend beginning your search there. Occasionally, you may encounter a report beyond the capabilities of *Relational Report Writer*. In the last year and a half of full-time programming, I have only encountered one such report specification.

A third area of weakness, particularly from the viewpoint of C or Pascal programmers, is Clipper's concept of inherited variables. This trait, another birthmark from dBASE, concerns the way Clipper treats memory variables. There are several different classes of memory:

Type	**Scope**
Public	the entire program
Private	the current function and those it calls
Unspecified	the current function and those it calls

The most potentially dangerous kind are unspecified, since you'll never know for sure how large the domain actually is. Far better to declare explicitly every variable you're going to use, at the top of the function in which it resides.

Whether you love or hate this behavior of Clipper, you should know that it occurs. If you're a C or Pascal programmer, be forewarned. It's simple enough to avoid any problems once you understand how Clipper scopes memory variables: just declare every variable you use Private at the top of every program.

Components of Clipper

The Clipper package comprises several files of various types. The compiler itself is CLIPPER.EXE. The linker supplied with Clipper is PLINK86.EXE, whose principal virtue is its ability to link overlays. To help manage your software development, a version of MAKE is supplied. For those unfamiliar with MAKE, it compares source and object files according to a dependency list, then automatically recompiles any programs which have changed since the last compile.

Clipper also comes with two libraries, CLIPPER.LIB (which contains all the "official" dBASE and Clipper keywords), and EXTEND.LIB (which contains Clipper-specific extensions to the language). Besides these, several object files are supplied which may be optionally linked into your Clipper program. The one you'll use most often is DEBUG.OBJ, the powerful Clipper debugger. I strongly suggest that you include the debugger in every program you create, leaving it in until you're ready to ship your program. Trying to debug software without it is as helpful as covering your monitor with a blanket.

Modular Programming

Clipper turned dBASE into a modular programming language. In doing so, it fundamentally changed the rules of dBASE programming.

Programmers already experienced in structured programming languages will immediately appreciate the full implications of this shift, but for many dBASE programmers Clipper is their first experience with a compiler.

For those readers, this section explores the concepts of modular programming, and attempts to illustrate how they transform your everyday programming behavior.

At the most general level is the world of your application program. Making it up are one or more procedure files, each handling some large purpose such as calculating the accounts receivable or maintaining a customer file. Each procedure file contains a number of procedures and/or functions which operate at the level of molecules. They in turn are made from commands, which correspond to atoms.

In Clipper, a function returns a value while a procedure does not. Depending upon your viewpoint, you either see a function as a procedure which returns a value, or see a procedure as a function whose return value is unimportant.

A couple of provisos here, deviations in Clipper from vanilla dBASE syntax. First, a Procedure file cannot contain a procedure or a function of the same name. Second, no Set Procedure command is required. (If you put one in, Clipper will simply ignore it.) Since your whole executable program will be in memory, Set Procedure is redundant.

We conceive the hierarchy of program components like this:

Component	Description
Application Programs	your main program
Procedure Files	not required, but often useful
Procedures	a throwback to dBASE code
Functions	our fundamental construction
Commands	the atoms of a program

Application programs perform a precisely defined task. They may combine several related tasks into a full-featured application, for example an order-entry program which handles inventory updates, form letters to customers, accounts receivable and re-order reports. Not every application program has to be full-featured, of course. Many are not.

Procedure files collect all the procedures related to one event or type of data. A procedure file for customer maintenance might contain routines to draw the screen, and to find, add, edit or delete records. These in turn may be further granulated - one block of code to load a record into memory, another to read the user's input, another to write the memory variables to disk.

Too many years invested in dBASE can make this final step painful and difficult. The limitations of dBASE (particularly the maximum of 32 procedures per procedure file) have ruled out complete granularity of code.

To get around this, most dBASE programmers have learned some bad habits such as copying blocks of code from one procedure file to another, then making minor changes to suit the new situation.

This approach effectively prevents any consideration of how the same block of code might handle both situations if passed the correct parameters.

Among the most important benefits of granularity is hidden detail. By hiding the details of each step in a process, you make each block of code more readable, to yourself or anyone else. Consider this simple function:

```
FUNCTION STRINT
PARAMETER number
RETURN LTRIM(STR(INT(number)))
```

Typically, this construction is used to format dates or numbers for printing, where part of the string is character data and another part numeric (i.e. November 15, 1989). More advanced dBASE users use the technique to fake an array (i.e. memvar&n). Whatever you do with it, with three pairs of parentheses for each use there are abundant chances for typos, eliminated in one stroke. Now whenever you need it, you simply write:

```
memvar = STRINT(number)
```

and you've got your character string, all trimmed and ready for use.

Programs undertake an action, rather than simply handing something back to us. That's not to say that functions cannot undertake actions - many of the functions in this book undertake considerable action. There's another way to look at the difference between programs and functions.

Functions, unfortunately, cannot be stored in a file of the same name. One way around this limitation is to create groups of functions and store them in what amount to procedure files, including them in your .LNK file for each application. This is the strategy suggested (by example, not explicitly) in the Clipper documentation.

The down-side to this strategy is its potential for fat code. All the functions you have requested will be included of course, but if one of these is in a source file which contains half a dozen others, the entire object file will be linked in, not just the function you requested. Your code is fatter than it needs to be.

Better to place each function in its own file, using a naming scheme that will readily identify the contents of each file. In the scheme employed here, all source files begin with the prefix "AA_", then conclude with a five-letter compression of the function name. For example, the function IS_DATE(), used to determine if a variable or field is a date, is contained in the file AA_ISDAT.PRG.

Functions behave like the dBASE functions you already know, such as TRIM() or MAX(). They return a value, as TRIM("waistline   ") returns "waistline". If that were the only difference, the choice between writing a function or a procedure would be arbitrary.

The unique power of a function is that it can be used in the middle of a line of code, and can even be nested. For example:

```
@ row, col SAY DTOC(DATE()) + ", " + AMPM(TIME())
```

Programs and procedures, in contrast, must be activated using the DO command, which means they occupy a command line of their own. They can take parameters, which gives you some flexibility, but you cannot write this:

```
@ row, col DO proc_name
```

The date-based example is trivial, and may not communicate the full significance of this difference. Let's try another example:

```
@ row, col GET mcust_code ;
VALID HELPFILL( mcust_code, ;
"Customer", ;
"company" )
```

With these parameters, HELPFILL() performs as follows. If the user types in a customer code, the function searches for it in the customer file. Finding a match, it returns true. Failing a match, it pops up a message to inform the user, waits for a keystroke, restores the screen and returns the user to the pending GET.

If the user presses F1 or Enter on a blank field, a window pops open allowing the user to scroll through the customer file, viewing the company names (the field company). When the user presses Enter, the corresponding customer code is stored into the variable cust_code, the screen is restored, and the READ continues on the next field — all in one function call. A screen with a half-dozen such lookups would require one line of code each.

HELPFILL() calls another library function, POP_MSG(). This function pops a message onto the screen, waits for a key, then restores the screen. Messages may have varying lengths, and may occupy more than one line of the screen. Also, you may want the message box displayed at a particular location. POP_MSG() takes these varying requirements in stride.

In the simplest case, you just want to let the user know you're waiting for a keystroke. Pass no parameters and the message popped is "Press any key". The next step up is a single-line message (along with the "any key" message). Pass a string. For a multi-line message, pass an array of strings. If the array contains more than eleven elements, POP_MSG() displays it single-spaced, otherwise it's double-spaced. In either case, POP_MSG() figures out how large a box to create, automatically centering it unless you also pass a row and column number. It also overrides impossible box locations and sizes. In short, it behaves. You can trust it.

A function may also occupy an entire command line, if you wish,and this quality turns out to be equally powerful. Early versions of Clipper insisted that you assign the result of a function to a variable:

```
throw_away = func(var1, var2, var3)
```

More recent versions dispense with the need to assign the return value. This command is quite acceptable:

```
func(var1, var2, var3)
```

Why is this so useful, particularly if you throw away the returned value? Consider this block of code:

```
x = "func( var_array )"
y = &x
```

In this case, as the variable x is macro-expanded, the function func() executes, placing its returned value in your variable y. Note that a slight change has occurred in the example. Clipper will not successfully execute this code:

```
x = "func( var1, var2, var3 )"
y = &x
```

Why? The commas are the killers — the moment Clipper arrives at the first comma, it thinks that's the end of the string, and thus attempts to execute only a portion of the command. As a result, the only parameter passed to your function func() is *var1*, while *var2* and *var3* are ignored. Hence the change in type of parameter passed, from a list of variables to an array. By changing the function func() to accommodate the arrival of an array, we can pass virtually anything to func(). If the need ever arose, we could even pass an array of arrays in the form of an array of array-names, macro- expanding them inside the function.

Few Clipper users have explored the concept of libraries, so a few words about them are in order.

As you know, Clipper comes with two libraries, CLIPPER.LIB and EXTEND.LIB. Besides these, a number of third- party libraries are available, *Tom Rettig's Library* or

Neil Weicher's *NETLIB* for example, which offer specialized functions not available within Clipper. Such libraries are typically written in C and/or assembly language. As a result, many Clipper programmers conclude that those languages are the only ones in which libraries can or should be created. Not so.

The library we'll build in the course of this book contains more than 150 functions, all stored in a single file. Imagine how much more difficult it would be to manage your hard disk if each library function were a separate file. The saving extends to disk space as well. No matter what kind of hard disk you have, it allocates space to files in blocks rather than the exact number of bytes required. Usually a block is 2 KB, so if you store a file containing only a single character, DOS saves that file with a 2000% airspace factor, like a single car in a shopping center parking lot.

The other important gain in using a library is conceptual. To gain access to every function contained in it, all you have to do is make the linker aware of the library. When the linker tries to put together your program, it reads the list of files to link, pulls all their object code into memory, constructing a table of procedures and/or functions. For each function it cannot find in your object files, the linker searches each library in the library list.

To a programmer who knows what to do with this freedom, it is a powerful gift. It means you are free to embellish the language to whatever extent you please. Any command you wish were a part of Clipper, you can add to Clipper yourself. All you do is write it, compile it, add the object code to your library, and then use it, just as if it were part of the Clipper language. You never need to concern yourself with trivialities and time-eaters such as specifically adding each function to your list of object files. Whenever you need a library function, you simply call for it as you would any Clipper command. The linker takes care of everything else. You thought you were writing programs, and it turns out you're writing a language.

Chapter 3

The Working Environment

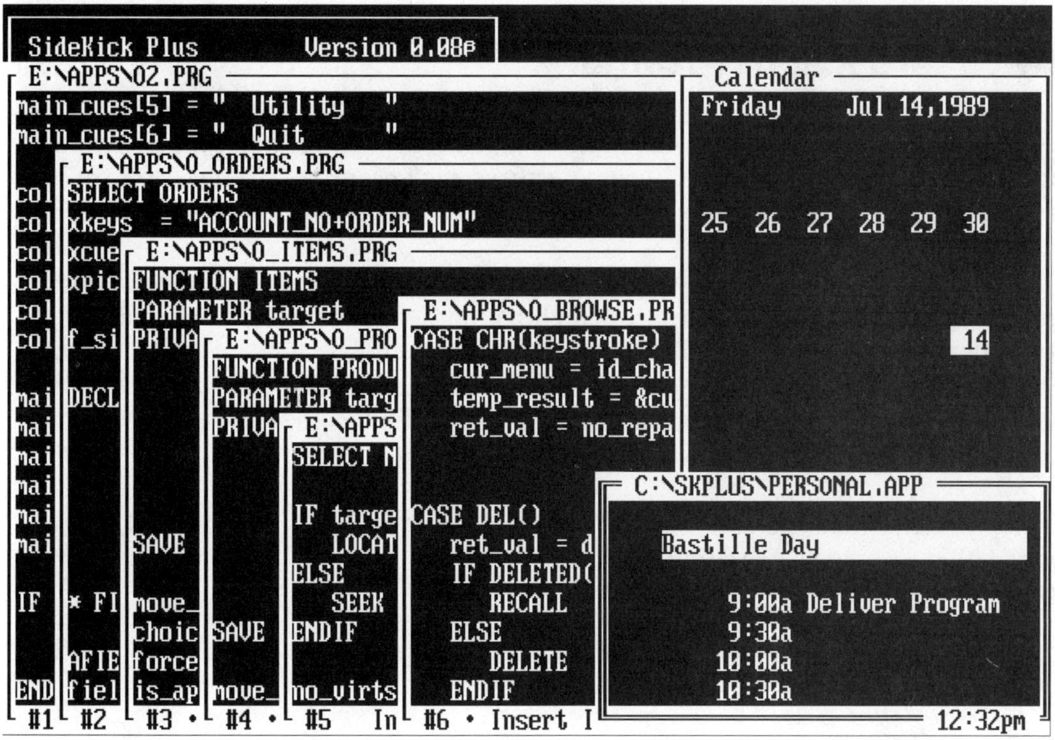

SideKick Plus optimized for editing source code — nine editors, a file manager, three outliners and a scheduler. The entire source code for O.EXE is loaded at once, with the executable running beneath SideKick Plus. It's difficult to imagine a superior programming environment.

The basic requirement of a professional Clipper programmer is a professional environment. Time is money, and a programmer's time is worth a considerable amount of money. A professional programming environment makes the most of a programmer's time. It begins at the software level and extends down into the hardware.

Grunts on Disk!

Clipper is only one component in your application development toolkit. It performs one of the essential tasks involved, but there are many essential tasks. All require specialized tools, and it is senseless to work without them.

Keyboard Macro Programs

A programmer without a keyboard macro program is working at half his or her potential productivity level, at best. Given how cheap such programs are, and how much of programming is repetitive, it is senseless to work without one.

The wonderful thing about keyboard macro programs is their ability to work with almost any other software you use. In combination with a text editor they can be truly formidable tools, reading in blocks of code from a template directory, typing dozens or hundreds of keystrokes for every one of yours, displaying pop-up help windows, and much more. The stylistic consistency of the code in *Professional Clipper* is due in large part to *SuperKey*, and is less work rather than more.

The program file headers, to cite only one example, are read in with one keystroke, which then prompts for program title, time-stamps the file, waits for parameters to be typed in, and more.

Text Editors

Even if I bothered to list all the programmer's editors available as I write this, by the time this book makes it into your hands there will be a dozen or two more.

Programmers seem to fall into two camps, those who favor RAM-resident editors and those who favor stand-alones.

For my money, the RAM-resident editor of choice is *SideKick Plus*, and at least for the moment I cannot imagine a better programmer's editor. Nine editors, nine outliners, a calendar expanded into a project scheduler, background communications and printing, a file manager resembling *Xtree*, and an ASCII table — all in RAM (or swapped to disk, RAMdisk or EMS) while you are writing or debugging your application: having tasted this, I won't settle for anything less.

The stand-alone editors bring different features to the party, many addressing *SideKick*'s most serious shortcoming, its extremely weak Undo command. Typically, stand- alone editors try to provide a programming environment, so you can run your compiler from within the editor, and jump directly to the appropriate source line in the event of a compiler error. The finest is *Brief*, whose most dramatic feature is nested undos (press Undo and your last change is negated; press Undo again and the change before that is negated). *Brief*'s programming language is a full-fledged language, with looping constructs, counters, conditionals, and even a macro compiler. An add-on package called *dBrief* is also available. Intended for dBASE programmers, the language overlap means that many of its capabilities are also useful to the Clipper programmer.

If the price of *SideKick Plus* places it out of range, consider Sammy Mitchell's program *QEDIT*, a shareware program available by modem from most bulletin boards. It boasts a pull-down menu interface, totally configurable keyboard, and as many windows as will fit into memory. *QEDIT* is extremely fast and occupies precious little RAM, but it offers no RAM-resident mode.

Whichever text editor you chose, make sure it is a text editor rather than a word processor. There's a world of difference between the two, and nothing around that does both jobs well.

Screen Painters

The problem with screen generators, especially the good ones, is that occasionally you look up and realize that for the past three weeks all you've been doing is drawing boxes!

The irony is, screens are the most trivial part of your applications. Even the screen generators that produce basic file maintenance code from the screens you draw are automating only the most banal portions of the final application.

That is precisely why a screen generator is essential. You have far too many things to do to be wasting time writing statements like these:

```
memvar = field
@ row, col SAY "Driver's License Number"
GET memvar
REPLACE field WITH memvar
```

In a real application, each of these statement types is typically an entire block of code, and if software can do it for you, splendid! Humans shouldn't be wasted on such things.

In the low-cost range, *SayWhat!?* stands out from the competition. It's very easy to use, generates code in a variety of languages, and includes both a screen-popping program and a light-bar menu system. As an added bonus, it can also be used in batch files, allowing you to knock together a gorgeous front end to your application in no time.

More sophisticated screen-generation programs include *The UI Programmer* and *Genifer*. *UI*'s 3-D screen-painting facility is a joy to use, it generates code in a variety of dBASE flavors, with or without calls to its screen- popper, and it provides a good template language you can tailor any way you please.

Genifer, written in Clipper (and thus an interesting example of the usefulness of Clipper to professional developers), takes a completely different approach, storing all your application specifications in a database. You maintain the application in exactly the same way as your end user will maintain his or her databases. In addition, *Genifer* includes a powerful report painter that writes code involving up to ten data files, with up to ten breakpoints. (I use both these products, and would part with neither.)

There are also shareware screen painters, available from many bulletin boards including *eBBS*, (the bulletin board mentioned in the Introduction and Overview). One of the nicest is Russell Freeland's *SCRIMAGE*, which works well, is easy to learn and very reasonably priced. Mr. Freeland also has a nice sense of humor, which makes his documentation more fun than usual.

Source Code Formatters

You also need a way of printing source code, whether or not such output is one of the deliverables in an application. You might think source files are enough, but they are not, for several reasons. Consider, for a moment, the prospect of your own smashing success. Suppose that the application you just completed reveals a bug in a few months, by which time half a dozen programmers are in your employ. Your system documentation should be good enough that a programmer who has never seen the source code before can grasp it quickly, and do the fix for you.

Unless you're a fanatic for comments, your source files alone won't be enough. The good source-printing utilities will enhance the appearance and readability of your code in several ways. Some print keywords in a different case from variables. Most will format your code according to your preferences, indenting each level precisely. Almost all can depict the flow of logic using graphic characters alongside the code, showing nesting levels, the destination of any EXITs, LOOPs, BREAKs and RETURNs.

Many of these programs will also print variable cross reference lists, and a few will even print flow charts of your application.

The competition in this category of utility is fierce, with dozens of companies at war for the spoils. Our needs are quite specific, and ironically a shareware program, *SNAP*, outperforms many of the commercial packages available. A particular strength of *SNAP* is its ability to recognize functions. At this writing, most of the commercial source code formatters lack this capability, though to be fair they make up for it in other ways. Far and away the finest of the commercial packages is Wallsoft's *The Documentor*, although it is also the most expensive. It provides very thorough system documentation, including formatted source, flow charts, cross reference tables and more.

Unfortunately, many of the code formatters are not geared toward advanced Clipper programming techniques. By asking several important questions, you can decide quickly whether a given formatter will be useful to you.

- Does the program allow user-definable keywords?
- Does the program recognize user-defined functions?
- Will the program accept a list of files to include in an analysis, rather than working from calls within each program?
- Will the program print file headers listing all functions and procedures contained in a given source file?
- Does the program allow separate control over the case and printing density of keywords, variables and text?

These capabilities will be indispensable in your Clipper programming. Think carefully before buying any product that does not offer them all.

C Compilers

Beginning with Summer '87, the Clipper development team moved from the Lattice C compiler to the Microsoft implementation. If you're planning to combine Clipper with C programs, you're therefore well advised to consider *Microsoft C*. You'll know from the outset that your object formats and floating-point routines will be compatible. If you don't yet own a C compiler but are interested in pursuing this avenue, you might try *Microsoft Quick C*. An added bonus is the LINK program that comes with *Quick C*. It's two or three times as fast as the old DOS *LINK* program.

The other major compiler in the market is Borland's *Turbo C*, whose speedy linker alone justifies the purchase price. The speed, however, comes at a price: it cannot link more than 128 program segments. Highly modular code often contains many more functions than 128, and virtually all complex programs do. No sooner do you fall in love with *TLINK* than you kiss it goodbye. That said, Turbo C is a good, low-priced compiler which generates Clipper-compatible code. An important qualification is that you cannot do floating-point calculations in a Turbo C routine destined for use in a Clipper program. If you want to do that, you must use the Microsoft product.

Third Party Libraries

One of the best reasons for programming in Clipper is the acknowledgement it has received in the form of third-party libraries. These include *Logitek's BREEZE.LIB*, which brings windowing capabilities to Clipper; *NETLIB*, which increases Clipper's networking capabilities substantially; *Tom Rettig's Library*, a collection of 300 functions written primarily in C and assembler. Several developers offer communications libraries, as well. If you make Clipper your business, chances are you'll need one or more of these. Many Clipper programmers buy them all.

Setting Up Shop

The hard disk arrangement suggested in the Clipper documentation is minimal, with everything in one directory. Fortunately, Clipper provides a number of flags on the command line to alter its behavior.

If you have already set up Clipper in a way that works well for you, excellent. If not, you may wish to consider setting it up along these lines, and use the batch files included here to simplify your relationship with the compiler, linker and library programs. You'll be dealing with six different classes of files. It's useful to create a directory for each of them, placing all files of that type there and setting the path and command line flags to play into this arrangement.

Directory Layout

File Type	Directory Location
executable files	\PGMS
batch files	\BAT
source files	\SRC
object files	\OBJ
library files	\LIB
data files and indexes	\app_name
link files	\LISTS

Why Manage Directories?

It makes sense to design your hard disk layout on the assumption that you'll be working on more than one program at once. In the event that you're working on only one, the system works, and in the event of success you're covered.

On this model, you set your DOS path to \PGMS;\BAT and whatever else your other activities require. Place Clipper, PLINK86 Plus and the other executables on the Clipper disks in the \PGMS directory. In addition, the linker will send your finished programs there.

The batch files that run your operation for you go in the \BAT directory.

Depending on the size and number of your applications, you may have more than one \SRC directory. Clipper compiles so quickly that you may come to regard .OBJ files as beneath backup, so even when working on several applications at once, you may send all the object files to a single \OBJ directory.

Store CLIPPER.LIB, EXTEND.LIB, your own library and any others you use in the \LIB directory, directing the linker to look there.

Finally you have the data directories, in which reside all data files, indexes and any other files germane to the application. It is important to separate the data from the program. At different times during the development process, the separation can work for you in different ways. Sometimes you'll want several versions of the program trained on a single data directory. Later on in development, when it's time to test batch updates and similar routines, it's useful to have several copies of the data on your hard disk. That way you lose the minimum amount of time recovering from small glitches.

The one optional item in this list of directories is the last, the \LISTS directory, which is only required if you link your programs using file lists rather than specifying them all on the command line. There are arguments both ways, and most programmers do it both ways. Linking from file lists is especially useful in complex programming projects, where you're stretching your knowledge. Having never faced a problem before, you may not know which of several options might be best. So you try several approaches, sharing as much code as possible and hiding the areas of difference in your file lists.

A Batch of Batch Files

Clipper provides several command-line options which produce slightly different files. From the viewpoint of structured programming, Clipper's default option is precisely the one we don't want, because it combines the named program and all those it calls into a single file. Much more useful is the - *m* parameter, which tells Clipper to compile this and only this module.

The batch files presented here assume the directories are named as suggested. If you want to give them different names, substitute them throughout the batch files and everything should work as expected.

Several of the batch files also call PUSHDIR.COM and POPDIR.COM, popular utilities widely available on bulletin boards. If you can't find them in the BBS's in your area, you can obtain them from *eBBS*.

Compiling Several Files at Once

To compile our source code, we'll use a batch file so that we won't have to enter all our command-line parameters every time we call Clipper. We almost never want the default parameters Clipper expects. We prefer that Clipper compiles the named module only, so we add the *-m* parameter. We want the object file output to go to our object directory, so we add the *-o* parameter. If you have a RAM disk available, you can add the *-t* parameter as well, instructing Clipper to write its temporary work files to your RAM disk.

While we're at it, we may as well overcome Clipper's inability to accept multiple file names in a single instruction. If you don't use loops in batch files, you may want to have a careful look at CL.BAT, absorb its technique and apply it in other batch files you write. Thanks to the loop, you can tell Clipper to compile about a dozen files in a single command, with each one resulting in its own object file, placed in the object directory.

```
ECHO OFF
REM I'm a compulsive timer. The line below calls Norton's TM.EXE
TM START
C:
:MORE
IF '%1'=='' GOTO NOMORE
CLIPPER \SRC\%1 -m -o\OBJ
REM Use this line instead if you have a ramdisk.
REM Change the drivespec to suit your machine.
REM The -t param tells Clipper to write its work
REM files to the named drive (D:)
REM CLIPPER \SRC\%1 -m -o\OBJ -tD:
SHIFT
GOTO MORE
:NOMORE
TM STOP
```

Updating a Library

The next batch file, UPD.BAT, exists in two versions, one for those who have *Marion the Librarian*, the library program that accompanies the Computer Innovations *C86* compiler, and another for those who will be using the DOS *LIB* program, which does the same thing less well. (Unlike *Marion*, *LIB* does not maintain checksums to guarantee the validity of the library modules.)

The *Marion* version of UPD.BAT lets you add up to a dozen or so modules to your library in a single command. (The limit is the length of the DOS command line.) The nice thing is, if the module already exists the previous version will be automatically replaced. It also makes invisible the fact that the object and library files are in different directories.

```
ECHO OFF
PUSHDIR
C:
CD \OBJ
IF '%1'=='' GOTO :NOARG
TM START
REM The next line allows you to update numerous modules at once.
MARION -ue \LIB\ARTFUL %1 %2 %3 %4 %5 %6 %7 %8 %9
GOTO :END
:NOARG
ECHO This batch file is used to update the Library
ECHO With it you can add or replace object files...
:END
POPDIR
TM STOP
```

The LIB version of UPD.BAT is less elegant but achieves the same result. Since LIB.EXE wants explicit instructions for each file passed on the command line, if you pass fewer parameters than anticipated the command line will have extraneous characters on it. Therefore it does a series of comparisons which determine how many parameters were passed, then goes to the appropriate command line. Note that the batch file does not accept an argument for a library, on the assumption that you'll always be updating the same library.

```
ECHO OFF
PUSHDIR
TM START
D:
IF '%5'=='' GOTO TRY4
LIB \LIB\ARTFUL -+%1 -+%2 -+%3 -+%4 -+%5,\LIB\ARTFUL.DOC;
GOTO DONE
:try4
if '%4'=='' goto try3
LIB \LIB\ARTFUL -+%1 -+%2 -+%3 -+%4,\LIB\ARTFUL.DOC;
GOTO DONE
:TRY3
```

```
IF '%3'=='' GOTO TRY2
LIB \LIB\ARTFUL -+%1 -+%2 -+%3,\LIB\ARTFUL.DOC;
GOTO DONE
:TRY2
IF '%2'=='' GOTO JUST1
LIB \LIB\ARTFUL -+%1 -+%2,LIB\ARTFUL.DOC;
GOTO DONE
:JUST1
LIB \LIB\ARTFUL -+%1,\LIB\ARTFUL.DOC;
:DONE
POPDIR
TM STOP
```

Removing a Library Module

LOSE.BAT deletes one or more modules from your library. The name of the library is hard-coded, since you'll usually work on only one.

```
ECHO OFF
TM START
LIB ARTFUL -%1,E:\LIB\ARTFUL.DOC;
TM STOP
```

Linking with Lists

L.BAT invokes the DOS linker rather than *Plink86*. The DOS linker is considerably faster, and as long as you're making *.EXE* files, it's most often better to use it. Of course, the moment your programs get large enough to demand overlays, you have to forget about the DOS linker. L.BAT assumes that you've made your file lists.

```
ECHO OFF
REM This batch file calls LINK to create an executable file from an
REM object-file list in the \LISTS directory and the list of
libraries you use,
REM contained in \LISTS\ARTFUL.LST
TM START
IF '%2'=='' GOTO DBUGGER
LINK D:%1,C:\PGMS\%1,,@\LISTS\ARTFUL.LST  /SE:1024 /NOE
GOTO END
:DBUGGER
```

```
LINK %1 DEBUG,\PGMS\%1,,@\LISTS\ARTFUL.LST /SE:1024 /NOE
:END
TM STOP
```

Linking with Overlays

Try as we might to avoid it, occasionally applications are so large as to demand overlay structures. The increase in link time is substantial — four or five times that of the DOS linker and ten times that of *TLINK*, but at that point we have no alternative to *Plink86+*. For those occasions, PL.BAT links the files listed in a *.LNK* file stored in the \LISTS directory.

```
ECHO OFF
IF '%1'=='' GOTO :NOARG
TM START
PUSHDIR
C:
CD \OBJ
PLINK86 @\LISTS\%1
GOTO END
:NOARG
ECHO This batch file calls PLINK86 to link files
ECHO listed in a ".LNK" file in the current directory.
ECHO You must supply a filename for the Linker to work.
:END
POPDIR
TM STOP
```

Linking with TLINK

The batch file TL.BAT calls *TLINK* to link one program module with whatever it requires from the libraries.

```
ECHO OFF
REM Remark out one or the other of the next two commands.
REM The first call assumes no ramdisk.
TLINK \OBJ\%1,\PGMS\%1,,@\LISTS\STANDARD.LST
REM The second assumes a RAM disk called Drive D:
TLINK D:%1,C:\PGMS\%1,,@\LISTS\STANDARD.LST
REM The file STANDARD.LST contains your library list:
```

```
REM   D:CLIPPER D:ARTFUL D:KEYS D:EXTEND
TM STOP
```

TLINK with Lists

It's handy to have a second version of this batch file, which links a list of files. Its second parameter allows you to override the default list of libraries to suit special purposes.

```
ECHO OFF
TM START
IF '%2'=='' GOTO STANDARD
REM otherwise override the standard list of libraries, using %2
REM
TLINK @\LISTS\%1,\PGMS\%1,,@\LISTS\%2.LST
GOTO END
REM
:STANDARD
TLINK @\LISTS\%1,\PGMS\%1,,\LIB\LISTS\STANDARD.LST
:END
TM STOP
```

Compiling Without Line Numbers

Once you're satisfied that an application works as intended, you'll do one more compile to remove the line numbers. This compile, while not strictly necessary, cuts the resultant executable down by about 10% of its size — three bytes per line. In a 250 KB application, this matters. Pass a wildcard filespec to TIGHTEN.BAT and it will compile all matching files without line numbers.

```
REM Arguments: this module only, no line numbers, quietly,
REM send output to \obj
FOR %%X IN (%1) DO clipper %%X -m -l -q -o\obj
TM STOP
```

Summary

Clipper is the most important software in your toolkit, certainly, but it is only one component in a suite of essential tools for software development. At this point, your hard disk should be laid out in a way that works well for you; your suite of software tools should be available on the directory path so that you can call it from anywhere; and most important, you should understand what a library is, why it's useful, and how to maintain one.

We now have everything in place for professional database development. Our assembly line is ready, so to speak. It's now time to consider what we're going to do with it.

Chapter 4

Core Tools

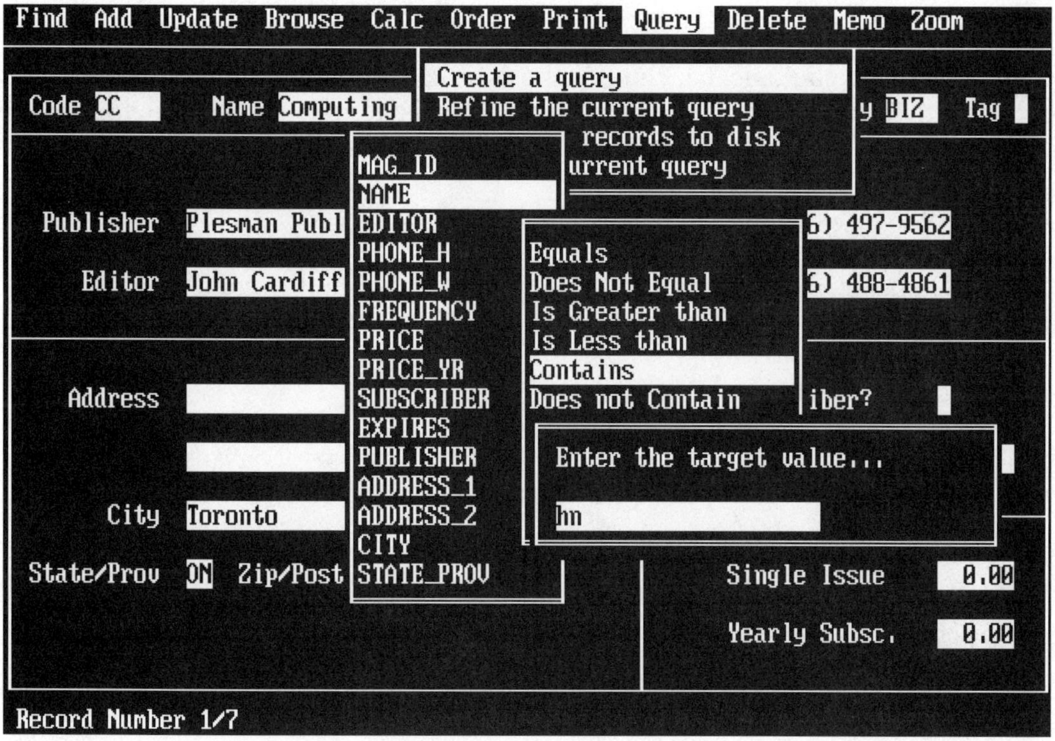

The function QUERY() at full extension. Depending on the user's selection, it will either loop or SET FILTER TO the resulting specification. At all points, ACHOICE() prevents inappropriate selections.

In this chapter we'll create several more of our more common library functions so that when you see calls to them, you'll have an idea what they do and how they do it. We'll begin simply, and quickly multiply the capabilities. We'll develop functions to draw a box, display a message, and ask for user input. Then we'll develop two more powerful functions: DB_OPEN(), which will perform all our file-handling tasks, and QUERY(), a generalized query facility which extends the power of any application, providing its users with the means to ask virtually any question about the contents of a file.

How to Draw a Box

Other things being equal, users prefer a program that looks good to one that does not. Users like boxes. They lend an aura of stability to a program, and used correctly they can provide a psychological anchor for the user. A box routine is a perfect candidate for a generalized function. Rather than hard-coding boxes into other functions, we can localize all such activities in a single function call, and use it everywhere.

DRAW_BOX() takes six parameters, one more than Clipper's BOX command, and accepts a number rather than a string as the fifth parameter. Rather than clutter our code with graphic strings in BOX commands, we move all the graphic strings we'll ever use directly into the DRAW_BOX() function — the only place we'll ever need them.

Sometimes we want to clear the screen before drawing a box, sometimes not — which explains the sixth parameter passed to DRAW_BOX(). It's optional and may be of any data type. Pass anything as parameter six and the screen will clear before the box appears.

We have several choices as to how we might store the graphic characters. We could create separate variables for each one, or declare an array and fill it with the types of boxes we want. Either of these approaches results in too many lines of code for such a simple task.

Instead we create a single character variable containing all our box strings, then use the box number as a pointer into the string. This type of offset calculation is common enough, especially once you learn to rely on arrays extensively, that it's worth noting the formula:

```
pointer = (box_no - 1) * length + 1
```

When the box number is 2, the first character of the box string is in position 9. When the box number is 4, the pointer points at character 25.

```
PROGRAM        AA_DRBOX.PRG
Function(s)    DRAW_BOX()
Purpose        Generalized box routine
Conventions    box types are numbered internally.
               Optional clear-screen parameter.
               Does not check validity of the parameters
Syntax         DRAW_BOX(r1,c1,r2,c2,box_no,clear_it)
Parameters     r1 - top row
               c1 - top column
               r2 - bottom row
               c2 - bottom column
               box_no - see below. Defaults to 11
               clear_it - any value causes screen to clear first
Example        DRAW_BOX(04,10,16,66,03)
Assumes        valid parameters
Side Effects   could crash with bad parameters
Returns        True always
Calls          SCROLL()
```

```
FUNCTION DRAW_BOX

PARAMETERS Top, Left, Bottom, Right, Border_no, Clear_scr
PRIVATE box_chars, bptr, box_str
IF TYPE("Border_no") != "N"
   Border_no = 11
ENDIF
boxchars = "ZD?3YD@3IM;:H:UM83MT3VD7:=DS:\\\[___[\\\^___]"+;
           "[[[[[[[[22222222111111110000000ZD?3MT3        "+;
           "BDB3MT3"
bptr = (box_no - 01) * 08 + 01
box_str = SUBSTR(box_chars, bptr, 08)
IF TYPE("Clear_scr") != "U"
   CLEAR
```

```
ENDIF
IF Border_no != 0
   SCROLL(Top, left, bottom, right, 0)
   @ Top,left,bottom,right BOX box_str
ENDIF
RETURN .T.
```

An increasingly popular box style is the shadow box, which creates a three-dimensional effect, lifting the contents of the box "above" the underlying screen. The next routine draws this kind of box, adding to it the capability of displaying a box heading as well. Note the way it compensates for the addition of a header.

```
PROGRAM        AA_SHBOX.PRG
Function(s)    SHADOWBOX()
Purpose        Draws boxes with a shadow behind them
Conventions    pass dimensions of the box you want, not
               the shadow
Syntax         SHADOWBOX( tr, tc, br, bc, hd, box_no )
Parameters     tr - top row
               tc - top column
               br - bottom row
               bc - bottom column
               hdr - string to use as header on box
               box_no - numeric, passed to DRAW_BOX()
Example        SHADOWBOX(08,15,20,65,"Shadow Box",03)
Assumes        nothing
Side Effects   bad data may cause crash
Returns        True always
Calls          POP_MSG(), SYSCOLOR(), SETCOLOR(),
               DRAW_BOX(), MIN(), MAX()
```

```
FUNCTION SHADOWBOX

PARAMETERS tr, tc, br, bc, hdr, box_no
IF TYPE("tr") != "N"
   RETURN POP_MSG("No parameters were passed")
ENDIF
IF TYPE("box_no") != "N"
   box_no = 03 && see DRAW_BOX() for string
ENDIF
```

```
IF TYPE("hdr") != "C"
   hdr = ""
ENDIF
tr = MAX(01, tr)
tc = MAX(01, tc)
br = MIN(22, br)
bc = MIN(78, bc)
br = IF(!EMPTY(hdr), br + 01, br)
SYSCOLOR(01)
DRAW_BOX(tr, tc, br, bc, box_no)
IF !EMPTY(hdr)
   SYSCOLOR(02)
   @ tr + 1, tc + 1 SAY MIDDLE( hdr, bc - tc - 1)
   SYSCOLOR(01)
ENDIF
IF TYPE("monochrome") = "U"
      monochrome = .F.
ENDIF
shadow = IF(monochrome, "", " ")
cur_color = SETCOLOR( "W/N" )
@ tr + 1, bc + 1, br + 1, bc + 1 BOX shadow
@ br + 1, tc + 1, br + 1, bc + 1 BOX shadow
SETCOLOR(cur_color)
RETURN .T.
```

Suppose you decide that all your warning messages, say, should have a new box style. If you have developed a style for your program and remained consistent with it, all you'll have to do is change the graphic string in function DRAW_BOX(), recompile and update the module in your library. As you re-link each program, the change ripples throughout.

A Word on Glitz

One of the most obvious giveaways of amateur software is glitz. Boxes and windows explode unpredictably, with no overall concept knitting them together. Everything is a different color, often with no relationship between the color and the status of the object painted.

Glitz alone is bad enough, but it invariably leads to maintenance complications. Where there is glitz you'll almost always find color assignments hard-coded in the routines, and then you *know* something is wrong.

In almost every case, less is better than more. Confine yourself to about four colors. When you draw a box, don't just pick a new box number each time. Consider the program in its entirety. Ask what place the given routine occupies in the scheme of things. Don't use the same box style for warnings and simple data displays. You'll only confuse your users.

Consistency at this level is one of the subtle, effective differences between professional software and amateur or student software.

How to Talk to a User

Throughout your programs you'll send messages to your users. One of the most common is "press any key to continue". There are other messages, however. They reduce to three groups:

- Error Messages, such as "File xyz is missing. Cannot continue without it".
- Working Messages, whose purpose is basically to tell the user that the computer has not malfunctioned. "Indexing file xyz."
- Result Messages, such as "I cannot find Customer xyz", usually specify bad results (if the program had found Customer xyz it would have displayed the record.)

Each group has a few variants, of course. Sometimes we want to halt the program until we get a keypress; other times we don't want a keypress but would like a blinking effect so the user doesn't think the program has hung; sometimes we need a "Press any key" message to accompany another message; and sometimes we just want the lowest common denominator, "Press any key".

In keeping with our strategy, we'll answer all of these requirements with a single function called MSG(). It handles all the messaging requirements of every program in this book.

Our strategy is fairly simple. We pass a varying number of parameters to activate switches within the function. Pass nothing at all and the result is the classic "Press any key". Pass a message and it is displayed, right-justified, on line 24.

There are three possibilities now. First, we do not want to wait for a keypress. Second, we want a keypress and a message saying so, in addition to the message we passed. Third, we don't need to say "Press any key", it's obvious from the context.

To implement this we pass a second parameter, a number from zero to three. Zero signifies no wait, one activates the "any key" message, and two waits without the message.

Looking over the code, you may wonder about two decisions. Given that only two values are used, why not use a logical rather than a numeric parameter? Second, and related, why the CASE statement for two cases, why not an IF? In a word, planning for the future. As other conditions arise that I did not anticipate, I can pass higher numbers and modify the code to deal with them, preserving the syntax. With a CASE statement rather than an IF, the modifications are minimized — just add a new case.

As users of *1-2-3* are well aware, blinking an entire message gives users headaches, not information. We are more ergonomically sensitive, and subtle too. We blink three dots after the message, and leave the message alone.

I hope this program covers all the messaging requirements you commonly encounter. If you do have others, just expand the CASE statement to include them.

```
PROGRAM      AA_MSG.PRG
Function(s)  MSG()
Purpose      General message service
Conventions  line 24 is used for these messages
Syntax       MSG(string, wait, blink)
Parameters   string - message to display,
             defaults to "Press any key"
             wait - 0 = no wait, 1 = wait
             blink - add 3 blinking dots to string
Example      MSG("Working",0,.T.)
Assumes      line 24 is the message area, right justified
Side Effects none
Returns      True always
Calls        ALLTRIM(), SYSCOLOR()
```

```
FUNCTION MSG

PARAMETERS message, number, blinking
```

```
PRIVATE    temp, row, col, sp, dots
temp = PCOUNT()
ak_msg  = " Press any key "
row = 24 && bottom line of the screen
sp = " "
dots = "..."
IF TYPE("message") != "C"             && press any key + dots
      message  = ak_msg
   number   = 01
   blinking = .T.
ENDIF
IF TYPE("blinking") = "U"             && default to no dots
   blinking = .F.
ENDIF
IF TYPE("number") != "N"              && default to no wait
   number = 00
ENDIF
message = sp + ALLTRIM(message) + sp + ;
         IF(number  0, ". " + ak_msg, "")
IF blinking
   col = (77 - LEN(message))          && account for dots
ELSE
   col = (80 - LEN(message))          && right-justify
ENDIF
IF !blinking
   SYSCOLOR(02)                       && reverse video
ENDIF
@ row, col SAY message
SYSCOLOR(01)                          && back to normal
IF blinking
      BLINK(dots, ROW(), COL())
ENDIF
IF number > 00
   DO WAIT
   @ row, col SAY SPACE(LEN(message))
   result = .T.
ENDIF
RETURN LASTKEY() = 27
```

How to Get What You Want Out of Users

One of our most common programming tasks involves prompting the user for input, then doing something with it. Typically we also want to be aware if the user pressed Escape or simply pressed Enter without typing in data, since we'll often want to trap these possible errors before proceeding.

ASK_FOR() illustrates another of our fundamental concepts: functions should be as versatile as possible, allowing us to pass different types of data to them without causing them to crash. As applied here, what we want to do is separate the prompting message and the type of data requested from the routine itself.

The separation is achieved by passing parameters: the display prompt, the variable to read, and the picture to use while reading it. From this information, ASK_FOR() figures out what to do. In this way, a single routine will do all our work, regardless of what type of data we're prompting the user for.

Before charging into it, let's consider what else can happen when we're asking the user for data. A common occurrence is validation of the input in some way; the types of validation that might occur are about as plentiful as applications. Let's pass an optional fourth parameter, a character string containing any desired validation instructions.

Note that this program calls a function called CENTRE() (to distinguish it from the CENTER() function supplied with Clipper). Not surprisingly, CENTRE() is used to center a string on the screen. It returns the column number at which to begin the display.

The question arises, where to display our prompt and GET variable, and how to keep this information separate from the routine itself. We can pass row and column numbers, either for both items or just for the SAY, using the construct:

```
@ row, col SAY string GET memvar
```

There are abundant complexities here: too many. This makes the problem into an ideal candidate for a pop-up window, which would free us completely from the underlying screen. It won't matter a whit what the screen looks like. With this approach, all we'll have to do is save the screen, figure out how large to make our window, pop it onto the screen, grab the user's input and restore the screen. Simple.

One thing to note about ASK_FOR() is its use of the PCOUNT() function, which returns the number of parameters passed to a procedure or function. Given our stated goal of writing functions to which a variable number of parameters can be passed, PCOUNT() becomes one of our most relied-upon Clipper tools.

Immediately upon entering ASK_FOR(), we grab the value of PCOUNT() and store it away. We do so at once because somewhere within our function we may want to call another function, which action would replace the value of PCOUNT() with some new number.

You'll see a lot of PCOUNT() in the pages that follow. Whenever we need to, we'll be grabbing its value for future reference, then using it to determine what should occur in a given function.

Note the simple technique of dealing with the problem of a variable number of parameters. We check each one in turn to see if it was passed, and if not, supply a default. This eliminates the problem, and all subsequent testing for parameters. Now we *know* they all exist, and can act accordingly. Thus we issue a single GET command, complete with PICTURE and VALID clauses.

```
PROGRAM       AA_ASK.PRG
Function(s)   ASK_FOR()
Purpose       Prompts the user for data
Conventions   pops up a box containing your msg_str,
              accepts data into memvar using pict_str,
              with optional validation using val_str and
              optional override of EXACT setting.
              Restores the screen after the READ.
Syntax        ASK_FOR(msg_str,memvar,pict_str,val_str,;
                   exact_on)
Parameters    msg_str - prompt string to display,
                   3 dots added to it automatically
memvar    -- initialized to correct data type
pict_str  -- defaults to GEN_PIC(memvar)
val_str   -- string containing valid condition
exact_on  -- default is OFF or false.
                   returns trim rather than entire memvar
                   pass anything as exact_on to set ON
Example       ASK_FOR("Enter a letter from A to F" ;
              memvar, "!", "memvar $ "ABCDEF")
Assumes       Calculates size of box according to the
              length of msg_str.
Side Effects  unpleasant cosmetics if msg_str is too long
Returns       memvar
Calls         PCOUNT(), CENTRE(), MAKE_STR(), DRAW_BOX()
```

```
FUNCTION ASK_FOR

PARAMETERS msg_str, memvar, pict_str, val_str, exact_on
CLEAR GETS
PRIVATE tr, tc, br, bc, add_space, ;
      pos, temp_scr, var_col, msg_col
IF TYPE("exact_on") = "U"              && nothing passed, go default
   exact_on = .F.
ENDIF
msg_str = TRIM(msg_str) + "..."
temp    = PCOUNT()
data    = TYPE("memvar")
msg_col = CENTRE(msg_str)
var_col = CENTRE(MAKE_STR(memvar))
tc      = MAX(0, MIN(var_col, msg_col) - 03)
bc      = 80 - tc
tr      = 05
br      = 12
IF TYPE("pict_str") != "C"
   pict_str  = GET_PIC(memvar)
ENDIF
IF TYPE("val_str") != "C"
   val_str  = ".T."
ENDIF
SAVESCREEN(tr, tc, br, bc, temp_scr)
SHADOWBOX(tr, tc, br, bc)
@ tr + 2, MSG_ = SAY msg_str
@ tr + 4, VAR_ = GET memvar ;
                 PICTURE pict_str ;
                 VALID &val_str
READ_IT()
RESTSCREEN(tr, tc, br, bc, temp_scr)
IF !exact_on .AND. TYPE("memvar") = "C"
   memvar = TRIM(memvar)
ENDIF
RETURN memvar
```

How to Give Users What They Want

The only reason to put data into files in the first place is to extract it later on. Not surprisingly, then, every program has some method of allowing the user to find records. The SEEK and FIND commands presuppose that the file in question is indexed, but it often happens that the file is indexed on more than one key. Rather than write an individual routine for each possible searching method, we follow our principle of generalization and abstract the process from its objects.

This is possible thanks in part to the SET ORDER command, which allows us to change the order of several indexes in use. Then we present the choices in the same sequence as the indexes in use, using the PULL_DOWN() function to display them as a menu and return the user's choice to us.

If the user presses Escape, the returned value will be zero, in which case we cancel the search and return to the program. Otherwise we SET ORDER to the selected choice, which might be 1, 2 or 3.

Then we ASK_FOR() the search target. If the user enters nothing or presses Escape, we cancel the search. Otherwise we perform the SEEK. If the SEEK fails we inform the user, and return to the record at which we began. Otherwise we simply return to our main loop, causing the found record to be displayed.

SEARCH() accepts from zero to four parameters. Pass nothing, and the function fabricates an array of index keys. More often you'll pass two or three parameters — the index key(s), their menu prompt (cues), and sometimes their picture masks. The fourth parameter is numeric, and if passed overrides the default row used for the menu of key values.

```
PROGRAM      AA_SRCH.PRG
Function(s)  SEARCH()
Purpose      Generalized search mechanism
Syntax       SEARCH(keys,cues,pics)
Parameters   keys - string or array of index key(s)
             cues - string or array of key identifiers
             pics - string or array of PICTUREs
             row - optional row to use for display
Example      SEARCH(xkeys, xcues, xpics)
Assumes      xkeys, xcues, and xpics are defined
             in preparation for a call to THE_USUAL()
             this function inherits those definitions
             if called from THE_USUAL().
Side Effects compound indexes with "@R" pictures can
             result in pictures that are too short.
             I'm working on it.
Returns      True only if search succeeds.
Calls        XCOUNT(), XFILL(), ASCAN(), L_MENU(),
```

```
ASK_FOR(), BLANK()
```

```
FUNCTION SEARCH

PARAMETERS keys, cues, pics, row
PRIVATE choice, record_no, temp, result, ht, width, temp_scr, ;
      msg, row, col
temp = PCOUNT()
record_no = RECNO()
choice = 01
result = .T.
msg = "Search for the "
row = 02
col = 02
ht = 00
width = 00
IF TYPE("row") != "N"
   row = 02                              && below THE_USUAL() menu row
ENDIF
IF temp = 00
   k_size = XCOUNT()
   IF k_size  01
      DECLARE keys[k_size], cues[k_size]
      XFILL(keys)
      XFILL(cues)
   ENDIF
ENDIF
IF TYPE("cues") = "A"                    && if an array of keys was passed
   choice = ASCAN(keys,INDEXKEY(0))
   PULL_DOWN(keys, row, col, choice)
   msg = msg + cues[choice]
   m_pic = pics
   target = BLANK(&keys)
ELSE
   msg = msg + cues
   m_pic = pics
   target = BLANK(&keys)
ENDIF
SET ORDER TO choice
ASK_FOR(msg, @target, m_pic)
IF !ESC()
   SEEK target
   IF !FOUND()
      POP_MSG("I can't find " + MAKE_STR(target))
      result = .F.
   ELSE
      record_no = RECNO()
   ENDIF
```

```
ELSE
   result = .F.
ENDIF
GO record_no
RETURN result
```

```
PROCEDURE PREV_PMT

PARAMETERS x, y, z
PRIVATE left, esc
left = 19
esc = 27
esc = 27
KEYBOARD CHR(esc) + CHR(left)
RETURN
```

```
PROCEDURE NEXT_PMT

PARAMETERS x, y, z
PRIVATE right, esc
right = 04
esc = 27
KEYBOARD CHR(esc) + CHR(right)
RETURN
```

How to Open a File

What could be more essential in database applications programming than a bulletproof means of opening files? Yet a surprising number of applications I've been called upon to debug or enhance contain no guaranteed way of checking for the presence of all the files associated with an application. Some didn't even have a way of creating missing indexes!

Time to introduce another fundamental design principle:

No program shall run before its time.

In every program we write, the first thing we'll do is check that all required files exist. If data files are missing, we'll tell the user which ones, then return to DOS to allow the user a chance to figure out where they went, copying them from a backup copy if need be.

This way, our program is guaranteed not to crash because of the absence of an essential file. Further, we can eliminate all subsequent file checking from the application, confident that all required files exist. This cleans our code up considerably. We can even close all the files if necessary (to run a tape backup program, for example), then reopen them afterwards. Each application will contain a function CHK_DBFS(), comprised of one call to our file-handler for each data file in the application.

Our file handler must be flexible enough to respond to the multitude of ways we can open a file. A file may be opened in any of 255 work areas, with anywhere from zero to 10 indexes open on it. Clipper frees us from the need to specify work areas, however, if we choose to use it. Instead of SELECTing a specific work area, SELECT 0. Clipper understands this to mean the next available area. If you refer to tables by their names or aliases, what do you care where Clipper opens them? What matters is that they *are* open.

This raises another issue, the maximum number of tables you may have open at once. Beginning with DOS 3.3, programs may open up to 255 files. You simply set the DOS environmental variable *Clipper = Fnn*, where *n* is the number of files your program will open. If your programs need lots of tables, put the SET command in your AUTOEXEC.BAT.

Earlier versions of DOS demand slightly trickier means. Fortunately, there is a public domain solution called HANDLES.ARC, available on most bulletin boards, including eBBS. With this method you link two files into your program, HANDLES.OBJ and HANDPROC.OBJ, then somewhere in your code call the function HANDLES(). If your software demands lots of tables open and also must run on all versions of DOS, your best bet is to include the HANDLES files in your link.

Naming Indexes

Quite a few programmers name indexes according to their keys rather than the table to which they point. In the short term this approach may appear to make sense, but it brings numerous disadvantages with it. Most important, you lose an immediate way of seeing which indexes relate to which data files.

This sacrifice in meaning occurs not only at the DOS directory level but inside your own program as well. Given that Clipper provides the INDEXKEY() function, which returns the key value of any index, you can always determine what was indexed when you need to. Therefore the index name can do something useful rather than redundant.

The pattern assumed here is quite simple. We take the left seven letters of the data file name and append a digit to them. The number indicates the importance of the index. The file INVOICES.DBF might have three indexes, which would be named INVOICE1.NTX, INVOICE2.NTX and INVOICE3.NTX. The first index is the one in which all records are unique.

This rule allows us to generate the names of the indexes, freeing us from the necessity to store them. There is no way around storing the keys, since without them our program would be hard pressed to deduce the information.

We'll pass all this information to our file-handler in parameters, preserving the generality of our routine. Within our file handler we'll rely on the Clipper function PCOUNT() to determine how many parameters were passed.

Much can be done to increase the power of functions by passing parameters in an intelligent order. In our first glimpse at this principle, we'll keep the application fairly simple, but later on we'll push the concept further and further.

```
PROGRAM        AA_DBOPN.PRG
Function(s)    DB_OPEN()
Purpose        File/Index handler
Conventions    Every application should begin with a call
               to DB_OPEN() for each file.
Syntax         DB_OPEN(file,no_indexes,keys,aka)
Parameters     file - name of file to open
               no_indexes - number of indexes on file
               keys - string (1 index) or array of keys
               aka - alias if any
Example        IF !DB_OPEN("CUSTOMER",01,"CUST_CODE")
Assumes        nothing
Side Effects   leaves the file open with indexes in use,
               order 1
Returns        True only if file and indexes were opened
               successfully
Calls          MSG(), STRINT(), MAKE_STR()
```

```
FUNCTION DB_OPEN

PARAMETERS dbf_name, indexes, index_key, aka
PRIVATE temp, root, pd_pos, temp_name, msg
```

```
temp       = PCOUNT()
ok_dbf     = .T.
pd_pos     = AT(".", dbf_name)
dbf_name   = IF(pd_pos  0, ;
                dbf_name, ;
                dbf_name + ".DBF")
pd_pos = AT(".", dbf_name)      && Redefine . location after append
root    = LEFT(dbf_name, MIN(pd_pos - 1,7))
IF TYPE("indexes") != "N"
   indexes = 0
ENDIF

SELECT 0
IF !FILE(dbf_name)
   POP_MSG( "I cannot locate the file " + dbf_name  )
   ok_dbf = .F.
   RETURN ok_dbf
ENDIF
IF TYPE("aka") != "C"
   USE &dbf_name
ELSE
   USE &dbf_name ALIAS &aka
ENDIF
IF indexes > 0
   IF TYPE("index_key") = "A"
      i = 1
      FOR i = 1 TO indexes
         n = STRINT(i)
         temp_name = root + n
         temp_key = TRIM(index_key[i])
         msg = "Indexing " + m->dbf_name + ;
               " on " + temp_key + ;
               " to " + temp_name
         IF !FILE(temp_name + ".NTX")
            MSG(msg, 0, .T.)
            INDEX ON &temp_key TO &temp_name
            @ 24,00
         ENDIF
      NEXT
   ELSE
      temp_key = TRIM(index_key)
      n = STRINT(indexes)
      temp_name = root + n
      msg = "Indexing "+m->dbf_name+" on "+temp_key+;
         " to "+temp_name
      IF !FILE(temp_name + ".NTX")
         MSG(msg, 0, .T.)
         INDEX ON &temp_key TO &temp_name
         @ 24,00
```

```
      ENDIF
   ENDIF
   SET ORDER TO 1
ENDIF
IF TYPE("index_key") = "A"
   i = 1
   FOR i = 1 TO indexes
      n = STRINT(i)
      ntx&n = root + n
   NEXT
   DO CASE
      CASE indexes > 06
         SET INDEX TO &ntx1, &ntx2, &ntx3, &ntx4,;
            &ntx5, &ntx6, &ntx7
      CASE indexes = 05
         SET INDEX TO &ntx1, &ntx2, &ntx3, &ntx4,;
            &ntx5
      CASE indexes = 04
         SET INDEX TO &ntx1, &ntx2, &ntx3, &ntx4
      CASE indexes = 03
         SET INDEX TO &ntx1, &ntx2, &ntx3
      CASE indexes = 02
         SET INDEX TO &ntx1, &ntx2
      CASE indexes = 01
         SET INDEX TO &ntx1
   ENDCASE
ENDIF
RETURN ok_dbf
```

Using a Data Dictionary

In a large application program, you may wish to include a data dictionary. A dictionary is itself a table, describing all the data tables in the application, and all the indexes on each table. It must have a certain minimal structure, beyond which it can expand according to your requirements.

In its most compact form the dictionary file would have fields for file name and one index key. You'd then add one record for every data file in the system, and another for every extra index beyond the first. This approach compacts the data but forces you to call DB_OPEN() once for every index, which is time-consuming and unnecessary.

Alternatively, you could expand the dictionary structure to include several fields for index keys, thus allowing you to use only one record per data file, and to call DB_OPEN() only once for each of them. On this model, you'll need as many indexkey fields as the maximum number of indexes open on any data file in the application. If many of the other files have fewer indexes, your dictionary will contain a lot of airspace.

The disk space taken is insignificant, to my mind, compared with the gains in speed and clarity of the dictionary. On this second model, if one of our files had five active indexes, we'd expand the structure of the dictionary accordingly:

Structure for database: DICT.DBF

Field	Field Name	Type	Width
1	FILE_NAME	Character	8
2	ALIAS	Character	10
3	NO_KEYS	Numeric	2
4	DESCRIPT	Character	50
5	KEY_1	Character	30
6	KEY_2	Character	30
7	KEY_3	Character	30
8	KEY_4	Character	30
9	KEY_5	Character	30
10	KEY_6	Character	30
11	KEY_7	Character	30
12	CUE_1	Character	10
13	CUE_2	Character	10
14	CUE_3	Character	10
15	CUE_4	Character	10
16	CUE_5	Character	10
17	CUE_6	Character	10
18	CUE_7	Character	10
19	PIC_1	Character	30
20	PIC_2	Character	30
21	PIC_3	Character	30
22	PIC_4	Character	30
23	PIC_5	Character	30
24	PIC_6	Character	30
25	PIC_7	Character	30
Total			561

```
PROGRAM        AA_DICT.PRG
Function(s)    CHK_DICT()
Purpose        Checks system files using a dictionary
               whose name is passed. Rebuilds missing
               indexes, warns of missing data files.
Conventions    Begin your program with CHK_DICT()
               returning to DOS if it returns false.
Syntax         CHK_DICT(dict_file)
Parameters     dict_file -- name of dictionary file
Example        CHK_DICT("APP_DICT")
Assumes        Structure of dict_file as in chart
Side Effects   Does not check disk space
               before re-indexing. It could, though.
Returns        True if all data files are present
Calls          DB_OPEN()
```

```
FUNCTION CHK_DICT

PARAMETER dict_file
PRIVATE i, s, file_name, alias, indexes
IF !DB_OPEN(dict_file)
   RETURN .F.
ENDIF
DO WHILE !EOF()
   file_name = File_name              && fields from dict_file
   alias = Alias
   DECLARE keys[7]                    && temp array
   indexes = 0                        && count 'em ourselves
   FOR i = 1 TO 7                     && index keys from file
      s = STR(i,1)
      IF key_&s != " "
         indexes = indexes + 1
         keys[indexes] = key_&s
      ENDIF
   NEXT
   IF indexes > 0
      DECLARE index_key[indexes]      && pass this array of keys...
         FOR i = 1 TO indexes
            index_key[i] = keys[i]
         NEXT
      ELSE
         index_key = ""               && or a null string
```

```
   ENDIF
   IF !DB_OPEN(file_name, indexes, index_key, alias)
      result = .F.                && return on first open err
   ENDIF
   SELECT &dict_file
   SKIP
ENDDO
USE                               && close the dictionary
RETURN result
```

Using DB_OPEN(), with or without a data dictionary, you gain in several important ways. First, you guarantee that your application will not crash because of missing files. Second, any time you (or your users) want to re-index, just delete all the index files and boot the application. Because missing indexes are automatically rebuilt, they require no backup.

With a data dictionary, you gain even more: any time a new file or index has to be added to an application, all you have to do is add a record to the dictionary — no recompile, no re-link, no possibility of introducing a new bug. Just fill in the blanks, as your users do.

You *Can* Get Good Help

WordStar pioneered the concept of respectful help. While its command syntax has long been the target of ridicule (misplaced, I think), the beauty of its help system has gone unnoticed, and unfortunately influenced too few programmers. *WordStar* gives users the power to roll back the help in stages, and what a sad loss that concept is. Almost all contemporary software has a fixed help system that remains the same no matter how adept the user becomes. Four years and a thousand spreadsheets into *1-2-3* press F1: you'll know exactly what I mean.

Why not pick up where *WordStar* left off, and give the user the ability to change the help? This seems not only sensible and respectful, but it's also useful to you the programmer.

The first gain is entirely yours. As you write the program, you can write the help. As you ship versions for testing, the inadequacies of the help will become clear and you can easily make the changes.

There's a subtler gain as well. You cannot possibly think of every question a new user might have six months or a year after the application has been delivered. By allowing the user to change the help, you build into your program the accumulated skills of the experienced user.

Your user knows more about his business than you ever will or should. If anyone can explain to a novice the gap between what the program does and what needs to be done, it's the experienced user. So let him, and he'll thank you.

You will have delivered software that evolves, that reflects its users, that they can shape. This is much more important than delivering an airtight system of menus. We are talking about the human spirit. Give your users commands and capabilities, not limits and choices.

Almost every application worth compiling has at least minimal help built into it. Help screens can be done in dozens of ways, more and less creative. On the least creative end of the spectrum are hard-coded screens, using the TEXT/ENDTEXT commands.

More creative is the use of format files as Help, since they can have up to 10 pages and include automatic interpretation of the PageUp and PageDown keys. It's easy to create these, using the dBASE Create Format command or more powerful editors. Just put a Read statement after every page, with a single variable at the end so the Read which activates the format file has a variable to Read. For lots of Help, this is one of the best ways available within dBASE itself.

Unfortunately, Clipper does not support format files as well as we might like. Even if it did, though, all we'd have gained is a new problem: every small change in the Help text would force another compile and link. More important, it becomes impossible for a user to change the Help to suit changing conditions such as new employees.

We're going to lay as much of the responsibility for our Help routine as we can on Nantucket's doorstep, exploiting several powerful features of Clipper.

Built into Clipper is automatic sensitivity to F1, with a little intelligence included in the form of three parameters:

- Procedure
- Line number
- Variable being read.

The second parameter has not proved very useful in my work, but the first and third give us all the context-sensitivity we could ask for. If the *variable* parameter is not empty, the user was reading that field when she pressed F1; otherwise she was elsewhere in the program, at a menu, perhaps, or listing records — and the first parameter can tell us where.

In a word, we're going to put all our Help in a data file, using memo fields. Then we'll index the file on a key derived from either the READ variable or the Procedure name parameter, in that order of preference. We grab the key, select the Help file and SEEK it, then display the memo field. We save the screen before and restore it afterward. Simple.

In some situations there may be too many files open to index the help, in which case we might LOCATE rather than SEEK.

Let's take the idea one step further, making the system just as powerful for ourselves as for the end user. If there's no Help aboard, we'll go into append mode and start writing it! Then we can write all the Help as we develop and test the system. At installation time, we can either remove the ability to add Help text, or leave it in for more experienced users to add help for less experienced users.

Structure for a HELP.DBF

Field	Field Name	Type	Width
1	PROC	Character	10
2	VARIABLE	Character	10
3	HELP_TEXT	Memo	10
4	HTR	Numeric	2
5	HTC	Numeric	2
6	HBR	Numeric	2
7	HBC	Numeric	2
Total			39

```
PROCEDURE HELP

PARAMETERS x, y, z
PRIVATE cur_file, target, memo_fld
IF x = "HELP"
   RETURN
ENDIF
memo_fld = "HELP"
```

```
cur_file = ALIAS()
target   = x + z
SELECT HELP
IF !EMPTY(INDEXKEY(0))
   SEEK target
ELSEIF EMPTY(z)
   LOCATE FOR Proc = x
ELSE
   LOCATE FOR Proc = x .AND. variable = z
ENDIF
IF !FOUND()
   IF VERIFY("This part of the program is help-less. " + ;
         Want to add some?")
      APPEND BLANK
      REPLACE Proc WITH x, Variable WITH z
      READ_MEMO(memo_fld)
   ENDIF
ELSE
   READ_MEMO(memo_fld)
ENDIF
IF !EMPTY(cur_file)
   SELECT &cur_file
ELSE
   SELECT A
ENDIF
RETURN
```

Ask Me Anything

The typical Clipper or dBASE program which bothers to implement a query facility usually botches it. The lazy approach is to use the same routine as the *add* function employs — initialize some variables, display them on the screen to blank the current record display, get the keys and remaining fields, READ_IT(), then check for the Escape key.

Rather than append a blank and perform the replaces, instead we examine all the variables, discarding the empty ones and from the others assembling a string. Several of the popular code generators take this approach. In a word, it ties the hands of the user almost as effectively as no query program at all.

The string we build takes the following form:

```
"'memvar = '" + query_value + "'.AND."
```

Suppose the user wants to isolate all the customers located in Sacramento, to print a list or do a run of labels. The Customer file has a field *City* into which the user types "Sacramento", then executes the Query. Our program examines all the fields, finds only City occupied, and constructs the following string:

```
City = 'Sacramento'.AND.
```

As we encounter non-blank entries, we assemble the new portion of the string and append it to whatever already exists, like so:

```
temp = "City = 'Sacramento'.AND."
qry_string = qry_string + temp
```

As soon as we've checked all the fields, we trim off the last five characters (the trailing .AND.), making an honest condition out of the string. Now we can pass it to Clipper, which will macro-expand it:

```
SET FILTER TO &qry_string
```

The current record may or may not satisfy the Query, so it's important to GO TOP immediately after setting the filter, forcing the record pointer to either the first legitimate member of the set or the end of file.

Data Types

This approach poses several important problems. Most obviously, the routine will crash the first time it encounters non-character data. We must devise a means of handling dates, numbers and logicals as well as strings. Before we can safely concatenate them to *qry_string* we'll have to turn all of them into strings.

With dates, we use the DTOC() function to create a string, then wrap that string in a CTOD() function call so Clipper can translate it back into a date at runtime. This double-translation trick demands a rather contorted expression.

```
date_str = DTOC( date_field )
qry_string = qry_string + date_field + "=CTOD('" + ;
date_str + "')" + ".AND."
```

For numeric data we can use LTRIM(STR()), taking advantage of Clipper's built-in ability to retain the decimals in a number-to-string conversion without being instructed to do so.

```
num_str = STR(num_value)
qry_string = qry_string + fieldname + "=" + ;
num_value + ".AND."
```

Logicals pose an additional problem. Since the default (empty) value of a logical is False, how can the user intentionally specify False values as one of the criteria? If we're trapping for empty values, how can we distinguish between an empty logical and an intentional False?

Since logicals are polar, there is no way to do it. Is the answer therefore to dispense with logicals, replacing them with character fields? Less radically, we might preserve them in the data structure and thus in the _FLD() and _SAY() functions, but treat them as character data in Query mode only. Instead of storing a False to the memory variable we'll store a space, then restrict entry to Y or N or blank. We'll have to translate these back into logicals as we assemble the string, of course, but here we have a way to offer the user this capability in an intuitive format.

On reflection, we see that a numeric field — or rather the type of selection we usually want to make on a numeric field — presents an additional problem. Typically we want to select records whose value falls above or below a specific value. Selecting records from the Line Item file, say, chances are far greater that we'll want to scan for quantities or dollar amounts over or under a boundary than quantities precisely equal to a value.

Actually, the same thing applies to dates. There will be occasions when we would like to search for an exact date, but far more often we'll want dates in — or not in — a range. To see this month's orders, we'd enter the first of the month while the system date supplied the cutoff.

We solve one problem and reveal another. How will the user indicate whether the intended range is over or under the number actually entered?

Finally, we return to our original character fields. Wouldn't it be useful to offer the ability to select above or below a specified string, as well?

The string we're assembling, recall, is based on this structure:

```
"fieldname = '" + variable + "'.AND."
```

which translates into an expression such as:

```
City = 'Sacramento' .AND.
```

The problem comes where the user wants to enter, say, "> Sacramento", making the whole string expand into:

```
City = '>Sacramento' .AND.
```

upon which Clipper, your application and you will stumble ungraciously.

For once, Clipper's built-in PICTURE abilities turn against us. We're not going to be able to prepend an operator of any sort to a field whose first position must be a number, and even if we could we'd still be short one position since date format is eight characters and no more.

All these problems arise from the decision to take the "easy" way out and use the input form already created. Realizing this, many programmers either cut back on the functionality or, if the client won't accept that, copy the existing form to a new function and make the changes there — hard-coding both the GETs and the assembly of the filter string field by field. Typically this adds several hundred dense, difficult lines of code to the program.

One quick way to solve most of these problems is based on the library function MAKE_STR(), which accepts one parameter of any data type and returns its string equivalent. Where the initialization code might have read:

```
mBalance = BLANK(Balance)
```

it will now read:

```
mBalance = MAKE_STR(BLANK(Balance))
```

At the assembly end of things we simply join the pieces, oblivious to data type:

```
temp = "Balance = " + mBalance + ".AND."
qry_string = qry_string + temp
```

We can refine this further and simplify our ultimate task by breaking the operator into its own component. To mask this from our user, we might trap for the presence of an operator in the first position of the field. Finding one, we won't supply it ourselves. Not finding one, we'll default the operator to *equals*
`("=").` `The code will look something like this:`

```
fld_name = "Balance"
memvar = "mBalance"
op = "="
and = ".AND."
temp = fld_name + op + memvar + and
qry_string = qry_string + temp
```

Now we have to trap any relational operators, some of which are more than one character long, " != " (not equal to) for example. The library function IS_OP() accepts one or more characters and returns true if the first character is a relational operator. We simply modify the initialization of *op*:

```
op = IF(IS_OP(memvar), "", "=")
```

Even with all our attempts to anticipate what can go wrong with a Query procedure based on our input form, we still end up with a form charitably described as inflexible.

It may be that this approach is entirely wrong. Let's try something completely different.

Query Freed from the Data

First, we divorce the function from the specifics of the application. Then we step the user through a sequence of events until s/he indicates that the query specification is complete. Stripped to the bones, our new approach is this:

- Ask for a field.
- Ask for a relational operator.
- Ask for a value.
- Ask for a connector.

For step one, we'll create an array of field names and present them as a menu. For step two, we'll present a menu of relational operators. For step three, we'll determine the field type, create a blank value of that type and present it to the user to be filled in. For step four, we'll present the choices "And", "Or" and "Done". If the user does not choose "Done", we create the new portion of the Query spec then repeat the steps.

At the outset, we'll save the screen. At each step we'll allow the user to backtrack using the Escape key. When the Query is complete, we'll SET FILTER to the condition, GO TOP, then restore the screen and continue. If no records match, following the GO TOP we'll be at EOF(), in which case we'll tell the user nothing matches the specification, cancel it and return to the original record number.

Expressed this way, suddenly all the previous complexities disappear. Certain problems remain, such as ensuring that the Query spec stays within the limits of Clipper's string-length boundary, but they are trivial while the gains are significant. We isolate all the problems of string construction into small routines and forget about ever having to write this mind-bending code again. The user also gains: the new query routine is flexible enough to isolate almost any combination of records.

One area of QUERY() which may not please you is its reliance upon the actual field names in the file. If the field names you have chosen seem inappropriate when turned into a menu, QUERY() may not be acceptable in a particular application.

Alternatively, a small or large number of fields in an application might be seen as not worth searching, and excluded from the array of fields. One wonders, though, if they're not worth searching, why are they being stored?

To satisfy these special situations, you might create application-specific versions of QUERY(), linking them into your program directly rather than from the library. If this is frequent, you may wish to modify QUERY() so that it accepts an array or two as parameters. Then you could send an array of selected field names and optionally a second array of field descriptions for the menu.

Let's look at the code.

```
PROGRAM         AA_QUERY.PRG
Function(s)     QUERY(), GET_QUERY(), GET_CLAUSE(),
                GET_OP(),ANDORDUN(),  PROCESS()
Purpose         Generalized query function.
Conventions     Called from THE_USUAL(). Allows create,
                refine undo and cancel commands.
Syntax          QUERY()
Parameters      none
Example         QUERY()
Assumes         a file is in use.
                xcues contains the index key(s) -
                not essential but more appealing.
Side Effects    SETS FILTER TO the conditions you specify,
                returns control to the caller.
Returns         True or False
Calls           DBFILTER(), EMPTY(), POP_MSG(), ESC(),
                ACHOICE(), MAKE_STR(), READ_IT(),
                SYSCOLOR(), DRAW_BOX(), L_MENU()
```

```
FUNCTION QUERY

PRIVATE result, temp_scr, row, choice, cur_rec, no_opts, choice
no_opts = 04
PRIVATE choices[no_opts], legals[no_opts]
result = .F.
query_str = ""
row = 02
choice = 01
cur_rec = RECNO()
row = 02
col = 47
ht = no_opts + 02
width = 32

SAVE SCREEN TO temp_scr

choices[01] = " Create a query                    "
choices[02] = " Refine the current query          "
choices[03] = " Save these records to disk        "
choices[04] = " Undo the current query            "
legals[01] = .T.
legals[02] = "!EMPTY(DBFILTER())"
legals[03] = "!EMPTY(DBFILTER())"
legals[04] = "!EMPTY(DBFILTER())"
DRAW_BOX(01,col -1, ht, col + width, 13)
choice = ACHOICE(row, col, ht, col + width - 1, choices, legals,
             .T., choice)
IF ESC()
   RESTORE SCREEN FROM temp_scr
   RETURN .F.                       && Out, without changing order
ENDIF

RETURN result
```

```
FUNCTION GET_QUERY

PRIVATE result, temp_scr
result = .F.
query_str  = ""
SAVE SCREEN TO temp_scr
DO WHILE .T.
   temp_str = GET_CLAUSE()
   IF ESC() .OR. EMPTY(temp_str)
      EXIT
   ENDIF
   joiner = ANDORDUN()
   IF joiner = "DONE" .OR. EMPTY(joiner)
```

```
      query_str = query_str + temp_str
        result = .T.
      EXIT
   ELSE
      query_str = query_str + temp_str + joiner
   ENDIF
   IF LEN(query_str) > 250
      POP_MSG("The string has reached maximum complexity")
        result = !ESC()
      EXIT
   ENDIF
ENDDO
RESTORE SCREEN FROM temp_scr
RETURN result
```

FUNCTION GET_CLAUSE

```
PRIVATE field, op, value, str, dollar, not_in, counter, ;
   temp_scr
str    = ""
dollar = "$"
not_in = "!$"
counter = 01
SAVE SCREEN TO temp_scr
DO WHILE .T.
   DO CASE
      CASE counter = 00
         RESTORE SCREEN FROM temp_scr
         EXIT
      CASE counter = 01
         field = GET_FIELD()
         counter = IF(EMPTY(field), ;
               counter - 01, ;
               counter + 01)
      CASE counter = 02
         op = GET_OP(field)
         counter = IF(EMPTY(op), ;
               counter - 01, ;
               counter + 01)
      CASE counter = 03
         value = GET_VALUE(field)
         counter = IF(EMPTY(value), ;
               counter - 01, ;
               counter + 01)
      CASE counter = 04
         str = PROCESS(field, op, value)
         counter = counter + 01
      CASE counter = 05
```

```
      EXIT
   ENDCASE
ENDDO
RETURN str
```

```
FUNCTION GET_FIELD

PARAMETERS file, tr, tc
PRIVATE temp, cur_file, temp_scr, br, bc
SAVE SCREEN TO temp_scr
temp = PCOUNT()
cur_file = ALIAS()
IF temp > 00
   SELECT &file
ELSE
   file = cur_file
ENDIF
IF EMPTY(file)
   RETURN POP_MSG("You must select a file first")
ENDIF
DECLARE fld_ra[FCOUNT()]
AFIELDS(fld_ra)
IF UN_DEF("tr")
   tr = 04
   tc = 26
ENDIF
br = MIN( 22, tr + MIN(16, LEN(fld_ra) + 01) )
bc = tc + 16
DRAW_BOX(tr, tc, br, bc, 03)
fld = ACHOICE(tr+1, tc+1, br-1, bc-1, fld_ra)
IF fld > 0
   SYSCOLOR(02)                        && highlight selected item
   @ ROW(), tc + 01 SAY fld_ra[fld]
   SYSCOLOR(01)
ELSE
   RESTORE SCREEN FROM temp_scr
ENDIF
SELECT &cur_file
RETURN IF(fld = 0, "", fld_ra[fld])
```

```
FUNCTION GET_OP

PARAMETERS field, tr, tc
PRIVATE result, br, bc, no_ops, width, height, temp_scr
SAVE SCREEN TO temp_scr
IF PCOUNT() < 02
```

```
   tr = 08
   tc = 38
ENDIF
result  = ""
no_ops = 10
width  = 20
br = tr + no_ops - 01
bc = tc + width
DECLARE ops[no_ops], op_chrs[no_ops], permits[no_ops]
ops[01] = "Equals                 "
ops[02] = "Does Not Equal         "
ops[03] = "Is Greater than        "
ops[04] = "Is Less than           "
ops[05] = "Contains               "
ops[06] = "Does not Contain       "
ops[07] = "Is in the List         "
ops[08] = "Is not in the List     "
ops[09] = "Is in the Range        "
ops[10] = "Is not in the Range    "
op_chrs[01] = "="
op_chrs[02] = "!="
op_chrs[03] = ""
op_chrs[04] = ""
op_chrs[05] = "$"
op_chrs[06] = "!$"
op_chrs[07] = "L"
op_chrs[08] = "!L"
op_chrs[09] = "R"
op_chrs[10] = "!R"
permits[01] = .T.
permits[02] = .T.
permits[03] = "TYPE(field)!='L'"
permits[04] = "TYPE(field)!='L'"
permits[05] = "TYPE(field)='C'"
permits[06] = "TYPE(field)='C'"
permits[07] = .T.
permits[08] = .T.
permits[09] = .T.
permits[10] = .T.
DRAW_BOX(tr - 1, tc - 1, br + 1, bc + 1, 03)
ch = ACHOICE(tr, tc, br, bc, ops, permits)
IF ch > 0
    result = op_chrs[ch]
   SYSCOLOR(02)
   @ ROW(), tc SAY ops[ch]
   SYSCOLOR(01)
ELSE
   RESTORE SCREEN FROM temp_scr
ENDIF
```

```
RETURN result
```

```
FUNCTION GET_VALUE

PARAMETER field
PRIVATE msg, width, get_data, temp_scr
msg = "Enter the target value..."
get_data = BLANK(&field)
IF TYPE("get_data") = "C"
   pic_str = IF( LEN(get_data)  20, "@S20", "@X" )
ELSE
    pic_str = GEN_PIC(field)
ENDIF
get_pos = MAX( 42, (40 + (35 -LEN(MAKE_STR(get_data)))/2
SAVE SCREEN TO temp_scr
DRAW_BOX( 14, 40, 18, 75, 03 )
@ 17,get_pos = get_data PICTURE pic_str
READ_IT()
IF ESC()
   RESTORE SCREEN FROM temp_scr
ENDIF
RETURN get_data
```

```
FUNCTION ANDORDUN

PRIVATE result, tr, tc, br, bc, no_ops, temp_scr
result  = ""
tr = 19
tc = 60
br = 21
bc = 70
no_ops = 03
DECLARE ops[no_ops]
ops[01] = "And       "
ops[02] = "Or        "
ops[03] = "Done      "
SAVE SCREEN TO temp_scr
DRAW_BOX(tr - 1, tc - 1, br + 1, bc + 1, 03)
ch = ACHOICE(tr, tc, br, bc, ops)
IF ch = 00
    result = ""
   RESTORE SCREEN FROM temp_scr
ELSE
   SYSCOLOR(02)
   @ ROW(), tc SAY ops[ch]
   SYSCOLOR(01)
```

```
ENDIF
DO CASE
   CASE ch = 01
      result = ".AND."
   CASE ch = 02
      result =  ".OR."
   CASE ch = 03
      result =  "DONE"
ENDCASE
RETURN result
```

```
FUNCTION PROCESS

PARAMETERS fieldname, op, contents
PRIVATE string
fieldname = TRIM(fieldname)
op = TRIM(op)
sp = " "
DO CASE
   CASE TYPE("contents") = "C"
      IF op = dollar
         string = "'" + TRIM(contents) + "'" + dollar + field
      ELSEIF op = not_in
         string = "!('" + TRIM(contents) + "'" + ;
         dollar + field + ")"
      ELSE
         string = field + op + "'" + TRIM(contents) + "'"
      ENDIF
   CASE TYPE("contents") = "D"
      string = field + op + "CTOD('" + DTOC(contents) + "')"
   CASE TYPE("contents") = "N"
      string = field + op + LTRIM(STR(contents))
   CASE TYPE(field) = "L"          && actual field
      x = LEFT(MAKE_STR(contents),1)
      string = IF(x $ "FN", "!", "") + field
ENDCASE
RETURN string
```

Summary — Core Tools

We now have almost all our high-level tools in place for rapid development of professional-quality Clipper applications:

- A bulletproof file-handler.
- A box-drawing routine.
- A very flexible routine to ask for input.
- A file-search mechanism for indexes.
- A flexible, easily modified help system.
- A powerful query facility divorced from any reference to the data.

Through a careful design which anticipates future complexities, we have managed to create a number of general- purpose functions upon which we can rest significant portions of our database management task.

Each function we have developed derives its power from one simple strategem: we separate the task from the data upon which it works. We never do anything literally, but always by reference or by pointing, or by building into the functions themselves the intelligence to derive what they need to know from the run-time situation.

In some cases, the functions first inquire whether a given variable has been defined and if so, what its data type is, taking action accordingly.

Whichever strategem we employ, our goal remains the same.

Write it once and once only.

Chapter 5

Meta-Functions

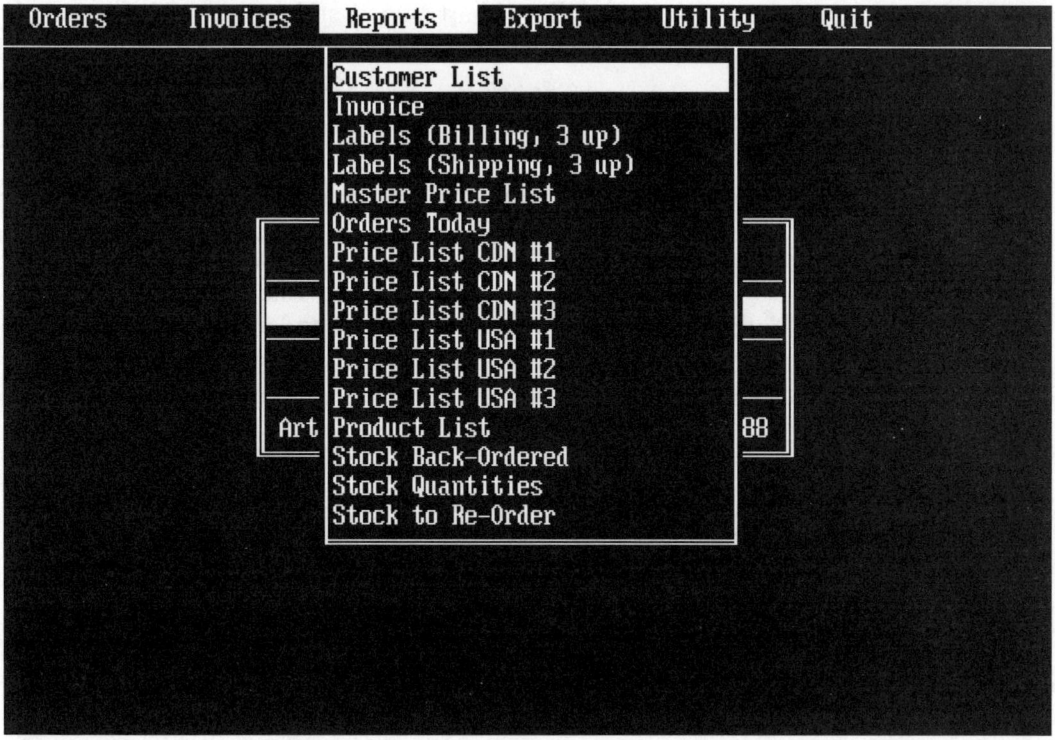

A pull-down menu system in action. Function PD_MENU() requires three parallel arrays for each pull-down (for prompts, permissions and udfs to execute), then administers the execution of the entire program, even including context-sensitive help.

Now that we have our core toolkit in place, we are equipped to create several of the most powerful functions in the library: DO_IT(), PD_MENU(), THE_USUAL(), and XBROWSER(). Think of these functions as *meta- functions* — very high level routines which do a great deal more than those we've explored so far. These functions provide, in various ways, the engine for your programs. You cite the specifics, and they take care of everything else.

How to Create Software

It is a common cliche in programming books to suggest that you postpone writing code as long as possible. Yet you itch to get into it, and for good reason: the tools available to you on a computer certainly beat a flow-chart stencil and notepad. Unfortunately, there remains a significant gap between your notepad and your source code.

Using just two tools from the library, you can design your software applications from the top down, freely changing them as you go, adding items to menus or moving them from one menu to another, planning the entire flow of the program before you write a line of genuine code.

The tools are DO_IT() and POP_MSG(). DO_IT() is an intelligent menu system, driven by arrays. All details about location of the prompts and messages, even execution of the appropriate function, are hidden from you. All you have to do is create arrays corresponding to the menus, messages and resultant actions, then call DO_IT().

POP_MSG() is a generalized function which pops a message box onto the screen, waits for a keystroke and then restores the screen. For each option on your menu, call POP_MSG() with an explanation of what should occur at that point in your program.

Then you compile, link and observe. Your program runs. You use it rather than imagine it. You realize this menu item actually belongs on another menu, so you move a block of code in your text editor and re-compile. Your program runs again.

This strategy allows you to concentrate on the layout and the commands, developing each level of detail in turn, until finally there is no choice but to actually write a routine. At that point, call POP_MSG() with an explanatory string such as "Here's where we print the production schedule".

Thanks to the robust menu functions in the library, you can knock together a working model in a morning. Wherever the code is missing, cover with a call to POP_MSG().

One by one, you remove each call to POP_MSG() and write the actual routine. At all points in the development process, your program runs.

Let's look at a program written like this.

```
SIGN_ON()
MAIN_MENU()
SIGN_OFF()
```

A tight little program, so far. Now we define the opening and closing functions.

```
FUNCTION SIGN_ON
POP_MSG("Hello world")
RETURN .T.
```

```
FUNCTION SIGN_OFF
POP_MSG("I've had all I can take. Returning to DOS")
```

Before you call DO_IT(), you must declare at least two arrays — one for the menu prompts and the other for the functions to execute. If you want your menu to have a message line, declare a third array to contain the messages. Let's whip up a menu for an *Insults or Abuse* program.

```
FUNCTION MAIN_MENU
choice = 01
menu_size = 06
DECLARE cues[menu_size],msgs[menu_size],udfs[menu_size]
cues[01] = " Arguments "
cues[02] = " Insults "
cues[03] = " Enough "
msgs[02] = "You swine. You're coming back for" + ;
           "more, aren't you?"
msgs[01] = "You won't choose this selection." + ;
           "I know your type."
msgs[03] = "What makes you think you can quit?"
udfs[01] = "POP_MSG(;
           'I knew you would pick me. Heh heh...')"
udfs[02] = "POP_MSG(INSULT())"
```

```
DO_IT(choice, cues, msgs, udfs)
```

It's as easy as that. DO_IT() absorbs this data, presents a light-bar menu. If you do not press Escape, DO_IT() looks in the *udfs* array for the name of the function to call, then attempts to execute it. I say *attempts* because it is not guaranteed to execute, unless you link the function into your program. Neither Clipper nor the linker can "see" the functions, if the only reference to them is within a text string. To Clipper and the linker, these are just strings.

You avoid the problem by declaring the functions so hidden *external*. In the example above, the explicit calls to POP_MSG() in SIGN_ON() and SIGN_OFF() will tell the linker that this function is required. The function INSULT(), however, is invisible to the linker. Unless you write it and either specifically include it or declare it external, your program will crash when the user selects the second menu choice.

Function DO_IT() calls another library function, L_MENU(), to execute the menu. Why? There will be times when we want to display a menu but not execute a function as a result, for example when we just want to set a flag such as report destination. By breaking the menu machine into a separate function, we can use it in both situations.

Let's look at the code for DO_IT().

```
PROGRAM        AA_DOIT.PRG
Function(s)    DO_IT()
Purpose        Generalized program administrator
Conventions    Usually a main menu, but doesn't have to be.
               Self-contained loop, so no external loop
               is required.
Syntax         DO_IT(choice, array1, array2, array3, ;
                      row1, row2)
Parameters     choice - default menu selection
               array1 - array of menu prompts
               array2 - optional array of messages
               array3 - array of udf names to execute
               row1 - display menu on row. default 00
               row2 - display messages on row. default 02
Example        DO_IT(choice, prompts, msgs, udfs)
Assumes        validity of array1 and array3.
               The other params are optional.
```

```
Side Effects executes the udf pointed to in array3.
Crashes
             if that function is not linked into the program.
Returns      The number of the selected choice, or 0 if
escape
Calls        L_MENU()
```

```
FUNCTION DO_IT

PARAMETERS choice, prompts, msgs, udfs, row1, row2
PRIVATE temp
SET CURSOR OFF
temp = choice
IF TYPE("row1") != "N"
   row1 = 00
ENDIF
IF TYPE("row2") != "N"
   row2 = row1 + 02
ENDIF
IF TYPE("msgs") != "A"
   msgs = .F.
ENDIF
DO WHILE .T.
   choice = L_MENU( choice, prompts, msgs, udfs, row1,
   IF choice > 0
      udf = udfs[choice]
      result = &udf
   ELSE
      EXIT
   ENDIF
ENDDO
RETURN choice
```

Get Me a Menu

The code could hardly be simpler. First it inquires whether the parameters *row1* and *row2* were passed. These are only necessary if you want to override the default locations, rows zero and two respectively. Next DO_IT() checks whether the variable *msgs* is an array. If not, it initializes *msgs* to zero.

All this is preparation for the call to L_MENU(), which creates and displays the menu, returning the number of the choice selected or zero if Escape was pressed. L_MENU() regains control, plucks the udf from the array and executes it.

Because DO_IT() is a loop, our main program does not require a loop. A simple call to DO_IT() administers the entire program.

Now let's delve one layer deeper, and see how L_MENU() creates the menu.

```
PROGRAM       AA_LMENU.PRG
Function(s)   L_MENU()
Purpose       Generalized Lotus-style menu administrator
Conventions   Use with or without messages, on any row
              adjusts to occupy a second row if nec.
Syntax        L_MENU(choice, array1[, array2])
Parameters    choice - start menu at; defaults to 1
Example       L_MENU(01,array1)
Assumes       choice and array1 must exist
Side Effects none
Returns       value of the prompt selected, or 0 if esc
Calls         ALENGTH() - to determine total length of menu
```

```
FUNCTION L_MENU

PARAMETERS choice, array1, array2, row1, row2
SET WRAP ON
PRIVATE temp, ra_len, show_msgs, msg, total_len
temp = PCOUNT()
ra_len = LEN(array1)
show_msgs = (TYPE("array2") = "A")
total_len = ALENGTH(array1)
IF temp < 04
   row1 = 00
ENDIF
g_row = row1 + IF(total_len  80, 02, 01)
IF temp < 05
   row2  = g_row + 01
ENDIF
@ row1,00 SAY SPACE(0)
IF row1 < 02
   @@ g_row,00 SAY REPL(CHR(196),80)
   IF show_msgs
```

```
      @ row2,00
   ENDIF
ENDIF
@ row1,00 SAY SPACE(0)
IF show_msgs
   SET MESSAGE TO row2
ELSE
   SET MESSAGE TO
ENDIF
FOR i = 1 TO ra_len
   IF show_msgs
      @ row1, COL() PROMPT  array1[i] ;
               MESSAGE array2[i]
   ELSE
      @ row1, COL() PROMPT array1[i]
   ENDIF
   IF i < ra_len
      IF COL() + LEN(array1[i+1])  80
         row1 = row1 + 1
         @ row1,00 SAY SPACE(0)
      ENDIF
   ENDIF
NEXT
MENU to choice
IF show_msgs
   @ row2,00
ENDIF
RETURN choice
```

Pull-Down Menus

PD_MENU() is a pull-down menu system which also controls your entire application. It works marvellously as a design tool, coming into play almost as soon as you begin thinking about the program you're going to write.

You can design a complex real-world application around PD_MENU(), concerning yourself only with the functionality of your program, oblivious to the details. PD_MENU() will automatically adapt to your needs, regardless of the number of options, the width of the pull-downs, or the tasks to execute when a selection is made.

Particularly in the design stages, this is invaluable: you can change your mind as often as you like. Moving this option or that entire menu to a new position in the scheme is no more difficult than moving a block of code in your text editor. A quick recompile and your program runs again.

Designing a Pull-down System

The beautiful thing about pull-down menus is the learning mechanism they present to your users. A beginning user can tour your program without actually doing anything, and very quickly grasp its overall concept and organization. If you take the pains to tie your help system into the menu, your users can learn most of your program without reference to printed documentation.

In this chapter we'll build a generalized pull-down menu system, which you can regard as a two-dimensional extension of DO_IT(). Our basic organizational tool will be arrays. We'll build some smarts into the pull-down system, as well — specifically, each pull-down menu will remember its last-selected option. ("Stupid" pull-downs default to the first element each time they're opened.) We'll also grab a copy of the screen just prior to executing any function, which we'll restore on completion — a little show biz.

As with DO_IT(), we create a set of arrays parallel to the menu options, which execute when the user selects the parallel option. Given the two-dimensional nature of the problem, a corresponding increase in setup is required before PD_MENU() can be executed.

Pull-down menus comprise a main or top-line menu, each option of which has a sub-menu which "pulls down" when the appropriate item is selected. We'll represent the main menu with an array, and each of the sub-menus with a pair of arrays, one for the prompts and the other for the user-defined functions to execute.

Just as DO_IT() serves us as a prototyping tool, so can its two-dimensional equivalent, PD_MENU(). Let's take PD_MENU() for a test drive — but before we take off, let's outline what we expect of a pull-down menu function.

At a minimum, PD_MENU() must have the prompts to display and the names of the functions to execute, so we acknowledge our responsiblity as supplier of those details.

We want to cut loose, however, at precisely that point: we should be able to declare some arrays and call the function, and on that information PD_MENU() should perform intelligently.

Selectable Options

Under certain conditions, some menu options will be irrelevant or illegal. The user should not be able to View a catalog until s/he has first selected one, for example. The wealth of options available in a pull-down menu scheme forces you the programmer to take special care. You must protect the data from inadvertent damage.

The Microsoft *Windows* interface, after the Macintosh, "screens out" various commands from selection, depicting them in italics and preventing the highlight bar from moving to the illegal choices. This is tricky programming, but fortunately for us it's all built into the Clipper function ACHOICE(), which turns an array into a menu and returns the choice selected.

ACHOICE() takes up to eight parameters. The first four dictate the location of the menu. The fifth is the array to menu. The sixth, if passed, is an array of logical expressions which parallels the first array. The seventh, if passed, is the name of the udf you want executed within ACHOICE(). The last two parameters indicate the default menu position and the relative window row.

By default, any item in the menu is accessible. If the second array contains a false expression in the parallel position, its matching menu item in the first array is declared off limits. If everything in a menu is accessible, you don't need to pass the second array. If some choices are allowed and some not, you need the array. The splendid thing about the design of ACHOICE() is its acceptance of logical expressions rather than simple logicals.

In this structure lies considerable power. For example, suppose a given command — List, for example — presupposes a file in use, but should be active no matter which file it happens to be. You could code it this way:

```
menu[n] = " List "
permit[n] = "!EMPTY(ALIAS())"
```

Specs

Let's outline our strategy before we go further. We'll construct a pair of arrays for the main or top-line menu, one for the prompts and the other for the functions to execute. We'll pass these to our function DO_IT().

For each pull-down menu, we'll have three arrays, containing prompts, permissions and functions to execute. We'll calculate the size of the pull-down box at run-time, and within each function we'll call ACHOICE(), passing the prompts and the permissions.

ACHOICE() will return a number to us. If it's greater than zero, we'll extract the function to which it points and fire it up.

Too literal.... We can do better. There's no reason to create separate functions for each pull-down — we can eliminate them, and the array containing their names, and the call to DO_IT() as well.

Instead let's build the loop right into PD_MENU(). We'll call L_MENU() instead to administer the top line. If L_MENU() returns a number greater than zero, we'll pass the number to our function PD_OPEN(), which pulls down the menu bearing that number.

How can PD_OPEN() know what to do? Since all the arrays must be declared and filled before the call, PD_MENU() simply has to figure out their names. We can simplify this task significantly by devising a simple naming scheme and sticking to it: then PD_MENU() can execute the rules defining the scheme and deduce the names of the arrays to use.

Why not pass the arrays themselves rather than a number? In a word, performance: it takes time to pass an array, and the larger the array the more time it takes. Far more efficient to pass a pointer to the array.

We'll name our three arrays *c*, *l* and *u* (cues, legals and udfs), followed by a number corresponding to the main menu choice. Thus the cues for pull-down menu 3 will be stored in array c3.

Now, we pass a number into PD_OPEN(). The udf STRINT()s the number, concatenates it to the three characters in turn, and presto, knows the names of the arrays.

To speed things up even more, we'll create an array of box-widths, and use the number passed into PD_OPEN() as a pointer into it. It's short work to calculate the height of the box, so we'll let PD_OPEN() do that for us as well.

Smart Defaults

A few details remain. We'll need a means of saving the selected item in each pull-down. We'll use an array, initialized to 1, and update it regularly.

There are four ways to leave each menu: escape, which closes the menu; enter, which executes the appropriate function; and the right and left arrow keys, which go to the next and previous menu, wrapping if necessary.

In the normal execution of ACHOICE(), as also in the MENU TO command, the arrow keys are redundantly mapped: up and left both have the same effect, while down and right share the opposite effect. In short, to write a pull-down menu system we must defeat this "feature" of ACHOICE(), forcing it to acknowledge that right-arrow and down-arrow are quite different events.

To do this we'll employ Clipper's SET KEY command, and persuade ACHOICE() that a right-arrow key is equivalent to three keystrokes — escape (which closes the menu and returns us to the top menu), right-arrow (which advances us one position on the main menu), and enter (which pulls down the newly-selected menu). We'll do the same with the left-arrow key, decrementing rather than advancing. Thus we'll need two procedures, NEXT_BOX and PREV_BOX, and we'll tie them to the arrow keys with the Clipper SET KEY command.

There is an interesting side effect to this approach. Though the arrow keys now provide an exit from ACHOICE(), they do not change its internal counter keeping track of the current selection. If the value upon entering the menu is 3, right or left arrow will exit the menu and leave the value at 3, regardless of your location when you left the menu. Thus we cannot trust it to supply the information we need.

The solution implemented here relies on the Clipper ROW() function to determine the current selection. Given that the first item in any menu is on row 2, PD_OPEN() has all the information it needs. It simply subtracts 1 from the row number and places the result in the array of defaults.

Given the tight relationship between the functions comprising the pull-down system, I have enclosed them all in a single source file. To some extent this is a trace of the debugging process, in which it was useful to have them all in one file. Since then, no occasion has arisen which called for one of the functions and not the others; as a result, they remain in one file.

I mention this in part because of the bad examples on the Clipper disks, EXAMPLEP.PRG and EXAMPLEA.ASM, which collect functions of widely disparate nature and purpose into a single file, perhaps misleading some users into thinking this is good programming practice. It is not. It is *bad* practice. The moment a function becomes useful in more than one context, it deserves its own file.

```
PROGRAM        AA_PDMNU.PRG
Function(s)    PD_MENU(),PD_OPEN(),NEXT_BOX,PREV_BOX,
               PD_UDF()
Purpose        Pull-down menu administrator
Conventions    3 sets of arrays ready to go
Syntax         PD_MENU(cues, sizes, menu_udf)
Parameters     cues - main menu prompts
               sizes - array of sub-menu sizes
               menu_udf - udf for achoice()
Example        PD_MENU(cues, sizes)
Assumes        existence and validity of arrays/contents/udfs
Side Effects   crash on bad data
Returns        True
Calls          AFILL(), DRAW_BOX(), L_MENU(), STRINT(), ESC()
               STUFF_RA() - you write this in setup
```

```
FUNCTION PD_MENU

PARAMETERS cues, sizes, menu_udf
PRIVATE choice, is_open, number
choice = 01
IF TYPE("menu_udf") = "U"
   menu_udf = "PD_UDF"
ENDIF
PRIVATE sels[m_size], ;
        wids[m_size], ;
AFILL(sels,01)
i = 01
FOR i = 01 TO m_size
   n = STRINT(i)
   DECLARE c&n[sizes[i]], ;
           u&n[sizes[i]], ;
           l&n[sizes[i]]
NEXT
STUFF_RA()  && You write this one...
is_open = .T.
DO WHILE .T.
   choice = L_MENU( choice, cues )
   IF choice  00
      PD_OPEN(choice, menu_udf)
   ELSE
      EXIT  && they pressed escape
```

```
   ENDIF
ENDDO
RETURN .T.
```

```
FUNCTION PD_OPEN

PARAMETERS number, pd_udf
PRIVATE choice, col, right, left, temp_scr
str_no = STRINT(number)
carray = "c" + str_no
uarray = "u" + str_no
larray = "l" + str_no
uwidth = wids[number]
choice = sels[number]
col = cols[number]
ht = sizes[number] + 02
left = 19
right = 04
SAVE SCREEN TO temp_scr
DO WHILE .T.
   SET KEY right TO NEXT_BOX
   SET KEY left TO PREV_BOX
   DRAW_BOX(01,col -1,ht,col + uwidth,13)
   choice = ACHOICE(02, col, ht-1, col+ uwidth-1, ;
            &carray, ;                && prompts
            &larray, ;                && legals
            pd_udf, ;                 && udf
            sels[number])             && default to
   SET KEY right TO
   SET KEY left TO
   IF choice  0
      SYSCOLOR(02)
      @ ROW(), col SAY &carray[choice]
      SYSCOLOR(01)
      sels[number] = ROW() - 01
      is_open = .T.
      udf = &uarray[choice]
      x = &udf && execute the udf
   ELSE
      EXIT
   ENDIF
ENDDO
RESTORE SCREEN FROM temp_scr
RETURN ""
```

```
PROCEDURE NEXT_BOX

sels[number] = ROW() - 01
KEYBOARD CHR(27) + CHR(04) + CHR(13)
RETURN
```

```
PROCEDURE PREV_BOX

sels[number] = ROW() - 01
KEYBOARD CHR(27) + CHR(19) + CHR(13)
RETURN
```

```
FUNCTION PD_UDF

PARAMETERS mode, curr_sel, relative
PRIVATE x
IF mode = 4
   keystroke = INKEY(0)
   x = 0
ELSE
   keystroke = LASTKEY()
   x = 2
ENDIF
IF mode = 3
   DO CASE
      CASE ENTER()
         x = 1
      CASE keystroke = 1
         KEYBOARD CHR(31)
      CASE keystroke = 6
         KEYBOARD CHR(30)
                  CASE IS_DATA(keystroke)
                         x = 3
   ENDCASE
ENDIF
RETURN x
```

Prototyping Software

You now have two powerful prototyping tools in our armory, each appropriate to a different type of application: DO_IT() and PD_MENU(). Both functions require little more from you than statements about what you want to happen, and in the latter case sometimes statements about when it may be permitted to happen.

DO_IT() suits the more traditional applications, in which records are displayed one at a time. PD_MENU() suits a different type of application, and to my mind, a different presentation. As the menu itself offers an overview of the program, so the presentation should offer an overview of the database.

So you can better see how to call PD_MENU(), let's design a complete menu system using it. In this exercise you'll see how easily you can hang a program on this framework. Later on, we'll be building a program called dCAT, which uses the pull-down interface. We'll begin with a few general job specifications.

Our assignment this time is to write a program which catalogs disks — floppy, hard or optical. It should catalog them automatically, of course. In addition, it should provide the ability to use multiple catalogs so that different types of files could be recorded in different catalogs. It should provide search mechanisms on several fields. It should allow notes about each file to be stored, and be able to import text files into the notes as well as to export the notes to disk or printer.

Given the nature of the task, it would be useful to have a variety of utilities available to run within the program. We might want a text editor, or a file maintenance program. Finally, the program should be able to produce a variety of reports from the catalog — by disk, filename, and space available.

With that spec, we can begin to design the pull-down menu system. Our main menu will offer five options: Catalog, Search, File, Report and Utility — each of which pulls down to reveal a sub-menu.

We have enough to begin.

```
PROGRAM        TESTMENU.PRG
Function(s)    PD_OPEN(), NEXT_BOX, PREV_BOX
Purpose        Demonstrate pull-down menu system
Conventions    a complete program administrator
Assumes        Arrays declared as outlined below
Side Effects   none
Returns        True always
Calls          SIGN_ON(), SYSCOLOR(), PD_MENU(),
               VERIFY(), SIGN_OFF()
```

```
exe_name = "Demonstration Menu System"
```

```
exe_desc = "Pull-down menus made simple"
SYSCOLOR(01)    && the usual colors
SIGN_ON(exe_name, exe_desc)
m_size = 05
PRIVATE r_flags[05]
PRIVATE cues[m_size], cols[m_size], sizes[m_size], ;
         sub_menu_sizes, sels[m_size]
cues[01] = " Catalog "
cues[02] = " Search  "
cues[03] = " File    "
cues[04] = " Report  "
cues[05] = " Utility "
cols[01] = 02
cols[02] = 10
cols[03] = 19
cols[04] = 28
cols[05] = 39
sizes[01] = 07
sizes[02] = 05
sizes[03] = 06
sizes[04] = 06
sizes[05] = 05
AFILL(sels,01)
i = 01
FOR i = 01 TO m_size
   n = STRINT(i)
   DECLARE c&n[sizes[i]], l&n[sizes[i]], u&n[sizes[i]]
NEXT
DO WHILE .T.
   SELECT A
   PD_MENU(cues, sizes)
   IF VERIFY("Leave this program and return to DOS")
      EXIT
   ENDIF
ENDDO
SIGN_OFF(exe_name)
RETURN
```

```
FUNCTION STUFF_RA

c1[01] = " Select   "
c1[02] = " View     "
c1[03] = " Disk     "
c1[04] = " Create   "
c1[05] = " Transfer "
c1[06] = " Purge    "
c1[07] = " Nuke     "
u1[01] = "SEL_CAT()"
```

```
u1[02] = "SHOW_CAT()"
u1[03] = "ADD_DISK()"
u1[04] = "NEW_CAT()"
u1[05] = "TRANSFER()"
u1[06] = "PACK_EM()"
u1[07] = "NUKE_EM(catalog)"
l1[01] = .T.   && permissions
l1[02] = "!EMPTY(ALIAS())"
l1[03] = "!EMPTY(ALIAS())"
l1[04] = .T.
l1[05] = .T.
l1[06] = "!EMPTY(ALIAS())"
l1[07] = "!EMPTY(ALIAS())"
c2[01] = " Disk ID      "
c2[02] = " File Name    "
c2[03] = " Volume Label "
c2[04] = " Extension    "
c2[05] = " Date Updated "
AFILL(l2, "!EMPTY(ALIAS())")
u2[01] = "RASK(01)"
u2[02] = "RASK(02)"
u2[03] = "RASK(03)"
u2[04] = "RASK(04)"
u2[05] = "RASK(05)"
c3[01] = " Query     "
c3[02] = " Directory "
c3[03] = " Label     "
c3[04] = " Import    "
c3[05] = " Export    "
c3[06] = " Order by  "
u3[01] = "QUERY()"
u3[02] = "RUN_DIR()"
u3[03] = "RUN_LBL()"
u3[04] = "READER(mmo_field)"
u3[05] = "WRITER(mmo_field)"
u3[06] = "MENU_ORD(cur_key)"
AFILL(l3,"!EMPTY(ALIAS())")
c4[01] = " Select        "
c4[02] = " Range         "
c4[03] = " Order by      "
c4[04] = " Destination   "
c4[05] = " Printer setup "
c4[06] = " GO!           "
AFILL(l4,"!EMPTY(ALIAS())")
u4[01] = "GET_FRM()"
u4[02] = "GET_SCOPE()"
u4[03] = "MENU_ORD( cur_key )"
u4[04] = "GET_DEST()"
u4[05] = "SET_PRN()"
```

```
u4[06] = "RUN_RPT( r_flags )"
c5[01] = " Configure  "                 && prompts
c5[02] = " DOS Window "
c5[03] = " Utility 1  "
c5[04] = " Utility 2  "
c5[05] = " Utility 3  "
u5[01] = "POP_MSG('Perform ' + c5[01])"
u5[02] = "POP_MSG('Perform ' + c5[02])"
u5[03] = "POP_MSG('Perform ' + c5[03])"
u5[04] = "POP_MSG('Perform ' + c5[04])"
u5[05] = "POP_MSG('Perform ' + c5[05])"
FOR i = 01 TO m_size
   n = STRINT(i)
   wids[i] = LEN(c&n[01])
NEXT
RETURN .T.
```

Faster Graphics

For those readers who have acted on the advice given earlier in this book and purchased Logitek's BREEZE.LIB, the next program is a pulldown menu system drawing on the functions in that library rather than the native Clipper functions.

This version is considerably faster than the Clipper version. On the other hand, it lacks the ability to screen out certain choices, as the former version can do.

You could certainly add this feature to the system, although with more work. You'll have to construct the traps yourself. You could employ a similar technique, using parallel arrays filled with logicals to determine the eligibility of a given choice.

Note that the functions in this second version are named slightly differently than those in the native Clipper version. This is to allow you to store both versions in your library, using the one appropriate to your needs at the time.

```
PROGRAM        PD.PRG
Function(s)    PDM(), PULLDOWN()
Purpose        Complete Pulldown menu system
Conventions    version based on LOGITEK BREEZE.LIB
Syntax         PDM()
Parameters     none
Example        PDM()
```

```
Assumes       arrays all set up as outlined below
Side Effects executes appropriate function
Returns       True
Calls         PULLDOWN(), POP_MSG(), SYSCOLOR()
              WPRINT(), WCLOSE(), WCOLOR(), WRELEASE(),
              WDISPLAY()
```

```
SET SCOREBOARD OFF
SET CURSOR OFF
exe_name = "A pulldown menu system"
exe_desc = "based on BREEZE.LIB"
m_size = 05
m_wno = 80
mono = 07
double = 02
single = 01
enter = 28
left = 75
right = 77
up = 72
down = 80
IF scrmode() = mono
   color1 = "w+/n"
   color2 = "n/w"
   color3 = "w+/n"
   color4 = "n/w"
   color5 = "n+/w"
   color6 = "w+/n"
   color7 = "w+/n"
   color8 = "w/n"
   color9 = "w+/n"
   color10 = "w+/n"
   color11 = color10
   color12 = "n/w"
   color13 = "w/n"
ELSE
   color1 = "r+/n"
   color2 = "n/bg"
   color3 = "rb/n"
   color4 = "w/b"
   color5 = "n/gr"
   color6 = "bg+/n"
   color7 = "bg/n"
   color8 = "b/n"
   color9 = "W/B"
   color10 = "gr+/n"
   color11 = "rb+/n"
```

```
   color12 = "+W/R"
   color13 = "w/n"
ENDIF
window = 81                          && submenu window number
m_high = 03                          && main menu window height
m_wide = 80                          && main menu window width
m_tr   = 01
m_tc   = 00
m_clr  = color9
DECLARE cols[m_size], ;
        cues[m_size], ;
        wids[m_size], ;
        dflts[m_size]
cols[01] = 02
cols[02] = 18
cols[03] = 33
cols[04] = 49
cols[05] = 64
cues[01] = "Menu 1"
cues[02] = "Menu 2"
cues[03] = "Menu 3"
cues[04] = "Menu 4"
cues[05] = "Menu 5"
AFILL(dflts,01)
AFILL(wids,20)
size = 03
DECLARE c1[size], u1[size]
c1[01] = "Choice 1"
c1[02] = "Choice 2"
c1[03] = "Choice 3"
u1[01] = 'POP_MSG("You selected choice 1")'
u1[02] = 'POP_MSG("You selected choice 2")'
u1[03] = 'POP_MSG("You selected choice 3")'
size = 05
DECLARE c2[size], u2[size]
c2[01] = "Choice 1"
c2[02] = "Choice 2"
c2[03] = "Choice 3"
c2[04] = "Choice 4"
c2[05] = "Choice 5"
u2[01] = 'POP_MSG("You selected choice 1")'
u2[02] = 'POP_MSG("You selected choice 2")'
u2[03] = 'POP_MSG("You selected choice 3")'
u2[04] = 'POP_MSG("You selected choice 4")'
u2[05] = 'POP_MSG("You selected choice 5")'
size = 03
DECLARE c3[size], u3[size]
c3[01] = "Choice 1"
c3[02] = "Choice 2"
```

```
c3[03] = "Choice 3"
u3[01] = 'POP_MSG("You selected choice 1")'
u3[02] = 'POP_MSG("You selected choice 2")'
u3[03] = 'POP_MSG("You selected choice 3")'
size = 05
DECLARE c4[size], u4[size]
c4[01] = "Choice 1"
c4[02] = "Choice 2"
c4[03] = "Choice 3"
c4[04] = "Choice 4"
c4[05] = "Choice 5"
u4[01] = 'POP_MSG("You selected choice 1")'
u4[02] = 'POP_MSG("You selected choice 2")'
u4[03] = 'POP_MSG("You selected choice 3")'
u4[04] = 'POP_MSG("You selected choice 4")'
u4[05] = 'POP_MSG("You selected choice 5")'
size = 05
DECLARE c5[size], u5[size]
c5[01] = "Choice 1"
c5[02] = "Choice 2"
c5[03] = "Choice 3"
c5[04] = "Choice 4"
c5[05] = "Choice 5"
u5[01] = 'POP_MSG("You selected choice 1")'
u5[02] = 'POP_MSG("You selected choice 2")'
u5[03] = 'POP_MSG("You selected choice 3")'
u5[04] = 'POP_MSG("You selected choice 4")'
u5[05] = 'POP_MSG("You selected choice 5")'
SYSCOLOR(01)
CLEAR
SIGN_ON(exe_name, exe_desc)
PDM()
SIGN_OFF(exe_name)
SET CURSOR ON
RETURN
```

FUNCTION PDM

```
WSELECT(m_wno)
WUSE(m_high, m_wide, m_tr, m_tc, m_clr)
WFRAME(double)
i = 01
FOR i = 01 TO m_size
   WPRINT(01, cols[i], cues[i])
NEXT
WCOLOR(color12)
WPRINT(01, cols[01], cues[01])
WCOLOR(color9)
```

```
WDISPLAY()
docode = .F.
oldcntr = 1
menucntr = 1
code = 28
DO while code > 1

   IF docode
      code = KEYCODE()
   ENDIF
   docode = .T.

   oldcntr = menucntr

   DO CASE
   CASE code = left
      menucntr = menucntr - 1
   CASE code = right
      menucntr = menucntr + 1
   CASE code = enter
      menucntr = menucntr
   OTHERWISE
      LOOP
   ENDCASE

   IF menucntr < 01
      menucntr = m_size
   ELSEIF menucntr  m_size
      menucntr = 01
   ENDIF

   WCOLOR(color9)
   WPRINT(1, cols[oldcntr], " " + cues[oldcntr] + " ")
   WCOLOR(color12)

   last_chosen = menucntr
   WPRINT(1, cols[menucntr], " " + cues[oldcntr] + " ")
   PULLDOWN(menucntr)
   IF menucntr  last_chosen
      docode = .F.
   ENDIF

   WCOLOR(color9)
   CLEAR typeahead

ENDDO
WCLOSE(m_wno)
WRELEASE(m_wno)
code = 28
```

```
RETURN .T.
```

```
FUNCTION PULLDOWN

PARAMETER menu_ptr
PRIVATE size
n = STRINT(menu_ptr)
array = "c" + n                          && array's name
funcs = "u" + n                          && function array
size  = LEN(&array)
high  = size + 02
wide  = wids[menu_ptr]
tr    = 03
tc    = cols[menu_ptr] - 02
tc    = MAX(01, tc)
tc    = MIN(tc, 79 - wids[menu_ptr])
w_no  = 81
clr   = color9
fr    = 03
dflt  = dflts[menu_ptr]
WSELECT(w_no)
WUSE(high,wide,tr,tc,clr)
WFRAME(fr)
FOR i = 01 TO size
   WPRINT(i,05," "+&array[i]+" ")
NEXT
WDISPLAY()
WCOLOR(color12)
WPRINT(dflt,05," " + &array[dflt] + " ")
s_code = 00
scntr = 01
soldcntr = 01
DO while s_code < 01 .AND. menucntr = menu_ptr
   s_code = keycode()
   soldcntr = scntr
   dflts[menu_ptr] = scntr
   DO CASE
      CASE s_code = up
         scntr = scntr - 01
      CASE s_code = down
         scntr = scntr + 01
      CASE s_code = enter
         scntr = scntr
         udf = &funcs[scntr]
         result = &udf
      CASE s_code = right
         menucntr = menucntr + 01
         IF menucntr  m_size
```

```
            menucntr = 01
         ENDIF
      CASE s_code = left
         menucntr = menucntr - 01
         IF menucntr  01
            menucntr = m_size
         ENDIF
      CASE s_code = 01
         menucntr = menucntr
      OTHERWISE
         LOOP
   ENDCASE
   IF scntr < 01
      scntr = size
   ELSEIF scntr > size
      scntr = 01
   ENDIF

   WCOLOR(color9)
   WPRINT(soldcntr,05," " + &array[soldcntr] + " ")
   WCOLOR(color12)
   WPRINT(scntr,05," " + &array[scntr] + " ")
   CLEAR typeahead
ENDDO
WCLOSE(w_no)
WRELEASE(w_no)
WSELECT(m_wno)
WCOLOR(color9)
WPRINT(01,cols[menu_ptr]," " + cues[menu_ptr] + " ")
WCOLOR(color12)
WPRINT( 01, ;
         cols[menucntr], ;
         " " + cues[menucntr] + " ")
WCOLOR(color9)
code = 28
RETURN .T.
```

```
EXTERNAL POP_MSG, WAIT
```

PD_MENU() and its BREEZE-based equivalent PDM(), as DO_IT() did earlier, achieve their power because of their separation of code from data. You should know see how easily function choice, and with it program flow, can be generalized. Now we bring this concept to a new task, equally universal.

I'll Have the Usual

The next meta-function is called THE_USUAL(). If you think you've seen powerful functions so far in *Professional Clipper*, then brace yourself. You are about to learn something about power.

From THE_USUAL() we expect nothing less than completely generalized file-handling, for use in situations or programs in which one record is presented at a time. We expect it to work without reference to the number of tables in use, the relationships between them, or the custom tasks we must perform at any given moment. THE_USUAL() should handle all of this.

Let's push it further. THE_USUAL() should not require a recompile when we do something as trivial as add a memo field to the file, or alter the indexing strategies.

Let's get even more demanding. THE_USUAL() should require only minimal changes in the event that we suddenly realize we have conceived the file relationships incorrectly, that an alleged parent file was in fact a child. Let's aim to design THE_USUAL() so that it can respond gracefully even to radical changes such as these, with a minimal effort on our part.

THE_USUAL() provides a foundation for traditional applications — programs oriented around the presentation of a single record at a time.

Due in large part to the phenomenal success of 1-2-3, users have come to realize that list format is more useful in situations where they must scan a large number of records, then take action on a selected few.

The Clipper function DBEDIT() provides an elegant foundation for window-based applications development. By encasing it in two library functions, we exploit its potential much more. The first function wraps around DBEDIT(), sugar-coating the call to that function. The partner function builds in many of the capabilities we will frequently require, in the same way as THE_USUAL(): through the magical medium of macro expansion. We store in strings the names of the custom routines we want executed at certain points. We link them into the final program. At the appropriate points, the functions execute.

Our goal this time is to create a general file-maintenance function, powerful enough to handle all the usual tasks we must perform on a file, yet flexible enough to accomodate the oddities of any given application. We call this function THE_USUAL().

Specifically, we want THE_USUAL() to be capable of the following functions, without reference to the details of the application:

Command	Description
Find	search using any available index
Add	add records to the file
Update	change existing records
Browse	list records on screen, 1 record per row
Delete	deletes the current record
Order	change the record display order
Next	go to the next record
Previous	go to the previous record
Top	go to the first record
Bottom	go to the last record
Calc	count the records currently selected
Query	allow a subset of the file to be isolated
Screen	where more than one screen is involved
Memo	automatic handling of memo field(s)

THE_USUAL() is a hybrid, combining the concept of a function table with certain specific routines which remain the same no matter what the file in use. These routines are so brief that we include them directly in the code for THE_USUAL(), rather than than breaking them out into functions of their own.

As with the functions you've already seen, we build into THE_USUAL() a system of intelligent defaults, so it can perform intelligently in the absence of specific instructions. Only when we want to override the defaults will we pass parameters into THE_USUAL().

We'll store the names of the functions to execute in an array and use the result of the MENU command as a pointer into it. Actually, our approach is a little more mnemonic than a table, but the idea is the same.

At strategic points throughout this code, we'll plant variables which may or may not contain the names of custom functions required at key points in the overall task. We default these to "the usual" functions, but anywhere a custom routine is required we simply substitute its name for the default.

Thus our program will alter its behaviour according to the contents of these variables. THE_USUAL() blindly executes the function chosen, without having any notion of its name or details, then regains control afterward. Anytime you need to override the default calls with custom versions, you simply replace the name of the default function in the array of names, write the routine and link it in. Often the alterations will be quite minor, but you're free to get as elaborate as you like, in confidence that THE_USUAL() will handle it gracefully.

So that you can fully appreciate the power of THE_USUAL(), let's examine a typical call to it.

```
THE_USUAL()
```

Complex, hmm? Of course, this won't do anything (except crash!) if you don't set the call up first. To call THE_USUAL(), you must perform these steps:

- Open all the files and indexes.
- Indicate the maximum number of screens.
- Set up the function table defaults.
- Declare variables for the index cues, the prompts to represent them and the picture statements to use when GETting them. These variables may be either strings or arrays. Use strings where only 1 index is active, otherwise use arrays.
- Create some memory variables to match the field names.

That's all there is to it. Let's take them one at a time.

Open all the Files

THE_USUAL() assumes that all required files are open and ready for use. In the previous chapter we created DB_OPEN(), our generalized file-handler. By convention, we write a function CHK_DBFS() unique to each application, hard-coded or driven from a file dictionary using CHK_DICT().

Indicate the Number of Screens

Here we have two variables, *screen_no* and *no_screens*. The first tells us which screen to display, the second how many screens are involved. In single-screen applications these variables are both set to one.

In theory there is no limit to the number of screens per table, though after a dozen or so the menu will grow a little too cluttered. In several years of writing applications, I have never come close to this limit.

Create a Table of Functions

Now you create a version of the function table, only stored in memory variables. Are you wondering why the function table is not an array, as in our earlier functions L_MENU() and DO_IT()? I admit it might be better to do it that way; in fact, I found it too complex to implement. So instead I chose to use a pseudo-array of mnemonic variables, hard-coding some of the options.

First, we arrange a pattern of default functions, calling some of the functions you have already seen. Here we store function names for our Add, Update, Query, Calc and Help routines.

```
udf_add  = "GET_STD(.T.)"          && id_char + "_ADD()"
udf_upd  = "GET_STD(.F.)"          && id_char + "_UPD()"
udf_calc = "COUNT_EM()"            && id_char + "_CAL()"
udf_qry  = "QUERY()"               && id_char + "_QBE()"
udf_rpl  = "RPL()"                 && id_char + "_RPL()"
udf_hlp  = "U_HELP"                && id_char + "_HELP"
```

As you already know, we have built so much flexibility into the defaults that they alone will suffice even in complex situations. But systems designed to work only so far will fail frequently, so we extend the flexibility even further, providing a doorway to any custom functions a given application might demand.

We can predict the areas which will require custom functions: Does this table have a child-file in which details are stored? Are there several children? Does the user want custom functions such as a WordPerfect emulation while editing text? Will the BROWSE command require custom commands, or the memo- field editing? If so, we store the names of the functions in our table of variables.

A table may have no children, in which case store False to *udf_zoom*. There may be no memo-fields in an application, or you may not require any extras in editing them. In that case store False to *udf_memo*. A minimal Browse routine may suffice; store False to *udf_brow*. The print routine is *always* custom.

```
udf_zoom = ".F."                          && udf for Zoom command
udf_brow = ".F."                          && udf for BROWSER()
udf_memo = ".F."                          && udf for MEMOEDIT()
udf_prt  = id_char + "_PRT()"
```

You can name these functions anything you like, so long as you store their names in the appropriate variables. If you stick with the names, however, you gain in code-writing speed: you can copy the table as is to a template file, then use it over and over again in each new application you create.

We want THE_USUAL() to be able to provide automatic control over all indexing considerations, without reference to the actual situation. All THE_USUAL() needs to know in order to provide this control is the location of the information.

The variables *xkeys*, *xcues* and *xpics* are used to store the indexing information. Depending on the number of indexes in the current file, your code will resemble either of these two blocks:

```
xkeys = ""                                && e.g. "CODE"
xcues = ""
xpics = ""                                && e.g. "@!"
```

or

```
DECLARE xkeys[no_keys], ;                 && arrays for
      xcues[no_keys], ;                   && multiple keys
      xpics[no_keys]
```

The easiest way to create a group of variables to match the field names is to let Clipper do it for you. By convention, we add the prefix "m" to the field names to distinguish the memory variable from the field itself. (Naming them identically can cause very subtle bugs which could keep you up many nights.)

This next fragment of code shows how GET_STD() does this. Look at it carefully. Note how it uses macros to point to addresses before assigning values to the variables at those locations:

```
i = 01    && manufacture memvar dupes
FOR i = 01 TO FCOUNT()                    && Clipper udf returns # fields
   f = FIELD(i)                           && grab the field name
   v = "m" + f                            && stick an em in front
   &v = BLANK(&f)                         && point, then shoot
NEXT
```

Here is a template which you can copy to your template directory and use as a starting point for every program your write that calls THE_USUAL().

```
FUNCTION whatever

PARAMETER blood_line                      && identifier from parent if any
PRIVATE result, temp_scr, id_char, ;
         old_file, curr_file, blood_line, ;
         screen_no, no_screens, no_kids, no_indexes
PRIVATE udf_add, udf_upd, udf_scr, udf_say, udf_key, ;
         udf_calc, udf_prt, udf_rpl, udf_qry, udf_fld, ;
         udf_zoom, udf_memo, udf_brow, udf_help
PRIVATE xkeys, xcues, xpics, kids, kkeys, kcues
SAVE SCREEN TO temp_scr
result = .F.
no_screens = 01
screen_no  = 01
curr_file = ""
blood_line = IF(TYPE("bood_line")="U","",blood_line)
SELECT &curr_file
SEEK   blood_line
id_char = ""
udf_scr  = id_char + "_SCR()"
udf_say  = id_char + "_SAY()"
udf_key  = id_char + "_KEY()"
udf_fld  = id_char + "_FLD()"
```

```
udf_prt   = "POP_MSG('Ask your programmer for a print routine')"
udf_add   = "GET_STD(.T.)"
udf_upd   = "GET_STD(.F.)"
udf_calc = "COUNT_EM()"
udf_qry   = "QUERY()"
udf_rpl   = "RPL()"
udf_help = "U_HELP"
udf_zoom = .F.
udf_brow = .F.
udf_memo = .F.
no_keys = 00
no_kids = 00
* Include one of the remark-blocks below:
* xkeys = ""
* xcues = ""
* xpics = ""
*   or
*  DECLARE xkeys[no_keys], ;          && arrays only necessary for
*  xcues[no_keys], ;                  && multiple keys
*  xpics[no_keys]
IF no_kids > 00
   DECLARE kids[no_kids], ;
         cues[no_kids]
   kids[01]  = ""
   kcues[01] = ""
ENDIF
i = 01
FOR i = 01 TO FCOUNT()
   f = FIELD(i)
   v = "m" + f
   &v = BLANK(&f)
NEXT
THE_USUAL()
result = .T.
RETURN result
```

The next template provides the scaffolding for the five required functions. For *char*, substitute the actual character which identifies this suite of functions (*id_char*, as declared above).

```
FUNCTION char_SCR
<your code goes here>
RETURN .T.
```

```
FUNCTION char_KEY

PRIVATE result
result = .F.
<your code goes here>
READ_IT()
result = !ESC()
RETURN result


FUNCTION char_FLD

PRIVATE result
result = .F.
<your code goes here>
READ_IT()
result = !ESC()
RETURN result


FUNCTION char_SAY

PRIVATE result
SYSCOLOR(02)
<your code goes here>
SYSCOLOR(01)
RETURN .T.
```

Now for the code to THE_USUAL().

```
PROGRAM        AA_USUAL.PRG
Function(s)    THE_USUAL()
Purpose        General purpose file maintenance
Conventions    file maintenance routine that handles
               multiple files, multiple screens, elaborate
               validations and custom functions required by
               the given application only.
               Because of the file naming scheme and the
               principle of macro substitution, this loop
               can control many different applications.
Syntax         THE_USUAL([array1, array2])
Parameters     array1 - prompts for extra udfs
               array2 - udfs to execute
Example        THE_USUAL()
```

```
Assumes         A great deal. Details below.
Side Effects crash if not all conventions adhered to
Returns          .T.
Calls           ACOPY(),BROWSER(),COUNT_EM(),GET_STD(),
                GO_BOT,GO_TOP,L_MENU(),MCOUNT(),MENU_ORD()
                PGDN(),PGUP(),POP_MSG(),QUERY(),READ_MEMO()
                RPL(),SEARCH(),SELE_SCR(),STAT_LINE(),U_HELP
Macro calls     udf_scr - display screen
                udf_key - get key
                udf_fld - get remaining fields
                udf_say - display a record
                udf_add  - default = "GET_STD(.T.)"
                udf_upd  - default = "GET_STD(.F.)"
                udf_calc - default = "COUNT_EM()"
                udf_qry  - default = "QUERY()"
                udf_rpl  - default = "RPL()"
                udf_help - default = "U_HELP"
                udf_brow - default = "XBROWSER"
                udf_memo - optional Memoedit customizer
                udf_zoom - only if file can be Zoomed
```

```
FUNCTION THE_USUAL

PARAMETERS so_cues, so_udfs
PRIVATE result, x, choice, memos, temp, is_append, ;
   memo_pos, zoom_pos, scr_pos, first_avail, ;
   cur_dbf, temp_scr, dead_recs
temp  = PCOUNT()

KEYS_ON()
IF TYPE("udf_help") != "C"
   udf_help = "U_HELP"
ENDIF
SET KEY 28 TO &udf_help
IF TYPE("udf_brow") != "U" .OR. EMPTY(udf_brow)
   udf_brow = .F.
ENDIF
IF TYPE("udf_memo") != "U" .OR. EMPTY(udf_memo)
   udf_memo = .F.
ENDIF
zoomable  = (no_kids  00)
multi_scr = (no_screens  01)
x = .T.
repaint = .T.
```

```
choice = 01
memo_pos = 00
zoom_pos = 00
scr_pos = 00
first_avail = 10
cur_dbf    = ALIAS()
dead_recs = .F.
is_memo    = (MCOUNT()  00)
DO CASE
   CASE TYPE("so_cues") = "U"
      extras = 00
   CASE TYPE("so_cues") = "A"
      extras = LEN(so_cues)
   OTHERWISE
      extras = 01
ENDCASE
size = 09 + IF( is_memo, 01, 00 ) + ;
   IF( multi_scr, 01, 00 ) + ;
   IF( zoomable, 01, 00 ) + ;
   extras   && add extra prompts
DECLARE choices[size]
choices[01] = " Find "
choices[02] = " Add "
choices[03] = " Update "
choices[04] = " Browse "
choices[05] = " Calc "
choices[06] = " Order "
choices[07] = " Print "
choices[08] = " Query "
choices[09] = " Delete "
next_pos = first_avail
IF is_memo
   memo_pos = next_pos
   choices[memo_pos] = " Memo "
   next_pos = next_pos + 1
ENDIF
IF no_screens >  01
   scr_pos = next_pos
   choices[scr_pos] = " Screen # "
   next_pos = next_pos + 1
ENDIF
IF zoomable
   zoom_pos = next_pos
   choices[zoom_pos] = IF(TYPE("kcues") = "C", kcues, " Zoom ")
   next_pos = next_pos + 1
ENDIF
IF extras = 01
   extra_pos = next_pos
   choices[extra_pos] = so_cues
```

```
ELSEIF extras  01
   ACOPY(so_cues, choices, next_pos)
ENDIF
DO WHILE .T.   && let's rock and roll
   IF repaint
      x = &udf_scr
      repaint = .F.
   ENDIF
   is_append = .F.
   nested = .F.
   x = &udf_say
   STAT_LINE()
   choice = L_MENU(choice, choices)
   DO CASE
      CASE choice = 00
         IF ESC()
            IF nested
               LOOP
            ELSE
               result = .T.
               EXIT
            ENDIF
         ENDIF
      CASE PGDN()
         SKIP
         IF EOF()
            SKIP -1
         ENDIF
      CASE PGUP()
         SKIP -1
      CASE choice = 01
         nested = .T.
         SEARCH(xkeys, xcues, xpics)
      CASE choice = 02
         add_one = .T.
         is_append = .T.
         KEYS_OFF()
         x = &udf_add
         KEYS_ON()
      CASE choice = 03
         is_append = .F.
         add_one = .F.
         KEYS_OFF()
         x = &udf_upd
         KEYS_ON()
      CASE choice = 04
         KEYS_OFF()
         BROWSER(03,00,23,79, udf_brow)
         KEYS_ON()
```

```
      CASE choice = 05
         x = &udf_calc
      CASE choice = 06
         MENU_ORD(xcues)
      CASE choice = 07
         x = &udf_prt
      CASE choice = 08
         x = &udf_qry
      CASE choice = 09
         IF DELETED()
            dead_recs = .T.
            RECALL
         ELSE
            DELETE
         ENDIF

* It's relative from here on in, handled by offset.
* If no_screens > 0, increment screen number
* If memo_pos > 0, call read_memo()
* If zoom_pos > 0 and chosen, do zoom
* If extras were passed, deal with them similarly
      CASE choice = scr_pos
         x = SELE_SCR(screen_no)
         IF x != screen_no
            screen_no = x
            repaint = .T.
         ENDIF
      CASE choice = memo_pos
         * READ_MEMO() will automatically menu
         * the memo fields if there are more than one.
         * everything is passed for you.
         READ_MEMO("", mtr, mtc, mbr, mbc, .T., udf_memo)
      CASE choice = zoom_pos
         SAVE SCREEN TO temp_scr
         @ 00,00
         x = &udf_zoom
         SELECT &cur_dbf
         RESTORE SCREEN FROM temp_scr
      CASE extras = 01
         x = &so_udfs
      OTHERWISE
         udf_pointer = LEN(choices) - first_avail
         func = so_udfs[udf_pointer]
         x = &func
   ENDCASE
ENDDO
IF dead_recs
   DUST_EM()
ENDIF
```

```
KEYS_OFF()
RETURN result
```

```
FUNCTION KEYS_OFF

SET KEY 31 TO
SET KEY 30 TO
SET KEY 29 TO
SET KEY 23 TO
SET KEY 28 TO
RETURN 01


FUNCTION KEYS_ON

SET KEY 31 TO GO_TOP                && ^Home or ^PgUp
SET KEY 29 TO GO_TOP
SET KEY 30 TO GO_BOT                && ^End or ^PgDn
SET KEY 23 TO GO_BOT
SET KEY 28 TO &udf_help && turn help back on
RETURN 01
```

```
PROCEDURE U_HELP

PARAMETERS x, y, z
POP_MSG("Help is for wimps and hairless dogs")
RETURN
EXTERNAL GO_TOP, GO_BOT, POP_MSG, QUERY, RPL, ;
   GET_STD, COUNT_EM
```

Memo Fields

One of the handiest built-in features of THE_USUAL() is its handling of memo fields. The function MCOUNT() returns the number of memo fields in the current file, optionally filling an array with their field names. You'll find the call to MCOUNT() near the top of THE_USUAL().

If there are memo fields, the prompt "Memo" is added to THE_USUAL() menu. If selected, it activates a call to READ_MEMO(), our generalized memo-field handler.

READ_MEMO() takes from zero to seven parameters. Pass none to go with all the built-in defaults - automatic construction of a menu of field names, an editing window from 04,05 to 22,74, the ability to edit, and no custom function to execute inside MEMOEDIT().

To edit a particular memo field, pass its name as the first parameter. To alter the size or location of the editing window, pass the new location as parameters 2 through 5. To make the editing window Read-only, pass a False as parameter 6. And finally, to execute a custom function within MEMOEDIT(), pass its name as parameter 7.

Several cosmetic details are worth noting. READ_MEMO() fabricates a window header from the field name and displays it in reverse video on the top row of the window. Thanks to the Clipper function SETCOLOR(), READ_MEMO() can change the color setting, then change back to the original setting, without knowing what the original setting was.

SETCOLOR() exhibits exactly the quality we prize in a library function - it works without reference to the current state of the machine. As you get ideas for new functions - and hopefully, this book will inspire your creative juices - keep this lesson in mind. Often it's enough just to ask, is there a way to write this so it works without reference to other facts?

Note that READ_MEMO() supplies the name of a user- defined function by default. I have included in this function a few basic capabilities, but encourage you to embellish it to your heart's content. If you or your users run WordPerfect, for example, you could redefine most of MEMOEDIT()'s behaviour to conform to that model.

Your imagination is really the only limit you face in customizing MEMOEDIT(), aside from the approximately 60 Kbyte maximum field size. A fairly simple feature to add is a means of defining and re-defining the function keys. If you like that idea, you might also wish to save the definitions in your system file.

Remember that a function key can contain carriage return/line-feed characters. The string "San Anselmo;California;90067;", assigned to a function key, prints:

```
San Anselmo
California
90067
```

Thanks to the structure of READ_MEMO(), you can exploit its strengths with no more than a call to the function. If you need more control, pass more information.

```
PROGRAM      AA_RMEMO.PRG
Purpose      A standard routine for reading memo fields
Comments     to control where pass r1, c1, r2, c2
             to stifle save/restore pass a .t.
             Three diffferent boxes are used.
             The frame is one box.
             Around it is another box, to create space.
             The actual edit area is 1 char smaller than
             the box, to allow an inner border
```

```
FUNCTION READ_MEMO

PARAMETERS memo_field, tr, tc, br, bc, edit_it, udf
PRIVATE   temp, no_memos, memo_buff, temp_scr, buff_size, row
IF TYPE("edit_it") != "L"
   edit_it = .F.
ENDIF
IF TYPE("udf") = "U"
   udf = ""
ENDIF
IF TYPE("tr") != "N"
   tr  = 04
   tc  = 05
   br  = 22
   bc  = 74
ENDIF
temp = PCOUNT()
row  = 02
IF TYPE("memo_field") = "U" .OR. EMPTY(memo_field)
   no_memos = MCOUNT()
   IF no_memos = 00
      POP_MSG("There are no memo fields in this file")
      RETURN .F.
   ELSEIF no_memos = 01
      memo_field = FIELD(MEMO_POS())
   ELSEIF no_memos  01
      DECLARE m_fields[no_memos]
      pos = 01
      FOR i = 1 TO FCOUNT()
         x = FIELD(i)
         IF TYPE(x) = "M"
            m_fields[pos] = " " + PROPER(x) + " "
            pos = pos + 01
```

```
   KEYBOARD CHR(4)
ENDIF
RESTSCREEN(tr,tc,br,bc, memo_buff)
keystroke = 0
SET CURSOR OFF
old_color =  SETCOLOR(cur_color)
@ ROW,00                                    && erase the sub-menu if there was on
RETURN CTRL_W()                             && was it a keeper?
```

DBEDIT() — Power Windows

DBEDIT() is among Clipper's most stunning extensions to the dBASE language. It began life as an emulation of the dBASE BROWSE command, but has evolved into one of the most powerful features of Clipper.

In essence, DBEDIT() creates a pannable, scrollable window into one or more databases. It accepts up to a dozen parameters, the most important of which is the name of the user-defined function you want executed within DBEDIT().

Even without this construct, DEBEDIT() surpasses dBASE BROWSE in its ability to control the size and location of the window, as well as its field headers and footers. To this DBEDIT() adds support of virtual fields and multiple files. In short, you can erect an entire application around the powers of this single function.

To call DBEDIT() successfully, all you have to do is open a file. More effort is rewarded, however. To exploit DBEDIT() fully, we require two functions, one to call DBEDIT() and a second to execute within DBEDIT(). The calling function supplies headings, defaults, picture statements and valid clauses.

The udf you pass into DBEDIT() can profoundly transform its behavior. As DBEDIT() executes, it calls your inner udf repeatedly, passing two parameters in automatically, and expecting one back:

```
FUNCTION your_udf

PARAMETERS mode, index
PRIVATE x
x = 00
<commands>
```

this DBEDIT() adds support of virtual fields and multiple files. In short, you can erect an entire application around the powers of this single function.

To call DBEDIT() successfully, all you have to do is open a file. More effort is rewarded, however. To exploit DBEDIT() fully, we require two functions, one to call DBEDIT() and a second to execute within DBEDIT(). The calling function supplies headings, defaults, picture statements and valid clauses.

The udf you pass into DBEDIT() can profoundly transform its behavior. As DBEDIT() executes, it calls your inner udf repeatedly, passing two parameters in automatically, and expecting one back:

```
FUNCTION your_udf

PARAMETERS mode, index
PRIVATE x
x = 00
<commands>
RETURN x
```

The first parameter your function receives, mode, describes the current state of the DBEDIT() process. It will contain one of five numbers:

- 0 — idle mode. no keystrokes are awaiting input.
- 1 — user has attempted to cursor past BOF().
- 2 — user has attempted to cursor past EOF().
- 3 — file is empty.
- 4 — user has pressed a key DBEDIT does not handle (i.e. generally a non-cursor key).

The second parameter your function receives, index, points to the current array element - which, remember, may or may not be a field.

DBEDIT() supplies automatic file movement control in both dimensions, panning the window when required, moving through the file in concert with the cursor - a remarkable feat of programming made more so through its acceptance of your user- defined function.

As it executes, DBEDIT() regularly calls your udf, passing its two parameters automatically.

Your UDF must always return a numeric value to DBEDIT(), instructing it according to the value you send:

- 0 — quit DBEDIT().
- 1 — continue DBEDIT().
- 2 — re-read data, repaint screen.
- 3 — open a blank row at the current location.

On this foundation you can build astonishing software. We'll explore the possibilities in detail in chapters to come, but in the meantime let's just consider some of the opportunities open to us.

In general, a function designed for use inside DBEDIT() should:

- Grab the last keystroke.
- Compare it to your list of hot-keys, probably in a CASE structure.
- Call any function tied to a hot-key.
- Send DBEDIT() a number between 0 and 3 inclusive, to instruct it what to do next.

We need an escape key, so let's use (surprise) escape. The first test in our CASE block might be nothing more than:

```
DO CASE
   CASE ESC()
      RETURN 0
   CASE <whatever>
```

```
ENDCASE
```

In function XBROWSER() we first check for Escape, then for each of the hot keys we've defined — Alt-R and Alt-W to read in text files and write out memo fields. The CASE structure could expand here to include as many possibilities as you can imagine.

The Browse command within THE_USUAL() calls our library function BROWSER(), itself a general-purpose file maintenance program and one of the most important functions in the library.

In essence, BROWSER() sugar-coats a call to the Clipper function DBEDIT(), passing it parameters describing the boundaries of the Browse window, and the name of any custom DBEDIT() function you have defined to override its default call to XBROWSER().

DBEDIT() is among Clipper's most important and amazing features. As you'll see in later chapters, this function can provide the basis for an extraordinary smart-windows interface that goes a long way toward our goal of invisible software.

As implemented here, however, BROWSER() provides only minimal capabilities — a pannable, scrollable window of up to 64 fields. One of the best things about it is that the record pointer moves along with the cursor, so that when the user leaves Browse mode, the current record is displayed full-screen. In many applications, a Browse command is precisely what is needed for updating the files. The eye scans several records at once, viewing only the fields of interest.

DBEDIT() can be customized to any extent through its optional fifth parameter, the name of a user-defined function you wish executed periodically within DBEDIT(). By default, THE_USUAL() supplies DBEDIT() with the name XBROWSER(), another of our library functions. To override this, place the name of your own function in the variable udf_brow before calling BROWSER().

BROWSER() requires very little outside information. At a minimum, a file must be in use. If you like, your program could consist of two lines:

```
USE table name
BROWSER()
```

You are encouraged to look over the code for XBROWSER() carefully, and to make any modifications you wish. Your goal is to set this inner function up to perform the way you like most of the time, so that most of the time you can eliminate the call and rely on the default. Here and elsewhere in the library, the functions expect you to do as little work as possible.

```
PROGRAM        AA_BROWS.PRG
Function(s)    BROWSER()
Purpose        General Browse function for DBEDIT()
Conventions    Assume use with DBEDIT()
Syntax         BROWSER(t,l,b,r,udf,fields,pics,heads)
Parameters     t - top left corner
               l - top left column
               b - bottom row
               r - bottom right column
               udf - custom function to override XBROWSER()
               fields - optional array of fields
               pics   - optional array of pictures
               heads - optional array of column headings
Example        BROWSER(02,00,22,77,udf_brow)
Assumes        called by THE_USUAL() but useful anywhere
Side Effects   none
Returns        True
Calls          POP_MSG(),
```

```
FUNCTION BROWSER

PARAMETERS t, l, b, r, udf, fields, pictures, heads
PRIVATE n, move_chrs, force_rec, ntx_expr, ntx_eval, prev_rec, ;
      is_append, any_append, keystroke, e_field, get_data,;
      f_size
IF EMPTY(FIELDNAME(1))
   POP_MSG("Sometimes I wonder about you as a programmer")
   RETURN .F.
ENDIF
move_chrs = CHR(24) + CHR(05) + CHR(03) + CHR(18) + CHR(31) +
CHR(30)
f_size = FCOUNT()
force_rec = .T.
is_append = .F.
any_append = .F.
prev_rec = 0
```

```
IF TYPE("pictures") != "A"
   DECLARE pictures[f_size]
   i = 01
   FOR i = 01 TO f_size
      pictures[i] = GEN_PIC(FIELD(i))
   NEXT
ENDIF
IF TYPE("heads") != "A"
   DECLARE heads[f_size]
   i = 01
   FOR i = 01 TO f_size
      heads[i] = PROPER(FIELD(i))
   NEXT
ENDIF
dummy = .F.
SAVE SCREEN
IF PCOUNT() < 4 .OR. TYPE("t") != "N"
   t = 01
   l = 00
   b = 23
   r = 79
ENDIF
SCROLL(t, l, b, r, 0)
@ t, l, b, r BOX "UM83MT3"
@ t + 3, l SAY "F"
@ t + 3, r SAY "5"
t = t + 1
l = l + 1
r = r - 1
IF TYPE("udf") $ "UL"
   udf = "XBROWSER"
ENDIF
IF TYPE("fields") != "A"
   DECLARE fields[f_size]
   FOR n = 1 TO f_size
      fields[n] = FIELD(n)
   NEXT
ENDIF
IF EOF()
   GO TOP
ENDIF
IF LASTREC() = 0
   KEYBOARD CHR(24)
ENDIF
DBEDIT(t + 1, l, b, r, ;
      fields, ;
      udf, ;
      pictures, ;
      heads,;
```

```
      dummy, dummy, "MOM", dummy)
RESTORE SCREEN
RETURN .T.
```

```
PROGRAM        AA_XBROW.PRG
Function(s)    XBROWSER()
Purpose        Inner function called by DBEDIT()
Conventions    Default function. Customize to suit your
defaults
               override call by BROWSE() by passing in a udf
Syntax         "XBROWSER" - stored as a string passed to
DBEDIT()
Parameters     mode, i - passed automatically by DBEDIT()
Example        udf = "XBROWSER"
Assumes        is_append, any_append, fields, pics
               (fields and pics are arrays manufactured
               in BROWSER() if not passed as params)
Side Effects   given all the freedom, hard to predict
Returns        a number from 0 to 4
Calls
```

```
FUNCTION XBROWSER

PARAMETERS mode, fld_ptr
PRIVATE ret_val, esc, home_key, end_key, ctrl_home, ctrl_end, ;
        ctrl_pgdn, ctrl_pgdn, right, left, down, up, ;
        right_key, left_key, down_key, up_key, ;
        do_repaint, no_repaint, ins_blank, cur_field, ;
        idle, bof, eof, empty, exception, m_row, m_col, exit
exit = 00
ret_val = 01
keystroke = LASTKEY()
esc_key    = CHR(27)
home_key   = CHR(01)
end_key    = CHR(06)
chome_key  = CHR(29)
cend_key   = CHR(23)
cpdn_key   = CHR(30)
cpup_key   = CHR(31)
right_key  = CHR(04)
left_key   = CHR(19)
down_key   = CHR(24)
up_key     = CHR(05)
```

```
enter_key = CHR(13)
enter = 13
esc = 27
home = 01
ctrl_home = 29
ctrl_end  = 23
ctrl_pgup = 31
ctrl_pgdn = 30
right = 04
left = 19
down = 24
up = 05
pgup = 18
pgdn = 03
idle = 00                          && dbedit idle mode
bof  = 01                          && bof hit in dbedit
eof  = 02                          && eof hit in dbedit
empty = 03                         && no records in file
exception = 04                     && keystroke exception
do_repaint = 02
no_repaint = 01
ins_blank  = 03
m_row = ROW()
m_col = COL()
cur_field = fields[fld_ptr]
IF prev_rec != RECNO()
   prev_rec = RECNO()
   force_rec = .T.
ENDIF
DO CASE
   CASE mode = idle
      IF CHR(keystroke) $ move_chrs .OR. force_rec
         STAT_LINE()
      ENDIF
   CASE mode = bof
      IF is_append
         ret_val = IF(any_append, do_repaint, ins_blank)
         is_append = .F.
         any_append = .F.
      ELSE
         STAT_LINE()
      ENDIF
      force_rec = .T.
   CASE mode = eof
      IF is_append
         IF keystroke = down .AND. !EOF()
            ret_val = ins_blank
         ELSE
            IF keystroke = ctrl_pgdn
```

```
                ret_val = IF(any_append, do_repaint, ins_blank)
                is_append = .F.
                any_append = .F.
             ELSE
                IF force_rec
                    STAT_LINE()
                ENDIF
             ENDIF
          ENDIF
       ELSE
          IF keystroke = down
             ret_val = ins_blank
             is_append = .T.
          ELSE
             STAT_LINE()
          ENDIF
       ENDIF
       force_rec = .T.
    CASE mode = empty
       IF keystroke = down
          ret_val = ins_blank
          is_append = .T.
          force_rec = .T.
       ELSE
          STAT_LINE()
       ENDIF
    CASE mode = exception
       DO CASE
          CASE ESC()
             ret_val = exit
          CASE DEL() .AND. !EOF() .AND. LASTREC() != 0
             IF DELETED()
                RECALL
             ELSE
                DELETE
             ENDIF
             STAT_LINE()
          CASE ENTER() .OR. INS() .OR. IS_DATA(keystroke) .AND. ;
             (is_append .OR. (!EOF() .AND. LASTREC() != 0))
             IF INS()
                is_append = .T.
             ENDIF
             IF IS_VIRTUAL(fld_ptr)
                ret_val = no_repaint
             ELSE
                ntx_expr = INDEXKEY(0)
                IF !EMPTY(ntx_expr)
                    ntx_eval = &ntx_expr
             ENDIF
```

```
IF keystroke != 13
      KEYBOARD CHR(keystroke)
   ENDIF
   IF TYPE(cur_field) = "M"
      READ_MEMO(cur_field)
   ELSE
       IF TYPE("valids") = "A"
         valid_exp = valids[fld_ptr]
         IF EMPTY(valid_exp)
            valid_exp = ".T."
         ENDIF
      ELSE
         valid_exp = ".T."
      ENDIF
      IF TYPE("pictures") = "A"
         pict_str = pictures[fld_ptr]
         IF EMPTY(pict_str)
            pict_str = GEN_PIC(cur_field)
         ENDIF
      ELSE
         pict_str = GEN_PIC(cur_field)
      ENDIF
      IF !is_append
         get_data = &cur_field
      ELSE
          IF TYPE("defaults") = "A"
            default = defaults[fld_ptr]
            IF EMPTY(default)
               default = BLANK(cur_field)
            ENDIF
         ELSE
            default = BLANK(cur_field)
         ENDIF
         get_data = default
      ENDIF
      SET KEY up TO clear_gets
      SET KEY down TO clear_gets
      @ m_row, m_col GET get_data ;
                     PICTURE pict_str ;
                     VALID &valid_exp
      READ_IT()
      keystroke = LASTKEY()
      * release keys
      SET KEY up TO
      SET KEY down TO
      IF UPDATED()
         IF is_append
            APPEND BLANK
            any_append = .T.
```

```
                  ENDIF
                  REPLACE &cur_field WITH get_data
                  KEYBOARD right_key
               ENDIF
            ENDIF
            ret_val = no_repaint
         ENDIF
         IF !EMPTY(ntx_expr) .AND. !is_append
            IF ntx_eval != (&ntx_expr)
               ret_val = do_repaint
            ENDIF
         ENDIF
         IF ret_val != do_repaint
            DO CASE
               CASE keystroke = up
                  IF is_append
                     ret_val = IF(any_append,;
                                  do_repaint,;
                                  ins_blank)
                     is_append = .F.
                     any_append = .F.
                  ELSE
                     KEYBOARD up_key
                  ENDIF
               CASE keystroke = PgUp
                  IF is_append
                     ret_val = IF(any_append,;
                                  do_repaint,;
                                  ins_blank)
                     is_append = .F.
                     any_append = .F.
                  ELSE
                     KEYBOARD up_key
                  ENDIF
               CASE keystroke = down
                  KEYBOARD down_key
               CASE keystroke = pgdn .AND. !is_append
                  KEYBOARD down_key
               CASE keystroke = enter
                  KEYBOARD right_key
            ENDCASE
         ENDIF
      ENDCASE
ENDCASE
RETURN ret_val
```

Summary

In this section we have created three functions powerful enough to tackle the most sophisticated microcomputer database applications:

- DO_IT — a generalized menu-machine which operates a light-bar menu system and executes the appropriate functions, with the intelligence built in to handle menus at any level of the program.

- PD_MENU — a two-dimensional version of DO_IT which add pull-down boxes to the menu system. It contains the intelligence to calculate box size and similar details, and doubles as a program executor.

- THE_USUAL — a generalized file-maintenance routine which divorced from the data it manipulates.

- BROWSER/XBROWSER — a pair of functions which encase DBEDIT() and result in a smart-windows interface.

The basic and high-level components of our toolkit are largely complete. By now, you're no doubt impatient to write some programs rather than just tools. A few subordinate functions called by our basic tools have not been presented, but let's postpone them until the last section of the book, the Function Library.

The next three chapters present three programs based on THE_USUAL(), each introducing new wrinkles and requirements at each step. You'll learn how to take each program from concept to completion, and to rely on the library to do the bulk of your work.

Chapter 6

A Simple Case of the Usual

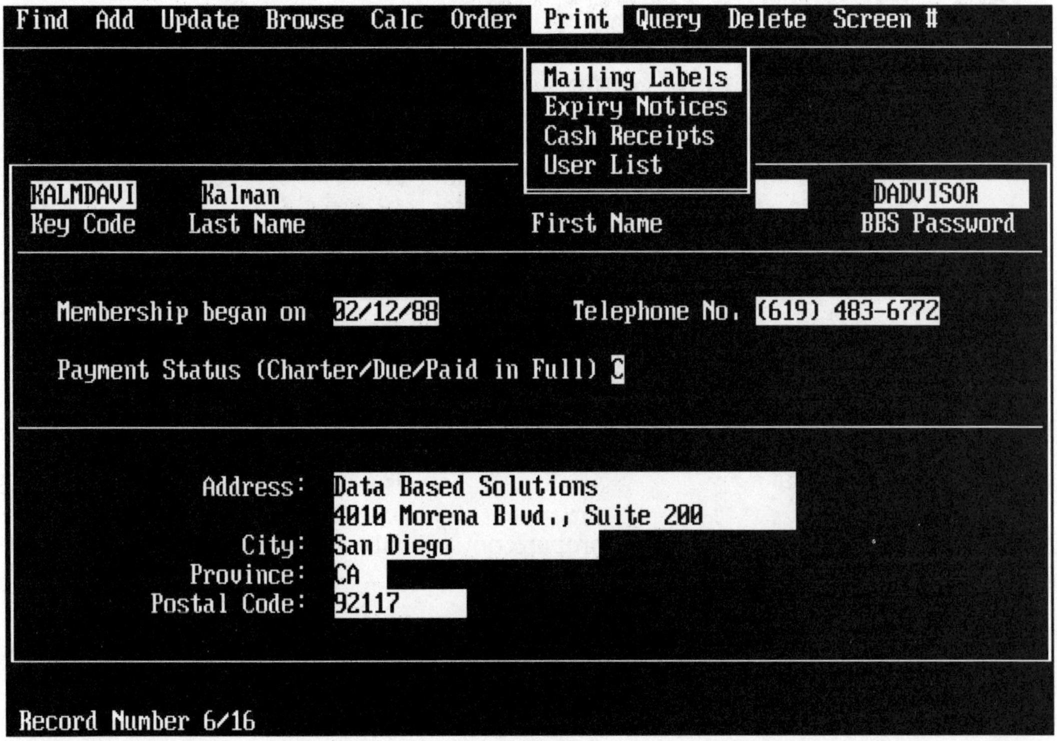

BBS.PRG, our first program based on THE_USUAL(). The Print command is active, displaying its sub-menu. THE_USUAL() senses that more than one screen is available, so it adds the Screen command automatically.

The preliminaries done, we can now construct our first program based on THE_USUAL().

In our first pass we'll keep everything simple. The application is based on a single data file USERS.DBF, containing the list of users of a bulletin board system. The screen is nothing fancy, nor is the file structure. We won't even bother with a main menu. We'll simply say hello, check the files and go straight into the application.

BBS.PRG is a complete program only in the sense that it runs. Capabilities such as printing a list of users are absent, although the design anticipates their eventual inclusion.

Table Structure of USERS.DBF

Field	Field Name	Type	Width
1	CODE	Character	8
2	LAST_NAME	Character	20
3	FIRSTNAME	Character	20
4	PASSWORD	Character	12
5	SIGNED_ON	Date	8
6	P_STATUS	Character	1
7	PHONE	Character	10
8	B_ADDR1	Character	35
9	B_ADDR2	Character	35
10	B_CITY	Character	20
11	B_PROV	Character	4
12	B_PCODE	Character	10
Total			184

Now for the calling program. We'll prepare our global variables, sign on, check out the data file and index, then call our main function.

```
PROGRAM        BBS.PRG
Function(s)    BBS, CHK_DBFS()
Purpose        a simple Clipper application
Conventions    A model program showing all components,
               and a first exposure to THE_USUAL().
Syntax         main program. Link with BBS1 or BBS2
Parameters     none
Example        LINK BBS BBS1,,,CLIPPER ARTFUL SMALLX KEYS
Assumes        existence of ARTFUL.LIB
```

```
Side Effects none
Returns      nothing
Calls        SYSCOLOR(), SIGN_ON(), DB_OPEN()
             USERS(), XBROWSER()
```

```
exe_name = "The eBBS User Maintenance Program"
exe_desc = "A Simple Case of The Usual"
SYSCOLOR(01)
SIGN_ON(exe_name, exe_desc)
IF !CHK_DBFS()
   SET CURSOR ON
   RETURN
ENDIF
USERS()
SIGN_OFF(exe_name)
```

```
FUNCTION CHK_DBFS

PRIVATE result, work_area, file_name, indexes, ntx_field
file_name = "USERS"
indexes   = 01
ntx_field = "CODE"
result = DB_OPEN( file_name, indexes, ntx_field )
RETURN result
EXTERNAL XBROWSER                     && Clipper doesn't know about it
```

```
PROGRAM      BBS1.PRG
Function(s)  USERS, CHK_DBFS()
Purpose      contains the main functions of BBS
Conventions  A model Clipper program
             and a first exposure to THE_USUAL().
Syntax       main program. Link with BBS1 or BBS2
Parameters   none
Example      LINK BBS BBS1,,,CLIPPER ARTFUL SMALLX KEYS
Assumes      existence of ARTFUL.LIB
Side Effects none
Returns      nothing
Calls        SYSCOLOR(), SIGN_ON(), DB_OPEN()
             USERS(), XBROWSER()
```

```
FUNCTION USERS

PRIVATE result, temp_scr, id_char, ;
         old_file, curr_file, blood_line, ;
         screen_no, no_screens, no_kids, no_indexes
PRIVATE udf_add, udf_upd, udf_scr, udf_say, udf_key, ;
         udf_calc, udf_prt, udf_rpl, udf_qry, udf_fld, ;
         udf_zoom, udf_memo, udf_brow, udf_help
PRIVATE xkeys, xcues, xpics, kids, kkeys, kcues
PRIVATE mtr, mtc, mbr, mbc
SAVE SCREEN TO temp_scr
old_file   = ALIAS()
curr_file  = "USERS"
blood_line = ""
id_char    = "U"
result      = .F.
no_screens = 01
screen_no  = 01
SELECT &curr_file
SEEK   blood_line
udf_scr   = id_char + "_SCR()"
udf_say   = id_char + "_SAY()"
udf_key   = id_char + "_KEY()"
udf_fld   = id_char + "_FLD()"
udf_prt   = "POP_MSG('Print Membership Expiring Reminders')"
udf_add   = "GET_STD(.T.)"
udf_upd   = "GET_STD(.F.)"
udf_calc = "COUNT_EM()"
udf_qry   = "QUERY()"
udf_rpl   = "RPL()"
udf_zoom = .F.
udf_brow = .F.
udf_memo = .F.
udf_help = .F.
mtr = .F.
mtc = .F.
mbr = .F.
mbc = .F.
no_keys = 01
no_kids = 00
xkeys = "CODE"
xcues = "User Code"
xpics = caps
IF no_kids > 00
   * copy these lines as required
   DECLARE kids[no_kids], kcues[no_kids]
   kids[01]   = ""
   kcues[01] = ""
ENDIF
THE_USUAL()
```

```
result = .T.
RETURN result
```

```
FUNCTION U_SCR

@ 05,00 CLEAR
DRAW_BOX(05,00,22,79,01)
@ 07,02 SAY "Key Code    Last Name                   First Name"+;
            SPACE(13) + "BBS Password"
@ 08,01 SAY REPL("D",78)
@ 10,04 SAY "Membership began on                     Telephone No."
@ 12,04 SAY "Payment Status (Charter/Due/Paid in Full)"
@ 14,01 SAY REPL("D",78)
@ 16,14 SAY "Address:"
@ 18,08 SAY "City:"
@ 19,12 SAY "Province:"
@ 20,11 SAY "Postal Code:"
RETURN .T.
```

```
FUNCTION U_KEY

PRIVATE result
result = .F.
name_pic = "!XXXXXXXXXXXXXXXXXXX"
@ 06, 15 GET mLAST_NAME PICTURE name_pic
@ 06, 41 GET mFIRST_NAME PICTURE name_pic
@ 06, 02 GET mCODE PICTURE caps VALID UNIQUE(mCODE)
READ_IT()
result = !ESC()
RETURN result
```

```
FUNCTION U_FLD

PRIVATE result
result = .F.
name_pic = "!XXXXXXXXXXXXXXXXXXX"
phone_pic = "@R (###) 999-9999"
caps = "@!"
date_pic = "@D"
@ 06, 66 GET mPASSWORD PICTURE caps
@ 10, 25 GET mSIGNED_ON PICTURE date_pic
@ 10, 57 GET mPHONE PICTURE phone_pic
@ 12, 46 GET mP_STATUS PICTURE caps VALID mP_STATUS $ "CPD"
@ 16, 25 GET mB_ADDR1
@ 17, 25 GET mB_ADDR2
```

```
@ 18, 25 GET mB_CITY PICTURE name_pic
@ 19, 25 GET mB_PROV PICTURE caps
@ 20, 25 GET mB_PCODE PICTURE caps
RETURN result
```

```
FUNCTION U_SAY

PRIVATE result
result = .T.
name_pic = "!XXXXXXXXXXXXXXXXXX"
phone_pic = "@R (###) 999-9999"
caps = "@!"
date_pic = "@D"
SYSCOLOR(02)
@ 06,02 SAY CODE PICTURE caps
@ 06,15 SAY LAST_NAME PICTURE name_pic
@ 06,41 SAY FIRST_NAME PICTURE name_pic
@ 06,66 SAY PASSWORD PICTURE caps
@ 10,25 SAY SIGNED_ON PICTURE date_pic
@ 10,57 SAY PHONE PICTURE phone_pic
@ 12,46 SAY P_STATUS PICTURE caps
@ 16,25 SAY B_ADDR1
@ 17,25 SAY B_ADDR2
@ 18,25 SAY B_CITY PICTURE name_pic
@ 19,25 SAY B_PROV PICTURE caps
@ 20,25 SAY B_PCODE PICTURE caps
SYSCOLOR(01)
RETURN result
```

Multiple Screens

Now that we have our basic engine in place, it's time to stretch it a little. Even in a simple one-file application, a possibility is a file requiring several screens. In dBASE we'd use SET FORMAT TO *file_name* and get automatic PageUp and PageDown control, but also lose Clipper's wonderful VALID clause.

Thanks to the structure of THE_USUAL(), we don't have to give this problem a second thought. All that is required is that our screen, display and get functions have the "pages" built into them, and that we keep aware which page we're supposed to be displaying.

That's easy: we'll create the variables *screen_no* and *no_screens*, the first a counter and the second a limiter. If *no_screens* is 1, we eliminate the Screen command from the menu since there is only one screen.

That alone, however, is not enough. Though it may "work", it denies the user the opportunity to select a page, then move through the file viewing only that page. Where there are a half dozen pages to view, the user interested only in the data on page 5 would be forced to enter six keystrokes per record. Let's not saddle our user so. Instead, we'll just track the screen number, defaulting it to 1 on each new call.

Another problem emerges. Since there is little point in duplicating essential (e.g. key) fields on every screen, what will we do when the user decides to add a record while viewing screen 5, on which no key fields appear? At this point, it's time to make up a rule: *any and all key fields in a multi-screen file maintenance routine must appear on the first screen.* I can't recall an occasion on which I wanted to do it otherwise, but let's realize the rules up front.

This rule simplifies the problem considerably: force the screen number back to 1, repaint the screen, then begin the add routine. This will ensure that they key fields are filled in and validated before the record is actually added.

In update mode, though, it will be neither necessary nor advantageous to switch to screen one. The user — or a specific user among a group — may wish only to view or update the information on a specific screen. The system should make it as easy as possible.

Let's return to our BBS program, adding more fields and a second screen to it. We've decided it would be useful to record our users' hardware, communications software and interests for future reference.

To make this change, first we need to alter the structure of our data file. Next we create the second screen and the blocks of SAY and GET statements to match. In our calling program, we must set the variable *no_screens* to the new total number of screens.

Finally, we must add a branching mechanism to our screen, key and field, so that depending on the value of screen_no they will behave appropriately.

First, the new file structure:

Here is the revised table structure for USERS.DBF.

Field	Field Name	Type	Width

1	CODE	Character	8
2	LAST_NAME	Character	20
3	FIRST_NAME	Character	20
4	PASSWORD	Character	12
5	SIGNED_ON	Date	8
6	P_STATUS	Character	1
7	PHONE	Character	10
8	B_ADDR1	Character	35
9	B_ADDR2	Character	35
10	B_CITY	Character	20
11	B_PROV	Character	4
12	B_PCODE	Character	10
13	HARDWARE	Character	40
14	COMM_PROG	Character	10
15	BAUD_RATE	Numeric	5
16	INTERESTS	Character	60
Total			299

Now let's look at the revised code. Comparing this to the original in BBS1.PRG, you'll see that actually very little has changed. We have set the variable *no_screens* to 2, and added an IF/ELSE/ENDIF structure to check the value of *screen_no* in the screen, say and get functions, and that's about it.

```
FUNCTION U_SCR

@ 05,00 CLEAR
DRAW_BOX(05,00,22,79,01)
@ 07,02 SAY ;
   "Key Code    Last Name
First Name"+;SPACE(13) + "BBS Password"
@ 08,01 SAY REPL("D",78)
IF screen_no = 01
   @ 10,04 SAY "Membership began on Telephone No."
   @ 12,04 SAY "Payment Status (Charter/Due/Paid in Full)"
   @ 14,01 SAY REPL("D",78)
   @ 16,14 SAY "Address:"
   @ 18,08 SAY "City:"
   @ 19,12 SAY "Province:"
   @ 20,11 SAY "Postal Code:"
ELSE
   @ 11,05 SAY "Hardware used:"
   @ 14,04 SAY "Comm. Software:                    Baud  Rate:"
   @ 17,21 SAY "Interests (separate entries with a '/')"
ENDIF
```

```
RETURN .T.
```

```
FUNCTION U_KEY

PRIVATE result
result = .F.
name_pic = "!XXXXXXXXXXXXXXXXXX"
caps = "@!"
@ 06, 15 GET mLAST_NAME PICTURE name_pic
@ 06, 41 GET mFIRST_NAME PICTURE name_pic
@ 06, 02 GET mCODE PICTURE caps VALID UNIQUE(mCODE)
READ_IT()
result = !ESC()
RETURN result
```

```
FUNCTION U_FLD

PRIVATE result
result = .F.
name_pic = "!XXXXXXXXXXXXXXXXXX"
phone_pic = "@R (###) 999-9999"
caps = "@!"
date_pic = "@D"
bauds = "300/1200/2400/9600/19200"
IF screen_no = 01
   @ 06, 66 GET mPASSWORD PICTURE caps
   @ 10, 25 GET mSIGNED_ON PICTURE date_pic
   @ 10, 57 GET mPHONE PICTURE phone_pic
   @ 12, 46 GET mP_STATUS PICTURE caps ;
      VALID mP_STATUS $ "CPD"
   @ 16, 25 GET mB_ADDR1
   @ 17, 25 GET mB_ADDR2
   @ 18, 25 GET mB_CITY PICTURE name_pic
   @ 19, 25 GET mB_PROV PICTURE caps
   @ 20, 25 GET mB_PCODE PICTURE caps
ELSE
   @ 11,22 GET mHARDWARE
   @ 14, 22 GET mCOMM_PROG PICTURE caps
   @ 14, 47 GET mBAUD_RATE PICTURE "99999" ;
         VALID STRINT(mBAUD_RATE) $ bauds
   @ 19, 10 GET mINTERESTS PICTURE caps
ENDIF
READ_IT()
result = !ESC()
```

```
RETURN result
```

```
FUNCTION U_SAY

PRIVATE result
result = .T.
phone_pic = "@R (###) 999-9999"
name_pic = "!XXXXXXXXXXXXXXXXXXX"
SYSCOLOR(02)
@ 06,02 SAY CODE PICTURE caps
@ 06,15 SAY LAST_NAME PICTURE name_pic
@ 06,41 SAY FIRST_NAME PICTURE name_pic
IF screen_no = 01
   @ 06,66 SAY PASSWORD PICTURE caps
   @ 10,25 SAY SIGNED_ON PICTURE date_pic
   @ 10,57 SAY PHONE PICTURE phone_pic
   @ 12,46 SAY P_STATUS PICTURE "!"
   @ 16,25 SAY B_ADDR1
   @ 17,25 SAY B_ADDR2
   @ 18,25 SAY B_CITY PICTURE name_pic
   @ 19,25 SAY B_PROV PICTURE caps
   @ 20,25 SAY B_PCODE PICTURE caps
ELSE
   @ 06,66 SAY PASSWORD PICTURE caps
   @ 11,22 SAY HARDWARE PICTURE "@X"
   @ 14,22 SAY COMM_PROG PICTURE "@X"
   @ 14,47 SAY BAUD_RATE PICTURE "99999"
   @ 19,10 SAY INTERESTS PICTURE "@X"
ENDIF
SYSCOLOR(01)
RETURN result
```

Compile and run the program and see how well THE_USUAL() responds to a simple, one-table problem, even if the application has validity checks and multiple screens. Of course, if your problems were all this simple, programming would be neither as lucrative nor as fun as it is. So now let's take on some real work.

In almost any application a client is going to pay you to write, there will be tasks or operations that THE_USUAL() doesn't anticipate. These extras might be transactional in nature, perhaps requiring an entire menu of their own; they might be file-oriented, such as posting a journal file to the General Ledger, copying selected records to a temporary file, appending sales orders placed overnight through a modem — a side-order of sausages, so to speak.

We deal with these possibilities by passing parameters into THE_USUAL(), shaping its behaviour from without. Whatever the custom function is, we can assume two facts: it must appear on the menu and it must have some code to execute. We can pass two strings into THE_USUAL(), one containing the cue to add to the menu, the other containing the name of the function. But what if there are several custom options to add?

We'll use our by-now familiar technique of checking the data type of the parameters passed in. If there are several options, we'll pass arrays. If there is only one option, we'll pass strings. If there are no custom options, we'll pass nothing.

This time I won't present the code, but simply a skeleton to follow. Returning to the BBS membership application, let's consider a few things it lacks which might be useful.

Most important, it lacks an output mechanism. We can't even print a list of members, let alone receipts, expiry notices or even mailing labels.All we have to do to create this routine is create a pair of arrays, one containing the prompts for the print menu and the other the names of the corresponding functions — which, for the moment, we'll fill with calls to POP_MSG(), reminding us what we have yet to write. We wrap those few lines of code in a function U_PRT(), then replace the line in the calling program that defaults the print routine to POP_MSG() with the new call to U_PRT(). Simple! We remark out the default print message, and un-remark the call below it:

```
udf_prt = "POP_MSG('Print Membership Expiring Reminders')"
udf_prt = id_char + "_PRT()"
```

Here's the code for U_PRT(), with calls to POP_MSG() until we get each of the subroutines written.

```
PROGRAM        BBS_UPRT.PRG
Function(s)    U_PRT()
Purpose        User-defined print routine for BBS.PRG
Conventions    Over-rides the default print routine
               in THE_USUAL()
Syntax         U_PRT()
Parameters     none
Example        udf_prt = id_char + "_PRT()"   - typical setup
Assumes        THE_USUAL() setup
```

```
Side Effects none
Returns      True
Calls        L_MENU()
```

```
FUNCTION  U_PRT

PRIVATE choice, opts[04], udfs[04]
choice = 01
opts[01] = " Labels "
opts[02] = " Expiry Notices "
opts[03] = " Receipts "
opts[04] = " User List "
udfs[01] = " POP_MSG('Here we print Labels ')"
udfs[02] = " POP_MSG('Here we print Expiry Notices')"
udfs[03] = " POP_MSG('Here we print Receipts')"
udfs[04] = " POP_MSG('Here we print a User List')"
choice = DO_IT(choice, opts, .F., udfs, 02)
RETURN .T.
```

You should now have a pretty good idea how well THE_USUAL() can accommodate the unusual, and how easily you can create such routines to plug into the slots awaiting them.

Now let's turn our attention to the *real* problem of database managment — multiple tables in an application.

Chapter 7

The Usual, with a Side

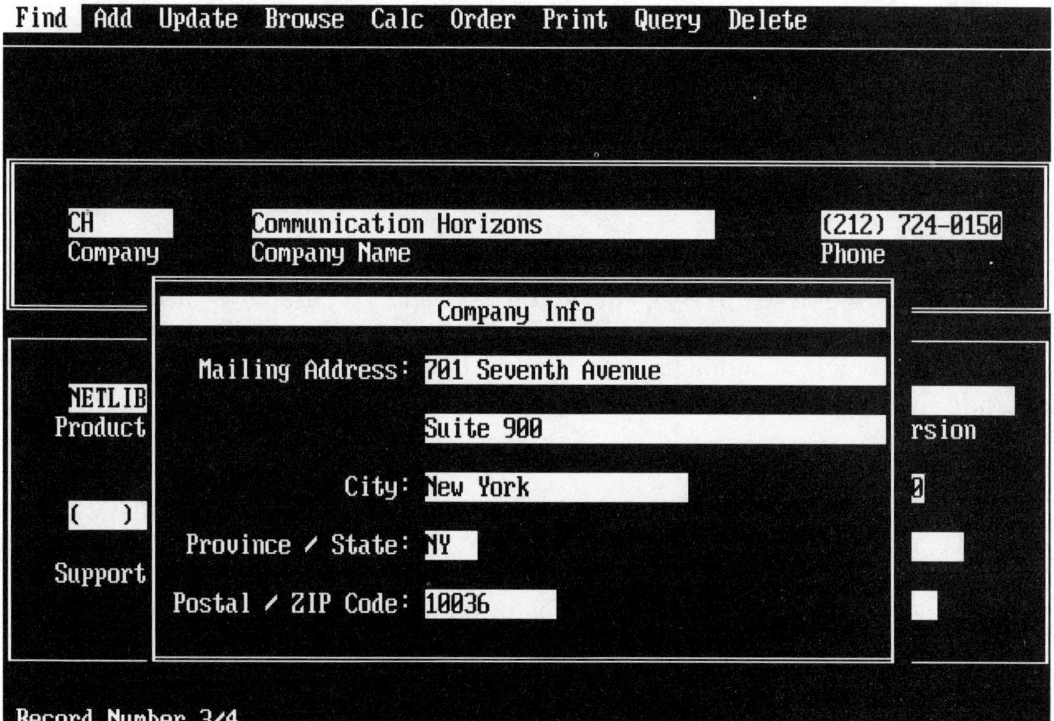

SOFT.PRG with its Zoom window open. Function SHADOWBOX() displays the window title, border and shadow. The Order command is active. Since no parameters were passed, MENU_ORD() dynamically generates a menu of sequences based on the active indexes plus the record numbers (order 0).

Tracking the Software You Buy

This pass we begin to tap the flexibility built into THE_USUAL(). This example is one of those programs you probably always meant to write but never got around to writing. (If you've already written it, congratulations! The shoemaker's children don't always go barefoot.) SOFT.PRG tracks the software you've purchased — name, serial number, date and place purchased, manufacturer's name, technical support phone number and so on. It is possible, even likely, that you have purchased more than one program from a given manufacturer, so these two information entities reside in separate tables.

This application could be written from either of two opposing viewpoints. The traditional view suggests that you begin with the parent file, then zoom to the children. In this case the parents are the manufacturers, the children the programs.

The opposing, user-oriented analysis views the software as the item of primary interest, while the manufacturers are only of interest when we need to talk to them. Viewed from here, the traditional approach forces the user to know the parent before locating one of its children, when in practice it is more likely that the user will know the name of a program than its manufacturer.

This second approach views the company file as a lookup table rather than a parent, but has problems of its own. When the user tries to add a program whose manufacturer is not yet on file, typically the record cannot be added. Instead, the user is forced to cancel the operation, abandon the software file, open the company file, add the record, return to the software file, and finally add the new program. In a word, user-hostile software.

To make the second approach workable, we need to add a routine which detects a non-existent company code, then asks the user if she wants to add it to the file. In the case of a typo she can try again. Where it is a new company, she can add it on the spot, then continue adding the software, with no interruption in the flow. In a word, useful software.

In a nutshell, it doesn't matter which of the two approaches to file relationships we use, zoom or lookup. All you have to do to restructure the application is change the number of children in each calling function, then change the line in your main program that calls the parent function. You might want to try this on your own, just to prove it works.

Table Structures

The Software Table

Field	Field Name	Type	Width	Dec
1	CODE	Character	8	
2	PROD_ID	Character	8	
3	PRODUCT	Character	30	
4	SERIAL_NO	Character	10	
5	VERSION	Character	10	
6	GENRE	Character	8	
7	PRICE	Numeric	7	2
8	PURCHASED	Date	8	
9	T_SUPPORT	Character	10	
10	CONTACT	Character	20	
11	DEALER	Character	10	
12	HISTORY	Memo	10	
13	NOTES	Memo	10	
Total			150	

The Hardware Table

Field	Field Name	Type	Width
1	CODE	Character	8
2	NAME	Character	35
3	PHONE	Character	10
4	B_ADDR1	Character	35
5	B_ADDR2	Character	35
6	B_CITY	Character	20
7	B_PROV	Character	4
8	B_PCODE	Character	10
Total			158

SOFT.EXE Source Code

As we have seen, the calling program does little more than sign on, check the files, call our main function, and sign off afterwards.

The function CHK_DBFS() localizes all our file-checking, and incidentally provides a concise summary of the data layout.

```
PROGRAM       SOFT.PRG
Function(s)   SOFT.PRG, CHK_DBFS()
Purpose       Software registration program
Conventions   main program
Syntax        SOFT mono
Parameters    mono
Example       SOFT M - forces monochrome execution
Assumes       pass anything to force monochrome
Side Effects  none
Returns       nothing
Calls         SYSCOLOR(), SIGN_ON(), SIGN_OFF(),
              DB_OPEN(), SOFTWARE()
```

```
PARAMETER monochrome
IF TYPE("monochrome") = "U"     && Guard against CGA/mono
   monochrome = .F.
ENDIF
exe_name = "The Soft Track"
exe_desc = "Software Registration System"
no_files = 02
phone_pic = "@R (###) 999-9999"
caps = "@!"
money42 = "####.##"
city_pic = "!XXXXXXXXXXXXXXXXXX"
phone_pic = "@R (###) 999-9999"
SYSCOLOR(01)
SIGN_ON(exe_name, exe_desc)
IF !CHK_DBFS()
   SET CURSOR ON
   RETURN
ENDIF
SOFTWARE()
SIGN_OFF(exe_name,exe_desc)
```

```
FUNCTION CHK_DBFS

PARAMETERS
PRIVATE result, x, work_area, file_name, indexes, ntx_field
result = .T.
x = .F.
file_name = "COMPANY"
```

```
indexes = 01
ntx_field = "CODE"
x = DB_OPEN( file_name, indexes, ntx_field )
IF !x                                 && postpone the RETURN
   result = .F.
ENDIF
file_name = "SOFTWARE"
indexes = 01
ntx_field = "CODE + UPPER(LEFT(PRODUCT,8))"
x = DB_OPEN( file_name, indexes, ntx_field )
IF !x
   result = .F.
ENDIF
RETURN result
```

```
PROGRAM        SOFT_SO.PRG
Function(s)    SOFTWARE(),S_SCR(),S_KEY(),S_FLD(), S_SAY()
Purpose        File maintenance function for SOFTWARE.DBF
Conventions    Called by SOFT.PRG
Syntax         SOFTWARE()
Parameters     none
Example        SOFTWARE()
Assumes        availability of THE_USUAL() functions
Side Effects   none
Returns        True
Calls          GET_STD(), COUNT_EM(), QUERY(), RPL()
               XBROWSER()
```

```
FUNCTION SOFTWARE

PRIVATE reply, temp_scr, id_char, ;
        curr_file, blood_line, ;
        screen_no, no_screens, no_kids, no_indexes
PRIVATE udf_add, udf_upd, udf_scr, udf_say, udf_key, ;
        udf_calc, udf_prt, udf_rpl, udf_qry, udf_fld, ;
        udf_zoom, udf_memo, udf_brow, udf_help
PRIVATE xkeys, xcues, xpics, ;
        kids, kkeys, kcues
PRIVATE mtr, mtc, mbr, mbc
SAVE SCREEN TO temp_scr
curr_file = "SOFTWARE"
blood_line = ""
id_char = "S"
reply = .F.
```

```
no_screens = 01
screen_no  = 01
SELECT &curr_file
SEEK   blood_line
udf_scr   = id_char + "_SCR()"
udf_say   = id_char + "_SAY()"
udf_key   = id_char + "_KEY()"
udf_fld   = id_char + "_FLD()"
udf_prt   = "POP_MSG('Ask for a print routine')"
udf_add   = "GET_STD(.T.)"
udf_upd   = "GET_STD(.F.)"
udf_calc = "COUNT_EM()"
udf_qry   = "QUERY()"
udf_rpl   = "RPL()"
udf_zoom = "COMPANY()"
udf_brow = .F.
udf_memo = .F.
udf_help = .F.
mtr = .F.
mtc = .F.
mbr = .F.
mbc = .F.
no_keys = 01
no_kids = 01
xkeys = "PROD_ID"
xcues = "Product Code"
xpics = caps
THE_USUAL()
reply = .T.
RETURN reply
```

```
FUNCTION S_SCR

PRIVATE reply, phone_pic

DRAW_BOX(05,00,10,79,02)
@ 08,05 SAY "Company       Company Name" +
               +space(31)+"Phone"
DRAW_BOX(11,00,22,79,01)
@ 14,04 SAY "Product Code   Product Name"
@ 14,40 SAY "Serial No.    Version"
@ 16,47 SAY "Purchase Price:"
@ 18,47 SAY "Purchased From:"
@ 19,04 SAY "Support Phone        Contact Person"
@ 20,47 SAY "Purchase Date:"
```

```
RETURN .T.
```

```
FUNCTION S_KEY

PRIVATE reply, phone_pic
reply = .F.
@ 07, 05 GET mCODE PICTURE caps ;
         VALID LOOKUP(mCODE,"COMPANY", "NAME", 07, 19)
SYSCOLOR(02)
@ 07, 62 SAY COMPANY->PHONE PICTURE phone_pic
SYSCOLOR(01)
@ 13, 05 GET mPROD_ID PICTURE caps ;
         VALID UNIQUE(mPROD_ID)
READ_IT()
reply = !ESC()
RETURN reply
```

```
FUNCTION S_FLD

PRIVATE reply
reply = .F.

date_pic = "@D"
@ 13, 19 GET mPRODUCT PICTURE caps
@ 13, 53 GET mSERIAL_NO PICTURE caps
@ 13, 67 GET mVERSION PICTURE caps
@ 16, 63 GET mPRICE PICTURE money42
@ 17, 05 GET mT_SUPPORT PICTURE phone_pic
@ 17, 24 GET mCONTACT
@ 18, 63 GET mDEALER
@ 20, 63 GET mPURCHASED PICTURE date_pic
READ_IT()
reply = !ESC()
RETURN reply
```

```
FUNCTION S_SAY

PRIVATE reply
reply = .T.
SYSCOLOR(02)
@ 07,05 SAY CODE PICTURE caps
@ 07,19 SAY FETCH(CODE, "COMPANY", "NAME")
@ 07,62 SAY COMPANY->PHONE PICTURE phone_pic
@ 13,05 SAY PROD_ID PICTURE caps
@ 13,19 SAY PRODUCT
```

```
@ 13,53 SAY SERIAL_NO PICTURE caps
@ 13,67 SAY VERSION PICTURE caps
@ 16,63 SAY PRICE PICTURE money42
@ 17,05 SAY T_SUPPORT PICTURE phone_pic
@ 17,24 SAY CONTACT
@ 18,63 SAY DEALER
@ 20,63 SAY PURCHASED PICTURE date_pic
SYSCOLOR(01)
RETURN reply
```

The functions which control the company table are quite similar to those controlling the software table, and that's the point of the exercise.

```
PROGRAM        SOFT_CO.PRG
Function(s)    COMPANY(),C_SCR(),C_KEY(),C_FLD(),C_SAY()
Purpose        Company file maintenance functions
Conventions    called by SOFTWARE()
Syntax         COMPANY()
Parameters     none
Example        COMPANY()
Assumes        THE_USUAL() functions are available
Side Effects   none
Returns        True
Calls          THE_USUAL()
```

```
FUNCTION COMPANY

PRIVATE reply, temp_scr, id_char, ;
        curr_file, blood_line, ;
        screen_no, no_screens, no_kids, no_indexes
PRIVATE udf_add, udf_upd, udf_scr, udf_say, udf_key, ;
        udf_calc, udf_prt, udf_rpl, udf_qry, udf_fld, ;
        udf_zoom, udf_memo, udf_brow, udf_help
PRIVATE xkeys, xcues, xpics, ;
        kids, kkeys, kcues
PRIVATE mtr, mtc, mbr, mbc
SAVE SCREEN TO temp_scr
curr_file  = "COMPANY"
blood_line = CODE
id_char = "C"
reply = .F.
no_screens = 01
```

```
screen_no  = 01
SELECT &curr_file
SEEK   blood_line
udf_scr = id_char + "_SCR()"
udf_say = id_char + "_SAY()"
udf_key = id_char + "_KEY()"
udf_fld = id_char + "_FLD()"
udf_prt = "POP_MSG('Ask for a print routine')"
udf_add = "GET_STD(.T.)"
udf_upd = "GET_STD(.F.)"
udf_calc = "COUNT_EM()"
udf_qry = "QUERY()"
udf_rpl = "RPL()"
udf_help = "U_HELP"
udf_zoom = ""
udf_brow = "XBROWSE"
udf_memo = ""
mtr = .F.
mtc = .F.
mbr = .F.
mbc = .F.
no_keys = 01
no_kids = 00
xkeys = "CODE"
xcues = "CODE"
xpics = caps
IF no_kids  00
DECLARE kids[no_kids], kcues[no_kids]
   kids[01]  = ""
   kcues[01] = ""
ENDIF
THE_USUAL()
reply = .T.
RETURN reply
```

```
FUNCTION C_SCR

PRIVATE reply
DRAW_BOX(05,00,10,79,02)
@ 08,05 SAY "Company        Company Name"+space(31)+"Phone"
SHADOWBOX(09,11,21,67,"Company Info",03)
@ 12,15 SAY "Mailing Address:"
@ 16,26 SAY "City:"
@ 18,14 SAY "Province / State:"
@ 20,13 SAY "Postal / ZIP Code:"
```

```
RETURN .T.
```

```
FUNCTION C_KEY

PRIVATE reply
reply = .F.
@ 07, 05 GET mCODE PICTURE caps VALID UNIQUE(MCODE)
READ_IT()
reply = !ESC()
RETURN reply
```

```
FUNCTION C_FLD

PRIVATE reply
reply = .F.
@ 07, 19 GET mNAME
@ 07, 62 GET mPHONE PICTURE phone_pic
@ 12, 32 GET mB_ADDR1
@ 14, 32 GET mB_ADDR2
@ 16, 32 GET mB_CITY PICTURE city_pic
@ 18, 32 GET mB_PROV PICTURE caps
@ 20, 32 GET mB_PCODE PICTURE caps
READ_IT()
reply = !ESC()
RETURN reply
```

```
FUNCTION C_SAY

PRIVATE reply, city_pic, phone_pic
reply = .T.
SYSCOLOR(02)
@ 07,05 SAY CODE PICTURE caps
@ 07,19 SAY NAME
@ 07,62 SAY PHONE PICTURE phone_pic
@ 12,32 SAY B_ADDR1
@ 14,32 SAY B_ADDR2
@ 16,32 SAY B_CITY PICTURE city_pic
@ 18,32 SAY B_PROV PICTURE caps
@ 20,32 SAY B_PCODE PICTURE caps
SYSCOLOR(01)
RETURN reply
```

```
EXTERNAL XBROWSER
```

Summary

SOFT.PRG illustrates how THE_USUAL() bends to accommodate a pair of data files held together in a relationship. This holds true, you'll be pleased to learn, for as many files as your system can handle. Before pushing THE_USUAL() even further, let's summarize what we've already learned.

- To write an application based on THE_USUAL(), you must first open all the files involved, then establish the relationships stitching them together.

- For each file you write a very similar program, consisting of five functions. Base the calling function on the template shown earlier. What changes from program to program are the number of indexes and children, the name of the local help program if any, and the four key functions, x_SCR(), x_SAY(), x_KEY() and x_FLD() — where x is the unique character identifying them.

Occasionally you'll encounter situations which require custom functions more sophisticated than are possible within the defaults. I stress: occasionally. Thanks to Clipper's incredibly powerful VALID clause, you can perform error-checking feats that do virtually anything you and your most demented client can imagine.

By hiding all these details inside user-defined functions tied to VALID clauses, you also hide them from THE_USUAL(), which simply gets a number from your user then blindly executes the function bearing that number — oblivious to all but its return value, which it hands back to the GET/READ statement presently underway. In a half-dozen lines of code you can have six incredibly complex tasks performed, all inside the default call to THE_USUAL().

The same power and flexibility is available in the display routine, thanks to its avoidance of one of the most popular programming constructs in the dBASE family of languages — the use of a block of GET statements (followed by a CLEAR GETS) as the means of displaying a record. Instead, we switch colors and actually SAY the data, avoiding the compromises that inevitably result from doing SAYs with GETs. Thus we are free to create as much difference as we wish between what we ask for at entry time, and what we display afterward. *We are free to display information rather than data.*

To keep the emphasis here on concept rather than application, we restricted SOFT.PRG to two tables. In business programming, you'll seldom find any jobs this easy. Now it's time to push THE_USUAL() further.

Chapter 8

The Usual, Stretched

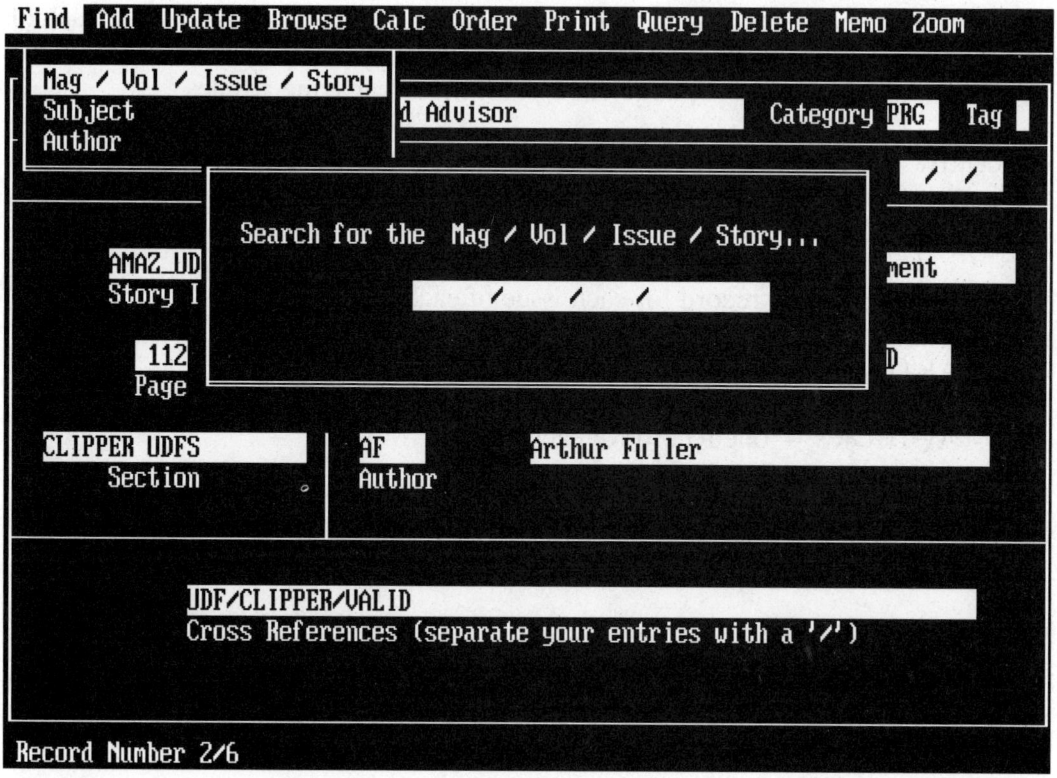

MAGS.PRG 3 zooms deep, with the Search menu active. The array *xcues* is presented as a menu. The parallel element in array *xpics* is used as the picture awaiting input, and passed to ASK_FOR(), which in turn calls SHADOW-BOX(). You fill the arrays and THE_USUAL() does the rest.

The Information Junkie

This time our hypothetical client is an information junkie with a bent for magazines on computing. He has an optical disk drive and wants to able able to say, "Show me all the articles about Clipper programming", and have the system respond instantly, allowing him to view or print any or all of the matches immediately. He wants instant access by subject, magazine, author, cross reference, and even whether the article contains a given word.

Thanks to a scanner and a modem, he has access to ASCII files of many of the articles he wants to track, and wants the facility to import new files into the system. In addition, he also wants to track detailed notes both on the magazines and on specific issues, as when they are theme issues. Clearly a case for memo fields — one in each of the files. Beginning with the Summer '87 version, Clipper expanded its comfortable size of memo fields to 64 KB, large enough for most magazine articles.

We identify four entities in this application:

- MAGAZINE — information on the particular publication.
- ISSUES — one record for each issue of each magazine.
- ARTICLES — one record for each article catalogued.
- AUTHORS — one record for each author.

Validations

Much of the data must be validated: all ISSUE records must not only be unique but also must contain a valid magazine code, meaning one that is present in the MAGAZINE file. Each article logged must be unique and also have valid magazine, issue and author codes. Each author must be unique.

To assist in these validations, we'll call two functions out of the library:

- UNIQUE(memvar, file), and
- LOOKUP(memvar, file, ret_field, row, col)

By default, UNIQUE() assumes that the item you want to check is in the current file, which is already indexed appropriately. You may override this assumption by passing the name of the file you wish to use instead as the second parameter. In that case, UNIQUE() also assumes that the file is open and indexed appropriately.

LOOKUP() is a *double function*, or perhaps a better description is a *deceptive function*. Designed for use in a VALID clause, it must return true or false, but before doing so it may perform a considerable amount of work.

LOOKUP() wants five parameters. The first is the object you wish to look up — it might be a customer code, general ledger account number or product code. Next, LOOKUP() needs to know where to look. Pass the name of the lookup file as parameter two. LOOKUP() assumes that the file is already open with the appropriate index in control. Parameter three is the name of the field from the lookup table you want to display. The last two parameters tell LOOKUP() the row and column at which to begin the display.

The displayed field is actually what we're after here, but the function is shaped this way because we intend to use it in a VALID clause, and thus it must return True or False. In the event of a failed search, LOOKUP() displays a blank value equivalent to an empty return field (the one we want to display).

LOOKUP() lends a feeling of immediacy to an application since it responds instantly to the user's keystrokes, refusing bad data in a helpful way. The unsure user can guess at the entry and see the result immediately. It is possible, after all, to enter a valid code which is nevertheless not the one you meant. Thanks to LOOKUP() you see the result immediately, and can correct it before proceeding, all in a smooth operation.

To help speed the data entry, we'll apply parental defaults to each new record. While the user is adding Issues, we'll default the magazine code to the current one in the magazine file. While the user adds articles, we'll default the magazine and issue codes to those of the current record in the Issues table.

The user begins with a new issue of a magazine, then searches the magazine file and either finds it or adds it. He then zooms to the Issue file, adds the issue and zooms to the articles file, adding each story in turn. Any new author will be detected as the story is entered, and can then be added to the Authors file.

In our determination to avoid displaying data when information can be displayed instead, we'll draw upon the library function FETCH() to display meaningful fields from related tables. In this application, our QUERY() function is going to shine, its "contains" operator even permitting searches of the memo fields.

For a print routine, we'll use a simple report form, illustrating a few techniques for dressing up the extremely limited capabilities available with the REPORT FORM command. Assuming it's written and linked, all we have to do to invoke it is insert its name in the variable *prt*.

A word on the screens. This time, they were designed to overlay each other, creating a "windows" effect. Because the screen is saved before the zoom command is executed, once the user is done with a child file we simply restore the screen and return to the parent program. Each main function has its own copy of the screen, so it's possible to go from the innermost file, AUTHORS, to the outermost, MAGAZINE, with three quick taps of the escape key, the screen restoring at each level. This technique helps persuade your users that your programs are blazingly fast — even with many thousands of records in the files. *In part, programming is show biz.*

Table Structures

The Magazine Table

Field	Field Name	Type	Width	Dec
1	MAG_ID	Character	5	
2	NAME	Character	35	
3	EDITOR	Character	30	
4	PHONE_H	Character	14	
5	PHONE_W	Character	14	
6	FREQUENCY	Numeric	2	
7	PRICE	Numeric	6	2
8	PRICE_YR	Numeric	6	2
9	SUBSCRIBER	Logical	1	
10	EXPIRES	Date	8	
11	PUBLISHER	Character	30	
12	ADDRESS_1	Character	30	
13	ADDRESS_2	Character	30	
14	CITY	Character	20	
15	STATE_PROV	Character	2	
16	ZIP	Character	10	
17	CATEGORY	Character	4	
18	TAG	Logical	1	
19	NOTES	Memo	10	
Total			259	

The Issues Table

Field	Field Name	Type	Width
1	MAG_ID	Character	5
2	VOLUME_ID	Character	3
3	ISSUE_ID	Character	2
4	DATE	Date	8
5	NOTES	Memo	10
Total			29

The Articles Table

Field	Field Name	Type	Width
1	MAG_ID	Character	5
2	VOLUME_ID	Character	3
3	ISSUE_ID	Character	2
4	STORY_ID	Character	8
5	TITLE	Character	50
6	SUBJECT	Character	45
7	CROSSREF	Character	60
8	PAGE	Numeric	4
9	SECTION	Character	20
10	AUTHOR	Character	5
11	NOTES	Memo	10
Total			213

The Authors Table

Field	Field Name	Type	Width
1	INITIALS	Character	6
2	NAME	Character	35
Total			41

MAGS Source Code

The calling program signs on, checks the files, calls the main function, then signs off.

```
PROGRAM       MAGS.PRG
Version       1.0
Comments      A magazine article index system.
              based on THE_USUAL().
```

```
PARAMETER monochrome
IF TYPE("monochrome") = "U"          && CGA + mono monitor?
   monochrome = .F.
ENDIF
exe_name = "M A G N U M   8 9"
exe_desc = "The Data Investigator"
exe_spec = "MAGS"
name_pic = "!" + REPL("X",34)        && pictures we'll need
publ_pic = "!" + REPL("X",29)
city_pic = "!" + REPL("X",19)
phone_pic = "@R (###) 999-9999"
money32 = "999.99"
caps = "@!"
yn = "Y"
date_pic = "@D"
title_pic = "!"+REPL("X",49)
SYSCOLOR(01)
SET SCOREBOARD OFF
SIGN_ON(exe_name, exe_desc)
IF !CHK_DBFS()
   SET CURSOR ON
   RETURN
ENDIF
MAG()
SIGN_OFF(exe_name,exe_desc)
```

```
FUNCTION CHK_DBFS

PRIVATE reply, work_area, file_name, indexes, ntx_field
reply = .T.
file_name = "MAGAZINE"
indexes = 01
ntx_field = "MAG_ID"
```

```
IF !DB_OPEN( file_name, indexes, ntx_field )
   reply = .F.
ENDIF
file_name = "ISSUES"
indexes = 01
ntx_field = "MAG_ID+VOLUME_ID+ISSUE_ID"
IF !DB_OPEN( file_name, indexes, ntx_field )
   reply = .F.
ENDIF
file_name = "ARTICLES"
indexes = 03
DECLARE ntx_field[indexes]
ntx_field[01] = "MAG_ID+VOLUME_ID+ISSUE_ID+STORY_ID"
ntx_field[02] = "SUBJECT"
ntx_field[03] = "AUTHOR"
IF !DB_OPEN( file_name, indexes, ntx_field )
   reply = .F.
ENDIF
file_name = "AUTHORS"
indexes = 01
ntx_field = "INITIALS"
IF !DB_OPEN( file_name, indexes, ntx_field )
   reply = .F.
ENDIF
RETURN reply
```

```
FUNCTION MAG

PRIVATE reply, temp_scr, id_char, ;
        old_file, curr_file, blood_line, ;
        screen_no, no_screens, no_kids, no_indexes
PRIVATE udf_add, udf_upd, udf_scr, udf_say, udf_key, ;
        udf_calc, udf_prt, udf_rpl, udf_qry, udf_fld, ;
        udf_zoom, udf_memo, udf_brow, udf_help
PRIVATE xkeys, xcues, xpics, ;
        kids, kkeys, kcues
SAVE SCREEN TO temp_scr
reply      = .F.
no_screens = 01
screen_no  = 01
cur_file = "MAGAZINE"
blood_line = ""
SELECT &curr_file
SEEK blood_line
id_char = "M"
udf_scr = id_char + "_SCR()"
udf_say = id_char + "_SAY()"
udf_key = id_char + "_KEY()"
```

```
udf_fld = id_char + "_FLD()"
udf_prt = "POP_MSG('Ask for a print routine')"
udf_add = "GET_STD(.T.)"
udf_upd = "GET_STD(.F.)"
udf_calc = "COUNT_EM()"
udf_qry = "QUERY()"
udf_rpl = "RPL()"
udf_help = "U_HELP"
udf_zoom = "ISSUES()"
udf_brow = "XBROWSER"
udf_memo = .F.
mtr = .F.
mtc = .F.
mbr = .F.
mbc = .F.
no_keys = 01
no_kids = 01
xkeys = "MAG_ID"
xcues = "MAG_ID"
xpics = "@!"
IF no_kids > 00
   DECLARE kids[no_kids], kcues[no_kids]
   kids[01]  = "ISSUE"
   kcues[01] = "Issues"
ENDIF
THE_USUAL()
reply = .T.
RETURN reply
```

```
FUNCTION M_SCR

PRIVATE reply
@ 04,00 CLEAR
DRAW_BOX(04,00,21,79,02)
@ 05,02 SAY "Code        "
@ 05,16 SAY "Name"+space(38)+"Category       Tag"
@ 06,01 SAY REPL("D",78)
@ 08,03 SAY "Publisher"+space(36)+"Phone  W:"
@ 10,06 SAY "Editor"+space(43)+"H:"
@ 12,05 SAY "Address"
@ 13,57 SAY "Subscriber?"
@ 15,57 SAY "Expires on"
@ 16,08 SAY "City"
@ 17,55 SAY "Single Issue"
@ 18,02 SAY "State/Prov      Zip/Postal"
@ 19,55 SAY "Yearly Subsc."
```

```
RETURN .T.
```

```
FUNCTION M_KEY

reply = .F.
@ 05, 07 GET mMAG_ID PICTURE "@!" VALID UNIQUE(mMAG_ID)
READ_IT()
reply = !ESC()
RETURN reply
```

```
FUNCTION M_FLD

PRIVATE reply
reply = .F.
@ 05, 21 GET mNAME PICTURE name_pic
@ 05, 67 GET mCATEGORY PICTURE caps
@ 05, 77 GET mTAG PICTURE yn
@ 08, 14 GET mPUBLISHER PICTURE publ_pic
@ 10, 14 GET mEDITOR PICTURE publ_pic
@ 12, 14 GET mADDRESS_1 PICTURE publ_pic
@ 14, 14 GET mADDRESS_2 PICTURE publ_pic
@ 16, 14 GET mCITY PICTURE city_pic
@ 18, 14 GET mSTATE_PROV PICTURE caps
@ 18, 29 GET mZIP PICTURE caps
@ 08, 58 GET mPHONE_W PICTURE phone_pic
@ 10, 58 GET mPHONE_H PICTURE phone_pic
@ 13, 70 GET mSUBSCRIBER PICTURE yn
@ 15, 69 GET mEXPIRES PICTURE date
@ 17, 71 GET mPRICE PICTURE money32
@ 19, 71 GET mPRICE_YR PICTURE money32
READ_IT()
reply = !ESC()
RETURN reply
```

```
FUNCTION M_SAY

PRIVATE reply
reply = .T.
SYSCOLOR(02)
@ 05,07 SAY MAG_ID PICTURE caps
@ 05,21 SAY NAME PICTURE name_pic
@ 05,67 SAY CATEGORY PICTURE caps
@ 05,77 SAY IF(TAG,CHR(251)," ")
@ 08,14 SAY PUBLISHER PICTURE publ_pic
@ 08,58 SAY PHONE_W PICTURE phone_pic
```

```
@ 10,14 SAY EDITOR PICTURE publ_pic
@ 10,58 SAY PHONE_H PICTURE phone_pic
@ 12,14 SAY ADDRESS_1 PICTURE publ_pic
@ 13,70 SAY IF(SUBSCRIBER,CHR(251)," ")
@ 14,14 SAY ADDRESS_2 PICTURE publ_pic
@ 15,69 SAY EXPIRES PICTURE date_pic
@ 16,14 SAY CITY PICTURE city_pic
@ 17,71 SAY PRICE PICTURE money32
@ 18,14 SAY STATE_PROV PICTURE caps
@ 18,29 SAY ZIP PICTURE caps
@ 19,71 SAY PRICE_YR PICTURE money32
SYSCOLOR(01)
RETURN reply
```

```
FUNCTION ISSUES

PRIVATE reply, temp_scr, id_char, ;
         old_file, curr_file, blood_line, ;
         screen_no, no_screens, no_kids, no_indexes
PRIVATE udf_add, udf_upd, udf_scr, udf_say, udf_key, ;
      udf_calc, udf_prt, udf_rpl, udf_qry, udf_fld, ;
      udf_zoom, udf_memo, udf_brow, udf_help
PRIVATE xkeys, xcues, xpics, ;
      kids, kkeys, kcues
PRIVATE mtr, mtc, mbr, mbc
SAVE SCREEN TO temp_scr
reply = .F.
no_screens = 01
screen_no = 01
curr_file = "ISSUES"
blood_line = MAG_ID
SELECT &curr_file
SEEK blood_line
id_char = "I"
udf_scr = id_char + "_SCR()"
udf_say = id_char + "_SAY()"
udf_key = id_char + "_KEY()"
udf_fld = id_char + "_FLD()"
udf_prt = "POP_MSG('Ask for a print routine')"
udf_add = "GET_STD(.T.)"
udf_upd = "GET_STD(.F.)"
udf_calc = "COUNT_EM()"
udf_qry = "QUERY()"
udf_rpl = "RPL()"
udf_help = "U_HELP"
udf_zoom = "ARTICLES()"     && zoom udf
udf_brow = "XBROWSER"
udf_memo = .F.
```

```
mtr = .F.
mtc = .F.
mbr = .F.
mbc = .F.
no_keys = 01
no_kids = 01
xkeys = "MAG_ID+VOLUME_ID+ISSUE_ID"     && Single key
xcues = "Magazine / Volume / Issue"
xpics = "@!"
THE_USUAL()
reply = .T.
RETURN reply
```

```
FUNCTION I_SCR

PRIVATE reply
CLEAR
DRAW_BOX(05,00,07,79,01)
@ 06,45 SAY "Vol.#      Iss.#    Date"
RETURN .T.
```

```
FUNCTION I_KEY

PRIVATE reply
reply = .F.
@ 06, 03 GET mMAG_ID PICTURE "@!" ;
         VALID LOOKUP(mMAG_ID,"MAGAZINE", "NAME", 06, 10)
@ 06, 51 GET mVOLUME_ID PICTURE "###"
@ 06, 62 GET mISSUE_ID PICTURE "##"
@ 06, 70 GET mDATE PICTURE date_pic
READ_IT()
reply = !ESC()
RETURN reply
```

```
FUNCTION I_FLD

PRIVATE reply
reply = .F.
@ 06, 70 GET mDATE PICTURE "@D"
READ_IT()
reply = !ESC()
RETURN reply
```

```
FUNCTION I_SAY

PRIVATE reply
reply = .T.
SYSCOLOR(02)
@ 06,03 SAY MAG_ID PICTURE "@!"
@ 06,10 SAY FETCH(MAG_ID, "MAGAZINE", "NAME")
@ 06,51 SAY VOLUME_ID PICTURE "###"
@ 06,62 SAY ISSUE_ID PICTURE "##"
@ 06,70 SAY DATE PICTURE date
SYSCOLOR(01)
RETURN reply
```

```
FUNCTION ARTICLES

PRIVATE reply, temp_scr, id_char, ;
         old_file, curr_file, blood_line, ;
         screen_no, no_screens, no_kids, no_indexes
PRIVATE udf_add, udf_upd, udf_scr, udf_say, udf_key, ;
         udf_calc, udf_prt, udf_rpl, udf_qry, udf_fld, ;
         udf_zoom, udf_memo, udf_brow, udf_help
PRIVATE xkeys, xcues, xpics, ;
         kids, kkeys, kcues
PRIVATE mtr, mtc, mbr, mbc
SAVE SCREEN TO temp_scr
reply = .F.
no_screens = 01
screen_no  = 01
id_char = "R"
old_file = ALIAS()
curr_file = "ARTICLES"
blood_line = MAG_ID+VOLUME_ID+ISSUE_ID
SELECT &curr_file
SEEK blood_line
udf_scr = id_char + "_SCR()"
udf_say = id_char + "_SAY()"
udf_key = id_char + "_KEY()"
udf_fld = id_char + "_FLD()"
udf_prt = "POP_MSG('Ask for a print routine')"
udf_add = "GET_STD(.T.)"
udf_upd = "GET_STD(.F.)"
udf_calc = "COUNT_EM()"
udf_qry = "QUERY()"
udf_rpl = "RPL()"
udf_help = "U_HELP"
udf_zoom = "AUTHORS()"        && zoom udf
udf_brow = "XBROWSER"
udf_memo = .F.
```

```
mtr = .F.
mtc = .F.
mbr = .F.
mbc = .F.
no_keys = 03
no_kids = 01
DECLARE xkeys[no_keys], ;      && multiple keys
         xcues[no_keys], ;
         xpics[no_keys]
xkeys[01] = "MAG_ID+VOLUME_ID+ISSUE_ID+STORY_ID"
xcues[01] = "Mag / Vol / Issue / Story"
xkeys[02] = "SUBJECT"
xcues[02] = "Subject"
xkeys[03] = "AUTHOR"
xcues[03] = "Author"
THE_USUAL()
reply = .T.
RETURN reply
```

```
FUNCTION R_SCR

PRIVATE reply
DRAW_BOX(08,00,23,79,01)
@ 10,05 SAY " Story ID:"
@ 10,53 SAY "Page:"
@ 12,07 SAY "Section:"
@ 14,09 SAY "Title:"
@ 16,07 SAY "Subject:"
@ 18,08 SAY "Author:"
@ 20,02 SAY "Cross Ref(s):"
RETURN .T.
```

```
FUNCTION R_KEY

PRIVATE reply
reply = .F.
IF EMPTY(mMAG_ID)       && This must be an add not edit
   mMAG_ID = ISSUES->MAG_ID
   mVOLUME_ID = ISSUES->mVOLUME_ID
   mISSUE_ID  = ISSUES->ISSUE_ID
ENDIF
@ 10, 20 GET mSTORY_ID PICTURE "@!" ;
         VALID UNIQUE(mMAG_ID+mVOLUME_ID+mISSUE_ID+mSTORY_ID)
READ_IT()
reply = !ESC()
```

```
RETURN reply
```

```
FUNCTION R_FLD

PRIVATE reply
reply = .F.
@ 10, 60 GET mPAGE PICTURE "###"
@ 12, 20 GET mSECTION PICTURE caps
@ 14, 20 GET mTITLE PICTURE title_pic
@ 16, 20 GET mSUBJECT PICTURE title_pic
@ 18, 20 GET mAUTHOR PICTURE caps ;
         VALID LOOKUP(mAUTHOR,"AUTHORS", "NAME", 18, 27)
@ 21, 10 GET mCROSSREF PICTURE caps
READ_IT()
reply = !ESC()
RETURN reply
```

```
FUNCTION R_SAY

PRIVATE reply
reply = .T.
SYSCOLOR(02)
@ 06,03 SAY MAG_ID PICTURE "@!"
@ 06,10 SAY FETCH(MAG_ID, "MAGAZINE", "NAME")
@ 06,51 SAY VOLUME_ID PICTURE "###"
@ 06,62 SAY ISSUE_ID PICTURE "##"
@ 06,70 SAY ISSUES->DATE PICTURE date_pic
@ 10,20 SAY STORY_ID PICTURE caps
@ 10,60 SAY PAGE PICTURE "###"
@ 12,20 SAY SECTION PICTURE caps
@ 14,20 SAY TITLE PICTURE title_pic
@ 16,20 SAY SUBJECT PICTURE title_pic
@ 18,20 SAY AUTHOR PICTURE caps
@ 18,27 SAY FETCH(AUTHOR, "AUTHORS", "NAME")
@ 21,10 SAY mCROSSREF PICTURE caps
SYSCOLOR(01)
RETURN reply
```

```
FUNCTION AUTHORS

PRIVATE reply, temp_scr, id_char, ;
        old_file, curr_file, blood_line, ;
        screen_no, no_screens, no_kids, no_indexes
PRIVATE udf_add, udf_upd, udf_scr, udf_say, udf_key, ;
        udf_calc, udf_prt, udf_rpl, udf_qry, udf_fld, ;
```

```
         udf_zoom, udf_memo, udf_brow, udf_help
PRIVATE xkeys, xcues, xpics, ;
         kids, kkeys, kcues
PRIVATE mtr, mtc, mbr, mbc
SAVE SCREEN TO temp_scr
reply = .F.
no_screens = 01
screen_no = 01
curr_file = "AUTHORS"
blood_line = AUTHOR
SELECT &curr_file
SEEK blood_line
id_char = "A"
udf_scr = id_char + "_SCR()"
udf_say = id_char + "_SAY()"
udf_key = id_char + "_KEY()"
udf_fld = id_char + "_FLD()"
udf_prt = "POP_MSG('Ask for a print routine')"
udf_add = "GET_STD(.T.)"
udf_upd = "GET_STD(.F.)"
udf_calc = "COUNT_EM()"
udf_qry = "QUERY()"
udf_rpl = "RPL()"
udf_help = "U_HELP"
udf_zoom = .F.
udf_brow = .F.
udf_memo = .F.
mtr = .F.
mtc = .F.
mbr = .F.
mbc = .F.
no_keys = 01
no_kids = 00
xkeys = "INITIALS"
xcues = "INITIALS"
xpics = "@!"
THE_USUAL()
reply = .T.
RETURN reply
```

```
FUNCTION A_SCR

PRIVATE reply
DRAW_BOX(08,11,16,66,01)
@ 10,15 SAY "Author's Code"
@ 13,24 SAY "Name"
```

```
RETURN .T.
```

```
FUNCTION A_KEY

PRIVATE reply
reply = .F.
@ 10, 30 GET mINITIALS PICTURE caps VALID UNIQUE(mINITIALS)
READ_IT()
reply = !ESC()
RETURN reply
```

```
FUNCTION A_FLD

PRIVATE reply
reply = .F.
@ 13, 30 GET mNAME PICTURE name_pic
READ_IT()
reply = !ESC()
RETURN reply
```

```
FUNCTION A_SAY

PRIVATE reply
reply = .T.
SYSCOLOR(02)
@ 10,30 SAY INITIALS PICTURE "@!"
@ 13,30 SAY NAME PICTURE name_pic
SYSCOLOR(01)
RETURN reply
```

Summary

In MAGS.PRG we revealed the robust nature of THE_USUAL(). You can push it considerably further than this, limited only by your adherence to the rules and your creative flair with user-defined functions.

- When you're designing screens, stay off the top two lines and the bottom line. These are used for menus and status messages respectively.

- If there is only one index, place its key in the variable *xkeys*, its menu cue in *xcues*, and its picture statement in *xpics*. Set the variable no_indexes to one. If there are several indexes, make these three variables arrays rather than strings and populate them appropriately.

- If your application requires several screens, ensure that the _SCR(), _SAY(), and _FLD() functions include checks on the screen number. Even though for two screens a simple IF/ELSE/ENDIF will suffice, it's a good habit to use a CASE structure. That way you can add another screen later with minimal revision.

- Place the names of any custom functions in their appropriate variables. Add any extras that may be required using the variables so_cues and so_udfs, making them strings for a single extra and arrays for several.

- Don't forget that anything hidden inside a string from the compiler and linker must be explicitly linked into your application, or declared external and available in a library whose name is included in the link command.

Chapter 9

Window-Based Programming

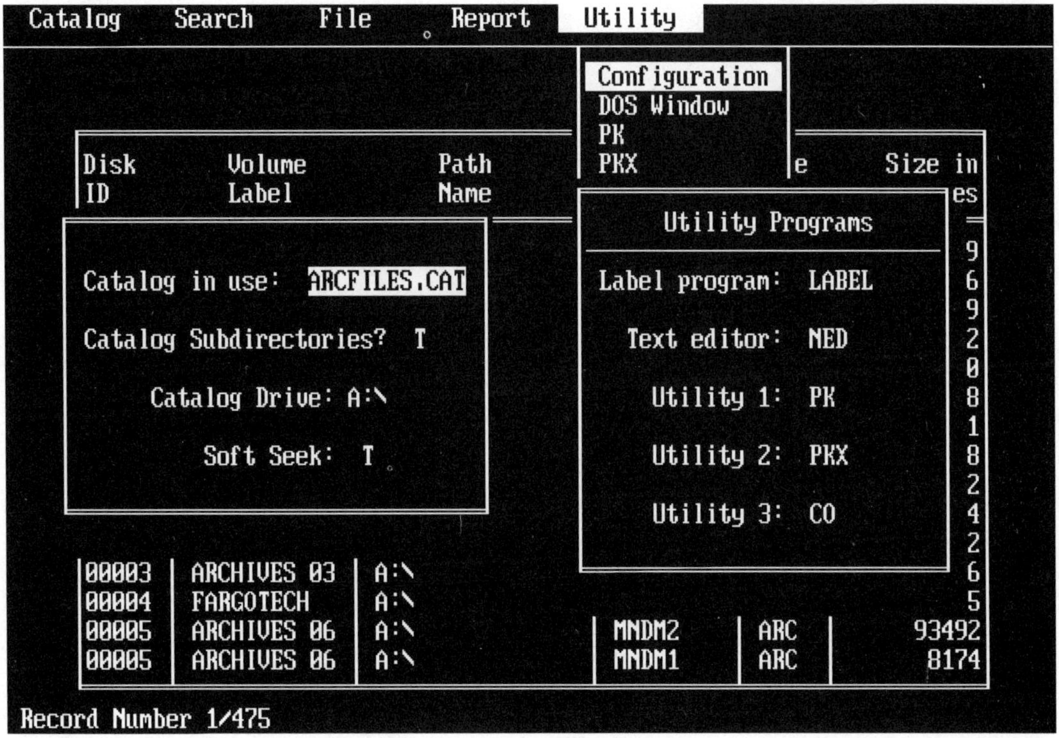

dCAT.PRG with its utility menu active and the editing windows open. Note that the utility programs installed by the user are displayed on the actual program menu.

dCAT — Designing for Performance

In Chapter 5, the section on PD_MENU() roughed in our design for a disk catalog utility, designed its pull-down menu system and generated a running demo. Now we turn to the specifics of the application.

How should the program work? Let's design for speed. The program intends to organize disk maintenance, an already boring activity — so it must be as automatic as possible. As the program comes up, it should load the catalog last in use, but allow us to choose another with a keystroke or two.

How should the program work? Let's design for speed. The program intends to organize disk maintenance, an already boring activity — so it must be as automatic as possible. As the program comes up, it should load the catalog last in use, but allow us to choose another with a keystroke or two.

dCAT should warn us when a disk has already been catalogued, and destroy the previous entries if we elect to proceed. As we catalog more and more disks, we'll probably take increasing advantage of the program's ability to use multiple catalogs. Therefore we'll want to ensure that we can switch between them easily and quickly. With multiple catalogs comes the chance that we'll read a disk into the wrong catalog, however, so we'd better have a command which allows us to delete all the entries corresponding to a disk ID; and another, to transfer selected records between catalogs. Most disks contain at least a few files which are beneath cataloguing, such as backup files, COMMAND.COM and CONFIG.SYS. Therefore it should be as easy as possible to delete entries.

Given the importance we have attached to speed, let's take the next large step in the pursuit of our larger target, invisible software. Let's eliminate the menu — or rather, hide it until it's required, while providing hot keys to activate the most frequent commands.

The three commands most users will use most often are Search, Catalog (a disk) and Delete (a particular file). We'll hot-key all of them: Alt-S will be our search key, the Insert key our Catalog key and the Delete key our delete key. Besides these, we'll assign Alt-R to read a disk file into the current record's memo field, and Alt-W to write the current memo field out to disk.

Using a System File

We'll take this programming opportunity to introduce a couple of new concepts, as well. dCAT will employ a system file, which is a data file like any other, used to contain the configuration parameters of the program. This is where we'll store the name of the catalog in use, for example, so that next time the program loads it will know which catalog to load first.

We'll store the program's colors in the system file, along with the names of the editor, disk-labeling program and other utilities the user wishes to add to the menu.

Even before we sign on, we'll attempt to open the system file. If we can't find it, we'll return to DOS. Finding it, we'll extract the name of the catalog last used, sign on and say hello.

Next we'll declare and load our arrays full of menu options, then call PD_MENU() to execute the entire program. Before we do, though, pause and think about that. A single function which executes your entire program, yet lets you re- think your application even as you develop it.

Table Stucture

The Catalog Table

Field	Field Name	Type	Width
1	DISK_ID	Character	5
2	VOLUME	Character	11
3	PATH	Character	15
4	FILE_NAME	Character	8
5	EXTENSION	Character	3
6	SIZE	Numeric	10
7	DATE	Date	8
8	TIME	Character	8
9	NOTES	Memo	10
Total			79

dCAT Source Code

```
PROGRAM        DCAT.PRG
Function(s)    DCAT.PRG, STUFF_RA(), CHK_DBFS()
Purpose        Master program for dCAT.EXE
Conventions    LINK with dCAT_2.PRG, ARTFUL.LIB, KEYS.LIB
Syntax         DCAT m
Parameters     m - to force monochrome
Example        dcat m
Assumes        nothing
Side Effects   may result in organized floppy disks
Returns        nothing
Calls          SIGN_ON(),SYSCOLOR(),POP_MSG(),
               PUBLICS()
```

```
PARAMETER monochrome
IF TYPE("monochrome") = "U"
   monochrome = .F.
ENDIF
sys_file = "dCAT.SYS"
IF !DB_OPEN(sys_file)
   RETURN
ENDIF
SET CURSOR OFF
SET SCOREBOARD OFF
PUBLICS()   && declare public vars
i = 01
FOR i = 1 TO FCOUNT()                  && declaration here so they're
   f = FIELDNAME(i)                    && thru the entire program
   &f = &f
NEXT
SYS_DFLT()
SYSCOLOR(1)
SIGN_ON(exe_name, exe_desc)
menu_key   = "/"
more_up    = CHR(24)
more_down  = CHR(25)
menu_open  = .T.
*
DECLARE dc_keys[no_indexes], ;
         dc_cues[no_indexes], ;
         dc_pics[no_indexes]
```

```
dc_keys[01] = "Disk_ID"
dc_keys[02] = "File_Name"
dc_keys[03] = "Volume"
dc_keys[04] = "Extension"
dc_keys[05] = "Date"
dc_cues[01] = " ID # "
dc_cues[02] = " File Name "
dc_cues[03] = " Volume Label "
dc_cues[04] = " Extension "
dc_cues[05] = " Date Saved "
dc_pics[01] = "99999"
dc_pics[02] = caps
dc_pics[03] = caps
dc_pics[04] = caps
dc_pics[05] = "@D"

m_size = 05
PRIVATE r_flags[05]
PRIVATE cues[m_size], cols[m_size], sizes[m_size]
cues[01] = "  Catalog  "
cues[02] = "  Search   "
cues[03] = "  File    "
cues[04] = "  Report  "
cues[05] = "  Utility  "
cols[01] = 02
cols[02] = 13
cols[03] = 24
cols[04] = 33
cols[05] = 44
sizes[01] = 07
sizes[02] = 05
sizes[03] = 07
sizes[04] = 06
sizes[05] = 05
new_cat = .F.
DO WHILE .T.
   SELECT A
   PD_MENU(cues, sizes)
   IF !new_cat
      IF VERIFY("Return to DOS")
         EXIT
      ENDIF
   ENDIF
ENDDO
SIGN_OFF(exe_name)
RETURN
```

```
EXTERNAL RUN_LBL, RUN_DIR, DOS, SIGN_OFF, ;
```

```
   OUT_OK, TRANSFER, DOS,SET_PRN, ;
   MENU_ORD, DUST_1, PACK_EM, NUKE_EM, QUERY
```

```
FUNCTION CHK_DBFS

PRIVATE root, ok_dbfs
ok_dbfs = .F.
root = LEFT(catalog, 7)

FOR i = 1 TO no_indexes
   n = STRINT(i)
   ntx&n = root + n
NEXT
ok_dbfs = DB_OPEN(catalog, no_indexes, dc_keys, alias)
IF ok_dbfs
   SET INDEX TO &ntx1, &ntx2, &ntx3, &ntx4, &ntx5
ENDIF
RETURN ok_dbfs
```

```
FUNCTION STUFF_RA

* CATALOG MENU
c1[01] = " Select a catalog  "
c1[02] = " Open the catalog "
c1[03] = " Add a new disk "
c1[04] = " Create a catalog "
c1[05] = " Transfer records "
c1[06] = " Purge the catalog "
c1[07] = " Nuke the catalog "
u1[01] = "SEL_CAT()"
u1[02] = "SHOW_CAT()"
u1[03] = "ADD_DISK()"
u1[04] = "NEW_CAT()"
u1[05] = "TRANSFER()"
u1[06] = "PACK_EM()"
u1[07] = "NUKE_EM(catalog)"
l1[01] = .T.
l1[02] = "!EMPTY(ALIAS())"
l1[03] = "!EMPTY(ALIAS())"
l1[04] = .T.
l1[05] = .T.
l1[06] = "!EMPTY(ALIAS())"
l1[07] = "!EMPTY(ALIAS())"
* SEARCH MENU
c2[01] = " Disk ID #     "
c2[02] = " Name of file "
```

```
c2[03] = " Volume Label "
c2[04] = " Extension    "
c2[05] = " Date Updated "
AFILL(12, "!EMPTY(ALIAS())")
u2[01] = "RASK(01)"
u2[02] = "RASK(02)"
u2[03] = "RASK(03)"
u2[04] = "RASK(04)"
u2[05] = "RASK(05)"
* FILE MENU
c3[01] = " Query the file "
c3[02] = " Read directory "
c3[03] = " Delete a disk  "
c3[04] = " Label a disk   "
c3[05] = " Import text    "
c3[06] = " Export text    "
c3[07] = " Order by field "
u3[01] = "QUERY()"
u3[02] = "RUN_DIR()"
u3[03] = "DEL_DISK()"
u3[04] = "RUN_LBL()"
u3[05] = "READER(mmo_field)"
      = ask for filename
u3[06] = "WRITER(mmo_field)"
u3[07] = "MENU_ORD(cur_key)"
      sets order
AFILL(13,"!EMPTY(ALIAS())")
* REPORT MENU
* this array is for the report machine
r_flags[01] = ""
r_flags[02] = ""
r_flags[03] = ""
r_flags[04] = ""
r_flags[05] = .F.
c4[01] = " Select a report "
c4[02] = " Range specs     "
c4[03] = " Order by field  "
c4[04] = " Destination...  "
c4[05] = " Printer setup   "
c4[06] = " GO! Print it    "
AFILL(14,"!EMPTY(ALIAS())")
u4[01] = "GET_FRM()"
u4[02] = "GET_SCOPE()"
u4[03] = "MENU_ORD(cur_key)"
u4[04] = "GET_DEST()"
u4[05] = "SET_PRN()"
u4[06] = "RUN_RPT(r_flags)"
* UTILITY MENU
c5[01] = " Configuration "
```

```
c5[02] = " DOS Window "
c5[03] = " " + Util_1
c5[04] = " " + Util_2
c5[05] = " " + Util_3
u5[01] = "DC_CONFIG()"
u5[02] = "DOS()"
u5[03] = "DOS(Util_1)"
u5[04] = "DOS(Util_2)"
u5[05] = "DOS(Util_3)"
FOR i = 01 TO m_size
   n = STRINT(i)
   wids[i] = LEN(c&n[01])
NEXT
RETURN .T.
```

```
FUNCTION PUBLICS

PUBLIC exe_name, exe_desc, alias, catalog,no_indexes, choice, ;
      mmo_field, refresh, cur_key, util_1, util_2, util_3, ;
      editor, labeler, bell_on, color_on, confirm_on, do_subs, ;
      high_lite, ram_disk, indx_drv, data_drv, dflt_drv, ;
      index_ext, index_date, help_prc, mem_free
exe_name  = " d C A T ! "
exe_desc  = "a Disk Catalog Program from"
help_prc  = "HELP"
alias     = "CATALOG"
choice    = 01
no_indexes= 05
mmo_field = "NOTES"
mem_free  = MEMORY(0)
RETURN .T.
```

Mapping the Terrain

dCAT calls quite a few small functions dedicated to performing single pieces of the overall task. These were written in a stepwise fashion, at each point hiding the details of the event.

The heart of dCAT is, of course, the routine that reads the directory of the disk and imports it into the catalog. The function ADD_DISK() simply creates a loop, then calls GET_SPECS() repeatedly until the user presses escape.

A detail worth noting is the style used to format the headings — exactly the same as the old dBASE report form conventions, with semicolons defining line breaks.

Next, GET_SPECS() creates arrays for the file information, determining their size with a call to the Clipper function ADIR(), then filling them with a second call. To let the user know what is happening, it pops up a box and writes each record to the screen while adding it to the file. (This slows the routine up slightly, and you may wish to remove it. If so, comment out the calls to FILE_BOX() and SHOW_FILE() and remove the functions from the source file. I prefer the information to the minor gain in speed, and so have left the display in.)

The function NEW_CAT() is straightforward, ensuring first that a catalog file is in use then copying its structure to a new file.

Function RASK() is a slight variation on ASK_FOR(). The "R" stands for relative, meaning that the location of the pop-up box is relative to the cursor. It also works slightly differently than ASK_FOR() in that it receives a number rather than a series of parameters. Using the number as a pointer into the arrays of index keys, cues and pictures, it constructs the pop-up with its message and GET variable, calls READ_IT() and executes the SEEK afterwards.

Function SEL_CAT() is interesting. It calls the library function GET_FILE(), which in turn calls ADIR() and ACHOICE() to dynamically construct a menu of catalog files. If you select a new catalog, the program calls CHK_DBFS() to ensure that all its indexes are present. It saves the screen upon entry and restores it afterwards. Note, too, its return value: it returns the function CHK_DBFS() — or in other words, instructs Clipper to execute the function and then return its return value.

Function SHOW_CAT() administers the catalog view, which involves declaring arrays of field names, pictures and headings for each column in the file. A detail worth noting is the style used to format the headings — exactly the same as the old dBASE report form conventions, with semicolons defining line breaks.

SHOW_CAT(), in keeping with our usual plan, names DBEDIT()'s inner function in the variable udf_brow. However, the behavior we expect from this function is singular to this application, so we'll override XBROWSER() with a custom function MBROWSER() — the "M" hopefully reminding us that we have hot- keyed the menu, and also the read/write keys for the memo field.

For the report mechanism, we try something a little different, constructing a state machine — the software equivalent of the *Game of Life*: you set a state and some rules, then see what evolves.

The reports required in a disk catalog utility are within the "capabilities" of the REPORT FORM command. While supplying several example report form files to our users, we nevertheless expect that they may modify them or create their own. Function GET_FRM() therefore relies on GET_FILE() to create a menu of report forms available in the current directory.

Functions GET_SCOPE() and GET_HDR() illustrate convenient methods of allowing run-time embellishment of standard reports. Function RUN_RPT() contains all the requisite trapping to detect and include these parameters in the report. Due to the way the parser works in Clipper, the trapping must be especially careful. Notes within the code detail the problem.

Note how the function RUN_RPT() phrases the call to REPORT FORM. Any condition or scope you specify is joined with a call to the library function OUT_OK(), which polls the keyboard throughout the report run. If escape has been pressed OUT_OK() interrupts the report, presenting a menu of actions the user can take: cancel or resume the report, and skip back a page before resuming. Thus the user has some flexibility in the face of printer jams, mistaken parameters or other unforeseen events.

In function MBROWSER() we first check for escape, then for each of the hot keys we've defined - Alt-R and Alt-W to read in text files and write out memo fields. The CASE structure could expand here to include as many possibilities as you can imagine.

dCAT Support Functions

```
FUNCTION RASK

PARAMETER key_num
PRIVATE row, col, temp_scr, reply, dots, msg, var, wid
SAVE SCREEN TO temp_scr
reply = .F.
row   = ROW()
col   = COL()
dots = "..."
target = dc_keys[key_num]
msg   = "Search for " + dc_cues[key_num] + dots
var   = BLANK(&target)
wid   = LEN(msg) + 18
DRAW_BOX(row,col,row + 02, col + wid, 02)
@ row + 01,col + 02 SAY msg GET var PICTURE dc_pics[key_num]
READ_IT()
IF !EMPTY(var)
   SET ORDER TO key_num
   SEEK var
   reply = FOUND()
   IF reply && force exit from menu.
      KEYBOARD CHR(27) + CHR(27)
   ENDIF
ENDIF
RESTORE SCREEN FROM temp_scr
@ ROW, COL SAY SPACE(0)
RETURN reply
```

```
FUNCTION ADD_DISK

PRIVATE dir_pict, t1, t2
dir_pict = "!:\" + repl("!",27)
t1 = time()
t2 = time()
DO WHILE .T.
   IF !GET_SPECS()
      EXIT
   ENDIF
ENDDO
RETURN .T.
```

```
FUNCTION GET_SPECS

PRIVATE reply, temp_scr
SET ORDER TO 1
reply   = .F.
disk_id = NEXT("disk_id")
volume  = SPACE(11)
path    = SPACE(15)
filearg = "*.*" + SPACE(9)
SAVE SCREEN TO temp_scr
DRAW_BOX(05,20,20,60,03)
@ 08,24 SAY "Disk_ID"
@ 11,24 SAY "Volume Label"
@ 14,24 SAY "Path"
@ 17,24 SAY "Files to Catalog"
@ 08,43 GET m->disk_id PICTURE "99999" ;
      VALID CHECK_ID(m->disk_id)
@ 11,43 GET m->volume PICTURE "@!"
@ 14,43 GET m->path PICTURE "@!"
@ 17,43 GET m->filearg PICTURE "@K!"
SET SCOREBOARD ON
READ_IT()
SET SCOREBOARD OFF
IF ESC() .OR. EMPTY(m-disk_id)
   reply = .f.
ELSE
   path = TRIM(m->path)
   IF !EMPTY(m->path)
      path = IF(RIGHT(m->path, 1) != "\", ;
           m->path + "\", m-path)
   ENDIF
   filespec = m->path + TRIM(filearg)
   t1 = TIME()
   n = ADIR(filespec)
   IF n = 0
      reply = .f.
   ELSE
      DECLARE name_ra[n],size_ra[n],date_ra[n],;
            time_ra[n],attr_ra[n]
      ADIR(filespec,name_ra,size_ra,date_ra,;
            time_ra,attr_ra)
      FILE_BOX()
      FOR x = 1 TO n
         APPEND BLANK
         where = AT(".",name_ra[x])
         SHOW_FILE()
         IF where > 0
            REPLACE file_name WITH LEFT(name_ra[x], where - 1),;
               extension WITH SUBSTR(name_ra[x], where + 1)
            ELSE
```

```
            REPLACE file_name WITH name_ra[x]
         ENDIF
         REPLACE Date WITH date_ra[x], ;
            Size WITH size_ra[x], ;
            Time WITH time_ra[x], ;
            Disk_id WITH m->disk_id,;
            Volume WITH m->volume,;
            Path WITH m->path
      NEXT
      t2 = TIME()
      result_msg = STRINT(n) + " Files added to the catalog"
      MSG(result_msg, 1, .T.)
      reply = .T.
   ENDIF
ENDIF
RESTORE SCREEN FROM temp_scr
RETURN reply
```

```
FUNCTION SHOW_FILE

@ 08,43 SAY name_ra[x], 12)
@ 11,43 SAY date_ra[x]
@ 14,43 SAY time_ra[x]
@ 17,43 SAY size_ra[x] PICTURE "#,###,###,###"
RETURN .T.
```

```
FUNCTION FILE_BOX

DRAW_BOX(05,20,20,60,02)
@ 08,24 SAY "File Name"
@ 11,24 SAY "Date last saved"
@ 14,24 SAY "Time last saved"
@ 17,24 SAY "Size in bytes"
RETURN .T.
```

```
FUNCTION CHECK_ID

PARAMETER target
SET ORDER TO 1
SEEK target
IF FOUND()
   IF VERIFY("Disk " + target + ;
         " has already been catalogued. " + ;
            "Destroy existing entries")
      DELETE WHILE Disk_id = target
```

```
   ENDIF
   * Otherwise new entries will simply be added...
ENDIF
RETURN .T.
```

```
PROCEDURE HELP

PARAMETERS x, y, z                  && proc, line_no, read_var
PRIVATE h_tr, h_tc, h_br, h_bc, help_scr
IF TYPE("x") = "C"
   IF x = "HELP"
      RETURN
   ENDIF
ENDIF
SAVE SCREEN TO help_scr
SELECT DCAT && system file
memo_field = "HELP"
h_tr = 04
h_tc = 01
h_br = 22
h_bc = 77
DRAW_BOX(h_tr + 1, h_tc + 1, h_br - 1, h_bc - 1, 02)
SYSCOLOR(02)
@ h_tr + 1,((7 = LEN(memo_field)) / 2) SAY "  " + memo_field + "  "
SYSCOLOR(01)
cur_color = SETCOLOR()
SYSCOLOR(10)
SET CURSOR ON
REPLACE &memo_field WITH ;
         MEMOEDIT(&memo_field, h_tr + 3, h_tc + 5, ;
               h_br - 3, h_bc - 5, .T.)
SET CURSOR OFF
SELECT A
old_color = SETCOLOR(cur_color)
RESTORE SCREEN FROM help_scr
RETURN
```

```
FUNCTION NEW_CAT

SELECT A
IF EMPTY(ALIAS())
   USE &catalog
ENDIF
reply    = .F.
temp_cat = SPACE(8)
temp_cat = ASK_FOR("Catalog File to Create?",
```

```
IF !EMPTY(temp_cat)
   temp_cat = temp_cat + ".CAT"
   COPY STRU TO &temp_cat
   MSG("Catalog " + temp_cat + " is ready to go", 1)
   reply = .T.
ENDIF
RETURN reply
```

```
FUNCTION SEL_CAT

PRIVATE filespec, temp_cat, temp_scr, reply
SAVE SCREEN TO temp_scr
reply    = .F.
filespec = "*.CAT                    "
temp_cat = GET_FILE(filespec)
IF !EMPTY(temp_cat)
   catalog = temp_cat
   refresh = .T.
   reply   = .T.
ENDIF
RESTORE SCREEN FROM temp_scr
RETURN CHK_DBFS()
```

```
FUNCTION SHOW_CAT

PRIVATE reply, dummy, tr, tc, br, bc, temp_scr, udf_brow
reply = .F.
dummy = .F.
tr = 05
tc = 06
br = 23
bc = 73
udf_brow = "MBROWSER"
IF EMPTY(catalog)
   POP_MSG("Select a catalog first, then Open it")
   RETURN reply
ENDIF
IF !CHK_DBFS()
   RETURN reply
ENDIF
GO TOP
DECLARE fields[FCOUNT()], ;
        headings[FCOUNT()], ;
        pics[FCOUNT()]
FOR n = 1 TO FCOUNT()
   fields[n] = FIELDNAME(n)
```

```
   x = TYPE(FIELDNAME(n))
   DO CASE
      CASE x = "C"
         pics[n] = "@!"
      CASE x = "N"
         pics[n] = "@9"
      CASE x = "L"
         pics[n] = "--- Y ---"
      CASE x = "M"
         pics[n] = .F.
   ENDCASE
NEXT
headings[01] = "Disk;ID"             && justify the headings
headings[02] = "   Volume;   Label"
headings[03] = "     Path;     Name"
headings[04] = "  File;  Name"
headings[05] = "File;Ext."
headings[06] = "   Size in;     Bytes"
headings[07] = " Saved;   On"
headings[08] = " Saved;   At"
headings[09] = "Notes or;Comments"
@ 04,00 CLEAR
BASIC_BOX()
DBEDIT(tr, tc, br, bc, fields, udf_brow,;
          pics, headings,;
         dummy, dummy, "", dummy)
@ 04,00 CLEAR
RETURN .T.
```

```
FUNCTION MBROWSER

PARAMETERS mode, i
PRIVATE m_row, m_col, temp_scr, idle, result
cur_field = fields[i]
force_rec = .T.
is_append = .F.
any_append = .F.
can_append = .F.
prev_alias = ""
prev_rec = 0
m_row = ROW()
m_col = COL()
keystroke = LASTKEY()
idle = 00                            && dbedit idle mode
bof  = 01                            && bof hit in dbedit
eof  = 02                            && eof hit in dbedit
empty = 03                           && no records in file
exception = 04                       && keystroke exception
```

```
finished = 00
no_repaint = 01
do_repaint = 02
ins_blank = 03

IF prev_rec != RECNO()
   prev_rec  = RECNO()
   force_rec = .T.
ENDIF
DO CASE
   CASE mode = idle
      IF CHR(keystroke) $ move_chrs .OR. force_rec
         STAT_LINE()
      ENDIF
         result = no_repaint
   CASE mode = bof
      IF !EOF()
         STAT_LINE()
      ENDIF
      result = no_repaint
   CASE mode = eof
      STAT_LINE()
      result = no_repaint
   CASE mode = empty
      STAT_LINE()
      result = no_repaint
   CASE mode = exception
      DO CASE
         CASE CHR(keystroke) = menu_key
            SAVE SCREEN TO temp_scr
            PD_MENU(cues, sizes)
            RESTORE SCREEN FROM temp_scr
            result = no_repaint
         CASE DEL()
            IF DELETED()
               RECALL
            ELSE
               DELETE
            ENDIF
            result = do_repaint
            STAT_LINE()
         CASE ESC()
            result = finished
         CASE (keystroke = 13 .OR. IS_DATA(keystroke)) .AND.;
            (is_append .OR. (!EOF() .AND. LASTREC() != 0))
            ntx_expr = INDEXKEY(0)
            IF !EMPTY(ntx_expr)
               ntx_eval = &ntx_expr
            ENDIF
```

```
            IF keystroke != enter
               KEYBOARD CHR(keystroke)
            ENDIF
            SET CURSOR ON
            IF TYPE(cur_field) = "M"
               READ_MEMO(cur_field)
            ELSE
               @ m_row, m_col GET &cur_field
               READ_IT()
            ENDIF
            SET CURSOR OFF
            result = no_repaint
         CASE F1()
            DO HELP
            result = no_repaint
         CASE ALT_R()
            memo_field = "Notes"
            READER(memo_field)
            result = no_repaint
         CASE ALT_W()
            memo_field = "Notes"
            WRITER(memo_field)
            result = no_repaint
         CASE INS()
            GO BOTTOM
            ADD_DISK()
            target = Disk_ID
            SEEK target
            result = ins_blank
         CASE ALT_S()
            SEARCH(dc_keys,dc_cues,dc_pics,cmd_row+1)
            STAT_LINE()
            result = do_repaint
         OTHERWISE
            result = no_repaint
      ENDCASE
ENDCASE
RETURN result
```

```
FUNCTION BASIC_BOX

CLEAR
DRAW_BOX(04,05,23,74,03)
@ 07,05 SAY "" = 07,74 SAY ""
RETURN .T.
```

```
FUNCTION PACK_EM

PRIVATE result
result = .T.
IF VERIFY("Waste everybody on the Hit List")
   x = LASTREC()
   MSG("No turning back now, earthling" , 0, .T.)
   PACK
   @ 24,00 CLEAR
   y = LASTREC()
   POP_MSG(STRINT(x - y) + " records were wasted. " + ;
            STRINT(y) + " records survived.")
ENDIF
RETURN result
```

```
FUNCTION NUKE_EM

PRIVATE result
result = .T.
IF VERIFY("Nuke the entire file? Like, no survivors")
   ZAP
   MSG(" Too late for sorry, earthling ", 1)
ENDIF
RETURN result
```

```
FUNCTION GET_FRM

PARAMETERS func_name, line_no, mem_var        && allow hot-key call
PRIVATE    result
m_row    = ROW()                              && save cursor location
m_col    = COL()
filespec = "*.FRM"
result     = GET_FILE(filespec)
r_flags[ 1 ] = result
@ m_row, m_col SAY SPACE(0)
RETURN result
```

```
FUNCTION GET_SCOPE

PRIVATE prompt_msg, x
DECLARE scp_msg[ 03 ]
prompt_msg = "Enter a valid (e.g. dBASE-compatible) scope
expression"
scp_msg[ 01 ] = "AI has some distance to go, if I'm any example,
heh heh..."
```

```
scp_msg[ 02 ] = "I think you've made a syntax error. Be that as it
may."
scp_msg[ 03 ] = "Please try again, bearing in mind my meager
skills."
x = SPACE(50)
x = ASK_FOR(prompt_msg, @x)
IF !ESC()
   IF TYPE(x) = "U"
      POP_MSG(scp_msg)
   ELSE
      r_flags[2] = x
   ENDIF
ENDIF
RETURN x
```

```
FUNCTION GET_HDR

PRIVATE message
x   = SPACE(40)
x   = ASK_FOR("Enter the Header you would like", @x)
IF !ESC()
   r_flags[4] = x
ENDIF
RETURN x
```

```
FUNCTION GET_LEV

PRIVATE message
summary = r_flags[5]
message = IF(summary,;
            "Print a Summary Only (no detail)", ;
           "Print all the gory details")
r_flags[5] = VERIFY(message)
RETURN x
```

```
FUNCTION RUN_RPT

PARAMETER array                    && flags to control report
IF EMPTY(array[1])
   RETURN POP_MSG("No report has been selected")
ENDIF
frm_file = array[1]
scope    = array[2]
dest     = array[3]
summary  = array[5]
```

```
SET CONSOLE OFF
SAVE SCREEN TO rpt_scr
IF !EMPTY(scope)
   IF TYPE(scope) != "U"
      SET FILTER TO &scope   && we know it's valid
      GO TOP
      IF BOF() .AND. EOF()
         POP_MSG("No records match that spec, earthling")
      ENDIF
   ENDIF
ENDIF
IF summary
   DO CASE
      CASE !EMPTY(array[3])
         REPORT FORM &frm_file SUMMARY HEADING array[4] ;
               WHILE OUT_OK(dest) TO FILE &dest
      CASE array[3] = "P"
         REPORT FORM &frm_file SUMMARY HEADING array[4] ;
               WHILE OUT_OK(dest) TO PRINT
      OTHERWISE
         SET CONSOLE ON
         CLEAR
         REPORT FORM &frm_file SUMMARY HEADING array[4] ;
               WHILE OUT_OK()
   ENDCASE
ELSE
   DO CASE
      CASE !EMPTY(array[3])
         REPORT FORM &frm_file HEADING array[4] ;
               WHILE OUT_OK(dest) TO FILE &dest
      CASE array[3] = "P"
         REPORT FORM &frm_file HEADING array[4] ;
               WHILE OUT_OK(dest) TO PRINT
      OTHERWISE
         SET CONSOLE ON
         CLEAR
         REPORT FORM &frm_file HEADING array[4] ;
               WHILE OUT_OK()
   ENDCASE
ENDIF
SET FILTER TO
GO TOP
RESTORE SCREEN FROM rpt_scr
RETURN .T.
```

```
FUNCTION SYS_DFLT

IF Soft_on
```

```
   SET SOFTSEEK ON
ENDIF
IF Confirm_on
   SET CONFIRM ON
ENDIF
RETURN .T.
```

```
FUNCTION GET_DEST

PRIVATE x, choice, dummy
PRIVATE row, col, temp_scr, tr, tc, br, bc
row = ROW()
col = COL()
tr  = IF(row  18, row - 03, row + 1)
tc  = 13
br  = tr + 02
bc  = 65
SAVE SCREEN TO temp_scr
DRAW_BOX(tr, tc, br, bc, 02)
@ tr + 1,15 SAY "Send this Report to"
@ tr + 1,36 PROMPT " Printer "
@ tr + 1,46 PROMPT " Screen "
@ tr + 1,56 PROMPT " File "
MENU TO d_choice
DO CASE
   CASE d_choice = 1
      result = "P"
   CASE d_choice = 2
      result = "D"
   CASE d_choice = 3
      tr1 = IF(br  18, tr - 04, br)
      tc1 = 12
      br1 = tr1 + 04
      bc1 = 66
      DRAW_BOX(tr1, tc1, br1, bc1, 02)
      @ tr1 + 02,tc1 + 03 SAY "File to Create ..." ;
         GET ri_outfile PICTURE "@!"
      READ_IT()
ENDCASE
r_flags[3] = result
REPLACE ri_printer WITH printer
RESTORE SCREEN FROM temp_scr
RETURN result
```

```
FUNCTION DEL_DISK
```

```
PRIVATE target
target = SPACE(05)
target = ASK_FOR("ID of disk to delete", @target, "@9")
IF !EMPTY(target)
   IF VERIFY("Delete all files with Disk ID " + target)
      SET ORDER TO 1
      SEEK target
      IF FOUND()
         DELE WHILE disk_id = target
      ENDIF
   ENDIF
ENDIF
RETURN .T.
```

```
FUNCTION DC_CONFIG

PRIVATE temp_scr, cur_dbf, m_cat
SAVE SCREEN TO temp_scr
cur_dbf = ALIAS()
m_cat = catalog
SELECT DCAT
SHADOWBOX(07,04,17,36,02)
@ 09,06 SAY "Catalog in use:"
@ 11,06 SAY "Catalog Subdirectories?"
@ 13,11 SAY "Catalog Drive:"
@ 15,15 SAY "Soft Seek:"
SHADOWBOX(06,43,19,71,02)
@ 07,50 SAY "Utility Programs"
@ 08,44 SAY RE = "",27)
@ 09,45 SAY "Label program:"
@ 11,47 SAY "Text editor:"
@ 13,49 SAY "Utility 1:"
@ 15,49 SAY "Utility 2:"
@ 17,49 SAY "Utility 3:"
@ 09,23 GET Catalog
@ 11,31 GET Do_subs
@ 13,26 GET Data_drv
@ 15,27 GET Soft_on
@ 09,61 GET Labeler
@ 11,61 GET Editor
@ 13,61 GET Util_1
@ 15,61 GET Util_2
@ 17,61 GET Util_3
READ_IT()
IF UPDATED() .AND. CATALOG != m_cat
   result = CHK_DBFS()
ELSE
   result = !ESC()
```

```
ENDIF
RETURN result
```

```
FUNCTION GET_NTXS

REPLACE DCAT->INDEX_DATE WITH ;
   VERIFY("Maintain an index on the file date")
IF !ESC()
   REPLACE DCAT->INDEX_EXT WITH ;
   VERIFY("Maintain an index on the file extensions")
ENDIF
RETURN .T.
```

Summary

In dCAT, we are coming closer to our goal of invisible software. By eliminating the menu except when it is required, we get out of the user's way completely. By making the list the fundamental window into the catalog, we provide more information per second, if you will. The user's eye can scan rapidly over the records, finding related items very close together.

When you suddenly need to find a copy of a file, chances are you'd like to know where all available copies are, and on what dates they were saved. dCAT offers that information very quickly.

The step from dCAT to a genuine text management program is not large. All the requisite tools are already part of dCAT's code, though you may wish to add a few more fields to the catalog file such as subject, author perhaps, and document title. A program I wrote recently for a government ministry used these components to create a correspondence management system in which all the letters were stored in the memo fields.

Clipper's handling of memo fields, while a big improvement over the dBASE standard it inherited, could stand further improvements such as more efficient text storage. Still, the speed of retrieval, the reasonably large memo space per record, and the excellent control over output make Clipper an ideal tool for Text Base Management Software (TBMS). I leave these possibilities to readers interested in exploring them.

- The functionality stored in our library is beginning to accumulate. Beginning with either DO_IT() or PD_MENU(), we can quickly flesh out our overall design, then building the functions we need one at a time until we have our finished program.

- dCAT also introduced some simple reporting techniques. Probably the most useful is the function OUT_OK(), called by RUN_RPT() as a WHILE clause. This simple trick brings some desperately-needed control to the otherwise primitive REPORT FORM command.

Reports for paying clients seldom fall within REPORT FORM's capabilities, however. For serious applications, considerably more power is necessary. In the next chapter, we look at more complex reporting requirements.

Chapter 10

The Intrepid Reporters

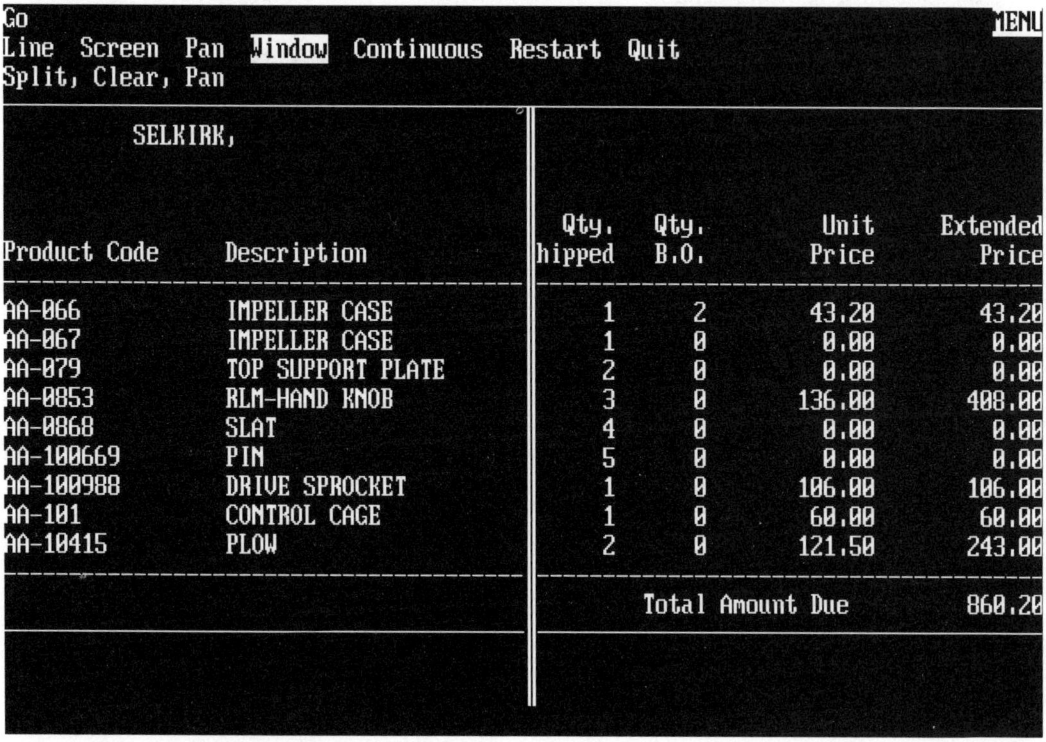

Relational Report Writer in *split window* mode. When you can include this sort of quality reporting without royalities, hard-coded reports are a waste of time.

Report Forms

The first fact of note about REPORT FORM is its limitations, which are charitably described as meager — two breakpoints, almost no control over headers, no control over footers; and horrid control over interrupts such as a printer off-line or a user-invoked halt.

If we could clean up the actual behavior of REPORT FORM, we'd see that more than a few business reports are within these limits. Thanks to user-defined functions, we can clean it up. Let's begin by addressing the good side of REPORT FORM.

We can total and subtotal on any valid break expression. We can request page breaks at both subtotal levels. We can control field width, heading and word wrap. We can include virtual fields (e.g. quantity * price). Thanks to user-defined functions, this means we can do a great deal in REPORT FORM that its creators never imagined we'd try.

We have run-time control over several clauses which can shape the output significantly:

Report Component	Example
Report Heading	'Orders for the Month of ' + CMONTH(DATE())
Report Scope	customers from 100 to 500
Report Condition	balance greater than $1000
Report Destination	screen, file or printer.

Less obvious: we can control the file reported. So long as it matches the one used when the report form was created, you can substitute any file you like: REPORT FORM will work oblivious. Particularly where you copy the contents of current files out to periodic files (e.g. JAN90.DBF), you can play the blindness to filename into powerfully compact report mechanisms.

To gain control over these possibilities, we must construct an effective (read bulletproof) front end. We should encase the user's access to all report forms in the system, providing the means to change all the variables mentioned above, as well as to run the reports. The application cries for a data-driven solution, since this would also allow the user (or us) to add reports to the system any time. We would simply create the new report form file, add a record to the reports table, and fill in the requisite data.

There is another aspect to this as well. If a Clipper program could handle report forms gracefully, then it might also allow the user to create new reports, and include them automatically in the menu of reports available. It brings us a little closer to the notion of software that evolves in the user's hands.

To incorporate new report forms automatically, we have two options. The first is to rely on our library function GET_FILE(), passing "*.FRM" as the selection parameter. A significant problem remains. We have no way of knowing whether the selected report has any connection at all with the current file setup. A mismatch will crash the program and send the user straight to DOS. Before we can trust our report form machine out in the world, we'll have to defend against this possibility.

The second approach uses a data file to contain all the information required by the report form manager. For complex reports, this could be quite a bit of information — files and indexes, relationships set, conditions, filters, scope and more. For one or two report forms it's more trouble than it's worth.

We Apologize for this Interruption

How can we bring gracefulness to REPORT FORM? With a udf, naturally; and to support it, a minor change in the usual way we call a report. To the usual calling convention,

```
REPORT FORM <frm_file> [TO PRINT] ;
   [FOR/WHILE <conditions>]
```

we simply tack our udf onto the <conditions>. Let's call our function OUT_OK(). The call becomes:

```
REPORT FORM <frm_file> [TO PRINT] ;
   [FOR/WHILE <conditions>] .AND. OUT_OK()
```

A small enough change. Now, what should our function do? Obviously, it should attend to the keyboard to see if a key has been pressed. Let's define Escape as the interrupt key. The user presses Escape and then what?

We could terminate the report at once, but that's hardly professional. Having detected an interrupt, all we really know is that the user wants to talk to us. Perhaps the printer jammed or the paper ran out. Perhaps the user chose the wrong report or supplied incorrect parameters. Our function should be able to deal gracefully with all these events. Since we can't really know what the user is thinking, let's present a menu of alternatives. The user can cancel the report, resume, or skip back one page and resume. If it's something like a paper jam, s/he can remedy the situation and then select one of the options.

```
PROGRAM        AA_OUTOK.PRG
Function(s)    OUT_OK()
Purpose        Make REPORT FORM graceful, like Gregory Hines
Conventions    append to any existing condition
Syntax         OUT_OK()
Parameters     none
Example        REPORT FORM <frm_file> WHILE
                    <conditions> .AND OUT_OK()
Assumes        files open and ready, .frm file exists
Side Effects   may eject page or re-start report
Returns        .T. unless report cancelled.
Calls          L_MENU(), VERIFY()
```

```
FUNCTION OUT_OK

PARAMETER dest
PRIVATE temp, choice, result, recs_on_pg, temp_scr
result = .T.
IF INKEY() = 27
   temp =  PCOUNT()
   choice =  01
   recs_on_pg = 55
   is_action = .F.
   SAVE SCREEN TO temp_scr
   SET CONSOLE ON
   DECLARE out_opts[03]
   out_opts[1] = " Resume "
   out_opts[2] = " Back up 1 page and Resume "
   out_opts[3] = " Cancel the report "
   choice = L_MENU(@choice, out_opts, .F., 00)
   DO CASE
      CASE choice = 0 .OR. choice = 3
         result = .F.
```

```
      CASE choice = 1
         result = .T.
      CASE choice = 2
         SKIP - recs_on_pg
         IF VERIFY("Eject the page before continuing")
            EJECT
         ENDIF
   ENDCASE
   RESTORE SCREEN FROM temp_scr
    IF temp > 0
      SET CONSOLE OFF
   ENDIF
ENDIF
RETURN result
```

Deviant Indexing

Multi-Line Breakpoint Headers

This example generates two different reports, one detailed and the second a summary. Fragments of their output follow. Note that in the first report, the breakpoint heading occupies several lines.

Although the file is indexed on the name of the customer, the first breakpoint defined is much more complex:

```
customer->company + CHR(13) + CHR(10) + ;
   SPACE(14)+  customer->b_addr1+ CHR(13) +  CHR(10)+;
   SPACE(14)+  customer->b_addr2+ CHR(13) +  CHR(10)+;
   SPACE(14)+  TRIM(customer->b_city)+;
   " " + customer->b_state + CHR(13) + CHR(10)
```

We embed carriage return-line feed characters directly in the break expression, so Clipper doesn't even notice. Given that our temporary index orders the records on company name + invoice number, our records come out in the right order.

Indexing on Related Data

Writing a compiler, you expose yourself and your product to events, data structures and instructions you cannot possibly imagine. To put it another way, your code has got to be robust, or it will crash the first time someone tries something unusual. I mention this because Clipper is very well coded, and remarkably robust. It gives you enough rope to hang your computer several times over! Just because something you'd like to try is not specifically listed in the documentation, that does not mean you cannot do it. Try it and see how Clipper reacts. A good example is multi-file indexing. Nowhere in the Clipper documentation does it say that you can index a file on data which is not in the file — but you can, and sometimes you can achieve sophisticated results with this simple technique.

Consider this problem: print a detailed list of invoices sorted by company name, with subtotals for each customer and a grand total at the end. Since you understand normalization and apply its principles in all your applications, all you have in the Invoice file is the customer code, which does not correspond to the Company name in terms of its sorting sequence. Since you need the detail as well, you're probably going to have to switch work areas several times during the report.

How would you code this, to get the job done with a minimal amount of work?

Thanks to Clipper's ability to index on data not present in the data file itself, we can make very short work of this problem. It may surprise you to realize that we can do it in twenty lines of code, using REPORT FORM. To do so, we must remain in a single work area. Therefore we drive the report from the Line Item table, indexing it on data not once removed, but twice — available thanks to the SET RELATION command. We set the files up like this:

Table Arrangment

```
Currently Selected table
Select area 1, table in Use: E:\O\INV_ITEM.DBF     Alias: INV_ITEM
Master index file       E:\O\TEMP.NTX  Key: CUSTOMER->COMPANY
Related into    PRODUCT
Relation ID
Related into    INVOICES
Relation ORDER_NUM
Select area:  2, table in Use: E:\O\PRODUCT.DBF     Alias: PRODUCT
   Master index file:    E:\O\PRODUCT1.NTX  Key: ID
            Memo file:    E:\O\PRODUCT.DBT
Select area:  3, table in Use: E:\O\INVOICES.DBF     Alias: INVOICES
```

```
   Master index file:    E:\O\INVOICE1.NTX  Key: ORDER_NUM
            Memo file:    E:\O\INVOICES.DBT
         Related into:    CUSTOMER
            Relation:    ACCOUNT_NO
Select area:  4, table in Use: E:\O\CUSTOMER.DBF    Alias: CUSTOMER
   Master index file:    E:\O\CUSTOME1.NTX  Key: ACCOUNT_NO
Memo file:    E:\O\CUSTOMER.DBT
```

```
PROGRAM       DEVIANT.PRG
Version       1 .0
Purpose       Demonstrate deviant indexing
Parameters    rept_num - identify which .frm
Assumes       invlist1, invlist2 - detail, summary
Comments      REPORT FORM stretched
```

```
PARAMETER rept_num
IF TYPE("rept_num") = "U"
   rept_num = "1"
ENDIF
frm_name = "INVLIST" + rept_num
CLEAR
IF !DB_OPEN("CUSTOMER", 01, "ACCOUNT_NO")
   RETURN
ENDIF
IF !DB_OPEN("PRODUCT", 01, "ID")
   RETURN
ENDIF
IF !DB_OPEN("INVOICES", 01, "Invoice_num")
   RETURN
ENDIF
SET RELATION TO Account_no INTO CUSTOMER
IF !DB_OPEN("INV_ITEM")
   RETURN
ENDIF
SET RELATION TO Invoice_num INTO INVOICES, ;
      TO ID INTO PRODUCT
MSG("Indexing. Please wait", 0, .T.)
INDEX ON CUSTOMER-> Name +  Invoice_num TO temp
GO TOP
IF FILE(frm_name +  ".FRM")
   REPORT FORM &frm_name WHILE OUT_OK()
ENDIF
ERASE TEMP.NTX
```

```
RETURN
```

Detailed Output

```
PAGE NO. 1
03/20/88
Detailed Sales Report by Invoice with Company
This report is is ordered on Company Name.
You can index a file on data not in the file.
In this case the company name is twice removed.

Product     Description       Qty.      Unit    Extended
Code                                    Price   Price

Company     ABCX INDUSTRIES LIMITED
            35 MERCY PARK
            SELKIRK, MD

Invoice # 89003
AA-105      CONTROL CAGE      3          60.30   180.90
AA-106      IMPELLER          4          22.00    88.00
AA-10x6 B   BUCKET BLANK      5         123.78   618.90
AA-10x6 P   BUCKET PUNCHED    1         136.00   136.00
AA-1159     TRUNION SHAFT     1          74.00    74.00
AA-116      CONTROL CAGE      2          44.00    88.00
AA-12       BLADES            3         106.00   318.00
AA-1201     CIRC.DEFLECTOR    4          60.00   240.00
AA-1202     LOWER SIDELINER   5         121.50   607.50
AA-1286     LOWER SIDE LINR   5         575.00  2875.00
Subsubtotal
                              33                5225.30
Invoice # 89124 ... etc.
```

Summary Output

```
PAGE NO.     1
03/20/88
Summary Sales Report by Invoice within Company.
This report stretches the capabilities of REPORT FORM
further than you may have imagined.
            Qty.                 Unit      Extended
                                 Price     Price

** Company: ABCX INDUSTRIES LIMITED

* Invoice # 89003
* Subsubtotal *
            33                   1322.58   5226.30

* Invoice # 89124
* Subsubtotal *
            1                     575.00    575.00

** Subtotal **
            34                   1897.58   5801.30

** Company: ALGORITHM STEEL CORPORATION

... etc.
```

Relational Report Writer

Let me phrase this as delicately as I can: if you don't buy *Relational Report Writer*, you need to be debugged. It's so powerful, flexible and easy to use — and the other means available to you so meager, that it can pay for itself in a day, even if your time is worth only $10 per hour.

As a licensed user of R&R, you may distribute the run-time and setup programs along with your program without paying royalty fees to Concentric Data Systems. You'll encounter reports R&R cannot deliver, particulary if you write very sophisticated programs, but the vast majority of business reports are easily within the range of this powerful product. In the face of this, you have no excuse for wasting time coding reports.

R&R is shipped as a group of executable files which include three programs — RR.EXE, which can create and run reports, RRUNTIME.EXE and RRUN.EXE, which can only run reports. RRUNTIME swaps the required memory out to disk, then calls RRUN.EXE, which loads in the space now freed. This arrangement minimizes the RAM demand of R&R within your Clipper program.

With a little extra work, you can make the link between our program and RRUNTIME virtually seamless, so that only an especially observant user would even notice.

The Job File

The next function, RPT(), is written to blend into a pull-down menu system. Unlike other menus you have seen, however, this one is data-driven. It assumes a file REPORTS.DBF, a standard R&R *job file*, a table containing one record for each report in the system, storing run-time parameters such as destination. A typical R&R job file has this structure:

Structure for table: REPORTS.DBF

Field	Name	Type	Len
1	RI_REPORT	C	30
2	RI_LIBRARY	C	80
3	RI_MASTER	C	80
4	RI_OUTFILE	C	80
5	RI_OUTAPPN	L	1
6	RI_PEQUIT	L	1

```
7       RI_CHKTIME  C       1
8       RI_NOESC    L       1
9       RI_PRINTER  C       1
10      RI_BEGPAGE  N       4
11      RI_ENDPAGE  N       4
12      RI_TEST     L       1
13      RI_SCOPE    C       1
14      RI_LOSCOPE  C       100
15      RI_HISCOPE  C       100
16      RI_COPIES   N       4
17      RI_FILTER   C       254
18      RI_QUERY    C       1
19      RI_DISPERR  L       1
```

In applications requiring only one job file, you may find it most convenient to name it REPORTS.DBF. Since R&R can print all the reports in a job file, you'll occasionally find reason to employ several job files. To deal with this possibility, RPT() anticipates a parameter *job_file*, defaulting it to REPORTS if you don't pass it.

Because RPT() is data-driven, it is unaffected by trivialities such as the number of reports in an application. Realistically, the number will be a small integer, probably smaller than 20 —, not that it matters, since ACHOICE() will scroll the menu automatically.

All we really need from this table are the report descriptions and the matching record numbers, so RPT() creates an array, fires the descriptions into it, and drops the menu down using a call to ACHOICE().

The number ACHOICE() returns is either zero (if Escape is pressed) or the number of the record you care about. You go to the appropriate record, then allow the user access to the run-time controls such as report destination. When everything is in place, you call RRUNTIME, passing it the name of the job_file and the record number.

```
FUNCTION RPT
PARAMETER job_file
PRIVATE dummy, x, tr, tc, br, bc, temp, cmd, job_file,;
    dest_row, top_area
SET KEY 28 TO RPT_HELP
job_file = IF(TYPE("job_file")="U","REPORTS",job_file)
temp  = PCOUNT()
dummy = .T.
SELECT &job_file
```

```
no_reports = LASTREC()
top_area = SAVESCREEN(00,00,01,79)
DECLARE rpt_list[no_reports]
FOR i = 01 TO no_reports
   GO i
   rpt_list[i] = RI_REPORT
NEXT
tr = 01
tc = 41
br = tr + no_reports + 01
bc = 78
dest_row = br
rpt_udf = .F.
logicals = .T.
DO WHILE .T.
   @ 02,00 CLEAR
   DRAW_BOX(tr,tc,br,bc,13)
   choice = ACHOICE(tr + 1, tc+ 1, br, bc - 1, ;
            rpt_list, logicals, rpt_udf, choice)
   IF EMPTY(choice)
      EXIT
   ELSE
      SELECT &job_file
      GO choice
      RUN_RPT()
   ENDIF
   RESTSCREEN(00,00,03,79,top_area)
ENDDO
SET KEY 28 TO
@ 02,00 CLEAR
RETURN .T.
```

State Machines

Once a report is selected, the function RUN_RPT() takes over. It declares an array, fills it with function names, then passes it to the library function AMACHINE(), a simple state machine.

If you're unfamiliar with the term *state machine*, think of it as a menu which increments its own default each time you complete an action, or decrements the default if you press Escape. Now remove the menu, and you have a state machine. This programming construct can grow as complex as you like — I once saw a machine with 112 states, each corresponding to a condition in the life of a pension fund. Most states caused some form of report to be printed — anything from a form letter requesting information to an annual summary.

RUN_RPT() is much simpler, yet illustrates how to handle a variety of states. The assumption is that the user wants to be able to back up at any point in the process. Enough Escape should leave the reporting module entirely.

Beginning with the first udf in the array, AMACHINE() executes them in sequence — unless the user presses Escape. In that case, the machine goes back to the previous function and continues from there. RUN_RPT() calls four functions, RR_DEST(), which controls the report destination, RR_SCOPE(), which allows the user to scope the report, RR_FILTER(), which calls QUERY() to set as complex a filter as you wish, and CALL_RR(), which executes the report.

```
FUNCTION RUN_RPT
PRIVATE result, actions[04]
result = 00
actions[01] = "RR_DEST(&job_file->ri_printer)"
actions[02] = "RR_SCOPE()"
actions[03] = "RR_FILTER()"
actions[04] = "CALL_RR()"
AMACHINE(actions,01)
RETURN result
```

Report Destination

The function RR_DEST() allows the user to control the output destination of RRUNTIME reports, selecting among display, printer or text file. Should the user select the latter, RR_DEST() prompts for the file name.

```
FUNCTION RR_DEST
PARAMETER cur_dest
PRIVATE row, col, temp_scr, tr, tc, br, bc, choice, result
row = dest_row
col = COL()
tr  = IF(row  18, row - 03, row + 1)
tc  = 13
br  = tr + 02
bc  = 65
result = 01
temp_scr = SAVESCREEN(tr,tc,br,bc)
DRAW_BOX(tr, tc, br, bc, 02)
@ tr + 1,15 SAY "Send this Report to"
@ tr + 1,36 PROMPT " Printer "
```

```
@ tr + 1,46 PROMPT " Screen "
@ tr + 1,56 PROMPT " File "
choice = MIN(01,AT(cur_dest,"1DA"))
MENU TO choice
DO CASE
   CASE choice = 0
      * do nothing
   CASE choice = 1
      cur_dest = "1"
   CASE choice = 2
      cur_dest = "D"
   CASE choice = 3
      tr1 = IF(br  18, tr - 04, br)
      tc1 = 12
      br1 = tr1 + 04
      bc1 = 66
   DRAW_BOX( tr1, tc1, br1, bc1, 02 )
   @ tr1 + 02,tc1 + 03 SAY "File to Create ..." ;
      GET ri_outfile PICTURE "@!"
   READ_IT()
   IF !EMPTY(ri_outfile)
      cur_dest = "A"
   ENDIF
ENDCASE
REPLACE &job_file-RI_PRINTER WITH cur_dest
IF ESC()
   result = -1
   RESTSCREEN(tr,tc,br,bc,temp_scr)
ELSE
   result = 1
ENDIF
RETURN result
```

Run-Time Specifications

R&R lets you control reports at run-time in three ways — scoping the report, using a parameter file, and applying a filter specification. Let's examine each of these in turn.

Report Scope

The first avenue of control available to you is the report scope. In R&R this has a very specific meaning: the controlling index dictates what can be scoped. If the controlling index were on Invoice Number rather than Invoice Date, you could not apply a date-sensitive scope. You could, however, enter a low and high invoice number into the fields RI_LOSCOPE and RI_HISCOPE, and RRUNTIME would report only records falling within those limits.

How can your program deduce what can be scoped? Assuming all the tables and indexes are open, the problem is trivial — all you need to add to REPORTS.DBF is a field RI_ORDER, containing the appropriate index number. Grab the number, and SET ORDER to it — easy.

To scope the report gracefully, though, you need a little more information, such as a picture statement through which to read the scope variables.

In some cases, the index used for a report is not maintained in general operations, but instead produced only at run-time. The field RI_ORDER will be no help. We therefore add the field RI_KEYEXP to REPORTS.DBF, using it only for run-time indexes. RPT() can therefore easily distinguish the situations. To keep the code as simple aspossible, name all such run-time indexes TEMP.NTX. Finally, for cosmetic reasons we add the field RI_KEYCUE, for use in the scoping prompt.

These new fields provide the basis for a routine which asks the user for report scope, without hard-coding such details, thus preserving the generality of the solution.We'll add these fields to REPORTS.DBF, sizing them as the application requires.

```
20    RI_KEYEXP    Character  20
21    RI_KEYCUE    Character  20
22    RI_KEYPIC    Character  15
23    RI_ORDER     Numeric    1
```

For reports in which run-time scoping is never required, we'll simply leave these fields blank. For reports the user can control in this way, we place the key expression, prompt string and picture statement in the new fields. At run-time, our report manager examines these fields. Finding data, it executes the function RR_SCOPE(). Using the appropriate index, RR_SCOPE() goes to the top and bottom of the file to obtain default values for low and high scope, supplying these to the user for confirmation or editing.

```
PROGRAM        AA_SCOPE.PRG
Function(s)    RR_SCOPE()
Purpose        GET upper and lower boundaries of a range
               With optional validation for RRUNTIME
Conventions    any VALIDs can be executed
```

```
Syntax        RR_SCOPE()
Parameters    none
Example       RR_SCOPE()
Assumes       tables open, job file selected
Side Effects  crash if files missing or closed
Returns       True unless escape is pressed
CallS         IS_CHAR,READ_IT,GEN_PIC,CENTRE,SHADOWBOX
```

```
FUNCTION RR_SCOPE

PRIVATE tr,tc,br,bc,r_header,box_no,temp_scr, result, file;
      msg, ntx_expr, pic, low, high, ord_no
file = RI_MASTER
msg = TRIM(RI_KEYCUE)
ntx_expr = RI_KEYEXP
pic = RI_KEYPIC
ord_no = RI_ORDER
SELECT &file
IF EMPTY(ntx_expr)
   SET ORDER TO ord_no
ELSE
   INDEX ON &ntx_expr TO TEMP
ENDIF
GO TOP
ntx_expr = INDEXKEY(0)
low = &ntx_expr
GO BOTTOM
high = &ntx_expr
tr = 04
tc = 11
br = 19
bc = 68
r_header = "Report Scope"
box_no = 02
result = 02
temp_scr = SAVESCREEN(tr,tc-1,br+1,bc+1)
SHADOWBOX(tr,tc,br,bc,r_header,box_no)
@ 09,15 SAY "Begin at " + msg + "..."
@ 14,15 SAY "End at " + msg + "..."
@ 11,15 GET low PICTURE pic
@ 16,15 GET high PICTURE pic
READ_IT()
IF !ESC()
   SELECT &job_file
   REPLACE ri_scope with "O", ;
      ri_loscope with low, ;
      ri_hiscope with high
```

```
ENDIF
RESTSCREEN(tr,tc-1,br+1,bc+1,temp_scr)
result = IF(ESC(),result -2,result)
RETURN result
```

Functions can only return one value, unfortunately, which explains why we don't return the values entered directly, and instead have to do the replaces within the function.

Parameter-Driven Reports

The second method is using a parameter file. You create a file (RPARAMS.DBF, say), containing fields similar to those you wish to use in delimiting the report. For example, you might have a field in RPARAMS.DBF called Lo_number. In R&R, you create a Query specification comparing Lo_number to a field in the file you're reporting (Qty_onhand, say). Your report query might specify all records whose Qty_onhand value is less than RPARAMS->Lo_number.

Typically, a parameter file has only one record, but it could have a hundred if that suited your purposes. A parameter file need have no more than the fields you require, but it's useful to generalize the structure so that it works with any report. To do this, you simply add a pair of fields for each data type.

Table Structure for RPARAMS.DBF

Field	Name	Type	Len	Dec
1	C1	C	20	0
2	C2	C	20	0
3	D1	D	8	0
4	D2	D	8	0
5	L1	L	1	0
6	L2	L	1	0
7	I1	N	5	0
8	I2	N	5	0
9	N1	N	10	2
10	N2	N	10	2

It's important to realize that this structure is merely a starting point. There's a pair for each data type; numeric possibilities are covered twice, with a pair of fields each for integers and money.

The point is, we can restructure this table any time we wish, with no changes in code. Add or remove fields from this table according to your program's requirements — this information is for R&R, not Clipper.

Creating your report in R&R, you specify a query comparing one or more fields in the database to parallel fields in RPARAMS. It will resemble this query:

```
Birthdate > RPARAMS->D1 .AND. Birthdate < RPARAMS->D2 .AND. ;
      Coverage > RPARAMS->N1
```

At run-time, you ask the user for the birthdate range and the level of insurance coverage, plug them into RPARAMS and call RRUNTIME.

Inside R&R, you create a calculated field and assign it a constant value equal to the record number in the parameter file (most often, 1). Next you relate theparameter file to your primary table through the calculated field — which effectively locks the parameter file at the record number specified, no matter what happens in the primary file.

Again in R&R, you'd supply a query specification which compares the field of interest to the contents of the matching field in the parameters file. For example, to create a list of new customers, you might create a field DATE in your customer file, defaulting it to today's date at entry time (to save the user typing it over and over). Just prior to running the report, you ask the user for a date and copy the response into the parameter file.

Now when the report runs, it compares each Customer's DATE field with the date supplied in the parameter file, printing the customer record only if it is greater than or equal to the date in the parameter file.

This avenue of influence is considerably more powerful than the former, in which only the field(s) in the primary key are subject to scoping specifications. On the other hand, this approach requires one more data file than the first, which may be a consideration in some circumstances.

Setting a Filter

The third and most powerful method of controlling a report at run-time is through setting a filter on the database. To filter a table at run-time, place an "O" (for override) in the field RI_QUERY and the filter expression in the the field RI_FILTER.

Thanks to the power of the library function QUERY(), you can offer your user a significant degree of run-time control, while preventing all but the most devious programmers from entering an expression which is syntactically incorrect.

Filtering the File

The function RR_FILTER() is a simple variant on QUERY, the difference being that it writes the resulting filter string to the RI_FILTER field in the REPORTS file, rather than actually setting the filter. RRUNTIME encounters the filter string and filters the file to those specifications. The nice thing about handling ad-hoc requests this way is the insulation from syntax that RR_FILTER() provides. Only a determined programmer could construct a string which contained faulty syntax. It is extremely unlikely that a normal user could do so.

```
FUNCTION RR_FILTER
PRIVATE result, file
SELECT &file
QUERY()
filt_str = DBFILTER()
REPLACE &job_file->RI_FILTER WITH filt_str
result = IF(ESC(), 0, 1)
RETURN result
```

Calling RRUNTIME

With everything now in order, the call to RRUNTIME is straightforward. You simply assemble the string to be passed to RRUNTIME, then call the program.

One minor problem arises — you must close REPORTS.DBF before calling RRUNTIME; in fact, to conserve memory you must close all files before the call. On the first call, you can assume that all required tables are open. After the report has run, you must re-open all the files — thus the call to CHK_DBFS().

```
FUNCTION CALL_RR
PRIVATE result
rr_rec = strint(RECNO())
rr_job = job_file
cmd = "RRUNTIME " + rr_job + " " + rr_rec
result = 0
IF FILE( "RRUNOUT.DBF" )
   ERASE rrunout.dbf
ENDIF
MSG("Working... Please be patient",0,.T.)
RUN &cmd
CHK_DBFS()
SELECT &job_file
GO &rr_rec
RETURN result
```

Help on Reports

Finally, you may decide to include some simple help text for your reporting module. This simple example is not dazzling, but it does the job. First it eliminates the bizarre behavior that can result from nested help calls, then it displays the help text.

```
PROCEDURE rpt_help
PARAMETERS x, y, z
IF x = "RPT_HELP"
   RETURN
ENDIF
SAVE SCREEN TO temp_scr
CLEAR SCREEN
TEXT
                       HELP ON PRINTING REPORTS


      The arrow keys move you from report to report.
      Page Up and Page Down work as expected.
      Ctrl-Page Up and Ctrl-Page Down go to the first and last
report.
      Point at the report you wish to print, then press Enter.
      Where applicable, scoping options (begin at, end at) will
appear.
```

```
      To change the report Destination, move to that field and
press Enter.
      To quit, press ESCape.



ENDTEXT
WAIT
RESTORE SCREEN FROM temp_scr
RETURN
```

Summary

If you do not yet own R&R, I hope this chapter has convinced you to purchase it. From a professional point of view, there is no better reporting tool available. Occasionally you will come across reports which it cannot handle — send them to Concentric Data Systems, by all means — but far more often you'll be able to deliver every report in a system using it, in a tenth the time it would take you to code. The fact is, R&R is so good I hope my competition *doesn't* buy it.

Chapter 11

The Story of O.EXE

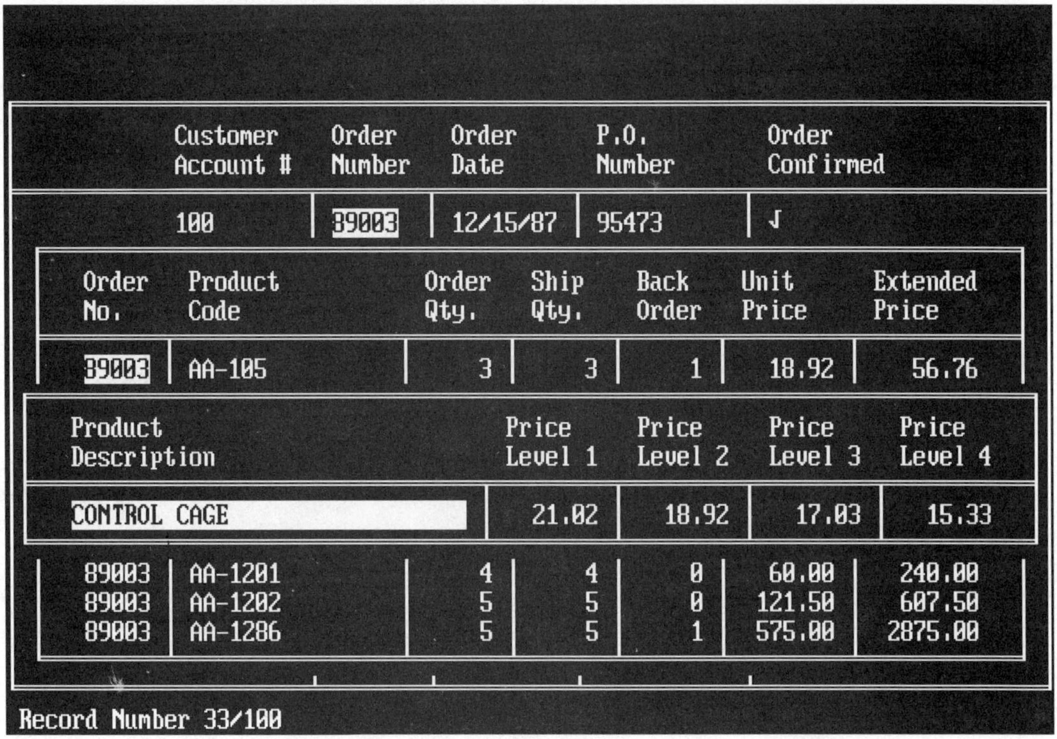

Smart Windows — O.EXE with all its windows open. Note that each window opens relative to the information already displayed, leaving a highlight in the previous window on the zoomed data. This way the user can easily follow exactly what was zoomed to arrive at the current position.

The Job Spec

In this chapter, you'll bring together everything you've learned so far, creating an order-entry program based on smart windows. Besides being dramatically different than typical database applications, smart-windows programs are a lot more fun to write — and to use.

Our client in this case sells replacement parts for hundreds of industrial machines. Lots of the parts are used in a variety of machines; unfortunately, this often means that one customer calls a given blade an *X09W*, a second calls the same blade a *GMQ 407*, while a third customer thinks it's an *ABC876*. They are all, of course, right.

From our client's view, though, they're all talking about a single blade which the firm may or may not have in stock. It is not his place to tell people to learn yet another number - rather, he wants you to write a system which will let his order takers enter whatever number the customer uses - while correctly handling the inventory updates of the single blade he orders from a single manufacturer.

There's another little catch, too, or rather six of them. The client has six price levels, and wants your program to pick the price from the appropriate column automatically - but also to allow the user to override the default price.

Your software must also handle stock receipts, of course, and provide mechanisms for adjusting quantities due to shrinkage, damage, error and theft.

In terms of output, the owner has all the usual requirements — print orders, invoices and packing slips, purchase orders by supplier, back-order reports, stock re-order reports, price lists, stock lists without prices.

In addition, your system must provide a set of management reports. Management wants to know which items move well and which are hardly selling at all. A report showing all deviations from the standard price is also required, so management can observe which salespeople are consistently selling below the default prices.

Identifying the Center of Events

Virtually all orders are placed over the phone, which is to say your system must respond very quickly - not in several seconds but in a fraction of a second. You visit the client's site, notebook on your lap, and watch the order takers in action. One of the order takers has a speaker phone, so you can hear both sides of the conversation.

"Hi Susan, it's Bob Rybak at HydroTech. Can I have price and delivery on a dozen RXT-11 blades?"

Susan reaches for a parts catalogue, fingers through it like a teller counting bills, slides a nail halfway down a page.

"Eighty-two dollars," she replies, turning to ask a co- worker, "We still got any RXT-11's?"

The co-worker nods.

"That's nine dollars more than Western is charging," the customer complains.

Susan makes a face. "Take two dozen and I'll meet their price."

"Oh, and a couple of weeks or maybe a month ago I bought some gaskets, I forget the number, " says the customer. "I need another box."

"I'll check through the invoices," says Susan. "I'll have to get back to you."

"Don't get back to me. Just send it."

The calls come every few minutes, for an average of about a hundred orders per day. Susan has been here for years, knows most of the parts and prices without reference to the table, has the authority to adjust prices. She hates telling customers she has items in stock when in fact they are not. It makes her — and the firm — look bad.

Far better to tell them the parts will arrive in five days when you think it will take three. Then she can call to say they're here early.

The complete application is beyond the scope of this book. We'll concentrate on the center of events, the data-entry section. We'll also include a report manager, to control and integrate any reports you wish to add to the system. In place of some of the other functions you'll find stubs based on a call to POP_MSG(). I encourage you to remove these at your pleasure, replacing them with working routines.

Smart Windows

dCAT allowed us to glimpse what an application built around DBEDIT() might look like. Now it's time to reveal the powers of DBEDIT(). Recall that DBEDIT() accepts as one of its parameters the name of a function. Normally that function is more or less like the XBROWSER() function we used in dCAT. You can, however, pass in anything you want, including a function which calls DBEDIT(). In other words, you can nest DBEDIT() windows. On this capability we can build a network of smart windows.

Smart windows take into consideration what is already on the screen before they appear. They open to complement the information already on the screen, embellishing or extending it with detail.

In O.PRG, we'll develop a system of interrelated windows which expand on the current information, calculating where they open according to the cursor location. To see any detail, press the Zoom key. To collapse any window, press the Escape key.

Figure 10.1 shows O.EXE in action, with three of its windows open. The largest and deepest window is the base of operations, the Orders window. The next window is the Order Items window, which shows only items belonging to the selected Order. The topmost window appears when any Order Item is zoomed, showing the description of the product, prices and stock levels. Note how each window opens relative to the highlighted item in the previous window.

Smart Keys

Optimizing for speed at entry time, we'll attach several commands to specific keys, and have them perform intelligently depending on which window is active.

Alt-P, for example, is the Pricing key. If the Order Items window is active when the user presses Alt-P, we'll copy the default customer price for the item into the price. On the other hand, the user may have zoomed from there to the Product window, and intend another price to be used. If the Product window is active, we'll check which field the cursor is in. If it's one of the price fields, we'll copy that price back into the Order Items window. Either way, the user can also over-write the price simply by typing a new one in.

Alt-B will activate the back-order process. Not every customer wants to back-order items, after all. If on the other hand the customer does want to back-order, why should the user have to enter more than one keystroke? Alt-B executes the process cleanly and invisibly.

Stock to fill an order is not allocated until the customer confirms the order. That may be at entry time, but it's also possible that the customer is simply calling for prices. Better to get the information into the system now rather than later, not least because it provides a means of tracking unconfirmed orders. The sales staff can call back and find out if the customer bought elsewhere or reconsidered or wants to confirm the order now.

Once an order is confirmed, we allocate stock to fill it. It's also important to ensure that we don't allocate the stock twice.

Alt-A invokes the function UPD_QTYAL(), which first checks to see if the stock has already been allocated.

We employ a similar routine in the back-order process to ensure that items are not back-ordered more than once — otherwise there would be chaos.

We know whether an item has been allocated or back- ordered thanks to a pair of logical fields in the Order Items file. As each record is added, these fields default to False. The allocate and back-order functions set their respective fields to True, so it's straightforward for us to check their status before permitting the action.

On the other side, if an item is deleted from an order, and has been allocated already, we must reverse the allocation to restore accuracy to the stock quantities. This is straightforward. The complication comes when an item is edited. The quantities allocated and back-ordered may have changed during the edit. The customer may call to tell you to double a given order. You've already allocated the first half, so when you re- allocate the stock, you want only to allocate the increase, not the entire quantity.

The same holds true for reduced orders. The customer orders ten blades and you allocate them. Then the customer calls back and reduces the order to six blades. You now must correct the over-allocation.

To cut through these complications, we make a rule: detecting an edit on the quantity ordered, shipped or back- ordered, we'll immediately reverse the transaction, so to speak. We'll de-allocate and de-back-order (I can hear my English teachers writhe) the item, restoring the stock quantities to their original state. Then we'll reset the flags in the Order Item file to False. With the integrity of the quantities restored, we can then proceed us usual.

These complications can only arise if the user edits an item which s/he has already either allocated or back-ordered or both. Thus what may at first seem a fairly complex problem is reduced to one of checking two flags before proceeding.

Data Structures

The Order Table

Field	Field Name	Type	Width
1	ACCOUNT_NO	Character	5
2	ORDER_NUM	Character	5
3	ORDER_DATE	Date	8
4	PO_NUM	Character	10
5	CONFIRMED	Logical	1
6	DETAILS	Character	35
7	FOB	Character	12
8	TERMS	Character	20
9	VIA	Character	10
10	NOTES	Memo	10
Total			117

The Order Item Table

Field	Field Name	Type	Width	Dec
1	ORDER_NUM	Character	5	
2	ID	Character	15	
3	QTY_ORDERD	Numeric	5	
4	QTY_SHIPPD	Numeric	5	
5	QTY_BO	Numeric	5	
6	PRICE	Numeric	10	2
7	ALLOCATED	Logical	1	
8	BACK_ORDRD	Logical	1	
Total			48	

The Product (Stock) Table

Field	Field Name	Type	Width	Dec
1	DESC	Character	30	
2	PRICE1	Numeric	8	2
3	PRICE2	Numeric	8	2
4	PRICE3	Numeric	8	2

5	PRICE4	Numeric	8	2
6	PRICE5	Numeric	8	2
7	PRICE6	Numeric	8	2
8	QTY_OH	Numeric	5	
9	QTY_AL	Numeric	5	
10	QTY_OO	Numeric	5	
11	QTY_BO	Numeric	5	
12	BIN	Character	8	
13	PACKED	Numeric	4	
14	COST	Numeric	8	2
15	MINORDER	Numeric	5	
16	MAXORDER	Numeric	5	
17	REORDER	Numeric	5	
18	UPDATED	Date	8	
19	WT_EACH	Numeric	7	2
20	NOTES	Memo	10	
21	ID	Character	15	
Total			174	

The O.E.M. Number Table

Field	Field Name	Type	Width
1	ID	Character	15
2	PROD_CODE	Character	15
Total			31

The Customer Table

Field	Field Name	Type	Width	Dec
1	ACCOUNT_NO	Character	5	
2	COMPANY	Character	35	
3	PHONE	Character	10	
4	PRICE_CODE	Character	1	
5	NOTES	Memo	10	
6	CREDIT	Numeric	10	2
7	CONTACT	Character	35	
8	SALESMAN	Character	5	
9	EXEMPT	Logical	1	
10	FSTNO	Character	15	
11	PSTNO	Character	15	
12	LANGUAGE	Character	1	
13	REGION	Character	5	
14	B_ADDR1	Character	35	
15	B_ADDR2	Character	35	
16	B_CITY	Character	20	

17	B_PROV	Character	4	
18	B_PCODE	Character	10	
19	SH_ADDR1	Character	35	
20	SH_ADDR2	Character	35	
21	SH_CITY	Character	20	
22	SH_PROV	Character	4	
23	SH_PCODE	Character	10	
24	TAX1	Numeric	10	3
25	TAX2	Numeric	10	3
Total				377

The System-Configuration Table

Field	Field Name	Type	Width	Dec
1	CO_PREFIX	Character	2	
2	CO_NAME	Character	40	
3	CO_ADDR1	Character	40	
4	CO_ADDR2	Character	40	
5	CO_CITY	Character	25	
6	CO_STATE	Character	2	
7	CO_PCODE	Character	10	
8	NEXT_ORDER	Character	5	
9	NEXT_INVCE	Character	5	
10	NEXT_PO	Character	5	
1	UTIL_1	Character	8	
12	UTIL_2	Character	8	
13	UTIL_3	Character	8	
14	EDITOR	Character	8	
15	SOFT_ON	Logical	1	
16	BELL_ON	Logical	1	
17	COLOR_ON	Logical	1	
18	CONFIRM_ON	Logical	1	
19	HELP	Memo	10	
Total			221	

Yes, We Have No Relations

You'll notice that each window-management function (except the first) receives a parameter from its caller, then immediately SEEKs it. You may be wondering why we don't simply SET RELATIONs among all the files and eliminate these SEEKs. Why do by hand what Clipper can do for us automatically?

In a word: speed. SET RELATION moves all the record pointers all the time, whether your program needs to or not. All this disk access places a heavy tax on performance. In reporting situations this cost is often irrelevant, since the printer is by far the slowest element in the loop. In programs which display only one record per screen, as well, you can often get away with the inefficiencies of SET RELATION.

When you rest an entire application on DBEDIT(), however, you can ill afford extraneous disk accesses. Your program will be significantly faster if you move the pointers yourself, only when necessary. Further, by creating a consistent pattern (passing a target parameter in and immediately SEEKing it), we make the relationships perfectly clear, reduce the complexity to two lines of code per window, and can even include those two lines in our production templates.

Locks On or Locks Off

None of the windows impose any parental locking on the records displayed. The user is not restricted to viewing only the related data, but may freely scroll through the file in any window. In certain applications this design is unacceptable (though they are far fewer than the prevalence of that constricted style can justify).

To lock a related window, to force it to show only the data related to its parent, you might set a filter. In the Order Item window, for example, you might deem it better to display only records relating to the Order zoomed. You could set a filter to achieve this automatically:

```
SELECT ORD_ITEM                        && Filter version
SET FILTER TO Order_num = target
GO TOP
```

Particularly in large files, this strategy is going to take time. With small files, however, it performs quite acceptably. The strategy here implemented applies no such filter, and performs much more quickly. When items are added to an order, the order number defaults to the highlighted record in the Orders window, so from that point of view the user loses nothing. Besides, the order number is displayed in the first column of the Item window, so it's always clear to which order a given item belongs.

```
SELECT ORD_ITEM                         && SEEK version
SEEK target                             && allows freedom of movement
```

In short, it depends on your point of view. I prefer unlimited movement within each window. Others may not. Occasionally, applications forbid it. Shape this part of the code according to your preferences. You might even want to employ a hybrid version, which relies on a trick to combine the speed and the filtering process:

```
SELECT ORD_ITEM                         && Speed/Filter version
SEEK target
SET FILTER TO Order_num = target
```

Usually you'll find, immediately following a SET FILTER command, a GO TOP command. This is because the filter you set is not actually applied to the file until the next instruction to move the record pointer. By performing the SEEK first, however, we turn this to our advantage.

If the SEEK lands on a record, the SET FILTER command will obviously apply to that record. If the SEEK fails, we'll be at EOF(), in which case it doesn't matter — we'll have stepped through the file in the fastest possible way. Should the user choose to add a record, our inheritance-principle will ensure that it receives the correct parental information.

Function Descriptions

O.EXE contains quite a few functions, distributed among several files for easier management. Before we get into the code, let's outline the purpose of each function.

Within O.PRG are STUFF_RA() and CHK_DBFS(), placed there primarily to facilitate a quick overview of the entire system. In one change we have made from the usual layout is that CHK_DBFS() accepts a parameter. The parameter enables us to turn CHK_DBFS() into a CASE block. Thus all file-opening code resides in a single function — an organizational advantage. It also paves the way for using the order-entry windows to display the invoices as well. Since most of the information and all the file relationships are similar, this simple act of passing a parameter allows us to re-use our code in a new situation.

ORDERS() is the master window control function. From the Orders window extend all the other windows in the system. Since the Orders window can Zoom in two directions (to the customer window or the order item window), its Zoom program is little more than a fork which tests the location of the cursor. Finding it in the customer account field, it Zooms to the Customer window. Finding the cursor anywhere else it opens the Order Item window.

ITEMS() administers the Order Item Window, passing O_BROWSER() to DBEDIT().

PRODUCTS() opens the Product window and handles all maintenance tasks associated with that file.

NUMBERS() opens the last window in the chain, revealing the table of translation codes on which the system rests. Each product code entered (in the Order Item window) may be either one of our own unique product numbers, or one of the "clone" numbers used by an OEM. In the interests of performance, no lookup or translation is done until the user requests it (by opening the Product window). This way no extraneous file manipulation slows down the system.

When the user opens the Product window, function XLATE() is called to test the value of the current product code (in the Order Item window). If this code begins with the company prefix identifying all internal product codes, we perform a simple SEEK to point at the appropriate product. If it begins with any other letters, we know it's an OEM number and call XLATE() to tell us what it "really" is. The numbers table, remember, is indexed on the OEM numbers, so we can perform this search very quickly. Finding the OEM number, we simply look at the other field and grab our internal number, then switch back to the Product file and perform our SEEK as usual. This way we guarantee that all legitimate product codes point at their correct products.

CUSTOMER() opens the customer window and handles all maintenance tasks associated with that file.

INVOICES() administers the Invoice file, using a browse window. The slash key ("/") activates a private menu.

O_BROWSER() is our custom udf written to execute inside DBEDIT(). We trap for the hot keys invoking various commands. Some of these are window-sensitive, so we have to check which window is active before taking certain of the actions.

O_UDFS.PRG houses all the utility functions comprising O.PRG. These include XLATE(), which translates between the unique product numbers and the OEM numbers which also represent them.

GET_PRICE() and DFLT_PRICE() are two different ways of pricing an item, depending on which window is open at the time. If the Order Item window is open, DFLT_PRICE() checks the customer file to determine which price this customer is usually charged, then copies that price into the appropriate field.

GET_PRICE() is invoked when the Product window is open; the assumption is that the user wants to see the range of prices, and may use a price other than the default. To select any other price, the user places the cursor on it then presses Alt-P, invoking GET_PRICE(). This function ensures that the cursor is in a price field, and if not tells the user so. If so, GET_PRICE() copies the selected price back into the Order Items window, then collapses the Product window (note the use of KEYBOARD CHR(27) to emulate a user pressing escape), returning the user to the Order Item window in preparation for the next item to add.

UPD_QTYAL() and UPD_QTYBO() handle the updates of quantities allocated and back-ordered.

The Browsing UDF

In many ways OBROWSER() resembles other functions we have written for use inside DBEDIT(). In fact, each time we need one we just make a local copy of the original and add what we require.

You'll see several new things in this code. First is the trap for a menu key, defined in this application as "/". As we have done often before, we call the menu function by reference, via macro expansion. There is an important gain here: it allows each window to have its own menu. Clearly the things you'll want to do while in the Customer window are quite different from those in the Product window. The indirect reference offers this capability within a single block of code.

OBROWSER()'s prime task is to trap for the hot-keys we've defined for the actions. Some of these commands, the Search command for example, have been assigned twice. Both the space bar and Alt-S activate Search.

At the top of OBROWSER() we assign the numbers corresponding to all the hot keys to a set of variables, then check the keystrokes by indirection. We could hard-code this, but we'd have more difficulty maintaining it in that form. More important, we are laying the groundwork here for future development. It's important to break the specific keystrokes away from the actions they invoke.Think of the form implemented here as halfway toward a system in which the user can define the hot keys while configuring the program. One user coming to your program from Word Perfect might set it up one way, another user with a different background will set it up differently. You could provide your favorite definitions as the defaults in the system file.

O Source Code

```
PROGRAM        O.PRG
Function(s)    Main program,STUFF_RA(),CHK_DBFS(),OPEN_SYS()
Purpose        Demonstrate the pull-down menu system
Conventions    Also a tool for prototyping applications
Syntax         O
Parameters     monochrome - pass anything to turn color off
Example        O
Assumes        Arrays declared as outlined below
Side Effects   none
Returns        True always
Calls          SIGN_ON(), PD_MENU(), SYSCOLOR(),
```

```
PARAMETERS user, monochrome
exe_name = "The Natural Order"
exe_desc = "Smart Window Order Entry"
o_keys = "ACCOUNT_NO+ORDER_NUM"
n_keys = "PROD_CODE+ID"
dummy = .F.
co_prefix = ""
menu_key = "/"
DATE_KEY(03)                         && assign system date to F3
IF UN_DEF("user")                    && This concept allows different users
   sys_rec = 1                       && to have different settings
ELSE                                 && and even different help!
   sys_rec = 2                       && you might want to store this field in
ENDIF                                && the system file as well.
IF !OPEN_SYS(sys_rec)
   SET CURSOR ON
   RETURN
```

```
ENDIF
IF TYPE("monochrome") = "U"
   monochrome = .F.
ENDIF
SYSCOLOR(01)
SIGN_ON(exe_name, exe_desc)
m_size = 06
PRIVATE main_cues[m_size], cols[m_size], main_sizes[m_size]
main_cues[1] = "  Orders     "
main_cues[2] = "  Invoices   "
main_cues[3] = "  Reports    "
main_cues[4] = "  Export     "
main_cues[5] = "  Utility    "
main_cues[6] = "  Quit       "
cols[1] = 02
cols[2] = 12
cols[3] = 23
cols[4] = 32
cols[5] = 42
cols[6] = 52
main_sizes[01] = 01
main_sizes[02] = 05
main_sizes[03] = 05
main_sizes[04] = 06
main_sizes[05] = 06
main_sizes[06] = 01
PD_MENU(main_cues, main_sizes)
SET CURSOR ON
SIGN_OFF(exe_name, exe_desc)
```

```
FUNCTION STUFF_RA

c1[01] = " Do Order Entry "
u1[01] = "ORDERS()"
c2[01] = " Browse Invoices  "
c2[02] = " Query the file   "
c2[03] = " Duplicate copy   "
c2[04] = " Pick List        "
c2[05] = " Today's Invoices "
u2[01] = "INVOICES()"
u2[02] = "POP_MSG('Ask questions about the Invoices')"
u2[03] = "POP_MSG('Print a second copy of an Invoice')"
u2[04] = "POP_MSG('Print the Shippers Pick List')"
u2[05] = "POP_MSG('Print todays invoices')"
c3[01] = " Orders by Date      "
c3[02] = " Invoices by Date    "
c3[03] = " Orders vs. Invoices "
c3[04] = " Accounts Receivable "
```

```
c3[05] = " Re-Order Report      "
u3[01] = "POP_MSG('List the orders taken for any period')"
u3[02] = "POP_MSG('List the invoices for any period')"
u3[03] = "POP_MSG('Compare orders taken with invoices printed')"
u3[04] = "POP_MSG('A short list, with phone numbers')"
u3[05] = "POP_MSG('Automatically re-order all required stock')"
c4[01] = " NewViews format    "
c4[02] = " PC Excel format    "
c4[03] = " 1-2-3 format       "
c4[04] = " Comma-separated    "
c4[05] = " Quotes + Commas    "
c4[06] = " Text in Columns    "
u4[01] = "POP_MSG('Send data out in New Views format')"
u4[02] = "POP_MSG('Send data out in PC Excel format')"
u4[03] = "POP_MSG('Send data out in 1-2-3 format')"
u4[04] = "POP_MSG('Send data out in Comma-separated fields')"
u4[05] = "POP_MSG('Send data out in Quotes plus commas')"
u4[06] = "POP_MSG('Send data to a text file in Columns')"
c5[01] = " Backup data files     "
c5[02] = " Restore data files    "
c5[03] = " Change Configuration "
c5[04] = " Edit Text Files       "
c5[05] = " Form Letter Setup     "
c5[06] = " Customer Labels       "
u5[01] = "POP_MSG('Emulate a smart user, for a change')"
u5[02] = "POP_MSG('Recover from your latest bungle')"
u5[03] = "POP_MSG('Change the colors and other settings')"
u5[04] = "POP_MSG('Run your text editor')"
u5[05] = "POP_MSG('Prepare a form letter to ' +;
       'send selected Customers')"
u5[06] = "POP_MSG('Print labels for one or more customers')"
c6[01] = "Return to DOS"
u6[01] = "SIGN_OFF(exe_name)"
cols[01] = 02
cols[02] = 13
cols[03] = 25
cols[04] = 37
cols[05] = 49
cols[06] = 61
i = 01
FOR i = 01 TO m_size                    && automatic, but takes time
   n = STRINT(i)
   wids[i] = LEN(c&n[01])               && length of 1st element
NEXT
*  wids[01] = 00
*  wids[02] = 00
*  wids[03] = 00
*  wids[04] = 00
*  wids[05] = 00
```

```
RETURN .T.
```

```
FUNCTION OPEN_SYS

PARAMETER sys_rec                           && record number
PRIVATE reply
reply = .T.
IF TYPE("sys_rec") != "N"
   sys_rec = 01
ENDIF
CLOSE DATA
IF DB_OPEN("System")
   reply = .T.
   GO sys_rec
   co_prefix  = Co_prefix
   next_order = Next_order
   next_invce = Next_invce
   next_po = Next_po
   util_1 = Util_1
   util_2 = Util_2
   util_3 = Util_3
   USE
ELSE
   reply = .F.
ENDIF
RETURN reply
```

```
FUNCTION CHK_DBFS

PARAMETER layout_no
PRIVATE result
IF !DB_OPEN("ORDERS", 1, o_keys)
   result = .F.
ENDIF
IF !DB_OPEN("ORD_ITEM", 1, "ORDER_NUM+ID")
   result = .F.
ENDIF
IF !DB_OPEN("PRODUCT", 1, "ID")
   result = .F.
ENDIF
IF !DB_OPEN("NUMBERS", 1, N_KEYS)
   result = .F.
ENDIF
IF !DB_OPEN("CUSTOMER", 1, "ACCOUNT_NO")
   result = .F.
ENDIF
```

```
RETURN reply
```

```
PROGRAM         O_ORDERS.PRG
Function(s)     SHOW_ORDERS(), O_ZOOM()
Purpose         ORDERS file administrator
Conventions     standard dbedit() setup file
Syntax          SHOW_ORDERS()
Parameters      none
Example         SHOW_ORDERS()
Assumes         nothing
Side Effects    none
Returns         .T.
Calls           POP_MSG, CHK_DBFS,
```

```
FUNCTION ORDERS

PRIVATE tr, tc, br, bc, fields, udf_brow, result, temp_scr, ;
      f_size, udf_zoom, xkeys, xcues, xpics, ;
      valids, defaults, virtuals, pictures, ;
      heads, m_row, m_col, from, to, cur_file, record_no, ;
      choice, move_chrs, force_rec, is_append, ;
      any_append, can_append, prev_alias
move_chrs = CHR(24) + CHR(5) + CHR(3) + CHR(18) + CHR(31) + CHR(30)
choice = 01
force_rec = .T.
is_append = .F.
any_append = .F.
can_append = .F.
prev_alias = ""
prev_rec = 00
IF !CHK_DBFS(01)
   POP_MSG("Copy the missing file(s) from a backup disk,"+;
      " and try again")
   SET CURSOR ON
   RETURN .F.
ENDIF
SELECT ORDERS
xkeys = "ACCOUNT_NO+ORDER_NUM"
xcues = " Customer Account / Order Number "
xpics = "@R !!!!! / 99999"
f_size = FCOUNT()
DECLARE fields[f_size], ;
        heads[f_size], ;
        pictures[f_size], ;
```

```
        defaults[f_size], ;
        valids[f_size], ;
        virtuals[f_size]
AFIELDS(fields)
fields[5] = "CHK_MARK(Confirmed)"  && virtual field
heads[01] = "Customer;Account #"
heads[02] = "Order;Number"
heads[03] = "Order;Date"
heads[04] = "P.O.;Number"
heads[05] = "Order;Confirmed"
heads[06] = "Details"
heads[07] = "F.O.B."
heads[08] = "Terms"
heads[09] = "Ship Via"
heads[10] = "Notes"
pictures[01] = "@!"
pictures[02] = "99999"
pictures[03] = "@D"
pictures[04] = "@!"
pictures[05] = .F.
pictures[06] = .F.
pictures[07] = .F.
pictures[08] = .F.
pictures[09] = "!XXXXXXXXXX"
pictures[10] = .F.
ABLANK(defaults, fields)          && stuff default array with strings
defaults[01] = "NEXT(Order_num)"   && override the ones we care about
defaults[03] = "DATE()"
defaults[08] = "2 % 10 Net 30        "
defaults[09] = "Courier    "
AFILL(valids,".T.")
valids[01] = "UNIQUE(Order_num)"
valids[02] = "EXIST(get_data,'CUSTOMER')"
AFILL(virtuals,.F.)               && fill them all quickly
virtuals[05] = .T.      && checkmark field is virtual
tr = 04
tc = 02
br = 23
bc = 77
id_char = "O"
udf_brow = "OBROWSER"
udf_zoom = "O_ZOOM()"
SYSCOLOR(01)
CLEAR
BASIC_BOX(tr -1,tc -2, br, bc +2)
DBEDIT(tr,tc,br,bc,;
      fields, ;
      udf_brow, ;
      pictures, ;
```

```
      heads, ;
      dummy,dummy, "", dummy)
SYSCOLOR(01)
RETURN .T.
```

```
FUNCTION O_ZOOM

* to force a repaint of parent,
* return 2, otherwise 1
PRIVATE result
result = 2
IF fld_name = "ACCOUNT_NO"
   CUSTOMER(Account_no)
ELSE
   ITEMS(Order_num)
ENDIF
SELECT ORDERS
RETURN  result
```

```
FUNCTION O_MENU

PRIVATE result
result = 2
POP_MSG("This is the sub-menu for the Orders Window")
RETURN result
```

```
PROGRAM        O_ITEMS.PRG
Function(s)    SHOW_ITEMS()
Purpose        Administrate Order Items file
Conventions    called (udf_zoom) by SHOW_ORDERS()
Syntax         SHOW_ITEMS()
Parameters     none
Example        SHOW_ITEMS()
Assumes        files are open and ready
Side Effects
Returns        .T.
Calls          nothing
```

```
FUNCTION ITEMS

PARAMETER target
```

```
PRIVATE tr, tc, br, bc, fields, udf_brow, reply, temp_scr, ;
        f_size, udf_zoom, xkeys, xcues, xpics, ;
        valids, defaults, virtuals, pictures, ;
        heads, m_row, m_col, from, to, cur_file, record_no, ;
        choice, move_chrs, force_rec, is_append, ;
        any_append, can_append, prev_alias
SAVE SCREEN TO temp_scr
move_chrs    = CHR(24) + CHR(5) + CHR(3) + CHR(18) + CHR(31) +
CHR(30)
choice       = 01
force_rec    = .T.
is_append    = .F.
any_append   = .F.
can_append   = .F.
prev_alias   = ""
prev_rec     = 00
cur_file     = ALIAS()
record_no    = RECNO()
m_row = ROW()
m_col = COL()
from = 01
to   = 06
id_char = "I"
x = 01                                  && return value: no repaint
SELECT ORD_ITEM                         && SEEK version
SEEK target                             && allows freedom of movement
IF EOF()
   KEYBOARD CHR(24)                     && down to force append
ENDIF
f_size = FCOUNT() + 1
DECLARE fields[f_size], ;
        heads[f_size], ;
        pictures[f_size], ;
        valids[f_size], ;
        defaults[f_size], ;
        virtuals[f_size]
AFIELDS(fields)
fields[07] = "qty_shippd * price"   && virtuals
fields[08] = "CHK_MARK(Allocated)"
fields[09] = "CHK_MARK(Back_Ordrd)"
heads[1] = "Order;No."
heads[2] = "Product;Code"
heads[3] = "Order;Qty."
heads[4] = "Ship;Qty."
heads[5] = "Back;Order"
heads[6] = "Unit;Price"
heads[7] = "Extended;Price"
heads[8] = "Allo;cated"
heads[9] = "Back;Ordered"
```

```
pictures[1] = "99999"
pictures[2] = "@!"
pictures[3] = "@9"
pictures[4] = "@9"
pictures[5] = "@9"
pictures[6] = "9999.99"
pictures[7] = "99999.99"
pictures[8] = "99999"
pictures[9] = "99999"
AFILL(valids, ".T.")                    && we accept everything
valids[01] = "EXIST(get_data,'ORDERS')"
ABLANK(defaults, fields)                && stuff array with blanks
defaults[1] = "ORDERS->Order_num"
AFILL(virtuals,.F.)
virtuals[07] = .T.                      && no edit extended price
virtuals[08] = .T.
virtuals[09] = .T.
tc = 04
bc = 75
IF m_row > 16                           && Open to max. possible size
    tr = 06                             && depending on relative loc
   br = m_row - 1
ELSE
   tr = m_row + 2
   br = 22
ENDIF
xkeys = "Order_num+id"
xcues = " Order Number (and Product Code)"
xpics = "@R 99999/!!!!!!!!!!!!!!!"
udf_brow = "OBROWSER"
udf_zoom = "PRODUCTS(ID)"               && pass current product id
SYSCOLOR(01)
BASIC_BOX(tr -1,tc -2, br, bc +2)
DBEDIT(tr,tc,br,bc,;                    && where it is
        fields, ;                       && what it is
      udf_brow, ;                       && what it does
      pictures, ;                       && how it looks
      heads, ;                          && what it says
        dummy,dummy, "", dummy)         && footings are for wimps
SELECT &cur_file
GO record_no
SYSCOLOR(01)
RESTORE SCREEN FROM temp_scr

RETURN x
```

```
FUNCTION I_MENU
```

```
PRIVATE result
result = 2
POP_MSG("This is the sub-menu for the Orders Items Window")
RETURN result
```

```
PROGRAM        O_PRODCT.PRG
Function(s)    PRODUCTS()
Purpose        Product file administrator
Conventions    called by ITEMS() as udf_zoom
Syntax         PRODUCTS()
Parameters     none
Example        PRODUCTS()
Assumes        files are open and ready
Side Effects   none
Returns        .T.
Calls
```

```
FUNCTION PRODUCTS

PARAMETER target
PRIVATE tr, tc, br, bc, fields, udf_brow, reply, temp_scr, ;
        f_size, udf_zoom, xkeys, xcues, xpics, ;
        valids, defaults, virtuals, pictures, ;
        heads, m_row, m_col, from, to, cur_file, record_no, ;
        choice, move_chrs, force_rec, is_append, ;
        any_append, can_append, prev_alias
SAVE SCREEN TO temp_scr
move_chrs = CHR(24) + CHR(5) + CHR(3) + CHR(18) + CHR(31) + CHR(30)
choice = 01
force_rec = .T.
is_append = .F.
any_append = .F.
can_append = .F.
prev_alias = ""
prev_rec = 0
cur_file = ALIAS()
record_no = RECNO()
m_row = ROW()
m_col = COL()
id_char = "P"
x = 01
IF target ! = co_prefix               && from system file
   target = XLATE(target)             && transl. oem#'s into our id#
ENDIF
```

```
SELECT PRODUCT
SEEK target
no_virts = 00
f_size = FCOUNT() + no_virts
DECLARE fields[f_size], ;
         heads[f_size], ;
         pictures[f_size], ;
         valids[f_size], ;
         defaults[f_size], ;
         virtuals[f_size]
AFIELDS(fields)
heads[01] = "Product;Description"
heads[02] = "Price;Level 1"
heads[03] = "Price;Level 2"
heads[04] = "Price;Level 3"
heads[05] = "Price;Level 4"
heads[06] = "Price;Level 5"
heads[07] = "Price;Level 6"
heads[08] = "On;Hand"
heads[09] = "Allo-;cated"
heads[10] = "On;Order"
heads[11] = "Back;Order"
heads[12] = "Bin"
heads[13] = "Packed;Qty"
heads[14] = "Cost;Price"
heads[15] = "Min.;Order"
heads[16] = "Max.;Order"
heads[17] = "ReOrder;Point"
heads[18] = "Last;Updated"
heads[19] = "Weight;Each"
heads[20] = "Notes"
heads[21] = "Product;Code"
pictures[01] = "@!"
pictures[02] = "9999.99"
pictures[03] = "9999.99"
pictures[04] = "9999.99"
pictures[05] = "9999.99"
pictures[06] = "9999.99"
pictures[07] = "9999.99"
pictures[08] = "99999"
pictures[09] = "99999"
pictures[10] = "99999"
pictures[11] = "99999"
pictures[12] = "@!"
pictures[13] = "99999"
pictures[14] = "9999.99"
pictures[15] = "999"
pictures[16] = "999"
pictures[17] = "999"
```

```
pictures[18] = "@D"
pictures[19] = "999.99"
pictures[20] = .F.
pictures[21] = "@!"
AFILL(valids, ".T.")
valids[FCOUNT()] = "UNIQUE(READVAR())"
virtuals = .F. && no array required
defaults = .F. && no array is required
tr = IF(m_row  17, m_row - 5, m_row + 2)
tc = 03
br = tr + 04
bc = 76
xkeys = "ID"
xcues = " Product Code "
xpics = co_prefix + "-!!!!!!!!!!!!" && unique code
udf_brow = "OBROWSER"
udf_zoom = "NUMBERS(ORD_ITEM->id)"
SYSCOLOR(01)
BASIC_BOX(tr -1,tc -2, br, bc +2)
DBEDIT(tr,tc,br,bc,;
      fields, ;
      udf_brow, ;
      pictures, ;
      heads, ;
      dummy,dummy, "", dummy)
SELECT &cur_file
GO record_no
SYSCOLOR(01)
RESTORE SCREEN FROM temp_scr
RETURN x
```

FUNCTION P_MENU

```
PRIVATE result
result = 2
POP_MSG("This is the sub-menu for the Products Window")
RETURN result
```

```
PROGRAM        O_NUMBER.PRG
Function(s)    NUMBERS()
Purpose        Numbers file administration
Conventions    called by PRODUCT() as udf_zoom
Syntax         NUMBERS(target)
Parameters     target - oem # to look up
Example        NUMBERS("CLIPPER")
Assumes        files are open and ready
Side Effects   none
Returns        True
Calls
```

```
FUNCTION NUMBERS

PARAMETER target
PRIVATE tr, tc, br, bc, fields, udf_brow, reply, temp_scr, ;
        f_size, udf_zoom, xkeys, xcues, xpics, ;
        valids, defaults, virtuals, pictures, ;
        heads, m_row, m_col, from, to, cur_file, record_no, ;
        choice, move_chrs, force_rec, is_append, ;
        any_append, can_append, prev_alias
SAVE SCREEN TO temp_scr
move_chrs = CHR(24) + CHR(5) + CHR(3) + CHR(18) + CHR(31) + CHR(30)
choice = 01
force_rec = .T.
is_append = .F.
any_append = .F.
can_append = .F.
prev_alias = ""
prev_rec = 00
cur_file = ALIAS()
record_no = RECNO()
m_row = ROW()
m_col = COL()
id_char = "N"
x = 01
xpics = caps
xcues = " O.E.M. Product Code "
xkeys = "PROD_CODE"
SELECT NUMBERS
IF target = co_prefix
   LOCATE FOR id = target
ELSE
   SEEK target
ENDIF
no_virts = 00
```

```
f_size = FCOUNT() + no_virts
DECLARE fields[f_size], ;
        heads[f_size], ;
        pictures[f_size], ;
        valids[f_size], ;
        defaults[f_size], ;
        virtuals[f_size]
AFIELDS(fields)
heads[1] = "Our Unique;Product Code"
heads[2] = "O.E.M.;Product Code"
pictures[01] = co_prefix + "-!!!!!!!!!!!"
pictures[02] = "@!"
AFILL(valids, ".T.")
valids[1]  = "EXIST(ID)"
valids[2]  = "UNIQUE(prod_code)"
virtuals = .F.
defaults[1] = "PRODUCT-id"
defaults[2] = "@!"
tr = m_row - 08
tc = 09
br = tr + 04
bc = 44
udf_brow = "OBROWSER"
udf_zoom = .F.                          && no zoom from here
eol = "End of the line, Jack"
SYSCOLOR(01)
BASIC_BOX(tr -1,tc -1, br, bc +1)
DBEDIT(tr,tc,br,bc,;
      fields, ;
      udf_brow, ;
      pictures, ;
      heads, ;
      dummy,dummy, "", dummy)
SELECT &cur_file
GO record_no
SYSCOLOR(01)
RESTORE SCREEN FROM temp_scr
RETURN x
```

```
FUNCTION N_MENU

PRIVATE result
result = 2
POP_MSG("This is the sub-menu for the OEM Numbers Window")
RETURN result
```

```
PROGRAM         AA_OCUST.PRG
Function(s)     CUSTOMER()
Purpose         Customer file administrator
Conventions     called from ORDERS()
Syntax          CUSTOMER(code)
Parameters      code - ORDERS-Account_no
Example         CUSTOMER("ARTFUL")
Assumes         files are open and ready
Side Effects    none
Returns         True
Calls
```

```
FUNCTION CUSTOMER

PARAMETER target
PRIVATE tr, tc, br, bc, fields, udf_brow, reply, temp_scr, ;
         f_size, udf_zoom, xkeys, xcues, xpics, ;
         valids, defaults, virtuals, pictures, ;
         heads, m_row, m_col, from, to, cur_file, record_no, ;
         choice, move_chrs, force_rec, is_append, ;
         any_append, can_append, prev_alias
SAVE SCREEN TO temp_scr
move_chrs = CHR(24) + CHR(5) + CHR(3) + CHR(18) + CHR(31) + CHR(30)
choice = 01
force_rec = .T.
is_append = .F.
any_append = .F.
can_append = .F.
prev_alias = ""
prev_rec = 00
cur_file = ALIAS()
record_no = RECNO()
m_row = ROW()
m_col = COL()
id_char = "C"
x = 01
SELECT CUSTOMER
SEEK target                             && ORDERS->Account_no
no_virts = 00
f_size = FCOUNT() + no_virts
DECLARE fields[f_size], ;
         heads[f_size], ;
         pictures[f_size], ;
         valids[f_size], ;
         defaults[f_size], ;
         virtuals[f_size]
```

```
AFIELDS(fields)
heads[1] = "Account;Number"
heads[2] = "Company Name"
heads[3] = "Phone;Number"
heads[4] = "Price;Code"
heads[5] = "Notes"
heads[6] = "Credit;Limit"
heads[7] = "Contact"
heads[8] = "Sales;Person"
heads[9] = "Tax;Exempt"
heads[10] = "F.S.T. #"
heads[11] = "P.S.T. #"
heads[12] = "Language"
heads[13] = "Region"
heads[14] = "Billing Address;Line 1"
heads[15] = "Billing Address;Line 2"
heads[16] = "City;(Billing)"
heads[17] = "Province;or State"
heads[18] = "Postal;or ZIP"
heads[19] = "Shipping Address;Line 1"
heads[20] = "Shipping Address;Line 2"
heads[21] = "City;(Shipping)"
heads[22] = "Porvince;(Shipping)"
heads[23] = "Postal;(Shipping)"
heads[24] = "Federal;Tax Rate"
heads[25] = "Provincial;Tax Rate"
pictures[1] = "@!"
pictures[2] = "!"+REPL("X",34)
pictures[3] = "@R (###) 999-9999"
pictures[4] = "9"
pictures[5] = .F.
pictures[6] = "99999.99"
pictures[7] = .F.
pictures[8] = "@!"
pictures[9] = "Y"
pictures[10] = "@!"
pictures[11] = "@!"
pictures[12] = "@!"
pictures[13] = "@!"
pictures[14] = .F.
pictures[15] = .F.
pictures[16] = "!"+REPL("X",19)
pictures[17] = "@!"
pictures[18] = "@!"
pictures[19] = "!"+REPL("X",34)
pictures[20] = "!"+REPL("X",34)
pictures[21] = "!"+REPL("X",19)
pictures[22] = "@!"
pictures[23] = "@!"
```

```
pictures[24] = "99.99%"
pictures[25] = "99.99%"
AFILL(valids, ".T.")
valids[1]  = "UNIQUE(Account_no)"
virtuals = .F.
ABLANK(defaults, fields)
tr = IF(m_row  17, m_row - 5, m_row + 2)
tc = 02
br = tr + 04
bc = 77
xkeys = "Account_no"
xcues = " Account Number "
xpics = caps
udf_brow = "OBROWSER"
udf_zoom = .F.
SYSCOLOR(01)
BASIC_BOX(tr -1,tc -1, br, bc +1)
DBEDIT(tr,tc,br,bc,;
      fields, ;
      udf_brow, ;
      pictures, ;
      heads, ;
      dummy,dummy, "", dummy)
SELECT &cur_file
GO record_no
SYSCOLOR(01)
RESTORE SCREEN FROM temp_scr
RETURN x
```

FUNCTION C_MENU

```
PRIVATE result
result = 2
POP_MSG("This is the sub-menu for the Customer Window")
RETURN result
```

```
PROGRAM         O_UDFS.PRG
Function(s)     XLATE(), GET_PRICE(), UPD_QTYAL(),
                UPD_QTYBO()
                W_COLOR()
Purpose         application-specific udfs for O.EXE
Conventions     LINK using STORYOFO.LST
```

```
FUNCTION XLATE

* Translates any product code into our
* unique code. not file-dependent.
PARAMETER target
PRIVATE reply, nyet, target, cur_file, cur_order, oem_order
reply = ""
nyet = "Don't recognize that sucker. Nope"
cur_file = ALIAS()
oem_order = 01
IF target = co_prefix
   reply = target
ELSE
   SELECT NUMBERS
   SEEK target
   IF !FOUND()
      POP_MSG(nyet)
      reply = ""
   ELSE
      reply = NUMBERS-> id          && send back our code
      SET ORDER TO cur_order        && previously-active ntx
   ENDIF
ENDIF
SELECT &cur_file
RETURN reply
```

```
FUNCTION GET_PRICE

PARAMETER choice
PRIVATE price_2_use, reply, err_msg
price_2_use = fld_name
reply = .F.
err_msg = "Move the cursor to the price field you wish to use,
first"
IF !(price_2_use = "PRICE")         && any of the price fields will do
   POP_MSG(err_msg)
ELSE
   REPLACE ORD_ITEM-> Price WITH PRODUCT-> &price_2_use
```

```
   reply = .T.
ENDIF
KEYBOARD CHR(27)                          && collapse the window
RETURN reply
```

```
FUNCTION DFLT_PRICE

PARAMETER target
PRIVATE price_no, mprice, x, cur_file
cur_file = ALIAS()
SELECT CUSTOMER
SEEK target
price_no = CUSTOMER-> Price_code
IF EMPTY(price_no)                        && new customer, incomplete data?
   price_no = "1"
ENDIF
mprice = "PRICE" + price_no
SELECT PRODUCT
SEEK XLATE(ORD_ITEM->ID)
IF !FOUND()
   BELL()
   x = 0.00
ELSE
   x = &mprice
ENDIF
SELECT &cur_file
RETURN x
```

```
FUNCTION UPD_QTYAL

* Updates the quantity allocated in the stock file,
* adding the number shipped on the current order item
* An additional function (UPD_QTYOH) takes care of On Hand when the
* item is actually shipped (denoted by Print_it = .T.)
PRIVATE amount, reply, err_msg
reply   = .F.
IF !(fld_name = "QTY_SHIPPD")
   amount = ORD_ITEM-> Qty_shippd
ELSE
   amount = &fld_name
ENDIF
already_done = ORD_ITEM-> Allocated
IF already_done
   POP_MSG("You've already allocated this item")
ELSE
   REPLACE PRODUCT-> QTY_AL WITH PRODUCT-> QTY_AL + amount
```

```
   REPLACE ORD_ITEM-> Allocated WITH .T.
ENDIF
reply = .T.
RETURN reply
```

```
FUNCTION UPD_QTYBO

* A VALID for the qty_bo field in ord_item
* also a hot-key process
* Updates the quantity back-ordered in the stock file,
* adding the number back-ordered on the current order item
PRIVATE amount, reply, err_msg
reply   = .F.
already_done = ORD_ITEM-> Back_Ordrd
IF already_done
   POP_MSG("You've already back-ordered this item")
ELSE
   IF !EMPTY(ORD_ITEM-> QTY_BO)
      amount = ORD_ITEM-> Qty_BO
   ELSE
      amount = ORD_ITEM-> QTY_ORDERD - ORD_ITEM-> QTY_SHIPPD
      REPLACE QTY_BO WITH amount
   ENDIF
   REPLACE PRODUCT-> QTY_BO WITH PRODUCT-> QTY_BO + amount
   REPLACE ORD_ITEM-> Back_Ordrd WITH .T.
ENDIF
reply = .T.
RETURN reply
```

```
PROCEDURE HELP

PARAMETERS proc, line_no, read_var
PRIVATE m_row, m_col, cur_file, record_no, viewer, tr, tc, br, bc
IF proc = 'HELP'    && Pre-empt nested calls to Help
   RETURN
ENDIF
m_row = ROW()
m_col = COL()
tr = 04
tc = 02
br = 22
bc = 77
cur_file = ALIAS()
record_no = RECNO()

IF DB_OPEN("SYSTEM")
```

```
   READ_MEMO("HELP", tr, tc, br, bc)
   SELECT SYSTEM
   USE
ENDIF
SELECT &cur_file
@ m_row, m_col SAY SPACE(0)
RETURN
```

```
PROGRAM        O_INVOIC.PRG
Function(s)    INVOICES()
Purpose        View Invoice file
Conventions    First whack at the Invoice routine. This
               will contain all udfs relating to invoicing.
Syntax         INVOICES()
Parameters     none
Example        INVOICES()
Assumes        invoice file
Side Effects   none
Returns        .T.
Calls          POP_MSG
```

```
FUNCTION INVOICES

POP_MSG("Browse the Invoice file")
RETURN .T.
```

```
PROGRAM        O_BROWSE.PRG
Function(s)    OBROWSER()
Purpose        inner udf for DBEDIT() in SHOW_ORDERS()
Conventions
Syntax         OBROWSER(mode, fld_pointer)
Parameters     mode, fld_pointer - passed automatically by
               DBEDIT()
Example        udf_brow = "OBROWSER"
Assumes        Standard DBEDIT() file setup
Side Effects
Returns        a number from 0 to 4 equal to dbedit() mode
```

Calls

```
FUNCTION OBROWSER

PARAMETERS mode, fld_pointer
PRIVATE fld_name, m_row, m_col, ret_val, keystroke, target, ;
         do_repaint, no_repaint, ins_blank
SYSCOLOR(01)
fld_name = fields[ fld_pointer ]
m_row = ROW()
m_col = COL()
idle = 00
bof_hit = 01
eof_hit = 02
empty_dbf = 03
exception = 04
ret_val = 01
keystroke = LASTKEY()
esc = CHR(27)
home_key = CHR(01)
end_key = CHR(06)
enter = 13
ctrl_home = CHR(29)
ctrl_end = CHR(23)
ctrl_pgdn = CHR(30)
ctrl_pgdn = CHR(30)
right = CHR(04)
left = CHR(19)
down = CHR(24)
up = CHR(05)
pgup = CHR(18)
pgdn = CHR(03)
do_repaint = 02
no_repaint = 01
ins_blank = 03
IF prev_rec != RECNO()
   prev_rec = RECNO()
   force_rec = .T.
ENDIF
DO CASE
   CASE mode = idle
      IF CHR(keystroke) $ move_chrs .OR. force_rec
         STAT_LINE()
      ENDIF
      ret_val = no_repaint
   CASE mode = bof_hit
      IF is_append
         ret_val = IF(any_append, do_repaint, ins_blank)
```

```
        is_append = .F.
        any_append = .F.
    ELSE
        IF !EOF()
            STAT_LINE()
        ENDIF
    ENDIF
    force_rec = .T.
CASE mode = eof_hit
    IF is_append
        IF keystroke = down .AND. !EOF()
            ret_val = ins_blank
        ELSE
            IF keystroke = ctrl_pgdn
                ret_val = IF(any_append, 2, 3)
                is_append = .F.
                any_append = .F.
            ELSE
                IF force_rec
                    STAT_LINE()
                ENDIF
            ENDIF
        NDIF
    ELSE
        IF keystroke = down .AND. can_append
            ret_val = ins_blank
            is_append = .T.
        ELSE
            IF !EOF()
                STAT_LINE()
            ENDIF
        ENDIF
    ENDIF
    force_rec = .T.
    STAT_LINE()
CASE mode = empty_dbf
    STAT_LINE()
    ret_val = no_repaint
CASE mode = exception
    DO CASE
        CASE F1()
            DO HELP
            ret_val = no_repaint
            CASE CHR(keystroke) = "/" .OR. F10()
            cur_menu = id_char + "_MENU()"
            temp_result = &cur_menu
            ret_val = no_repaint
            SAVE SCREEN TO temp_scr
            PD_MENU(main_cues, main_sizes)
```

```
            RESTORE SCREEN FROM temp_scr
         CASE DEL()
            ret_val = do_repaint
            IF DELETED()
               RECALL
            ELSE
               DELETE
            ENDIF
            STAT_LINE()
      CASE ESC()
         ret_val = 0
      CASE ENTER() .OR. IS_DATA(keystroke) .AND. ;
         (is_append .OR. (!EOF() .AND. LASTREC() != 0))
         IF IS_VIRTUAL(fld_pointer)
            ret_val = no_repaint
         ELSE
            ntx_expr = INDEXKEY(0)
            IF !EMPTY(ntx_expr) t
               ntx_eval = &ntx_expr
            ENDIF
            IF keystroke != enter
               KEYBOARD CHR(keystroke)
            ENDIF
            IF TYPE(fld_name) = "M"
               READ_MEMO(fld_name)
            ELSE
               IF TYPE("valids") = "A"
                   valid_exp = valids[fld_pointer]
                   IF EMPTY(valid_exp)
                        valid_exp = ".T."
                   ENDIF
               ELSE
                   valid_exp = ".T."
               ENDIF
               IF TYPE("pictures") = "A"
                   pict_str = pictures[fld_pointer]
                   IF EMPTY(pict_str)
                       pict_str = GEN_PIC(fld_name)
                   ENDIF
               ELSE
                   pict_str = GEN_PIC(fld_name)
               ENDIF
               get_data = &fld_name
               IF EMPTY(get_data)
                   IF TYPE("defaults") = "A"
                       default = defaults[fld_pointer]
                       IF EMPTY(default)
                           default = BLANK(fld_name)
                       ENDIF
```

```
            ELSE
                default = BLANK(fld_name)
            ENDIF
            get_data = &default
        ENDIF
        @ m_row, m_col GET get_data PICTURE pict_str VALID &valid_ex
        READ_IT()
        IF UPDATED()
            REPLACE &fld_name WITH get_data
            KEYBOARD right
        ENDIF
     ENDIF
     ret_val = no_repaint
  ENDIF
CASE INS()
  is_append = .T.
  IF !IS_VIRTUAL(fld_pointer)
     IF TYPE("valids") = "A"
        valid_exp = valids[fld_pointer]
        IF EMPTY(valid_exp)
            valid_exp = ".T."
        ENDIF
     ELSE
        valid_exp = ".T."
     ENDIF
     IF TYPE("pictures") = "A"
        pict_str = pictures[fld_pointer]
        IF EMPTY(pict_str)
            pict_str = GEN_PIC(fld_name)
        ENDIF
     ELSE
        pict_str = GEN_PIC(fld_name)
     ENDIF
     get_data = &fld_name
     IF EMPTY(get_data)
        IF TYPE("defaults") = "A"
            default = defaults[fld_pointer]
            IF EMPTY(default)
                default = BLANK(fld_name)
            ENDIF
        ELSE
            default = BLANK(fld_name)
        ENDIF
        get_data = &default
     ENDIF
     @ m_row, m_col GET get_data PICTURE pict_str VALID &valid_exp
     READ_IT()
     IF UPDATED()
        APPEND BLANK
```

```
            REPLACE &fld_name WITH get_data
            KEYBOARD right
         ENDIF
      ENDIF
      ret_val = do_repaint
   CASE F9() .OR. F2() .OR. ALT_Z()
      IF EMPTY(udf_zoom)          && don't just ignore keystroke
         POP_MSG("This is the lowest level of detail")
         ret_val = no_repaint
      ELSE
         SYSCOLOR(02)             && leave a marker
         @ m_row, m_col SAY &fld_name
         SYSCOLOR(01)
         ret_val = &udf_zoom      && 2 for repaint, else 1
      ENDIF
   CASE ALT_R()
      memo_field = "Notes"
      READER(memo_field)
      ret_val = no_repaint
   CASE ALT_W()                   && WRITE MEMO FIELD TO A FILE
      memo_field = "Notes"
      WRITER(memo_field)
      ret_val = no_repaint
   CASE ALT_S() .OR. SPACEBAR()
      SEARCH(xkeys, xcues, xpics)
      ret_val = do_repaint
      STAT_LINE()
   CASE ALT_A()
      IF ALIAS() = "ORD_ITEM"
         UPD_QTYAL()
         ret_val = do_repaint
      ELSE
         ret_val = no_repaint
      ENDIF
   CASE ALT_B()
      IF ALIAS() = "ORD_ITEM"
         UPD_QTYBO()
         ret_val = do_repaint
      ELSE
         ret_val = no_repaint
      ENDIF
   CASE F4() .OR. ALT_M()         && mark order toggle
      IF ALIAS() = "ORDERS"
         REPLACE Confirmed WITH !Confirmed
      ENDIF
      ret_val = no_repaint
   CASE ALT_P()                   && P is for PRICE
      IF ALIAS() = "PRODUCT"
         GET_PRICE()
```

```
            ret_val = no_repaint
         ELSEIF ALIAS() = "ORD_ITEM"
            target = ORDERS-> Account_no
            REPLACE PRICE WITH DFLT_PRICE(target)
            ret_val = no_repaint
         ENDIF
      OTHERWISE
         ret_val = no_repaint
   ENDCASE
ENDCASE
RETURN ret_val
```

Summary

Complex code is unpleasurable reading, and if you made it through all that, congratulations. If you had trouble understanding it, compile and run the program, then play with it for a while. Don't be afraid to try your own application based on it. That's the best way you can learn the principles.

- Turn the programs in this chapter into a template, stripping out all the specific data and leaving only the declarations.
- Design your data structure, figuring the tables you'll need and their relationships.
- Fill in the blanks with your data structure's specifications.
- Proceed one layer at a time. POP_MSG() everything that is not immediately obvious.
- Save your elaborate validation schemes for a late pass through the code. Introduce the changes one function per pass, so you can trace errors easily.
- Draw from the library. Functions such as HELP_FILL(), EXIST(), UNIQUE() and NEXT() do almost all the work for you — fill their names into the appropriate places and compile.
- Don't forget to declare *external* any functions hidden within strings.

Conclusion — Future Mods

O.EXE is obviously incomplete, yet you have the scaffolding on which to hang the new capabilities. That, after all, has been the point of the entire exercise — to develop a programming style based on the *certainty* of change — to build a vehicle which can respond intelligently to the problem.

I have tried to provide the most difficult part of O.EXE. The areas I left unfinished are the ones you'll have to re-write for almost every application you design on this model. So you don't feel abandoned, let's go over some likely scenarios and outline the modifications you might make.

Numbers Table not Required

In most small businesses, the problem of translating O.E.M. numbers does not arise. We dealt with it here to demonstrate that our smart-windows mechanism is robust enough to handle such complexity. In simpler applications, eliminate NUMBERS.DBF, then adjust the code in O_ITEMS.PRG, setting the variables *no_kids* to zero and *udf_brow* to False. Remove O_NUMBER.OBJ from the link list and you're done.

Invoice Routines

The Invoice file routines are absent in the program as presented here. The significant difference between an invoice and an order is that an invoice is history, and thus cannot be changed. Depending on the application, however, invoices can be processed in a number of other ways: you might copy them to another file for archival purposes, record payments against them, print duplicate copies or reports based on them.

Receiving

You must also provide a means of receiving stock shipments. At a minimum you'll need a RECEIPTS.DBF file and a child for each received item, REC_ITEMS.DBF. Upon receipt of a stock item, you SEEK the product number, decrement the quanity on order by the number received, and increment the quantity on hand the by number received. Since it's possible your supplier could ship more than you ordered, you may have to trap to ensure that the quantity on order never falls below zero. (On the other hand, minus quantities here would provide a handy means to scan the file for repeated over-shipments. It could be that one of your suppliers consistently overships, in hopes you'll say nothing and simply pay.

Time and Billing

Many professionals bill for time rather than for a product they sell, but the essence remains the same. They sell hours in various quantities, usually recorded against a particular project.

The easy version equates an invoice with a project; the slightly more difficult version distinguishes these entities, often because more than one project is underway with each customer. This type of system usually involves the further wrinkle that not every item outstanding is included on the invoice. All this requires, of course, is a logical field handled in the same way we handled the *Confirmed* field in the Orders table.

Yes, but Does it Do Accounting?

How far you go beyond these minimal requirements is up to you and your clients. You might provide a bridge to an accounting system, or expand O.EXE into a full-blown accounting program in its own right. You might start with a library of accounting source code, and front-end it with the library developed here.

However far you decide to go, *keep it modular*. In many cases, you can add entirely new branches of the program simply by copying one of the DBEDIT() calling files (e.g. O_ORDERS.PRG), then making the appropriate modifications.

If the total number of data files grows too large, you may have to move each file-opening function into the appropriate calling function, rather than having all the files open at the Main Menu.

DBEDIT() is such a powerful function that we can rest an application of this magnitude upon it. The concept of smart windows provides what I feel is a pretty good shot at the target of *invisible software*. But I hasten to point out that this is only the beginning. The possibilities of customization are limited only by your imagination.

New Directions

To help stimulate your investigations, let me point out a couple of directions. The commands themselves are hard-coded, and if this book has had any effect on you at all, this should make you uneasy. You might want to generalize the browsing function, replacing the hard-coded keystroke tests with indirect references. Add fields to the system file, one for each hard- coded command:

Variable Name	**Signals**
add_key	the desire to add a record
del_key	the desire to dust a record
zoom_key	the desire to know more
seek_key	dissatisfaction with the present

Default the commands to whichever keys you prefer, but allow your user to change them. Your user can thus make your software work in a familiar way, using the knowledge acquired in some other program. This versatility requires no extra work on your part. Even better, different users could define their own sets of commands!

Think of it: the same program, employing entirely different command keys depending on who's using it! Just add a record to the system file for every user. Add a trap for user I.D. on entry to the program, and LOCATE for user_id in the system file, initializing to the settings in that record. Depending on the security requirements of the system, your routine to add a user might vary, but you might use record 1 for the system defaults, and offer the user the chance to copy this set of commands.

Lots of markets out there *ache* for intelligent software. You now have a powerful toolkit you can use to address these markets. based on smart windows. Clipper is your foundation tool. The library presented here is your means of turning Clipper into a high-quality, high-quantity software production machine.

Now get out there and make some money!

Chapter 12

Array Functions

- ABLANK — fills an array with blanks mirroring the fields in a table.
- ACOUNT — returns the number of occurrences of a variable in an array.
- AEXIST — checks the existence of a variable in a file.
- AFULL — returns the number of the first undeclared element of an array.
- AGET — GETs an array element at the specified row and column.
- AINDEX — fills an array with the active indexes.
- ALENGTH — returns the total length of an array of strings.
- AMACHINE — a state machine which operates either in incremental or in sudden-death mode.
- ARRAY_DIR — creates a sorted array of filenames.
- ASAY — displays an array element at the specified row and column.
- ASEEK — searches an array for a value, then returns the corresponding value from a second array.
- AVALID — checks user input via an array of conditions.

• ABLANK()

```
PROGRAM         AA_ABLAN.PRG
Function(s)     ABLANK()
Purpose         Fill an array with blank values
Conventions     works using an array of field names, but
Syntax          ABLANK(value_ra,field_ra,from_pos,to_pos])
Parameters      value_ra - array to fill
                field_ra - optional array of field specs
                from_pos - start at element
                to_pos - stop at element
Example         ABLANK(array)
Assumes         If no field_ra passed, current file is used
```

```
FUNCTION ABLANK

PARAMETERS d_ra, f_ra, from_pos, to_pos
PRIVATE temp, reply, i
temp = PCOUNT()
reply = .F.
DO CASE
   CASE temp = 0
      POP_MSG("You forgot to pass params, idiot")
      RETURN .F.
   CASE temp = 1
      DECLARE f_ra[FCOUNT()]
      AFIELDS(f_ra)
ENDCASE
IF temp = 03
   from_pos = 01
ENDIF
IF temp  04
   to_pos = LEN(f_ra)
ENDIF
i = from_pos
FOR i = from_pos TO to_pos
      x = f_ra[i]
      d_ra[i] = BLANK(&x)
NEXT
reply = .T.
RETURN reply
```

• ACOUNT()

```
PROGRAM         AA_ACOUN.PRG
Function(s)     ACOUNT()
Purpose         Count occurrences in an array
Conventions     target and array must exist
Syntax          ACOUNT( target, array)
Parameters      target - item to search for
                array - array to search in
Example         x = ACOUNT(target, array)
Assumes         existence and validity of target and array
Side Effects    bad data could cause crash
Returns         0 or number of occurrences
Calls           IS_TYPE()
```

```
FUNCTION ACOUNT

PARAMETERS target, array
PRIVATE i, hits
i = 01
hits = 00
FOR i = 01 TO LEN(array)
   IF IS_TYPE(array[i], target)
         Hits = IF(array[i] = target, hits + 1, hits)
   ENDIF
NEXT
RETURN hits
```

• AEXIST()

```
PROGRAM         AA_AEXIST.PRG
Function(s)     AEXIST()
Purpose         Array-based version of EXIST()
Conventions     Used when you want to hide an EXIST()
validation
                in a character string (raising the problem
                of commas within the string). This avoids the p:
Syntax          AEXIST(array)
Parameters      array - mapped parallel to EXIST()'s params:
                array[01] - item to search for
                array[02] - file to search
                array[03] - udf to execute: optional
Example         DECLARE array[03]
                array[01] - "cust_code"
                array[02] - "customer"
                array[03] - "POP_MSG(comp_name)"
                pops up a box containing the company name if th
                data entered exists, returning True.
Assumes         validity of all data to be macro'd
Side Effects    depend on nature of udf if passed
Returns         True if found
Calls           AFULL(), POP_MSG()
                whatever you may have hidden in array[03]
```

```
FUNCTION AEXIST

PARAMETER array
PRIVATE reply, temp, workfile, record_no, target
temp = AFULL(array)
reply = .F.
work_file = ALIAS()
record_no = RECNO()
target = array[1]
IF temp > 1
   file = array[2]
   SELECT &file
ENDIF
SEEK target
reply = FOUND()
IF temp = 3
```

```
   udf = array[3]
   x = &udf
ENDIF
SELECT &work_file
GO record_no
RETURN reply
```

• AFULL()

```
PROGRAM        AA_AFULL.PRG
Function(s)    AFULL()
Purpose        Returns the number of the last defined element
               in an array, e.g. TYPE(array[n])!="U"
Conventions    useful when you're not sure how many items
               have been filled
Syntax         AFULL(array)
Parameters     array - the array to check
Example        empty_pos = AFULL(array) + 01
Assumes        contiguous population in array
Side Effects   crashes on bad data
Returns        number of last declared array element
Calls          ASCAN()
```

```
FUNCTION AFULL

PARAMETER array
PRIVATE i, result
SET EXACT ON
result = ASCAN(array, "")
SET EXACT OFF
IF result = 0
   result = LEN(array)
ELSE                               && element of first null string - 1
   result = result - 1
ENDIF
RETURN result
```

• AGET()

```
PROGRAM        AA_GET.PRG
Function(s)    AGET()
Purpose        GETs an array element
Conventions    array must exist. Used in tight loops where
               calculated rows and columns are used for
               GETs.
Syntax         AGET(ra_name, lmnt_no, row, col, lmnt_no, ;
                           pic_string, val_string)
Parameters     ra_name - name of the array
               lmnt_no - element number
               row - GET at row
               col - GET at col
               pic_str - PICTURE string
               val_str - VALID clause
Example        AGET(array,pointer,row,col,"@!","!ESC()"
               gets array[pointer], prevents Escape
               termination
Asumes         existence and validity of all data
Side Effects   Crash on bad data
Returns        .T.
Calls          nothing
```

```
FUNCTION AGET

PARAMETERS ra_name, lmnt_no, row, col, pic_string, val_string
@ row, col GET ra_name[lmnt_no] ;
        PICTURE pic_string ;
        VALID val_string
RETURN .T.
```

• AINDEX()

```
PROGRAM         AA_AINDEX.PRG
Function(s)     AINDEX()
Purpose         Fill an array with index keys from the
                current file
Conventions     current file is used
Syntax          AINDEX(array)
Parameters      array - predeclared array to fill
                determine its size using XCOUNT()
Example         DECLARE array[XCOUNT()]
                AINDEX(array)
Assumes         a file is in use, returns False otherwise
Side Effects    none
Returns         .T. if success, else .F.
Calls           INDEXKEY()
```

```
FUNCTION AINDEX

PARAMETER key_array
PRIVATE i, result
IF EMPTY(INDEXKEY(0))
   result = .F.
ELSE
   FOR i = 1 TO LEN(key_array)
         key_array[i] = INDEXKEY(i)
   NEXT
   result = .T.
ENDIF
RETURN result
```

• ALENGTH()

```
PROGRAM        AA_ALEN.PRG
Function(s)    ALENGTH()
Purpose        "Length" of an array of strings
Conventions    as if they were concatenated
Syntax         ALENGTH(array)
Parameters     array - an array of strings
Example        n = RLENGTH(array)
Assumes        array is valid, contains strings
Side Effects   none
Returns        total string length of an array
Calls          nothing
```

```
FUNCTION ALENGTH

PARAMETER array
PRIVATE i, x

i = 01
x = 00
FOR i = 01 TO LEN(array)
   x = x + LEN(array[i])
NEXT

RETURN x
```

• ALOAD()

```
PROGRAM        AA_ALOAD.PRG
Function(s)    ALOAD()
Purpose        Fills an array with values derived either
               from fields in current file or from an array
               of fieldnames/expressions
Conventions    by default just pass the array to fill
               determine its size with a call to FCOUNT().
               the second array if passed can contain not
               only field names but virtuals and / or udfs
               (If udfs, they must be declared external)
               by default, fill the entire array, unless
               offsets are also passed.
Syntax         ALOAD(d_ra[, f_ra[, from_pos[, to_pos]]])
Parameters     d_ra - array to fill
               f_ra - array of fieldnames or expressions
               from_pos - offset if required
               to_pos - boundary if required
Example        DECLARE data_ra[FCOUNT()]
               ALOAD(data_ra)
Assumes        a file is in use
Side Effects depend on the contents of f_ra (if passed)
Returns        .T. unless error
Calls          AFIELDS()
               POP_MSG()
```

```
FUNCTION ALOAD

PARAMETERS d_ra, f_ra, from_pos, to_pos
PRIVATE temp, reply, i
temp  = PCOUNT()
reply = .F.
DO CASE
   CASE temp = 0
      POP_MSG("You forgot to pass params, idiot")
      RETURN .F.
   CASE temp = 1
      DECLARE f_ra[FCOUNT()]
      AFIELDS(f_ra)
ENDCASE
IF temp < 03
```

```
   from_pos = 01
ENDIF
IF temp < 04
   to_pos = LEN(f_ra)
ENDIF
i = from_pos
FOR i = from_pos TO to_pos
      x = f_ra[i]
      d_ra[i] = (&x)
NEXT
reply = .T.
RETURN reply
```

• AMACHINE()

```
PROGRAM       AA_STMCH.PRG
Function(s)   AMACHINE()
Purpose       General purpose state machine
Conventions   two flavors - sudden death or incremental
              incremental  - increment to completion
              sudden death - first false terminatesu
Syntax        AMACHINE(array,flag)
Parameters    array - containing udf names as strings
              flag  - determines flavor of machine
Example       AMACHINE(udfs,01)
Assumes       validity of expressions contained in udfs[]
Side Effects  highly unpredictable due to freedom it
              allows
Returns       True on successful completion, else false.
Calls         Nothing directly.
```

```
FUNCTION AMACHINE

PARAMETERS array, flag
PRIVATE reply
reply = .T.
* this block of code handles the increment/decrement scenario
IF flag = 01
   n = 0
   i = 1
   FOR i = 1 to 7
      x = array[i]
      i = &x
      IF i  0
         reply = .F.
         EXIT
      ENDIF
   NEXT
ELSE
* this block of code handles the instant-death scenario
   n = 0
   i = 1
   FOR i = 1 to 7
      x = array[i]
      i = &x
      IF !i
```

```
         reply = .F.
         EXIT
      ENDIF
   NEXT

ENDIF
RETURN reply
```

• ASAY()

```
PROGRAM       AA _ASAY.PRG.
Function(s)   ASAY()
Purpose       SAY an array element at row, col
Conventions   array must exist. Companion to GET_LMNT().
              useful in calculated row, col situations.
Syntax        ASAY(array,lmnt_no,row,col,pict)
Parameters    array - array to use
              lmnt_no - element to display
              row - display at row
              col - display at col
              pict - using PICTURE mask
Example       ASAY(array,02,04,10,"999.99")
Assumes       all parameters exist and are correct type
Side Effects  display in reverse (SYSCOLOR(02))
Returns       .T.
Calls         SYSCOLOR()
```

```
FUNCTION ASAY

PARAMETERS ra_name, lmnt_no, row, col, pic_string
SYSCOLOR(02)
@ row, col SAY ra_name[lmnt_no] PICTURE pic_string
SYSCOLOR(01)
RETURN .T.
```

• ASEEK()

PROGRAM	AA_ASEEK.PRG
Function(s)	ASEEK()
Purpose	Search array1 for data, return corresponding element from array2
Conventions	target and both arrays must exist
Syntax	ASEEK(target,array1,array2)
Parameters	target - item to search for array1 - array of codes array2 - array of return values
Example	ASEEK(target, array1, array2)
Assumes	elements in each array are the same data type
Side Effects	crash on bad data
Returns	corresponding value or BLANK(array2[01])
Calls	ASCAN(), BLANK()

```
FUNCTION ASEEK

PARAMETERS memvar, array1, array2
result = BLANK( array2[ 1 ] )          && supply blank data type
limit = LEN( array1 )                  && how we'd do it in Clipper
IF !EMPTY( memvar )                    && without the ASCAN() udf
   FOR i = 1 TO limit
      IF array1[ i ] = memvar
         result = array2[ i ]
         i = limit
      ENDIF
   NEXT
ENDIF
n = ASCAN( array1, memvar )
IF n 0
   result = array2[ n ]
ELSE
   result = BLANK( array2[ 1 ] )
ENDIF
RETURN result
```

• AVALID()

```
PROGRAM         AA_VALID.PRG
Function(s)     AVALID()
Purpose         Array-based VALIDation routine, verfies
                input against an array and translates
                any acceptable code.
Conventions     2 arrays, codes, translations
                you want displayed at row, col
                On error display optional error message
                at same location.
Syntax          AVALID( target, array1, array2, ;
                  row, col[, err_msg] )
Parameters      target - item to validate
                array1 - array of codes
                array2 - array of translation strings
                row - row at which to display result
                col - column at which to display result
                err_msg - error message on failed search
Example         @ row, col GET mWEIGHT ;
                VALID AVALID(mWEIGHT,WEIGHTS,RATES,10,20)
                As mWEIGHT is entered, the udf
                displays the shipping cost at 10,20
                Useful in a GET statement so you can put
                something up on the screen without the READ
Assumes         validity of all parameters
Side Effects    the display is actually a side effect since
                the function must return True or False.
Returns         True or False.
Calls           ASCAN(), SYSCOLOR()
```

```
FUNCTION AVALID

PARAMETERS target, array1, array2, row, col, err_msg
PRIVATE pos, found, msg, temp
temp = PCOUNT()
pos = ASCAN(array1, target)
found = (pos  0)
IF found
   msg = array2[pos]
ELSE
```

```
   CHR(07)
   IF temp > 5
      msg = err_msg
   ENDIF
ENDIF
SYSCOLOR(01)
RETURN found
```

Chapter 13

Date Functions

- BOM — beginning of month.
- BONM — beginning of next month.
- BOW — beginning of week.
- BOY — beginning of year.
- DATE_KEY — sets specified function key to system date.
- EOM — end of month.
- EOW — end of week.
- EOY — end of year.
- IS_LEAP — true if the specified year is a leap year.
- LDATE — returns long string date, e.g. "Monday, May 3, 1989".

• BOM()

```
PROGRAM         AA_BOM.PRG
Function(s)     BOM()
Purpose         Beginning of month
Conventions     handy in date calculations
Syntax          BOM([date])
Parameters      date - optional date expression
Example         BOM() returns first of this month
Assumes         nothing
Side Effects    none
Returns         beginning of month as a date
Calls           nothing
```

```
FUNCTION BOM

PARAMETER date
IF TYPE("date") = "U"
   date = DATE()
ENDIF
RETURN date - DAY(date) + 1
```

- **BONM()**

```
PROGRAM        AA_BONM.PRG
Function(s)    BONM()
Purpose        Beginning of next month
Conventions    handy in date calculations
Syntax         BONM([date])
Parameters     date - optional date expression
Example        BONM() returns first of this month
Assumes        nothing
Side Effects   none
Returns        beginning of month as a date
Calls          nothing
```

```
FUNCTION BONM

PARAMETER date_valu
PRIVATE month, year, yr_inc, day, result
yr_inc = 0
month = MONTH(date_valu)+1
day = '/01/'

IF month = 13
   month = 1
   yr_inc = 1
ENDIF

cyear = STRINT(YEAR(date_valu)+yr_inc)
cmonth = STRINT(month)
result = CTOD(cmonth+day+cyear)

RETURN result
```

• BOW()

```
PROGRAM        AA_BOW.PRG
Function(s)    BOW()
Purpose        beginning of week
Conventions    handy in calculating dates
Syntax         BOW([date])
Parameters     date - optional date to use, default today
Example        BOW() ... returns the date of Monday this week
Assumes        nothing
Side Effects   none
Returns        Monday of the specified week as a date
Calls          nothing
```

```
FUNCTION BOW

PARAMETER date
IF TYPE("date") = "U"
   date = DATE()
ENDIF
RETURN IF(DOW(date)=1,(date-6),(date-(DOW(date)-2)))
```

• BOY()

```
PROGRAM       AA_BOY.PRG
Function(s)   BOY()
Purpose       beginning of year
Conventions   useful in date calculations
Syntax        BOY([date])
Parameters    date - optional date, default today
Example       BOY()
Assumes       nothing
Side Effects  none
Returns       January 1 of the year specified
Calls         STRINT()
```

```
FUNCTION BOY

PARAMETER date
IF TYPE("date") = "U"
   date = DATE()
ENDIF
year = YEAR(date)
RETURN CTOD("01/01/" + STRINT(year))
```

• DATE_KEY()

```
PROGRAM        AA_DTKEY.PRG
Function(s)    DATE_KEY()
Purpose        Set a function key to the system date
Conventions    a good candidate for a user-definable key
               (e.g. a field date_key (N2) in the system
               file, and allow the user to change it.)
Syntax         DATE_KEY(key_no)
Parameters     key_no - the number of the function key
               you want to define.
Example        DATE_KEY(03)
Assumes        nothing
Side Effects   none
Returns        True
Calls          nothing
```

```
FUNCTION DATE_KEY

PARAMETER key_no
PRIVATE reply
IF TYPE("key_no") != "N"
   reply = .F.
ELSE
   key_no = MAX(01,MIN(40,key_no))
   reply = .T.
   x = DTOC(DATE())
   SET FUNCTION key_no TO SUBSTR(x,1,2)+SUBSTR(x,4,2)+SUBSTR(x,7)
ENDIF
RETURN reply
```

• EOM()

```
PROGRAM      AA_EOM.PRG
Function(s)  EOM()
Purpose      end of the month
Conventions  useful in date calculations
Syntax       EOM([date])
Parameters   date - optional, default today
Example      EOM()
Assumes      nothing
Side Effects none
Returns      last day in month as a date
Calls        nothing
```

```
FUNCTION EOM

PARAMETER date
IF TYPE("date") = "U"
   date = DATE()
ENDIF
nxt_mnth = STRINT(MONTH(date) + 1)
day_one = "01"
this_year = STRINT(YEAR(date))
new_date = CTOD(nxt_mnth+"/"+day_one+"/"+this_year)
RETURN new_date - 1
```

• EOW()

```
PROGRAM       AA_EOW.PRG
Function(s)   EOW()
Purpose       end of week
Conventions   Sunday is the last day of the business week
Syntax        EOW([date])
Parameters    date - optional, default today
Example       EOW(DATE()+07) ... returns a week Sunday
Assumes       nothing
Side Effects  none
Returns       Sunday of the specified week as a date
Calls         nothing
```

```
FUNCTION EOW

PARAMETER date
PRIVATE result
IF TYPE("date") = "U"
   date = DATE()
ENDIF
IF DOW(date) = 2
   result = date + 6
ELSE
   result = date + (8 - DOW(date))
ENDIF
RETURN result
```

• EOY()

```
PROGRAM         AA_EOY.PRG
Function(s)     EOY()
Purpose         end of year
Conventions     useful in date calculations
Syntax          EOY([date])
Parameters      date - optional, defaults to today
Example         EOY()
Assumes         nothing
Side Effects    none
Returns         December 31 of the specified year as a date
Calls           nothing
```

```
FUNCTION EOY

PARAMETER date
IF TYPE("date") = "U"
   date = DATE()
ENDIF
year = YEAR(date)
RETURN CTOD("12/31/" + STRINT(year))
```

• IS_LEAP()

```
PROGRAM        AA_ISLEAP.PRG
Function(s)    IS_LEAP()
Purpose        Determines if a date is in a leap year
Conventions
Syntax         IS_LEAP([date])
Parameters     date - optional, defaults to today
Example        ? IS_LEAP() returns True in 1988
Assumes        if you pass bad data it uses today
Side Effects   none
Returns        True or False
Calls          EMPTY(), MOD()
```

```
FUNCTION IS_LEAP

PARAMETER date
IF TYPE("date") != "D"
   date = DATE()
ENDIF
RETURN EMPTY(MOD(YEAR(date),4))
```

• LDATE()

```
PROGRAM        AA_LDATE.PRG
Function(s)    LDATE()       (long date)
Purpose        present day and date as a string
Conventions    usful in report and screen headers
Syntax         LDATE([date])
Parameters     date - optional, default today
Example        LDATE(DATE()+07)
Assumes        nothing
Side Effects   none
Returns        string,e.g. "Wednesday, February 22, 1989"
Calls          STRINT()
```

```
FUNCTION LDATE

PARAMETER date
PRIVATE temp, result
temp = PCOUNT()
IF temp = 0
   date = DATE()
ENDIF
result = CDOW(date) + ', ' + CMONTH(date) + ' ' + ;
         STRINT(DAY(date)) + ', ' + STRINT(YEAR(date))
RETURN result
```

Chapter 14

File-oriented Functions

- BLANK — returns a blank of the field name passed.
- BROWSER — a generalized file-browse routine which can be customized by passing a udf to execute within DBEDIT().
- CHK_DICT — combines DB_OPEN() with a file dictionary.
- DB_OPEN — file-handler, opens all files/indexes in a program.
- DUST_1 — deletes/recalls the current record, on confirmation.
- DUST_EM — packs the current file.
- EXIST — checks for existence in a lookup table
- GET_FILE — creates a pop-up menu of filenames, returns selected name.
- GO_BOT — goes to the bottom of the current file.
- GO_TOP — goes to the top of the current file.
- GET_STD — a powerful, generalized add/update routine which executes intelligent defaults or any custom validations or behavior you may require.
- HELP_FILL — creates a scrolling window containing records from a lookup table so the user can select a valid field entry (e.g. scroll the customer file to fill in the customer code on an invoice).
- LOOKUP — provides validation with lookup table display.
- MENU_REC — turns a table into a scrolling menu, returns either a field value, the record number or the result of a udf.
- NEXT — increments the last value in a key field.
- NEXT_REC — moves to the next record in a table.
- PREV_REC — moves to the previous record in a table.
- QUERY — allows the user to find virtually anything in a database. Contains several sub-functions including GET_QUERY(), GET_CLAUSE(), GET_FIELD(), GET_OP(), GET_VALUE(), ANDORDUN() and PROCESS().
- RPL — automates replacing fields with memory variables.

- SELE_SCR — allows the user to select among several screens.
- STAT_LINE — provides status information on line 24.
- THE_USUAL — generalized file-maintenance meta-function.
- TRANSFER — transfers data from one table to another, creating the target if necessary.
- UNIQUE — returns true if the data passed is either not in the current index, or is but represents the current record.
- XBROWSER — provides default functionality to routines based on BROWSER.

• BLANK()

```
PROGRAM       AA_BLANK.PRG
Function(s)   BLANK()
Purpose       returns an empty memvar
Conventions   useful in numerous situations
Syntax        memvar = BLANK(expression)
Parameters    expression - must be legitimate
Example       BLANK(cust_code)
Assumes       validity of expression
Side Effects  crash on bad data
Returns       blank variable the right size and type
Calls         nothing
```

```
FUNCTION BLANK
PARAMETER memvar
DO CASE
   CASE TYPE("memvar") = "C"
      result = SPACE(LEN(memvar))
   CASE TYPE("memvar") = "D"
      result = CTOD("  /  /  ")
   CASE TYPE("memvar") = "M"
      result = SPACE(10)
   CASE TYPE("memvar") = "N"
      result = 0
   OTHERWISE
      result = .F.
ENDCASE
RETURN result
```

• BROWSER()

```
PROGRAM        AA_BROWS.PRG
Function(s)    BROWSER()
Purpose        sugar-coated calling function for DBEDIT()
Conventions    Assume use with DBEDIT()
Syntax         BROWSE()
Parameters     t - top left corner
               l - top left column
               b - bottom row
               r - bottom right column
               udf - to over-ride XBROWSER()
               fields - optional array of fields
               pictures - optional array of pictures
               heads - optional array of column headings
Example        BROWSER(02,00,22,77,udf_brow)
Assumes        data file is open
Side Effects   none
Returns        True
Calls
```

```
FUNCTION BROWSER

PARAMETERS t, l, b, r, udf, fields, pictures, heads
PRIVATE n, move_chrs, force_rec, ntx_expr, ntx_eval, prev_rec, ;
      is_append, any_append, keystroke, e_field, get_data,;
      f_size, temp_scr
IF EMPTY(FIELDNAME(1))              && no database in use
      POP_MSG("Sometimes I wonder about you as a programmer")
      RETURN .F.
ENDIF
move_chrs = CHR(24) + CHR(05) + CHR(03) + ; CHR(18) + CHR(31) +
CHR(30)
f_size = FCOUNT()                   && needed if no arrays passed
force_rec = .T.
is_append = .F.
any_append = .F.
prev_rec = 0
IF TYPE("pictures") != "A"
   DECLARE pictures[f_size]
   i = 01
   FOR i = 01 TO f_size
      pictures[i] = GEN_PIC(FIELD(i))
```

```
   NEXT
ENDIF
IF TYPE("heads") != "A"
   DECLARE heads[f_size]
   i = 01
   FOR i = 01 TO f_size
      heads[i] = PROPER(FIELD(i))
   NEXT
ENDIF
dummy = .F.
temp_scr = SAVESCREEN(t,l,b,r)
IF PCOUNT() < 4 .OR. TYPE("t") != "N"
   t = 01
   l = 00
   b = 23
   r = 79
ENDIF
BASIC_BOX()

IF TYPE("udf") $ "UL"                && allow customization, but
   udf = "XBROWSER"                  && also cover with minimal udf
ENDIF
IF TYPE("fields") != "A"             && no array of fields?
   DECLARE fields[f_size]
   AFIELDS(fields)
ENDIF
IF EOF()
   GO TOP
ENDIF
IF LASTREC() = 0                     && empty ...force append mode
   KEYBOARD CHR(24)
ENDIF
DBEDIT(t + 1, l, b, r, ;
      fields, ;
      udf, ;
      pictures, ;
      heads,;
      dummy, dummy, "MOM", dummy)
RESTSCREEN(t,l,b,r,temp_scr)
RETURN .T.
```

• CHK_DICT()

```
PROGRAM        AA_DICT.PRG
Function(s)    CHK_DICT()
Purpose        Checks files with reference to a dictionary
               passed as a param. Re-builds missing
               indexes, warns of missing data files.
Conventions    begin all programs with CHK_DICT(),
               returning to dos if CHK_DICT() returns .F.
Syntax         CHK_DICT(dict_file)
Parameters     dict_file - name of dictionary file
Example        CHK_DICT("APP_DICT")
Assumes        Structure of APP.DICT as in Chapter 4
Side Effects   crash on bad data.
Returns        True if all data files are present
               (all indexes will be).
Calls          DB_OPEN()
```

```
FUNCTION CHK_DICT

PARAMETER dict_file
PRIVATE i, s, file_name, alias, indexes
IF !DB_OPEN(dict_file)
   RETURN .F.
ENDIF
DO WHILE !EOF()
   file_name = File_name               && fields from dict_file
   alias = Alias
   DECLARE keys[7]                     && temp array
   indexes = 0                         && count 'em ourselves
   FOR i = 1 TO 7                      && index keys from file
      s = STR(i,1)
      IF !EMPTY(key_&s)
         indexes = indexes + 1
         keys[indexes] = key_&s
      ENDIF
   NEXT
   IF indexes > 0
      DECLARE index_key[indexes]       && pass this array of keys...
      FOR i = 1 TO indexes
         index_key[i] = keys[i]
      NEXT
   ELSE
```

```
      index_key = ""                    && or a null string
   ENDIF
   IF !DB_OPEN(file_name, indexes, index_key, alias)
      result = .F.                      && return on first open err
   ENDIF
   SELECT &dict_file
   SKIP
ENDDO
USE                                     && close the dictionary
RETURN result
```

• DB_OPEN()

```
PROGRAM       AA_DBOPN.PRG
Function(s)   DB_OPEN()
Purpose       File/Index handler
Conventions   recreates missing indexes automatically
              Every application begins with a call to
              DB_OPEN() for each file.
Syntax        DB_OPEN(file,no_indexes,keys,)
Parameters    file - name of file to open
              no_indexes - number of indexes on file
              keys - string (1 index) or array of keys
              aka  - alias if any
Example       x = !DB_OPEN("CUSTOMER",01,"CUST_CODE")
Assumes       nothing
Side Effects leaves the file open with all indexes in
              use, order 1
Returns       True only if files were opened successfully
Calls         MSG(), STRINT(), MAKE_STR()
```

```
FUNCTION DB_OPEN

PARAMETERS dbf_name, indexes, index_key, aka
PRIVATE temp, root, pd_pos, temp_name, msg
temp = PCOUNT()
result = .T.
pd_pos = AT( ".", dbf_name )
dbf_name = IF( pd_pos > 0, ;
               dbf_name, ;
               dbf_name + ".DBF" )
pd_pos = AT( ".", dbf_name )        && Redefine location of period
root   = LEFT(dbf_name, MIN(pd_pos - 1,7))
IF TYPE("indexes") != "N"
   indexes = 0
ENDIF
SELECT 0
IF !FILE( dbf_name )
   POP_MSG( "I cannot locate the file " + dbf_name  )
   result = .F.
   RETURN result
ENDIF
IF TYPE("aka") != "C"
   USE &dbf_name
```

```
ELSE
   USE &dbf_name ALIAS &aka
ENDIF
IF indexes > 0
   IF TYPE("index_key") = "A"
      i = 1
      FOR i = 1 TO indexes
         n = STRINT(i)
         temp_name = root + n
         temp_key  = TRIM( index_key[ i ] )
         msg = "Indexing " + m->dbf_name + " on " + ;
               temp_key + " to " + temp_name
         IF !FILE( temp_name + ".NTX")
            MSG( msg, 0, .T. )
            INDEX ON &temp_key TO &temp_name
            @ 24,00
         ENDIF
      NEXT
   ELSE
      temp_key = TRIM( index_key )
      n = STRINT( indexes )
      temp_name = root + n
      msg = "Indexing " + m->dbf_name + " on " + ;
            temp_key + " to " + temp_name
      IF !FILE( temp_name + ".NTX")
         MSG( msg, 0, .T. )
         INDEX ON &temp_key TO &temp_name
         @ 24,00
      ELSE
         SET INDEX TO &temp_name
      ENDIF
   ENDIF
ENDIF
IF TYPE("index_key") = "A"
   i = 1
   FOR i = 1 TO indexes
      n = STRINT(i)
      ntx&n = root + n
   NEXT
   DO CASE
      CASE indexes > 06
         SET INDEX TO &ntx1, &ntx2, &ntx3, &ntx4, ;
            &ntx5, &ntx6, &ntx7
      CASE indexes = 05
         SET INDEX TO &ntx1, &ntx2, &ntx3, &ntx4, &ntx5
      CASE indexes = 04
         SET INDEX TO &ntx1, &ntx2, &ntx3, &ntx4
      CASE indexes = 03
         SET INDEX TO &ntx1, &ntx2, &ntx3
```

```
      CASE indexes = 02
         SET INDEX TO &ntx1, &ntx2
      CASE indexes = 01
         SET INDEX TO &ntx1
   ENDCASE
ENDIF
RETURN result
```

• DUST_1()

```
PROGRAM        AA_DUST1.PRG
Function(s)    DUST_1()
Purpose        Delete/recall function
Conventions    calls STAT_LINE() for update
Syntax         DUST_1()
Parameters     none
Example        DUST_1()
Assumes        file is open
Side Effects   none
Returns        .T.
Calls          STAT_LINE()
```

```
FUNCTION DUST_1

IF DELETED()
   RECALL
ELSE
   DELETE
ENDIF
STAT_LINE()
RETURN .T.
```

• DUST_EM()

```
PROGRAM         AA_DUSTM.PRG
Function(s)     DUST_EM()
Purpose         PACKs all open files
Conventions     to pack just one file, pass its name
Syntax          DUST_EM([file])
Parameters      file - optional. If not passed, pack all
                open files
Example         DUST_EM("CUSTOMER")
Assumes         nothing
Side Effects    none
Returns         .T.
Calls           T_INDEX(), VERIFY(), MSG()
```

```
FUNCTION DUST_EM

PARAMETER file
PRIVATE result, msg1, msg2, pack_all, max_files, area
pack_all = (TYPE("file") != "C")
result = .F.
msg1 = "Remove all records marked for deletion"
msg2 = "Hang on"
max_files = 255
IF !VERIFY(msg1)
   RETURN .F.
ENDIF
MSG( msg2, 0, .T. )                 && no wait, plus blinking dots
IF !pack_all
   SELECT &file
   T_INDEX()   && sidestep a clipper bug
   PACK                             && see below
   result = .T.
ELSE
   cur_file  = ALIAS()
   FOR x = 1 TO max_files
      SELECT x
      IF !EMPTY(ALIAS())
         T_INDEX()
         PACK
      ELSE
         EXIT
      ENDIF
   NEXT
```

```
   result = .T.
ENDIF
IF FILE("TEMP.NTX")
   ERASE TEMP.NTX
ENDIF
@ 24,00                              && trash any message remains
RETURN result
```

- **T_INDEX**

```
FUNCTION T_INDEX                     && Temporary index

IF EMPTY(INDEXKEY(0))                && cover a bug in PACK
   temp_field = FIELD(1)             && corrupts records every 64K
   INDEX ON &temp_field TO temp      && packing an unindexed file
ENDIF
RETURN 01
```

• EXIST()

```
PROGRAM         AA_EXIST.PRG
Function(s)     EXIST()
Purpose         VALIDate input to items in a file
Conventions     converse of UNIQUE()
Syntax          GET memvar VALID EXIST(memvar[,file[,udf]])
Parameters      memvar - item to validate
                file - lookup table
                udf - function whose value you want instead
                (use to create complex criteria)
Example         @ row, col GET mCUST_CODE VALID ;
                EXIST(mCUST_CODE, "CUSTOMER")
Assumes         good data, file is open and indexed
Side Effects    unpredictable, given the power of
Returns         True if found, or True if udf returns True
Calls           POP_MSG(), MAKE_STR()
```

```
FUNCTION EXIST

PARAMETERS target, file, udf
PRIVATE temp, cur_file, record_no, reply
temp = PCOUNT()
cur_file = ALIAS()
record_no = RECNO()
reply = .F.
IF temp > 1
   SELECT &file
ENDIF
SEEK target
reply = FOUND()
IF !reply
   POP_MSG(MAKE_STR(target) + " is not on file")
ELSEIF
   IF TYPE("udf") = "C"
      reply = &udf                    && udf must return a logical!
   ENDIF
ENDIF
SELECT &cur_file
GO record_no
RETURN reply
```

• FETCH()

```
PROGRAM        AA_FETCH.PRG
Function(s)    FETCH()
Purpose        Display data from "related" files
Conventions    All files are open and indexed appropriately
Syntax         FETCH(target, file, field, message)
Parameters     target - item to search for. any data type
               file - file to look in. open/indexed.
               field - field to display. may also be udf name
               message - optional. error message to display
Example        @ row, col SAY FETCH(mCUST_CODE, "CUSTOMER" ;
               "Company")
Assumes        nothing
Side Effects    displays data from another table
Returns        from matching file, or BLANK()
Calls          BLANK()
```

```
FUNCTION FETCH

PARAMETERS target, file, field, message
PRIVATE cur_dbf, temp, reply
cur_dbf = ALIAS()                    && so where we can return
temp = &file->&field                 && obtain a sample
reply = ""  && prepare return value
IF TYPE("exact_on") = "U"            && you forgot to define it...
   exact_on = .F.
ENDIF
IF TYPE("target") = "C" .AND. !exact_on
   target = TRIM(target)
ENDIF
IF EMPTY(target) .OR. TYPE("message") = "U"
   reply = BLANK(temp)
ELSE
   reply = message
ENDIF
SELECT &file
SEEK target
IF FOUND()
   reply = &file->&field
ELSE
   ?? CHR(7)
   IF TYPE("message") = "C"
```

```
      reply = message
   ENDIF
ENDIF
SELECT &cur_dbf
RETURN reply
```

• GET_FILE()

```
PROGRAM        AA_GFILE.PRG
Function(s)    GET_FILE()
Purpose        get a filename from the user
Conventions    point and shoot file selector
Syntax         GET_FILE([filespec])
Parameters     filespec - defaults to "*.DBF"
Example        dbf = GET_FILE()
Assumes        the current directory is displayed
Side Effects   none
Returns        name of selected file
Calls          ADIR(), ACHOICE(), DRAW_BOX(), ESC()
```

```
FUNCTION GET_FILE

PARAMETERS filespec, top_row, top_col
PRIVATE temp_scr, m_row, m_col
m_row = IF( TYPE("top_row") = "U", ROW(), top_row)
m_col = IF( TYPE("top_col") = "U", COL(), top_col)
IF UN_DEF("filespec")
   filespec = "*.*"
ENDIF
DECLARE files[ADIR(filespec)]       && how big should it be?
ADIR(filespec, files)

bw = 12  && box width
tr = m_row + 02                     && top row
tc = m_col + 02                     && top column
IF tc + bw > 78
   tc = m_col - bw - 02
ENDIF
br = MIN(20,tr+LEN(files))          && bottom row
bc = tc + bw   && bottom column
temp_scr = SPACE((br - tr +1) * (bc - tc + 1))
SAVESCREEN(tr -1, tc -1, br + 1, bc + 1, temp_scr)
DRAW_BOX( tr -1, tc -1, br + 1, bc + 1, 2 )
ch = ACHOICE(tr, tc, br, bc, files)
IF ESC()
   reply = ""
ELSE
   reply = files[ch]
ENDIF
```

```
RESTSCREEN(tr -1, tc -1, br + 1, bc + 1, temp_scr)
RETURN reply
```

• GET_STD()

```
PROGRAM        AA_GSTD.PRG
Function(s)    GET_STD()
Purpose        Standard GET routine
Conventions    all THE_USUAL() assumptions
Syntax         GET_STD(append_flag)
Parameters     append_flag - logical signals append
               (Add vs. update)
Example        GET_STD(.T.)  ... call to add a record
Assumes        udf_??? variables have all been declared
Side Effects   could crash if not set up properly
Returns        True if escape not pressed
Calls          BLANK(), STAT_LINE(), VERIFY()
               udf_scr, udf_say, udf_key, udf_fld, udf_rpl
```

```
FUNCTION GET_STD

PARAMETER add_one
PRIVATE reply, msg, record_no
reply = .F.
msg = IF(add_one, "Add this record to the file", ;
         "Write the changes to disk")
record_no = RECNO()

IF add_one
   i = 01                           && manufacture some blanks
   FOR i = 01 TO FCOUNT()
      f = FIELD(i)                  && grab field name
      v = "m" + f                   && char name = "m" + field name
      &v = BLANK(&f)                && fill it with a blank
   NEXT
ELSE
   i = 01                           && manufacture memvars for editing
   FOR i = 01 TO FCOUNT()
      f = FIELD(i)                  && fieldname
      v = "m" + f                   && variable = "m" + fieldname
      &v = &f && variable = field
   NEXT
ENDIF
IF add_one .AND. screen_no != 01
   screen_no = 01                   && force it to screen 1 for keys
   x = &udf_scr                     && repaint
ENDIF
```

```
x = &udf_say                            && display blanks or current record
STAT_LINE()                             && update the status display
IF &udf_key                             && do everything involved to get the
   IF &udf_fld                          && if success, get remaining fields
      IF VERIFY(msg)                    && get user confirmation
         IF add_one
            APPEND BLANK
            reply = &udf_rpl            && replace udf if nec.
            DO WHILE screen_no < no_screens
               screen_no = screen_no + 01
               x = &udf_scr
               GET_STD(.F.)             && RECURSION
            ENDDO
            record_no = RECNO()
         ENDIF
         reply = &udf_rpl
      ENDIF
   ENDIF
ENDIF
GO record_no
RETURN reply
```

• GO_BOT()

```
PROGRAM       AA_GOBOT.PRG
Function(s)   GO_BOT()
Purpose       Go to the bottom record of a file
Conventions   Called by THE_USUAL() via SET KEY.
Syntax        GO_BOT()
Parameters    x, y, z - hot keystrokesNone
Example       SET KEY ## TO GO_BOT
Assumes       udf_say (displays record)
Side Effects  crash if udf_say unknown
Returns       True
Calls         a udf of yours whose name is in udf_say
```

```
FUNCTION GO_BOT

PARAMETERS x, y, z
GO BOTTOM
x = &udf_say                          && execute display record udf
RETURN .T.
```

• GO_TOP()

```
PROGRAM         AA_GOTOP.PRG
Function(s)     GO_TOP()
Purpose         Go to the top record of a file
Conventions     Called by THE_USUAL() via SET KEY.
Syntax          GO_TOP()
Parameters      x, y, z - hot keystrokes
Example         SET KEY ## TO GO_TOP
Assumes         udf_say (displays record)
Side Effects    crash if udf_say unknown
Returns         True
Calls           a udf of yours whose name is in udf_say
```

```
FUNCTION GO_TOP

GO TOP
x = &udf_say                            && execute record display udf
RETURN .T.
```

• HELP_FILL()

```
PROGRAM        AA_HFILL.PRG
Function(s)    HELP_FILL()
Purpose        VALIDation routine to scroll a lookup table
               in a window, returning True if user selects
               a record, else False. This traps the user
               in the GET until a legit entry is made.
Conventions    lookup table must be open and ready for use.
               return field must be in array position 1
Syntax         VALID HELP_FILL(@memvar, file, fld_ra, ;
                 udf, condition, tr, tc, br, bc)
PARAMETERS     memvar - item to validate
               file - lookup table
               array - of fields to display in window
               udf - to execute with dbedit()
               condition - used to set filter to...
               tr, tc, br, bc - window co-ordinates
Example        @ 10,10 SAY "ENTER BRANCH" GET m_branch ;
               PICT "9999" ;
               VALID HELP_FILL( @m_branch, file, fld_ra )
Assumes        all data are legitimate
Side Effects    crash on bad data
Returns        True if target exists, else False
Calls          MAKE_STR(), DRAW_BOX(), HF_UDF()
```

```
FUNCTION HELP_FILL

PARAMETERS memvar, file, fld_array, udf, condition, tr, tc, br, bc
PRIVATE not_eof, cur_file, m_row, m_col, fld1, fld2
cur_file = ALIAS()
m_row = ROW()
m_col = COL()
SELECT &file
IF !EMPTY(memvar)
   SEEK memvar
   IF FOUND()
      RETURN .T.
   ENDIF
ENDIF
SAVE SCREEN
IF TYPE("udf") != "C"                 && pass a logical to activate default
```

```
   udf = "HF_UDF"
ENDIF
IF TYPE("tr") != "N"
   tr = 04
   fld1 = fld_array[1]
   fld2 = fld_array[2]
   * The next line is followed by a stepwise explanation
   window_width = LEN(MAKE_STR(&fld1)) + LEN(MAKE_STR(&fld2)) + 06
   * item1 = &fld1
   * item2 = &fld2
   * width1 = LEN(MAKE_STR( item1))
   * width2 = LEN(MAKE_STR( item2))
   * white_space = 06
   * window_width = width1 + width2 + white_space
   tc = CENTRE(SPACE(window_width))
   br = 20
   bc = tc + window_width + 06       && a little white space
   window_ht = br - 05               && grabbed by dbedit headline
ENDIF
SELECT &file
IF TYPE("condition") != "C"
   SET FILTER TO
ELSEIF !EMPTY(condition)
   SET FILTER TO &condition
ENDIF
IF EOF()                             && conditional to allow for SOFTSEEK
   GO TOP
ENDIF
DRAW_BOX(tr-1, tc-1, br+1, bc+1, 03)
DBEDIT( tr, tc, br, bc, fld_array, udf )
SET FILTER TO
SELECT &cur_file
RESTORE SCREEN
SYSCOLOR(02)
@ m_row, m_col SAY memvar
SYSCOLOR(01)
RETURN (!EMPTY(memvar))
```

• HF_UDF()

```
FUNCTION HF_UDF

PARAMETERS mode, i
PRIVATE result
key_we_want = fld_array[1]
DO CASE
   CASE mode = 0
```

```
      * idle mode..display record number
      result = 1
   CASE mode < 4
      * case action can be implemented for each mode
      result = 1
   * mode 4..a keystroke not handled by DBEDIT
   CASE LASTKEY() = 13
      memvar = &key_we_want         && points to contents of field
      result = 0
   CASE LASTKEY() = 27
      result = 0
   OTHERWISE
      * Ignore the keystroke
ENDCASE
RETURN result
```

• LOOKUP()

```
PROGRAM        AA_LOOKU.PRG
Function(s)    LOOKUP()
Purpose        VALIDation with display of a lookup table
Conventions    Single-lookup display
Syntax         @ row, col GET target VALID ;
               LOOKUP(target,file, field, row, col)
Parameters     target - object to look up
               file - file to look in
               field - field to display
               row - display at row
               col - display at column
Example        @ row, col GET mCust_code VALID ;
               LOOKUP(mCust_code,"CUSTOMER","COMPANY",10,12)
Assumes        file is open and indexed appropriately
               exact_on flags trim of character fields
Side Effects   displays field at row,col,
               or blank if the search fails.
Returns        True if the search is successful, else False.
Calls          SYSCOLOR(n), MAKE_STR(), POP_MSG()
```

```
FUNCTION LOOKUP

PARAMETERS target, table, say_field, row, col
PRIVATE cur_file
cur_file = ALIAS()
SELECT &table
IF TYPE("target") = "C" .AND. !exact_on
   target = TRIM(target)
ENDIF
SEEK target
SYSCOLOR(02)
IF FOUND()
   @ row,col SAY &table->&say_field
ELSE
   ? CHR(7)
   POP_MSG( MAKE_STR(target) + " is not on file..." )
ENDIF
```

```
SELECT &cur_file
SYSCOLOR(01)                        && back to normal
RETURN FOUND()
```

• MENU_REC()

```
PROGRAM       AA_MNREC.PRG
Function(s)   MENU_REC()
Purpose       Turns a table into a menu.
              presents field(s) as prompts.
Returns       either a field value,
              the result of a udf, or the record number.
Conventions   double-function function:
              pass empty filename to browse current file,
              on finish go to pointed-at record
              pass a filename = pop open a lookup table,
              restore screen afterwards.
              disp_fld - any valid macro expression.
              ret_value - any valid expression, or 0.
              if ret_fld = 0, return recno().
              disp_fld may be any character string, not
              necessarily one field only. for example:
              "Company+space(4)+contact+space(4)+phone"
              results in a wide menu.
              It puts information right up front
              instead of forcing the user to ask for it.
              Equally important, ret_value could contain
              a udf name which could in turn contain
              1 parameter. (Can't pass two in a macro.
              To pass 2 params, use an array.)
Syntax        MENU_REC(file, disp_fld, ret_value)
Parameters    file      - file to use
              disp_fld  - field to display
              ret_value - anything you want back
Example       MENU_REC("CUSTOMER","COMPANY","CUST_CODE")
Assumes       file is open, disp_fld and ret_value
Side Effects  crash on bad data. It loads the file's fields
              into array without checking memory availability.
              (Summer '87 MEMORY() function doesn't
              work.) Since it's all in 1 array, the max.
              size is 2048 recs.
              If memory is a problem, you can cut down
              the load to fewer records and use a paging-
              load scheme instead.
Returns       &ret_value: for recno() pass "recno()"
```

	if a function name is passed as ret_value, its return value is returned if you don't pass ret_value, disp_fld is returned
Calls	CENTRE(), BLANK(), DRAW_BOX()

```
FUNCTION MENU_REC

PARAMETERS file, disp_fld, ret_value
PRIVATE tcount, cur_file, result, reply, screen_no, max_scrs, ;
      max_recs, n, tlr, ch, y, col, m_row, m_col, recno_wtd, ;
   dummy, temp_scr
tcount = PCOUNT()
m_row = ROW()  && save current cursor location
m_col = COL()
cur_file = ALIAS()
max_recs = 16
n = 0
screen_no = 1
tlr = 05
ch = 01
y = 01
sp = " "
temp_scr = ""
IF EMPTY(file)
   File = ALIAS()
ENDIF
SELECT &file
result = LASTREC()
col = CENTRE( &disp_fld )
PRIVATE fld_val[result], rec_num[result]
DECLARE fld_val[result], rec_num[result]
FOR n = 1 TO LASTREC()
   rec_num[n] = RECNO()
   fld_val[n] = sp + &disp_fld
   SKIP
NEXT
bw = LEN(&disp_fld) + 3             && box width
tr = 06
tc = 10
br = 20
bc = tc + bw
st = 01  && start pos
os = 00  && relative location (offset)
func = "MR_UDF"
r1 = "fld_val"
r2 = .f.
```

```
temp_scr = (br - tr + 1) * (bc - tc + 1)   && calculate window size
SAVESCREEN(tr -1, tc -1, br + 1, bc + 1, temp_scr)
DRAW_BOX(tr -1, tc -1, br + 1, bc + 1, 2 )
ch = ACHOICE(tr, tc, br, bc, &r1, .T., func)      &&, st, os)
IF ch > 0
   GO rec_num[ch]
   result = &ret_value                 && note the freedom from
ELSE  && data type this phrasing
   result = BLANK(&ret_value)          && provides
ENDIF
RESTSCREEN(tr -1, tc -1, br + 1, bc + 1, temp_scr)
RETURN result
```

• MR_UDF()

```
Syntax        MR_UDF( expN, expN  )
Returns       a number
Notes         Params passed automatically by ACHOICE()
```

```
FUNCTION MR_UDF

PARAMETERS mode, i
PRIVATE reply
reply = 2
DO CASE
   CASE mode = 0
      reply = 2
   CASE mode = 1
      reply = 2
   CASE mode = 2
      reply = 2
   CASE LASTKEY() = 27
      reply = 0
   CASE LASTKEY() = 13
      reply = 1
   OTHERWISE
      reply = 3
ENDCASE
RETURN(reply)
```

• NEXT()

```
PROGRAM        AA_NEXT.PRG
Function(s)    NEXT()
Purpose        Get next available item (usually in a
               sequential index).
               Increments character and numeric fields.
Conventions    Won't yet increment "ABC-999" to "ABD-000"
Syntax         NEXT(fieldspec [, filespec])
Parameters     fieldspec - name of the field to increment
               filespec  - optional, file to look in
Example        (field Invoice_no is char 5, last record is
               "08765"
               ? NEXT(Invoice_no) returns "08766"
Assumes        the file is indexed on the field you wish to
               increment
Side Effects   none
Returns        the next field item in ascending order
Calls          STRZERO()
```

```
FUNCTION NEXT

PARAMETERS fld_name, file
temp      = PCOUNT()
cur_file  = ALIAS()
record_no = RECNO()
IF temp > 1
   SELECT &file
ENDIF
GO BOTTOM
IF TYPE(fld_name) = "N"                 && is it a number, or string?
   nextone = &fld_name + 1
ELSE
   nextone = STRZERO( VAL( &fld_name ) + 1, LEN( &fld_name ) )
ENDIF
SELECT &cur_file
GO record_no
RETURN nextone
```

• NEXT_REC()

```
PROGRAM         AA_NXREC.PRG
Function(s)     NEXT_REC()
Purpose         Goes to next record, with message at EOF()
Conventions     line 24 is the message area
Syntax          NEXT_REC()
Parameters      none
Example         NEXT_REC()
Assumes         file is open
Side Effects    none
Returns         .T.
Calls           MSG()
```

```
FUNCTION NEXT_REC

PRIVATE msg
msg = "Last record in the file"
SKIP
IF EOF()
   SKIP -1
   MSG( msg, 1 )
ENDIF
RETURN .T.
```

• PREV_REC()

```
PROGRAM        AA_PVREC.PRG
Function(s)    PREV_REC()
Purpose        Go to previous record, with message at BOF()
Conventions    line 24 is the message line
Syntax         PREV_REC()
Parameters     none
Example        PREV_REC()
Assumes        file is open
Side Effects   possible message on line 24
Returns        True
Calls          MSG()
```

```
FUNCTION PREV_REC

PRIVATE reply, msg
reply = .T.
msg = "First record in the file"
SKIP -1
IF BOF()
   MSG( msg, 1 )
ENDIF
RETURN reply
```

• QUERY()

```
PROGRAM       AA_QUERY.PRG
Function(s)   QUERY(), GET_QUERY(), GET_CLAUSE(),
              GET_OP(), ANDORDUN(), PROCESS()
Purpose       Generalized query function.
Conventions   Called by default from THE_USUAL(). Allows
              create, refine undo and cancel commands.
Syntax        QUERY()
Parameters    none
Example       QUERY()
Assumes       a file is in use.
              xcues contains the index key(s) -
              cosmetically more appealing than keys.
Side Effects  SETS FILTER TO conditions you specify, then
              returns control to the caller.
Returns       True
Calls         DBFILTER(),EMPTY(),POP_MSG(),ESC(),
              ACHOICE(),MAKE_STR(),READ_IT(),SYSCOLOR(),
              DRAW_BOX(),L_MENU()
```

```
FUNCTION QUERY

PRIVATE result, temp_scr, row, choice, cur_rec, no_opts, choice
no_opts = 04
PRIVATE choices[no_opts], legals[no_opts]
result = .F.
query_str = ""
row = 02
choice = 01
cur_rec = RECNO()
row = 02
col = 47
ht = no_opts + 02
width = 32

SAVE SCREEN TO temp_scr

choices[01] = " Create a query                  "
choices[02] = " Refine the current query        "
choices[03] = " Save these records to disk      "
choices[04] = " Undo the current query          "
legals[01] = .T.
```

```
legals[02] = "!EMPTY(DBFILTER())"
legals[03] = "!EMPTY(DBFILTER())"
legals[04] = "!EMPTY(DBFILTER())"
DRAW_BOX(01,col -1, ht, col + width, 13)     && joiner box
choice = ACHOICE(row, col, ht, col + width - 1, choices, legals,
.T., choice)

IF ESC()
   RESTORE SCREEN FROM temp_scr
   RETURN .F.                && Out, without changing order
ENDIF

RETURN result
```

```
FUNCTION GET_QUERY

PRIVATE result, temp_scr
result = .F.
query_str  = ""
SAVE SCREEN TO temp_scr
DO WHILE .T.
   temp_str = GET_CLAUSE()
   IF ESC() .OR. EMPTY(temp_str)
      EXIT
   ENDIF
   joiner = ANDORDUN()
   IF joiner = "DONE" .OR. EMPTY(joiner)
      query_str = query_str + temp_str
      result = .T.
      EXIT
   ELSE
      query_str = query_str + temp_str + joiner
   ENDIF
   IF LEN(query_str) > 250
      POP_MSG("The string has reached maximum complexity")
      result = !ESC()
      EXIT
   ENDIF
ENDDO
RESTORE SCREEN FROM temp_scr
RETURN result
```

```
FUNCTION GET_CLAUSE

PRIVATE field, op, value, str, dollar, not_in, counter, ;
   temp_scr
```

```
str    = ""
dollar = "$"
not_in = "!$"
counter = 01
SAVE SCREEN TO temp_scr
DO WHILE .T.
   DO CASE
      CASE counter = 00
         RESTORE SCREEN FROM temp_scr
         EXIT
      CASE counter = 01
         field = GET_FIELD()
         counter = IF(EMPTY(field), ;
               counter - 01, ;
               counter + 01)
      CASE counter = 02
         op = GET_OP(field)
         counter = IF(EMPTY(op), ;
               counter - 01, ;
               counter + 01)
      CASE counter = 03
         value = GET_VALUE(field)
         counter = IF(EMPTY(value), ;
               counter - 01, ;
               counter + 01)
      CASE counter = 04
         str = PROCESS(field, op, value)
         counter = counter + 01
      CASE counter = 05
         EXIT
   ENDCASE
ENDDO
RETURN str
```

```
FUNCTION GET_FIELD

PARAMETERS file, tr, tc
PRIVATE temp, cur_file, temp_scr, br, bc
SAVE SCREEN TO temp_scr
temp = PCOUNT()
cur_file = ALIAS()
IF temp > 00
   SELECT &file
ELSE
   file = cur_file
ENDIF
IF EMPTY(file)
   RETURN POP_MSG("You must select a file first")
```

```
ENDIF
DECLARE fld_ra[FCOUNT()]
AFIELDS(fld_ra)
IF UN_DEF("tr")
   tr = 04
   tc = 26
ENDIF
br = MIN( 22, tr + MIN(16, LEN(fld_ra) + 01) )
bc = tc + 16
DRAW_BOX(tr, tc, br, bc, 03)
fld = ACHOICE(tr+1, tc+1, br-1, bc-1, fld_ra)
IF fld > 0
   SYSCOLOR(02)                       && highlight selected item
   @ ROW(), tc + 01 SAY fld_ra[fld]
   SYSCOLOR(01)
ELSE
   RESTORE SCREEN FROM temp_scr
ENDIF
SELECT &cur_file
RETURN IF(fld = 0, "", fld_ra[fld])
```

FUNCTION GET_OP

```
PARAMETERS field, tr, tc
PRIVATE result, br, bc, no_ops, width, height, temp_scr
SAVE SCREEN TO temp_scr
IF PCOUNT() < 02
   tr = 08
   tc = 38
ENDIF
result  = ""
no_ops = 10
width  = 20
br = tr + no_ops - 01
bc = tc + width
DECLARE ops[no_ops], op_chrs[no_ops], permits[no_ops]
ops[01] = "Equals              "
ops[02] = "Does Not Equal      "
ops[03] = "Is Greater than     "
ops[04] = "Is Less than        "
ops[05] = "Contains            "
ops[06] = "Does not Contain    "
ops[07] = "Is in the List      "
ops[08] = "Is not in the List  "
ops[09] = "Is in the Range     "
ops[10] = "Is not in the Range "
op_chrs[01] = "="
op_chrs[02] = "!="
```

```
op_chrs[03] = ""
op_chrs[04] = ""
op_chrs[05] = "$"
op_chrs[06] = "!$"
op_chrs[07] = "L"
op_chrs[08] = "!L"
op_chrs[09] = "R"
op_chrs[10] = "!R"
permits[01] = .T.
permits[02] = .T.
permits[03] = "TYPE(field)!='L'"
permits[04] = "TYPE(field)!='L'"
permits[05] = "TYPE(field)='C'"
permits[06] = "TYPE(field)='C'"
permits[07] = .T.
permits[08] = .T.
permits[09] = .T.
permits[10] = .T.
DRAW_BOX(tr - 1, tc - 1, br + 1, bc + 1, 03)
ch = ACHOICE(tr, tc, br, bc, ops, permits)
IF ch > 0
   result = op_chrs[ch]
   SYSCOLOR(02)
   @ ROW(), tc SAY ops[ch]
   SYSCOLOR(01)
ELSE
   RESTORE SCREEN FROM temp_scr
ENDIF
RETURN result
```

```
FUNCTION GET_VALUE

PARAMETER field
PRIVATE msg, width, get_data, temp_scr
msg = "Enter the target value..."
get_data = BLANK(&field)
IF TYPE("get_data") = "C"
   pic_str = IF( LEN(get_data)  20, "@S20", "@X" )
ELSE
   pic_str = GEN_PIC(field)
ENDIF
get_pos = MAX( 42, (40 + (35 -LEN(MAKE_STR(get_data)))/2
SAVE SCREEN TO temp_scr
DRAW_BOX( 14, 40, 18, 75, 03 )
@ 17,get_pos = get_data PICTURE pic_str
READ_IT()
IF ESC()
   RESTORE SCREEN FROM temp_scr
```

```
ENDIF
RETURN get_data
```

```
FUNCTION ANDORDUN

PRIVATE result, tr, tc, br, bc, no_ops, temp_scr
result  = ""
tr = 19
tc = 60
br = 21
bc = 70
no_ops = 03
DECLARE ops[no_ops]
ops[01] = "And       "
ops[02] = "Or        "
ops[03] = "Done      "
SAVE SCREEN TO temp_scr
DRAW_BOX(tr - 1, tc - 1, br + 1, bc + 1, 03)
ch = ACHOICE(tr, tc, br, bc, ops)
IF ch = 00
   result = ""
   RESTORE SCREEN FROM temp_scr
ELSE
   SYSCOLOR(02)
   @ ROW(), tc SAY ops[ch]
   SYSCOLOR(01)
ENDIF
DO CASE
   CASE ch = 01
      result = ".AND."
   CASE ch = 02
      result =  ".OR."
   CASE ch = 03
      result =  "DONE"
ENDCASE
RETURN result
```

```
FUNCTION PROCESS

PARAMETERS fieldname, op, contents
PRIVATE string
fieldname = TRIM(fieldname)
op = TRIM(op)
sp = " "
DO CASE
   CASE TYPE("contents") = "C"
```

```
      IF op = dollar
         string = "'" + TRIM(contents) + "'" + dollar + field
      ELSEIF op = not_in
         string = "!('" + TRIM(contents) + "'" + ;
         dollar + field + ")"
      ELSE
         string = field + op + "'" + TRIM(contents) + "'"
      ENDIF
   CASE TYPE("contents") = "D"
      string = field + op + "CTOD('" + DTOC(contents) + "')"
   CASE TYPE("contents") = "N"
      string = field + op + LTRIM(STR(contents))
   CASE TYPE(field) = "L"           && actual field
      x = LEFT(MAKE_STR(contents),1)
      string = IF(x $ "FN", "!", "") + field
ENDCASE
RETURN string
```

• RPL()

```
PROGRAM        AA_RPL.PRG
Function(s)    RPL()
Purpose        General purpose REPLACE function
Conventions    generates names from field names (e.g.
mCUST_CODE)
               assumes these exist, replaces into record
               GET_STD() automatically defines the vars.
               Do whatever you want to the vars, then call RPL()
Syntax         RPL()
Parameters     none
Example        RPL()
Assumes        existence of vars whose names it will generate
Side Effects   crash on bad or non-existent data
Returns        .T.
Calls          nothing
```

```
FUNCTION RPL

PARAMETER add_one
PRIVATE i, reply
reply = .F.
i = 01
FOR i = 01 TO FCOUNT()
   f = FIELD(i)                          && grab field name
   v = "m" + f                           && var name = "m" + field name
   REPLACE &f WITH &v                    && write it to disk
NEXT
reply = .T.
RETURN reply
```

• SELE_SCR()

```
PROGRAM        AA_SLSCR.PRG
Function(s)    SELE_SCR()
Purpose        called by THE_USUAL() to change screen number
Conventions    constructs a menu of screen numbers
Syntax         SELE_SCR(curr_no)
Parameters     curr_no - current screen number
Example        SELE_SCR(02) defaults the menu to Screen 2
Assumes        all THE_USUAL() conventions
Side Effects   crash if above not respected
Returns        new screen number
Calls
```

```
FUNCTION SELE_SCR

PARAMETER cur_screen
PRIVATE x, row, chars, choice, screens[no_screens], row, col, ;
      temp_scr
row = 02
col = 64
chars = "1st2nd3rd"
choice = cur_screen
SAVE SCREEN TO temp_scr

IF no_screens = 01                     && in case somehow it got thru
   POP_MSG("There's only one screen declared here")
   RETURN cur_screen
ENDIF

DECLARE screens[no_screens]            && make an array

FOR i = 1 TO no_screens
    IF i < 4
       screens[i] = SUBSTR(chars,(i * 3 - 2), 3) + " Screen    "
    ELSE
       screens[i] = STRINT(i) + "th Screen    "
    ENDIF
NEXT

choice = cur_screen
ht = LEN(screens) + 02
width = LEN(screens[01])               && pad element 1 out
DRAW_BOX(01,col -1, ht, col + width, 13)
```

```
choice = ACHOICE(row, col+1, ht-1, col + width - 1, screens, .T.,
            .T., choice)

RESTORE SCREEN FROM temp_scr
IF ESC()
   result = cur_screen
ELSE
   result = MAX( 01, choice )       && screen_no can never = 0
ENDIF

RETURN result
```

• STAT_LINE()

```
PROGRAM       AA_STLIN.PRG
Function(s)   STAT_LINE()
Purpose       Displays record status on Line 24
Conventions   called by THE_USUAL()
Syntax        STAT_LINE()
Parameters    none
Example       STAT_LINE()
Assumes       a file is in use
Side Effects  none
Returns       0
Calls         PAD()
```

```
FUNCTION STAT_LINE

PRIVATE rcount_msg, rstat_msg, boundary_msg
rc_msg = " Record Number " + PAD( STRINT( RECNO() ) + "/" + ;
         STRINT( LASTREC() ), 21)
rstat_msg = IF(DELETED(), "<Deleted>", "          ")
DO CASE
   CASE LASTREC() = 0 .AND. !is_append
      boundary_msg = "EMPTY"
      rcount_msg = SPACE(21)
   CASE EOF()
      boundary_msg = IF( is_append, "<new>", "<eof>" )
      rcount_msg = SPACE(21)
   CASE BOF()
      boundary_msg = "<bof>"
      rcount_msg = rc_msg
   CASE is_append
      boundary_msg = "<new>"
      rcount_msg = SPACE(21)
      is_append = .F.
   OTHERWISE
      boundary_msg = "      "
      rcount_msg = rc_msg
ENDCASE


@ 24,00
@ 24,00 SAY rcount_msg
@ 24,40 SAY boundary_msg
@ 24,61 SAY rstat_msg                 && status line is current
```

```
force_rec = .F.
RETURN 0
```

• THE_USUAL()

```
PROGRAM        AA_USUAL.PRG
Function(s)    THE_USUAL()
Purpose        General purpose file maintenance
Conventions    One of the most powerful udfs
               A complete file maintenance routine -
               multiple files, multiple screens, elaborate
               validations and custom functions required by
               the given application only.
               Because of the file naming scheme and
               macro substitution, this loop can control
               many different multi-file applications.
Syntax         THE_USUAL([array1, array2])
Parameters     array1 - prompts for extra udfs to add
               array2 - udfs to execute
Example        THE_USUAL(so_cues, so_udfs)
Assumes        A great deal. Details below.
Side Effects   crash if not all conventions adhered to
Returns        .T.
Calls          ACOPY(),BROWSER(),COUNT_EM(),GET_STD(),
               GO_BOT,GO_TOP,L_MENU(),MCOUNT(),MENU_ORD()
               PGDN(),PGUP(),POP_MSG(),QUERY(),READ_MEMO()
               RPL(),SEARCH(),SELE_SCR(),STAT_LINE(),
               U_HELP
Macro calls    udf_scr - display screen (required)
               udf_key - get key (required)
               udf_fld - get remaining fields (required)
               udf_say - display a record (required)
               udf_add - default = "GET_STD(.T.)"
               udf_upd - default = "GET_STD(.F.)"
               udf_calc - default = "COUNT_EM()"
               udf_qry - default = "QUERY()"
               udf_rpl - default = "RPL()"
               udf_help - default = "U_HELP"
               udf_brow - default = "XBROWSER"
               udf_memo - optional Memoedit customizer
               udf_zoom - only if file can be Zoomed
```

```
FUNCTION THE_USUAL

PARAMETERS so_cues, so_udfs
PRIVATE reply, x, choice, memos, temp, is_append, ;
         memo_pos, zoom_pos, scr_pos, first_avail, ;
         cur_dbf, temp_scr, dead_recs
temp = PCOUNT()                     && how many params passed?
* Define some hot keys which are not on the menu. These have to
* be hot-keyed because Clipper cannot see them through the
* MENU command. Note that two keys are assigned to both GO TOP
* and GO BOTTOM - depending on your viewpoint, a redundancy or
* a feature.
KEYS_ON()
IF TYPE("udf_help") != "C"          && could be false or undefined
   udf_help = "U_HELP"              && if so, go with the minimum
ENDIF
SET KEY 28 TO &udf_help             && MENU won't see F1
IF TYPE("udf_brow") != "U" .OR. EMPTY(udf_brow)
   udf_brow = .F.                   && to pass in turn to Browse
ENDIF
IF TYPE("udf_memo") != "U" .OR. EMPTY(udf_memo)
   udf_memo = .F.                   && to pass in turn to Memoedit
ENDIF
zoomable = (no_kids > 00)           && declared in calling program
multi_scr = (no_screens > 01)       && declared in calling program
reply = .T.                         && our return value
x = .T.                             && a throw-away value
is_append = .F.                     && are we appending?
repaint = .T.                       && should we paint the screen?
choice = 01     && menu default
memo_pos = 00   && column location of Memo prompt
zoom_pos  = 00                      && column location of Zoom prompt
scr_pos = 00    && column location of Screen prompt
first_avail = 10                    && 9 items on no-frills menu
cur_dbf = ALIAS()                   && so we know where home is
dead_recs = .F.                     && have we dusted anybody?
is_memo = (MCOUNT() > 00)           && are there any memo fields?
DO CASE                             && deal with side orders if any
   CASE TYPE("so_cues") = "U"
      extras = 00
   CASE TYPE("so_cues") = "A"       && an array of extra commands
      extras = LEN(so_cues)
   OTHERWISE
      extras = 01
ENDCASE
* now we know how large the array should be
size = 09 + IF( is_memo, 01, 00 ) + ;
         IF( multi_scr, 01, 00 ) + ;
```

```
         IF( zoomable, 01, 00 ) + ;
         extras
DECLARE choices[size]
choices[01] = " Find "                && all the usual commands
choices[02] = " Add "
choices[03] = " Update "
choices[04] = " Browse "
choices[05] = " Calc "
choices[06] = " Order "
choices[07] = " Print "
choices[08] = " Query "
choices[09] = " Delete "
next_pos = first_avail                && in case we add to the 9
IF is_memo
   memo_pos = next_pos
   choices[memo_pos] = " Memo "
   next_pos = next_pos + 1
ENDIF
IF no_screens > 01
   scr_pos = next_pos
   choices[scr_pos] = " Screen # "
   next_pos = next_pos + 1
ENDIF
IF zoomable
   zoom_pos = next_pos
   choices[zoom_pos] = IF(TYPE("kcues") = "C", kcues, " Zoom ")
   next_pos = next_pos + 1
ENDIF
IF extras = 01
   extra_pos = next_pos               && into the next available
   choices[extra_pos] = so_cues       && array position
ELSEIF extras > 01
   ACOPY(so_cues,choices,next_pos)    && copy array of cues into choices
ENDIF
DO WHILE .T.
   IF repaint
      x = &udf_scr                    && draw the screen
      repaint = .F.
   ENDIF
   is_append = .F.
   nested = .F.
   x = &udf_say
   STAT_LINE()
   choice = L_MENU(choice, choices) && menu the command array
   DO CASE
      CASE choice = 00                && escape pressed
         IF ESC()
            IF nested                 && detect ESC from a subcommand
               LOOP
```

```
         ELSE                          && as opposed to ESC from main
            reply = .T.
            EXIT
         ENDIF
      ENDIF
   CASE PGDN()                         && Next record
      SKIP
   CASE PGUP()                         && Previous record
      SKIP -1
   CASE choice = 01                    && Find
      nested = .T.                     && permit escape
      SEARCH(xkeys, xcues, xpics)&& names, not objects
   CASE choice = 02                    && Add
      add_one = .T.
      is_append = .T.
      KEYS_OFF()
      x = &udf_add
      KEYS_ON()
   CASE choice = 03                    && Update
      is_append = .F.
      add_one = .F.
      KEYS_OFF()
      x = &udf_upd                     && execute custom udf
      KEYS_ON()
   CASE choice = 04                    && Browse w/wo udf
      KEYS_OFF()
      BROWSER(03,00,23,79, udf_brow)
      KEYS_ON()
   CASE choice = 05                    && Calc routine
      x = &udf_calc
   CASE choice = 06                    && Order routine
      MENU_ORD(xcues)
   CASE choice = 07                    && Print routine
      x = &udf_prt
   CASE choice = 08                    && Query routine
      x = &udf_qry
   CASE choice = 09                    && Any delete sets
      IF DELETED()                     && dead_recs true
         dead_recs = .T.               && even if record is
         RECALL                        && recalled. not a bug,
      ELSE                             && a feature! allows
         DELETE                        && packing at a later
      ENDIF                            && time. (del, recall)
* There may be pages and/or memos and/or zooms and/or custom funcs.
* It's relative from here on in, handled by offset.
* If no_screens > 0, increment screen number
* If memo_pos > 0, call read_memo()
* If zoom_pos > 0 and chosen, do zoom
* If extras were passed, deal with them similarly
```

```
      CASE choice = scr_pos          && change screen
         x = SELE_SCR(screen_no)
         IF x != screen_no
            screen_no = x
            paint = .T.
         ENDIF
      CASE choice = memo_pos
         * READ_MEMO() will automatically menu
         * the memo fields if there are more than one.
         * everything is passed for you.
         KEYS_OFF()
         READ_MEMO("", mtr, mtc, mbr, mbc, .T., udf_memo)
         KEYS_ON()
      CASE choice = zoom_pos         && if there are children
         SAVE SCREEN TO temp_scr
         @ 00,00                     && clean menu line for new menu
         x = &udf_zoom               && execute the zoom udf
         SELECT &cur_dbf
         RESTORE SCREEN FROM temp_scr
      CASE extras = 01               && if only 1 extra function
         x = &so_udfs                && execute it
      OTHERWISE                      && execute selected udf
         udf_ptr = LEN(choices) - first_avail
         func = so_udfs[udf_ptr]     && grab its name
         x = &func                   && execute it
   ENDCASE
ENDDO
IF dead_recs
   DUST_EM()
ENDIF
KEYS_OFF()
RETURN reply
```

- **KEYS_OFF()**

```
FUNCTION KEYS_OFF

SET KEY 31 TO
SET KEY 30 TO
SET KEY 29 TO
SET KEY 23 TO
SET KEY 28 TO  && turn help off
RETURN 01
```

- **KEYS_ON()**

```
FUNCTION KEYS_ON

SET KEY 31 TO GO_TOP                    && ^Home  or  ^PgUp
SET KEY 29 TO GO_TOP
SET KEY 30 TO GO_BOT                    && ^End  or  ^PgDn
SET KEY 23 TO GO_BOT
SET KEY 28 TO &udf_help                 && help back on
RETURN 01
```

• U_HELP

```
PROCEDURE U_HELP

PARAMETERS x, y, z
POP_MSG("Help is for wimps and hairless dogs")
RETURN
```

```
* Clipper & linker can't see SET KEY procs
EXTERNAL GO_TOP, GO_BOT, POP_MSG, QUERY, RPL, GET_STD, COUNT_EM
```

• TRANSFER()

```
PROGRAM        AA_XFER.PRG
Function(s)    TRANSFER()
Purpose        transfers records to another table
Conventions    No params, on the theory that if you
               know what to transfer where,
               you don't need this routine.
Syntax         TRANSFER()
Parameters     none
Example        TRANSFER()
Assumes        files have at least some fields in common
Side Effects   although confirmation is required,
               could trash data by over-writing a file.
Returns        True if successful.
Calls          MSG(), GET_FILE(), EMPTY()
```

```
FUNCTION TRANSFER

PRIVATE dummy, choice, source, target, row
DECLARE array[2]
array[1] = " Add records to the file "
array[2]= " Over-write existing records "
dummy  = .F.
choice  = 01
row = 02
source = ""
target = ""
DO WHILE .T.
   MSG("Select the source file",0)
   source = GET_FILE("*.DBF")
   IF EMPTY(source)
      reply = .F.
      EXIT
   ENDIF
   MSG("Select the target file",0)
   target = GET_FILE("*.DBF")
   IF EMPTY(target)
      reply = .F.
      EXIT
   ENDIF
   USE &target
   IF LASTREC() > 0
      choice = L_MENU( choice, array, dummy, row )
```

```
      IF choice = 00
         LOOP
      ELSEIF choice = 2
         IF VERIFY( "Over-write (e.g. destroy) " + target )
            ZAP
         ELSE
            LOOP
         ENDIF
      ENDIF
   ENDIF
   MSG( "Now transferring data" )
   APPEND FROM &source
   @ row,00
ENDDO
RETURN .T.
```

• UNIQUE()

```
PROGRAM        AA_UNIQ.PRG
Function(s)    UNIQUE()
Purpose        Ensure that indexed data is unique
Conventions    use in a VALID clause
               where uniqueness is required.
Syntax         @ row, col GET memvar VALID ;
               UNIQUE(memvar,file)
Parameters     memvar - item to check
               file - optional file
Example        @ row, col GET mCUST_CODE VALID ;
               UNIQUE(mCUST_CODE)
Assumes        file is open and ready, if passed.
Side Effects crash if files aren't ready
Returns        True if memvar is unique.
Calls
```

```
FUNCTION UNIQUE

PARAMETER target
temp  = RECNO()
reply = .T.
SEEK target
IF FOUND()
   IF RECNO() != temp
      ?? CHR(7)
      reply = .F.
   ENDIF
ENDIF
RETURN reply
```

- XBROWSER()

```
PROGRAM        AA_XBROW.PRG
Function(s)  XBROWSER()
Purpose        Inner function called by DBEDIT()
Conventions  Default function. Customize to suit your
defaults
               or over-ride call by BROWSE() by passing in a udf
Syntax         "XBROWSER" - stored as a string passed to
DBEDIT()
Parameters   mode, i - passed automatically by DBEDIT()
Example        udf = "XBROWSER"
Assumes        is_append, any_append, fields, pictures
               (fields and pictures are arrays manufactured
               in BROWSER() if not passed as params)
Side Effects given all the freedom, hard to predict
Returns        a number from 0 to 4
Calls
```

```
FUNCTION XBROWSER

PARAMETERS mode, fld_ptr
PRIVATE ret_val, esc, home_key, end_key, ctrl_home, ctrl_end, ;
   ctrl_pgdn, ctrl_pgdn, right, left, down, up, ;
   right_key, left_key, down_key, up_key, ;
   do_repaint, no_repaint, ins_blank, cur_field, ;
   idle, bof, eof, empty, exception, m_row, m_col, exit
exit = 00
ret_val = 01
keystroke = LASTKEY()
esc_key = CHR(27)
home_key = CHR(01)
end_key  = CHR(06)
chome_key = CHR(29)
cend_key = CHR(23)
cpdn_key = CHR(30)
cpup_key  = CHR(31)
right_key = CHR(04)
left_key  = CHR(19)
down_key  = CHR(24)
up_key  = CHR(05)
enter_key = CHR(13)
enter  = 13
```

```
esc       = 27
home      = 01
ctrl_home = 29
ctrl_end  = 23
ctrl_pgup = 31
ctrl_pgdn = 30
right = 04
left  = 19
down  = 24
up    = 05
pgup  = 18
pgdn  = 03
idle = 00
bof  = 01
eof  = 02
empty = 03
exception = 04
do_repaint = 02
no_repaint = 01
ins_blank  = 03
m_row = ROW()
m_col = COL()
* get fieldspec into normal variable
cur_field = fields[fld_ptr]
IF prev_rec != RECNO()              && record pointer has been moved
   prev_rec = RECNO()
   force_rec = .T.
ENDIF
DO CASE
   CASE mode = idle
      IF CHR(keystroke) $ move_chrs .OR. force_rec
         STAT_LINE()
      ENDIF
   CASE mode = bof
      IF is_append                  && done append, refresh if any new
         ret_val = IF(any_append, do_repaint, ins_blank)
         is_append = .F.
         any_append = .F.
      ELSE
         STAT_LINE()
      ENDIF
      force_rec = .T.
   CASE mode = eof
      IF is_append                  && append mode active
         IF keystroke = down .AND. !EOF()
            ret_val = ins_blank
         ELSE
            IF keystroke = ctrl_pgdn
               ret_val = IF(any_append, do_repaint, ins_blank)
```

```
            is_append = .F.
            any_append = .F.
            ELSE                    && downs for days
               IF force_rec
                  STAT_LINE()
               ENDIF
            ENDIF
         ENDIF
      ELSE
         IF keystroke = down     && enter append mode
            ret_val = ins_blank
            is_append = .T.
         ELSE
            STAT_LINE()
      ENDIF
   ENDIF
   force_rec = .T.
CASE mode = empty
   IF keystroke = down           && enter append mode
      ret_val = ins_blank
      is_append = .T.
      force_rec = .T.
   ELSE                          && just display status
      STAT_LINE()
   ENDIF
CASE mode = exception            && keystroke exception
   DO CASE
      CASE ESC()                 && quit dbedit
         ret_val = exit
      CASE DEL() .AND. !EOF() .AND. LASTREC() != 0
         IF DELETED()
            RECALL
         ELSE
            DELETE
         ENDIF
         STAT_LINE()
      CASE ENTER() .OR. INS() .OR. IS_DATA(keystroke) .AND. ;
         (is_append .OR. (!EOF() .AND. LASTREC() != 0))
         IF INS()
            is_append = .T.
         ENDIF
         IF IS_VIRTUAL(fld_ptr)  && nyet edit virtuals!
            ret_val = no_repaint
         ELSE                    && edit the current field
            ntx_expr = INDEXKEY(0)
            IF !EMPTY(ntx_expr)  && expand for comparison after edit
               ntx_eval = &ntx_expr
            ENDIF
            IF keystroke != 13   && forward data keystroke to GET
```

```
   KEYBOARD CHR(keystroke)
ENDIF
IF TYPE(cur_field) = "M"
   READ_MEMO(cur_field)
ELSE
   * Look for an array of VALIDS. Invent if necessary
   IF TYPE("valids") = "A"
         valid_exp = valids[fld_ptr]
      IF EMPTY(valid_exp)
             valid_exp = ".T."
       ENDIF
   ELSE
         valid_exp = ".T."
  ENDIF
 * Look for an array of pictures. Invent if necessary
 IF TYPE("pictures") = "A"
        pict_str = pictures[fld_ptr]
  IF EMPTY(pict_str)
       pict_str = GEN_PIC(cur_field)
   ENDIF
  ELSE
    pict_str = GEN_PIC(cur_field)
  ENDIF
   IF  !is_append    && it must be an edit
   get_data = &cur_field
  ELSE
   * Look for an array of defaults.  Invent if necessary
   IF TYPE("defaults") = "A"
         default = defaults[fld_ptr]
      IF EMPTY(default)
            default = BLANK(cur_field)
       ENDIF
   ELSE
        default = BLANK(cur_field)
   ENDIF
    get_data = default
 ENDIF
  * up and down arrows will exit read
   SET KEY up TO clear_gets
   SET KEY down TO clear_gets
    @ m_row, m_col GET get_data ;
   PICTURE pict_str ;
   VALID &valid_exp
READ_IT()
keystroke = LASTKEY()
* release keys
SET KEY up TO
SET KEY down TO
IF UPDATED()
```

```
                IF is_append
                  APPEND BLANK
                     any_append = .T.
                  ENDIF
                REPLACE &cur_field WITH get_data
                KEYBOARD right_key
           ENDIF
        ENDIF
        ret_val = no_repaint    && continue DBEDIT()
     ENDIF
     IF !EMPTY(ntx_expr) .AND. !is_append
        * file indexed..check for altered key field
        IF ntx_eval != (&ntx_expr)
           ret_val = do_repaint
        ENDIF
     ENDIF
     IF ret_val != do_repaint   && certain keys move cursor after
        DO CASE                 && edit if no refresh
           CASE keystroke = up
                IF is_append    && done append, refresh if new
                     ret_val = IF(any_append, do_repaint, ins_blank)
                      is_append = .F.
                      any_append = .F.
               ELSE
                  KEYBOARD up_key
               ENDIF
           CASE keystroke = PgUp
                IF is_append
                     * no more append mode..refresh if new records
                      ret_val = IF(any_append, do_repaint, ins_blank)
                       is_append = .F.
                      any_append = .F.
               ELSE
                   KEYBOARD up_key
               ENDIF
           CASE keystroke = down
               KEYBOARD down_key
           CASE keystroke = pgdn .AND. !is_append
               KEYBOARD down_key
           CASE keystroke = enter
              KEYBOARD right_key
        ENDCASE
     ENDIF
  ENDCASE
ENDCASE
RETURN ret_val
```

Chapter 15

Logical Functions

- AND — returns true if all conditions or functions stored in an array return true.
- CASE_OF — translates input into one of a series of outputs. Equivalent to a DO CASE, but works as a function.
- IS_ARRAY — returns true if the parameter passed is an array.
- IS_BTW — determines if an input is between two boundaries.
- IS_CHAR — returns true if the parameter passed is character.
- IS_DATE — returns true if the parameter passed is a date.
- IS_DEF — returns true if the parameter passed has been defined.
- IS_DATA — returns true if the character input is alpha or numeric.
- IS_EVEN — returns true if a number is even.
- IS_FIELD — returns true if the parameter passed is the name of a field.
- IS_IN — returns true if a variable is "in" another. This function works with strings or arrays.
- IS_INT — returns true if the parameter passed is an integer.
- IS_KEY — returns true if the expression passed is an active index key.
- IS_LOGIC — returns true if the parameter passed is a logical.
- IS_MEMO — returns true if the parameter passed is memo.
- IS_NUM — returns true if the parameter passed is numeric..
- IS_OP —returns true if the string passed is a relational operator.
- IS_OPEN — returns true if the file passed is open.
- IS_PHONE — returns true if the parameter passed is a valid phone number.
- IS_TIME — returns true if the string passed is a valid time.
- IS_TYPE — compares two inputs, returning true if they are the same data type.
- IS_VIRTUAL — returns true if the expression passed in is not a field. Protects against attempting to edit a virtual field (e.g. "qty*price").

- NOR — checks an array of conditions, returning true if any condition is false. Equivalent to Not Or
- OR — checks an array of conditions, returning true if any condition is true.
- UN_DEF — returns true if the parameter passed has not been defined.
- VERIFY — pops up any message with OK and Cancel buttons, returning true if OK is selected.

• AND()

```
PROGRAM       AA_AND.PRG
Function(s)   AND()
Purpose       Check an array full of conditions for True
Conventions   array must exist. Strings must be valid.
Syntax        AND(array)
Parameters    array - of strings containing conditions
Example       AND(array)
Assume        all strings can be macro-expanded without
crashing
Side Effects can crash on bad data
Returns       True only if all conditions result in True
Calls
```

```
FUNCTION AND

PARAMETERS array
PRIVATE i, size
size = LEN( array_1 )
FOR i = 1 TO size
   Condition = array_1[ i ]
      IF TYPE("condition") = "C"
         IF !&condition
         RETURN .F.
      ENDIF
   ENDIF
NEXT
RETURN .T.
```

• CASE_OF()

```
PROGRAM        AA_CASOF.PRG
Function(s)    CASE_OF()
Purpose        return one of a small set of values to complex
               to express conveniently in nested if's
Conventions    useful in report forms, lists etc.
Syntax         CASE_OF(target,array1,array2)
Parameters     target - item to represent
               array1 - object to search
               array2 - translation table
Example        CASE_OF(claim_code, code_ra, xlate_ra)
Assumes        existence of both arrays
Side Effects   bad data can crash
Returns        array element from array2 or SPACE(0)
Calls          ASCAN()
```

```
FUNCTION CASE_OF

PARAMETERS target, codes, expansions
PRIVATE where, reply
where = ASCAN( target, codes )
reply = ""
IF where > 0
   reply = expansions[where]
ENDIF
RETURN reply
```

• IS_ARRAY()

```
PROGRAM       AA_ISRA.PRG
Function(s)   IS_ARRAY()
Purpose       Determine if data is an array
Conventions
Syntax        IS_ARRAY(memvar)
Parameters    memvar - any valid data
Example       IS_ARRAY(main_opts) ... probably True
Assumes       existence of memvar
Side Effects  none
Returns       True if memvar is type A
Calls         nothing
```

```
FUNCTION IS_ARRAY

PARAMETER memvar
RETURN ( TYPE( "memvar" ) = "A" )
```

• IS_BTW()

```
PROGRAM        AA_ISBTW.PRG
Function(s)    IS_BTW()
Purpose        Returns true if target is between low_val and
               high_val
Conventions    any data type. INCLUSIVE True.
Syntax         IS_BTW(    arget,low_val,high_val)
Parameters     target - item to check
               low_val - lower range
               high_val - upper range
Example        IS_BTW("G","A","Z") returns true
Assumes        target and ?bound are the same data type
Side Effects   crash on bad data
Returns        True if between, else false
Calls
```

```
FUNCTION IS_BTW

PARAMETERS target, low_val, high_val
IF PCOUNT()  03
   RETURN .F.
ENDIF
RETURN ( target >= low_val .AND. target <= high_val )
```

• IS_CHAR()

```
PROGRAM         AA_ISCHR.PRG
Function(s)     IS_CHAR()
Purpose         Determine if data is type character
Conventions     ar must be valid data
Syntax          IS_CHAR(memvar)
Parameters      memvar - object to check
Example         IS_CHAR(56) returns .F.
Assumes         validity of data
Side Effects    none
Returns         True if TYPE("memvar") = "C"
Calls
```

```
FUNCTION IS_CHAR

PARAMETER memvar
RETURN ( TYPE( "memvar" ) = "C" )
```

• IS_DATE()

```
PROGRAM       AA_ISDAT.PRG
Function(s)   IS_DATE()
Purpose       Determine if data is type date
Conventions
Syntax        IS_DATE(memvar)
Parameters    memvar - any valid data
Example       IS_DATE("Thursday") returns .F.
Assumes       nothing
Side Effects  none
Returns       True only if memvar is type D
Calls
```

```
FUNCTION IS_DATE

PARAMETER memvar
RETURN ( TYPE( "memvar" ) = "D" )
```

• IS_DEF()

```
PROGRAM        AA_ISDEF.PRG
Function(s)    IS_DEF()
Purpose        Returns true if memvar is defined
Conventions
Syntax         IS_DEF(memvar)
Parameters     memvar - name of memory variable
Example        IS_DEF("X")
Assumes        nothing
Side Effects
Returns        True if TYPE("memvar") != "U"
Calls
```

```
FUNCTION IS_DEF

PARAMETER memvar
RETURN ( TYPE( "memvar" ) != "U" )
```

• IS_DATA()

```
ROGRAM        AA_ISDTA.PRG
Function(s)   IS_DATA()
Purpose       Return true if key pressed is a data keystroke
Conventions   used polling keyboard, to act on arrows but
              recognize data
Syntax        IS_DATA(key_no)
Parameters    key_no - LASTKEY()
Example       k = LASTKEY()
              IF IS_DATA(k)...
Assumes       nothing
Side Effects  none
Returns       True if the last key was a data keystroke
Calls
```

```
FUNCTION IS_DATA

PARAMETER key_hit
reply = ( key_hit >= 32 .AND. key_hit < 249 ;
        .AND. key_hit <> 219 .AND. CHR(key_hit) <> ";" )
reply = ( key_hit = 32 .AND. key_hit  249 ;
        .AND. key_hit  219 .AND. CHR(key_hit)  ";" )
RETURN reply
```

• IS_EVEN()

```
PROGRAM       AA_ISEVN.PRG
Function(s)   IS_EVEN()
Purpose       Determine if a number is odd or even
Conventions   doesn't check data type
Syntax        IS_EVEN(number)
Parameters    number - numeric expression you want checked
Example       IS_EVEN(3 * 5) ... returns .F.
Assumes       validity of numeric expression passed
Side Effects  crash on bad data
Returns       True if the number is evenly divisible by 2
Calls         MOD()
```

```
FUNCTION IS_EVEN

PARAMETER number
RETURN (MOD(number,2) = 0)
```

• IS_FIELD()

```
PROGRAM       AA_ISFLD.PRG
Function(s)   IS_FIELD()
Purpose       Determines if memvar is a field
Conventions
Syntax        IS_FIELD(memvar)
Parameters    memvar - name of object you want to check
              file   - optional, if you don't mean current fi:
Example       IS_FIELD("cust_code")
Assumes       nothing
Side Effects none
Returns       True if memvar is a field in current file
Calls
```

```
FUNCTION IS_FLD

PARAMETERS field, file
PRIVATE temp, cur_file, record_no, answer
field = UPPER(field)
temp = PCOUNT()
cur_file = ALIAS()
record_no = RECNO()
answer = .F.
IF temp > 1
   SELECT &file
ENDIF

FOR i = 1 TO FCOUNT()
   IF FIELD( i ) = field
      answer = .T.
      EXIT
   ENDIF
NEXT
SELECT &cur_file
GO record_no
RETURN answer
```

- IS_IN()

```
PROGRAM        AA_IN.PRG
Function(s)    IS_IN()
Purpose         Returns True if str1 is in str2
Conventions    data could be char, memo or array
Syntax         IS_IN(str1, str2)
Parameters     str1 - item to search for
               str2 - object to search
Example        IS_IN("is a", "This is a string")... returns .T.
Assumes
Side Effects
Returns        True if str1 is in str2@CODE HEAD END = Calls
```

```
FUNCTION IS_IN

PARAMETERS str1, str2
PRIVATE reply
reply = .F.
DO CASE
   CASE TYPE("str2") = "A"
      reply = ( ASCAN( str2, str1 ) > 0 )
   CASE TYPE("str2") $ "CM"
      reply = ( str1 $ str2 )
   OTHERWISE
      CHR(07)
      reply = .F.
ENDCASE
RETURN reply
```

• IS_INT()

```
PROGRAM       AA_ISINT.PRG
Function(s)   IS_INT()
Purpose       Determine if a number is an integer
Conventions
Syntax        IS_INT(number)
Parameters    number - quantity to check
Example       IS_INT(5.41) returns .F.
Assumes       nothing
Side Effects  none
Returns       True if number is an integer
Calls         MOD()
```

```
FUNCTION IS_INT

PARAMETER number
PRIVATE temp
temp = INT(number)
RETURN (MOD(number,temp) = 0)
```

• IS_KEY()

```
PROGRAM        AA_ISKEY.PRG
Function(s)    IS_KEY()
Purpose        Determine if a field is a key field
Conventions    assumes if it is, its index must be open
Syntax         IS_KEY(fieldname[, array]))
Parameters     fieldname - object you wish to check
               array     - of key values if declared already
Example        IS_KEY("city") probably returns .F.
Assumes        validity of data. A file is open and Indexed.
Side Effects
Returns        True if fieldname is one of the active indexes.
Calls
```

```
FUNCTION IS_KEY

PARAMETERS key_expr, key_ra
PRIVATE i, max_open, position
i = 1
max_open = 7
position = 0
IF TYPE("key_ra") = "U"              && build the array if required
   DECLARE key_ra[max_open]
   AFILL( key_ra, "" )
   FOR i = 1 TO max_open
      IF !EMPTY( INDEXKEY(i) )
         key_ra[i] = INDEXKEY(i)
      ELSE
         EXIT
      ENDIF
   NEXT
ENDIF
RETURN ( ASCAN( key_ra, key_expr ) > 0 )
```

• IS_LOGIC()

```
PROGRAM        AA_ISLOG.PRG
Function(s)    IS_LOGIC()
Purpose        Determine if a value is logical
Conventions
Syntax         IS_LOGIC(memvar)
Parameters     memvar - object to check
Example        IS_LOGIC("XXX") probably returns .F.
Assumes        nothing
Side Effects   none
Returns        True if memvar is type L
Calls
```

```
FUNCTION IS_LOGIC

PARAMETER exp
RETURN ( TYPE( "exp" ) = "L" )
```

• IS_MEMO()

```
PROGRAM        AA_ISMMO.PRG
Function(s)    IS_MEMO()
Purpose        Determine if data is a memo field
Conventions
Syntax         IS_MEMO(memvar)
Parameters     memvar - any data type
Example        IS_MEMO(cust_code)... probably returns .F.
Assumes        valid data is passed in
Side Effects   could crash on invalid input
Returns        True only if memvar is type M
Calls
```

```
FUNCTION IS_MEMO

PARAMETER memvar
RETURN ( TYPE( "memvar" ) = "M" )
```

• IS_NUM()

```
PROGRAM        AA_ISNUM.PRG
Function(s)    IS_NUM()
Purpose        Determine if data is numeric
Conventions
Syntax         IS_NUM(memvar)
Parameters     memvar - any type of data
Example        IS_NUM(34.56) ... returns True
Assumes        nothing
Side Effects   none
Returns        True only if memvar is type N
Calls
```

```
FUNCTION IS_NUM

PARAMETER memvar
RETURN ( TYPE( "memvar" ) = "N" )
```

• IS_OP()

```
PROGRAM        AA_ISOP.PRG
Function(s)    IS_OP()
Purpose        determine if a string is an operator
Conventions    used to parse strings
Syntax         IS_OP(string)
Parameters     string - operator
Example        IS_OP("!=") returns .T.
Assumes        nothing
Side Effects   none
Returns        True only if string $ "=,!=,>=,<=,<>,or !$"
Calls          nothing
```

```
FUNCTION IS_OP

PARAMETER string
PRIVATE i, size
RETURN string $ "!=<=>=!$"
```

• IS_OPEN()

```
PROGRAM        AA_ISOPN.PRG
Function(s)    IS_OPEN()
Purpose        Determine if a file is already open
Conventions
Syntax         IS_OPEN(file)
Parameters     file - name or alias of file to check
Example        IS_OPEN("CUSTOMER")
Assumes        nothing
Side Effects   none
Returns        True if file is already open
Calls
```

```
FUNCTION IS_OPEN

PARAMETER file
PRIVATE i, reply
i = 01
reply = .F.
max_dbfs = 10
file = UPPER(file)
FOR i = 1 TO max_dbfs
   IF ALIAS(i) = file
      reply = .T.
      EXIT
   ENDIF
NEXT
RETURN reply
```

• IS_PHONE()

```
PROGRAM        AA_ISFON.PRG
Function(s)    IS_PHONE()
Purpose        VALIDate a phone number
Conventions
               Ranges are: area code: 2-9  0-1  0-9
               Exchange: 1st digit must be 2-9
               this function expects 10 digits input
               no trapping for parentheses, spaces or dash
               on the assumption you'll use
               PICT "@R (###) 999-9999"
               The # signs permit blanks, the 9's do not.
Syntax         IS_PHONE(string)
Parameters     string - a phone number stored as a string
Example        GET m_phone VALID(IS_PHONE(m_phone))
               IS_PHONE("9891234578") returns .F.
Assumes        phone number conventions
Side Effects   none
Returns        .T. if string conforms to phone number mask
Calls          nothing
```

```
FUNCTION IS_PHONE

PARAMETER ph_string
PRIVATE answer
answer = .T.
DO CASE
   CASE VAL( SUBSTR( ph_string, 1, 1 ) ) < 2
      answer = .F.
   CASE VAL( SUBSTR( ph_string, 2, 1 ) ) > 1
      answer = .F.
   CASE VAL( SUBSTR( ph_string, 4, 1 ) ) < 2
      answer = .F.
ENDCASE
RETURN answer
```

• IS_TIME()

```
PROGRAM        AA_ISTIM.PRG
Function(s)    IS_TIME()
Purpose        Determine if a time string is a valid time
Conventions    24 hour clock (e.g. 24:59:59 highest value)
Syntax         IS_TIME(string)
Parameters     string - format "99:99:99"
Example        IS_TIME("99:44:00") returns .F.
Assumes        the hour after midnight is 24:##
Side Effects   none
Returns        True if string conforms to time rules
Calls          nothing
```

```
FUNCTION IS_TIME

PARAMETER time_str
hours   = VAL( time_str )
minutes = VAL( SUBSTR( time_str, 3 ) )
seconds = VAL( SUBSTR( time_str, 6 ) )
RETURN ( hours < 24 .AND. minutes < 61 .AND. seconds < 61 )
```

• IS_TYPE()

```
PROGRAM       AA_ISTYP.PRG
Function(s)   IS_TYPE()
Purpose       Determine if two values are same data type
Conventions   both parameters must be passed
Syntax        IS_TYPE(value1, value2)
Parameters    value1 - first object
              value2 - second object
Example       IS_TYPE(05,188.1) returns .T.
Assumes
Side Effects  Crash on unknown data
Returns       true if both values are the same data type
Calls
```

```
FUNCTION IS_TYPE

PARAMETERS exp1, exp2
PRIVATE t1, t2
RETURN ( TYPE("t1") = TYPE("t2") )
```

• IS_VIRTUAL()

```
PROGRAM        AA_ISVRT.PRG
Function(s)    IS_VIRTUAL()
Purpose        Determine if a field is virtual or physical
Conventions    used to stifle editing of a virtual field in
               BROWSER() - type udfs
Syntax         IS_VIRTUAL(pointer)
Parameters     pointer - 2nd param passed in from DBEDIT()
Example        IS_VIRTUAL(02)
Assumes        virtuals, if declared, is either an
               array[f_size] or .f.
Side Effects   none
Returns        True if the virtuals[pointer] is True
Calls          nothing
```

```
FUNCTION IS_VIRTUAL

PARAMETER pointer
PRIVATE result
result = .F.                          && probably not virtual
IF TYPE("virtuals") = "A"             && they declared the array
   result = virtuals[pointer]         && so it might be virtual
ENDIF
RETURN result
```

• NOR()

```
PROGRAM        AA_NOR.PRG
Function(s)    NOR()
Purpose        Determine if any condition in an array is
True
Conventions    (Neither...nor) - any True returns False
Syntax         NOR(array)
Parameters     array - containing strings to VALIDate
Example        ra[01] = "!EOF()"
               ra[02] = "!BOF()"
               result = NOR(ra)
Assumes        existence of array and validity of expressions
               in it
Side Effects   crash on bad data
Returns        True only if all conditions in the array are
False.
Calls          nothing
```

```
FUNCTION NOR

PARAMETER array
PRIVATE i, reply, size
reply = .T.
i = 1
size = LEN( array )
FOR i = 1 TO size
   condition = array[ i ]
   IF TYPE("condition") = "C"
      IF &condition
         reply = .F.
         EXIT
      ENDIF
   ENDIF
NEXT
RETURN reply
```

• OR()

```
PROGRAM        AA_OR.PRG
Function(s)    OR()
Purpose        Check an array full of VALID conditions
Conventions    Any True condition returns True
Syntax         OR(array)
Parameters     array - full of conditions
Example        OR(array)
Assumes        all array elements are character or ignored
Side Effects   crashes on bad data or non-linked udfs
               (hidden)
Returns        True if any element returns True
Calls          nothing
```

```
FUNCTION OR

PARAMETER array
PRIVATE i, size, reply
i = 01
size = LEN(array)
reply = .F.
FOR i = 1 TO size
   condition = array[ i ]
   IF TYPE("condition") = "C"
      IF &condition
         RETURN .T.
      ENDIF
   ENDIF
NEXT
RETURN reply
```

• UN_DEF

```
PROGRAM       AA_UNDEF.PRG
Function(s)   UN_DEF()
Purpose       Determine if a variable has been defined
Conventions   pass the name of the data in. If you could
              pass the data, you wouldn't need the udf.
Syntax        UN_DEF(memvar)
Parameters    memvar - any string
Example       UN_DEF("ZXCV") ... probably returns .T.
Assumes       validity of data passed in
Side Effects  crash on bad data
Returns       True if macro-referenced data is type "U"
Calls         nothing
```

```
FUNCTION UN_DEF

PARAMETER memvar
RETURN ( TYPE( "&memvar" ) = "U" )  && point to data
```

• VERIFY()

```
PROGRAM        AA_VERIF.PRG
Function(s)    VERIFY()
Purpose        Get OK or Cancel
Conventions    displays string + "...", menus OK / Cancel
Syntax         VERIFY(string)
Example        IF VERIFY("Format your hard disk")
Assumes        a valid string
Side Effects   saves, restores screen
Returns        True if "Ok" is selected
Calls          CENTRE()
               DRAW_BOX()
               SCROLL()
```

```
FUNCTION VERIFY

PARAMETER msg_string
PRIVATE choice, temp_scr, row, lc, width, dots
SAVE SCREEN TO temp_scr
choice = 01
row = 07
dots = "..."
width = LEN( msg_string + dots ) + 06
lc = CENTRE( SPACE( width ) )
SCROLL( 07, lc, 15, lc + width, 0 )
DRAW_BOX( 07, lc, 15, lc + width, 03 )
@ 09, LC + 03 = msg_string + dots
@ 12,32 PROMPT = Ok "
@ 12,39 PROMPT = Cancel "
MENU TO choice
restore screen from temp_scr
RETURN ( choice = 1 )
```

Chapter 16

Mathmetical Functions

- COUNT_EM — counts the records in the current table, modifying its behavior slightly if a filter is in effect.
- KCOUNT — searches a child-file for records belonging to the current parent, returning the count. You may specify a further condition as well.
- LONGEST — returns the length of the longest element in an array of strings.
- MCOUNT — returns the number of memo fields in a table.
- MOD — returns the modulus of two numbers.
- XCOUNT — returns the number of active indexes in the current work area.

• COUNT_EM()

```
PROGRAM        AA_COUN.PRG
Function(s)    COUNT_EM()
Purpose        Counts records in a file, optionally for a
               condition
Conventions    file is selected
Syntax         COUNT_EM([condition])
Parameters     condition - a valid expression
Example        COUNT_EM("over_30 > 100")
Assumes        file is selected
Side Effects   none
Returns        number of matching records
Calls
```

```
FUNCTION COUNT_EM

PARAMETER condition
PRIVATE x, msg, record_no, cur_count
IF TYPE("condition") = "U"
   condition = ""
ENDIF
msg = ""
record_no = RECNO()
cur_count = 0
IF EMPTY(DBFILTER() + condition)
   msg = "There are " + STRINT(LASTREC()) + " records on file"
ELSE
   IF VERIFY("This could take some time. Proceed")
      IF !EMPTY(condition)
         * The inflexible (SLOW) approach...
         * COUNT TO cur_count FOR &condition
         * much faster if indexed, but
         * you have to do the SEEK yourself
         COUNT TO cur_count WHILE &condition
      ELSE
         COUNT TO cur_count
      ENDIF
      msg = STRINT(cur_count) + " records in the current set"
   ENDIF
ENDIF
GO record_no
IF EMPTY(msg)                         && cancelled count
   MSG()
```

```
ELSE
   POP_MSG(msg)
ENDIF
RETURN 0
```

• KCOUNT()

```
PROGRAM        AA_KCOUN.PRG
Function(s)    KCOUNT()
Purpose        Counts the children of the current parent record
               optionally for a condition
               Use in the absence of relations by using param 3
               to indicate the relationship
Conventions    Both files open, at least the child indexed
Syntax         result = KCOUNT(child[, condition][, rel_key])
Parameters     child - child file, open and indexed on
rel_key
Example        (customer and invoice files open, customer
selected)
               condition = "!Paid"        && logical field PAI
               SELECT cust_file
               LIST Cust_ID, Company, ;
               KCOUNT(inv_file, condition)
Assumes        files are open, condition if passed is valid,
               rel_key if passed is valid
Side Effects   bad data can cause crash
Returns        number of matching records
Calls          MSG()
```

```
FUNCTION KCOUNT

PARAMETERS child, condition, rel_key
PRIVATE temp, parent, cur_file
temp = PCOUNT()
parent = ALIAS()
cur_rec = RECNO()
hits = 00
related = (temp > 02)             && If actually related, pass no rel_k
I even bulletproof against myself...
DO CASE
   CASE temp = 00
      MSG( "You have to pass a file name at least, bozo!", 1 )
      RETURN hits
   CASE temp = 01
      condition = "!EOF()"
   OTHERWISE
      condition = condition + ".AND. !EOF()"
```

```
ENDCASE
SELECT &child
IF !related                           && you want it done right,
   SEEK rel_key                       && you do it yourself.
ENDIF
COUNT WHILE &condition TO hits
* Put everything back in place before returning
SELECT &parent
GO cur_rec
RETURN hits
```

• LONGEST()

```
PROGRAM        AA_LNGST.PRG
Function(s)    LONGEST()
Purpose        Find length of longest element in an array
Conventions    useful for calculating box sizes etc.
               elements not strings are MAKE_STR()'d
               for calculation
Syntax         LONGEST(array)
Parameters     array - array to measure
Example        n = LONGEST(array)
Assumes        array is full of strings
Side Effects   none
Returns        number = length of longest array element
Calls
```

```
FUNCTION LONGEST

PARAMETER array
PRIVATE i, x, number
x = 0
number = 0
IF TYPE("array") = "A"
   FOR i = 1 TO LEN( array )
      number  = LEN( MAKE_STR( array[ i ] ) )
      x    = MAX( number, x )
   NEXT
ENDIF
RETURN x
```

• MCOUNT()

```
PROGRAM        AA_MCOUN.PRG
Function(s)    MCOUNT()
Purpose        Count the memo fields in a file
Conventions    called by READ_MEMO() to find out if a menu
               is required
Syntax         MCOUNT([array])
Parameters     array - if passed, fill it with names
Example        DECLARE mfields[MCOUNT()]     && size it
               MCOUNT(mfields) && fill it
Assumes        file in use
Side Effects   fills the array if passed
Returns        number of memo fields in current file
Calls          nothing
```

```
FUNCTION MCOUNT

PARAMETER array
PRIVATE reply, n, temp, ra_passed
ra_passed = PCOUNT() > 00
reply = 00
n     = 01
IF EMPTY(ALIAS())
   RETURN -1
ENDIF
FOR n = 01 TO FCOUNT()
   temp = FIELD(n)
   IF TYPE(FIELD(n)) = "M"
      reply  = reply + 01
   ENDIF
   IF ra_passed
      array[n] = FIELD(n)
   ENDIF
NEXT
RETURN reply
```

• MOD()

```
PROGRAM        AA_MOD.PRG
Function(s)    MOD()
Purpose        Counts records in a file, optionally for a
               condition
Conventions    some differences with dBASE
Syntax         MOD(n1, n2)
Parameters     n1 - denominator
               n2 - divisor
Example        MOD(42,10) = 2
Assumes        n2 != 0
Side Effects   none
Returns        modulus of n1, n2
Calls          nothing
```

```
FUNCTION MOD

PARAMETERS n1, n2

PRIVATE result
IF n2 = 00
   result = n1
ELSE
   result = n1 % n2
   IF result * n2 < 0
      result = result + n2
   ENDIF
ENDIF
RETURN result
```

• XCOUNT()

```
PROGRAM        AA_XCOUN.PRG
Function(s)    XCOUNT()
Purpose        Determines number of indexes open on dbf
Conventions    if no file in use, returns -1
Syntax         XCOUNT([array])
Parameters     array - optional, filled with keys if passed
Example        DECLARE keys[XCOUNT()]&& size it
               XCOUNT(keys)&& fill it
Assumes        nothing
Side Effects   none
Returns        # indexes in use, or -1 if no file in use
Calls          nothing
```

```
FUNCTION XCOUNT

PARAMETER array
PRIVATE x, n, temp, ra_passed, max_open
IF EMPTY(ALIAS())
   RETURN -1
ENDIF
ra_passed = PCOUNT() > 00
x = 00
n = 01
max_open = 10                         && logically 15...
FOR n = 01 TO max_open
   temp = INDEXKEY(n)
   IF !EMPTY(temp)
      x  = x + 01
   ENDIF
   IF ra_passed
      array[n] = temp
   ENDIF
NEXT
RETURN x
```

Chapter 17

Memo Functions

- MEMO_POS — returns the field number of the next memo field, defaulting the starting position at 1.
- READER — reads a text file into a memo field, presenting a menu of filenames if none is passed.
- READ_MEMO — displays/edits a memo field in a pop-up window of the specified dimensions, defaulting if none are passed.
- WRITER — writes a memo field to a disk file, prompting for the filename if none is passed.
- NOTEPAD — administers a generalized notepad, allowing the user to store information about anything yet search by subject etc.

• MEMO_POS()

```
PROGRAM        AA_MOPOS.PRG
Function(s)    MEMO_POS()
Purpose        return the field number of a memo field
Conventions    param allows reading from offset
               to get at 2nd, 3rd etc. fields
Syntax         MEMO_POS([offset])
Parameters     offset - begin read at field number
               default 1
Example        x = MEMO_POS()
Assumes        dbf is already open and selected
Side Effects   none
Returns        -1 if no file in use
               0 if no memo fields in file
               # position of next memo field
Calls
```

```
FUNCTION MEMO_POS

PARAMETER offset
PRIVATE temp, x, i
x = 0
temp = PCOUNT()
IF temp = 0
   offset = 0
ENDIF

i = 1 + offset                          && enable edit of 2nd, 3rd memo
j = i
IF !EMPTY(ALIAS())
   FOR i = j TO FCOUNT()
      IF TYPE(FIELD(i)) = "M"
         x = i
         EXIT
      ENDIF
   NEXT
ELSE
   x = -1
ENDIF
RETURN x
```

• READER()

```
PROGRAM        AA_READF.PRG
Function(s)    READER()
Purpose        Read a text file into a memo field
Conventions    hot-key text importer
Syntax         READER(memo_field)
Parameters     memo_field - must be a valid name of memo
field
Example        READER("notes")
Assumes        memo_field is valid
Side Effects   crash on bad data
Returns        True if successful
Calls          GET_FILE()
```

```
FUNCTION READER

PARAMETER  mmo_field
PRIVATE reply, temp, filespec, m_row, m_col, ret
ret = CHR(17)+CHR(196)+CHR(217)
m_row = ROW()  && save cursor location
m_col = COL()
filespec = "*.*                       "
filespec = ASK_FOR( "Enter a file name, or press " + ;
            ret + " for a menu", @filespec, caps )
IF !LASTKEY() = 27
   file   = GET_FILE(filespec)
   REPLACE &mmo_field WITH MEMOREAD( file )
   reply = .T.
ELSE
   reply = .F.
ENDIF
@ M_ROW, M_COL SAY SPACE(0)
RETURN reply
```

• READ_MEMO()

```
PROGRAM       AA_RMEMO.PRG
Programmer    Arthur Fuller
Copyright     ARTFUL APPLICATIONS (c) 1988
Version       1 .1
Purpose       A standard routine for reading memo fields
Comments      to control where pass r1, c1, r2, c2
              to stifle save/restore pass a .t.
              Three diffferent boxes are used.
              The frame is one box.
              Around it is another box, to create space.
              The actual edit area is onw char smaller than
              the box, to allow an inner border
```

```
FUNCTION READ_MEMO

PARAMETERS memo_field, tr, tc, br, bc, edit_it, udf
PRIVATE   temp, no_memos, memo_buff, temp_scr, buff_size, row
* Step backwards through params, checking
IF TYPE("edit_it") != "L"           && default to YES edit
   edit_it = .T.                    && to pass into memoedit
ENDIF
IF TYPE("udf") = "U"                && manufacture a dummy
   udf = ""                         && to pass into memoedit
ENDIF
IF TYPE("tr") != "N"                && no locations or dummy params
   tr = 04                          && set these defaults to
   tc = 05                          && whatever you like
   br  = 22
   bc = 74
ENDIF
temp = PCOUNT()
row = 02

IF TYPE("memo_field") = "U" .OR. EMPTY(memo_field)
   no_memos = MCOUNT()
   DO CASE
      CASE no_memos = 00    && in case somehow it got thru
         POP_MSG("There are no memo fields in this file")
         RETURN .F.
   CASE no_memos = 01
      memo_field = FIELD(MEMO_POS()) && find out its name
   CASE no_memos > 01
```

```
      DECLARE m_fields[no_memos]     && make an array
      pos = 01

      FOR i = 1 TO FCOUNT()          && field it with names
         x = FIELD(i)                && of memo fields
         IF TYPE(x) = "M"
            m_fields[pos] = " " + PROPER(x) + " "  && cosmetics
            pos = pos + 01
         ENDIF
      NEXT
      ht = LEN(m_fields) + 02
      col = 63
      width = 12
      SAVE SCREEN TO temp_scr
      DRAW_BOX(01,col -1, ht, col + width, 13)
      choice = ACHOICE(row, col, ht-1, col + width - 1, m_fields, ;
            .T., .T., choice)
      IF ESC()
         RESTORE SCREEN FROM temp_scr
         RETURN .F.                  && Out, without changing order
      ENDIF
      memo_field = m_fields[x]
   ENDIF
ENDIF

temp_scr = SAVESCREEN(tr,tc,br,bc)
DRAW_BOX(tr + 1, tc + 1, br - 1, bc - 1, 02)
cur_color = SETCOLOR()
SYSCOLOR(10)
memo_field + SPACE(4)) SAY "  " + memo_field + "  "
old_color = SETCOLOR(cur_color)

* edit the memo field
SET CURSOR ON
get_data = MEMOEDIT( &memo_field, tr + 3, tc + 5, br - 3, bc - 5, ;
            .T.)
IF LASTKEY() = 23                    && ^W
   REPLACE &memo_field WITH M-get_data
   KEYBOARD CHR(4)
ENDIF

RESTSCREEN(tr,tc,br,bc, temp_scr)
keystroke = 0
SET CURSOR OFF
old_color = SETCOLOR(cur_color)
RETURN CTRL_W()                      && was it a keeper?
```

• WRITER()

```
PROGRAM       AA_WRITE.PRG
Programmer    Arthur Fuller
Copyright     ARTFUL APPLICATIONS (c) 1987
Version       1.0
Purpose       Writes memo fields to text files
Comments      assumes file is open and selected
              SET KEY works if the field is named Notes
              otherwise trap for the key in a CASE statement
              and pass in the field name
              second param allows you to skip the internal
              prompt for file name
```

```
FUNCTION WRITER

PARAMETERS mmo_field, output_txt
PRIVATE reply, msg, temp
temp = PCOUNT()

IF temp < 2
   DO WHILE .T.
      output_txt = SPACE(12)
      output_txt = ASK_FOR( "File to Write", @output_txt, caps )
      IF EMPTY( output_txt )
         RETURN .F.
      ENDIF
      IF FILE( output_txt )
         IF !VERIFY( output_txt + " exists. Overwrite it" )
            LOOP
         ENDIF
      ENDIF
      EXIT
   ENDDO
ENDIF

IF MEMOWRIT( output_txt, &mmo_field )
   msg = output_txt + " successfully written"
   reply = .T.
ELSE
   msg = "Error writing file"
   reply = .F.
ENDIF
```

```
MSG( msg, 1 )
RETURN reply
```

• NOTEPAD()

```
PROGRAM       NOTEPAD.PRG
Programmer    Arthur Fuller
Copyright     ARTFUL APPLICATIONS (c) 1987
Version       1.0
Purpose       POP-UP NOTEPAD
Comments
```

NOTEPADPRG

```
PARAMETERS proc_name, line_no, read_var
PRIVATE temp_scr, file,
IF PCOUNT() > 00                     && prevent self-calling
   IF proc_name = "NOTEPAD"
      RETURN
   ENDIF
ENDIF
SAVE SCREEN TO temp_scr
old_row = ROW()
old_col = COL()
old_dbf = ALIAS()
no_keys = 00    && an index makes it 3 files!
file = "NOTEPAD"
udf_brow = .F.                       && default to XBROWSE
is_open = IS_OPEN(file)
IF !is_open
   IF !DB_OPEN( 00, file )           && Next available area
      RETURN
   ENDIF
ENDIF
* made it. Show them the notes
SELECT &file
BROWSER(03,00,23,79, udf_brow)
RESTORE SCREEN FROM temp_scr
@ old_row,old_col SAY SPACE(0)
IF !is_open && wasn't open, so close it
   USE
ENDIF
SELECT &old_dbf
RETURN
```

Chapter 18

Menu Functions

- CHOOSE — presents an on-the-spot menu of strings, returning the corresponding character from a string of characters. Useful for instantly translating user input in a data-entry routine.
- DO_IT — a generalized menu and program executor based on L_MENU
- L_MENU — turns one or two arrays into a light-bar menu, using the second array (if passed) as messages. The display defaults to rows 0 and 2 with a graphic line between, unless row(s) are specified.
- MENU_ORD — presents a menu of the possible orders in which the current file may be viewed (based on the active indexes as well as record number order).
- PD_MENU — a generalized pull-down menu interface which also administers the entire program.
- PDM — same as PD_MENU but based on BREEZE.LIB and much faster.
- V_MENU — presents a pop-up vertical menu in a box at the location specified, executing the appropriate function.

• CHOOSE()

```
PROGRAM        AA_CHOOS.PRG
Function(s)    CHOOSE()
Purpose        menus the characters in a string
Conventions    creates an on-the-spot menu
Syntax         CHOOSE(char, array, row, col)
Parameters     char - start the menu at
               array - menu of translations or expansions
Example        CHOOSE(char, descrips, 10, 40)
Assumes        nothing
Side Effects   displays the expanded choice at row, col
Returns        the character chosen
Calls          nothing
Notes          If you know the codes just type one in
               and exit the routine. If not, use the
               arrow keys to see what's available.
```

```
FUNCTION CHOOSE

PARAMETERS char, array, row, col
PRIVATE choice, options
options = LEN(array)
choice = MAX(1, AT(char, char_list))

FOR i = 1 TO options
   n = STRINT(i)
   @ row, col PROMPT array[i]
NEXT

MENU TO choice
RETURN IF(choice = 0, "", SUBSTR(char_list, choice, 1))
```

• DO_IT()

```
PROGRAM       AA_DOIT.PRG
Function(s)   DO_IT()
Purpose       Generalized program administrator
Conventions   Usually a main menu, but doesn't have to be.
              Self-contained loop, so no external loop
              is required.
Syntax        DO_IT(choice, array1, array2, array3, ;
                          row1, row2)
Parameters    choice - default menu selection
              array1 - array of menu prompts
              array2 - optional array of messages
              array3 - array of udf names to execute
              row1 - menu on row... defaults to 00
              row2 - messages on row... defaults to 02
Example       DO_IT(choice, prompts, msgs, udfs)
Assumes       validity of array1 and array3.
              The other params are optional.
Side Effects  executes the function pointed to. Crashes
              if that function is not linked in.
Returns       The number of selected choice, or 0 if esc.
Calls         L_MENU()
```

```
FUNCTION DO_IT

PARAMETERS choice, prompts, msgs, udfs, row1, row2
PRIVATE temp
SET CURSOR OFF
temp = choice
IF TYPE("row1") != "N"
   row1 = 00
ENDIF
IF TYPE("row2") != "N"
   row2 = row1 + 02
ENDIF
DO WHILE .T.
   choice = L_MENU( choice, prompts, msgs, row1, row2 )
   @ row2,00
   IF choice > 0
      udf = udfs[choice]            && grab the function pointed to
      reply = &udf                  && execute it
```

```
   ELSE
      EXIT
   ENDIF
ENDDO

RETURN choice
```

• H_MENU()

```
PROGRAM       AA_HMENU.PRG
Function(s)   H_MENU()
Purpose       Simple horizontal menu with optional message
Conventions   a smaller call than L_MENU(), for q&d menus
Syntax        H_MENU(choice, array, message, row, col)
Parameters    choice  - default menu selection
              array   - of menu prompts
              message - defaults to "Commands >"
              row - menu row
              col - menu column
Example       choice = H_MENU(choice,prompts)
Assumes       nothing
Side Effects  none
Returns       the number of the selected choice
Calls
```

```
FUNCTION H_MENU

PARAMETERS choice, array, msg, row, col
PRIVATE temp, limit, i, sp, r_tri
SET WRAP ON
SET MESSAGE TO
temp = PCOUNT()
msg_sent = (TYPE("msg") = "C")
sp = " "
r_tri = CHR(16)

IF TYPE("choice") != "N"
   choice = 01
ENDIF
IF TYPE("msg") != "C"
   msg = ""
ENDIF
IF TYPE("row") != "N"                    && pass dummy for other params
row = 02                                 && sub-menu under L_MENU()
ENDIF
@ row, col                               && clear line, park cursor

IF !EMPTY(msg)
   msg = ALLTRIM(msg)
   @ row, col SAY msg + sp + r_tri + sp
```

```
ENDIF
limit = LEN(array)

FOR i = 1 to limit
   IF EMPTY(array[i])
      EXIT
   ELSE
      @ ROW(), COL() PROMPT array[i]
   ENDIF
NEXT

MENU to choice
RETURN choice
```

• L_MENU()

```
PROGRAM        AA_LMENU.PRG
Function(s)    L_MENU()
Purpose        Generalized Lotus-style menu administrator
Conventions    Use with or without messages, on any row
               With too many items for one row,
               it adjusts to occupy a second row.
Syntax         L_MENU(choice, array1[, array2])
Parameters     choice - start menu at; defaults to 1
Example        L_MENU(01,array1)
Assumes        choice and array1 must exist
Side Effects   none
Returns        value of prompt selected, or 0 if escape
Calls          ALENGTH() - for total length of menu
```

```
FUNCTION L_MENU

PARAMETERS choice, array1, array2, row1, row2
SET WRAP ON
PRIVATE temp, ra_len, show_msgs, msg, total_len
temp = PCOUNT()
ra_len = LEN(array1)
show_msgs = (TYPE("array2") = "A")
total_len = ALENGTH(array1)
IF temp < 04
   row1 = 00
ENDIF
g_row = row1 + IF(total_len  80, 02, 01)
IF temp < 05
   row2 = g_row + 01
ENDIF
@ row1,00 SAY SPACE(0)
IF row1 < 02   && sub-menu, no graphic line
   @ g_row,00 SAY REPL(CHR(196),80)
ENDIF
@ row2,00
@ row1,00 SAY SPACE(0)

IF show_msgs
   SET MESSAGE TO row2
ELSE
   SET MESSAGE TO
ENDIF
```

```
FOR i = 1 TO ra_len
   IF show_msgs
      @ row1, COL() PROMPT  array1[i] ;
               MESSAGE array2[i]
   ELSE
      @ row1, COL() PROMPT array1[i]
   ENDIF
   IF i < ra_len
      IF COL() + LEN(array1[i+1])  80
         row1 = row1 + 1
         @ row1,00 SAY SPACE(0)     && new value for COL()
      ENDIF
   ENDIF
NEXT

MENU to choice

IF show_msgs
   @ row2,00                        && Blank the line
ENDIF
```

```
RETURN choice
```

• MENU_ORD()

```
PROGRAM        AA_MNORD.PRG
Function(s)    MENU_ORD()
Purpose        Allow user to change record display order
Conventions    menus the available orders (+ record #)
               creates an array from the currently active
               indexes, presents the keys as a menu.
               if the user does not press escape,
               order is set to choice
               Since ORDER 0 (e.g. recno() ) is always
               possible, the routine presents it as
               selection 1, and sets order to choice - 1
Syntax         MENU_ORD(array)
Parameters     array – contains cues to menu
               row – optional display row, default 02
Example        MENU_ORD(xcues)
Assumes        xcues, xkeys and xpics are defined
               This udf will be called from THE_USUAL()
               in which case place it menu one line below
               the graphic line (e.g. the message row).
               But let's make the routine useful in
               other circumstances, too.
Side Effects crash on bad data
Returns        number (order) selected
Calls LONGEST(), DRAW_BOX()
```

```
FUNCTION MENU_ORD

PARAMETERS array, row                   && menu cues for indexes
PRIVATE result, no_indexes, choice, temp_scr, col, ht, width
SAVE SCREEN TO temp_scr
col = 33
choice = 01

IF TYPE("row") = "U"
   row = 02
ENDIF

DO CASE
   CASE TYPE("array") = "A"
      no_indexes = LEN(array)
```

```
   CASE TYPE("array") = "C"           && only 1 index
      no_indexes = 01

   OTHERWISE
      no_indexes = XCOUNT()

ENDCASE

IF no_indexes > 0                     && are indexes in use?
   choice = INDEXORD()+01             && default the menu
   DECLARE keys[no_indexes + 01]
   keys[01] = " Record # "            && always an option
ENDIF

IF TYPE("array") = "C"
   keys[02] = array
ELSE
   ACOPY(array,keys,01,LEN(array),02)
ENDIF

ht = LEN(keys) + 02
width = LONGEST(keys)
DRAW_BOX(01,col -1, ht, col + width, 13)
choice = ACHOICE(row, col, ht-1, col + width - 1, keys, .T., .T.,
            choice)
IF ESC()
   RESTORE SCREEN FROM temp_scr
   RETURN .F.                         && Out, without changing order
ELSE
   SET ORDER TO choice - 01           && 1 = record order (0)
   GO RECNO()                         && enforce new order
ENDIF

RESTORE SCREEN FROM temp_scr
RETURN choice
```

• PDM()

```
PROGRAM       AA_PDM.PRG
Function(s)   PDM(), PULLDOWN()
Purpose       Pull-down menu system using BREEZE.LIB
Conventions   color9 and color12 are called as
normal/reverse
Syntax        PDM()
Parameters    none
Example       PDM()
Assumes       all arrays are declared and filled with valid
data
Side Effects  crash on bad data
Returns       .T.
Calls         WSELECT, WDISPLAY, WUSE, WPRINT, WCOLOR,
              WFRAME
```

```
FUNCTION PDM

WSELECT(m_wno)
WUSE(m_high, m_wide, m_tr, m_tc, m_clr)
WFRAME(double)
i = 01
FOR i = 01 TO m_size
   WPRINT(01, cols[i], cues[i])
NEXT
WCOLOR(color12)
WPRINT(01, cols[01], cues[01])
WCOLOR(color9)
WDISPLAY()
docode = .F.
oldcntr = 1
menucntr = 1
code = 28
DO while code != 1
   IF docode
      code = keycode()
   ENDIF
   docode = .T.
   oldcntr = menucntr
   DO CASE
      CASE code = left
         menucntr = menucntr - 1
      CASE code = right
```

```
         menucntr = menucntr + 1
      CASE code = enter
         menucntr = menucntr
      OTHERWISE
         LOOP
   ENDCASE
   IF menucntr < 01
      menucntr = m_size
   ENDIF
   IF menucntr > m_size
      menucntr = 01
   ENDIF
   WCOLOR(color9)
   WPRINT(1, cols[oldcntr], cues[oldcntr])
   WCOLOR(color12)
   last_chosen = menucntr
   WPRINT(1, cols[menucntr], cues[menucntr])
   PULLDOWN(menucntr)
   IF menucntr != last_chosen
      docode = .F.
   ENDIF
   WCOLOR(color9)
   CLEAR typeahead
ENDDO
WCLOSE(m_wno)
WRELEASE(m_wno)
code = 28
RETURN .T.
```

- PULLDOWN()

```
FUNCTION PULLDOWN

PARAMETER menu_ptr                    && current option
PRIVATE size
n = STRINT(menu_ptr)
array = "c" + n                       && determine array's name
funcs = "u" + n                       && point to function array
size = LEN(&array)
high = size + 02
wide = wids[menu_ptr]                 && width of current box
tr = 03                               && all start at 3
tc = cols[menu_ptr] - 02              && where do you want it?
tc = MAX(01, tc)
tc = MIN(tc, 79 - wids[menu_ptr])
w_no = 81
clr = color9
fr = 03
dflt = dflts[menu_ptr]                && current default
WSELECT(w_no)
WUSE(high,wide,tr,tc,clr)             && 05,20,7,1,color9)
WFRAME(fr)
FOR i = 01 TO size
   WPRINT(i,06,&array[i])             && say all the options
NEXT
WDISPLAY()
WCOLOR(color12)
WPRINT(dflt,6,&array[dflt])           && higlight current default
s_code = 0
scntr = 1
soldcntr = 1
DO while s_code != 1 .AND. menucntr = menu_ptr
   s_code = keycode()
   soldcntr = scntr
   dflts[menu_ptr] = scntr
   DO CASE
      CASE s_code = up
         scntr = scntr - 01
      CASE s_code = down
         scntr = scntr + 01
      CASE s_code = enter
         scntr = scntr
         udf = &funcs[scntr]
         result = &udf
      CASE s_code = right
         menucntr = menucntr + 01
```

```
         IF menucntr > m_size
            menucntr = 01
         ENDIF
      CASE s_code = left
         menucntr = menucntr - 01
         IF menucntr < 01
            menucntr = m_size
         ENDIF
      CASE s_code = 01
         menucntr = menucntr
      OTHERWISE
         LOOP
   ENDCASE
   IF scntr < 01
      scntr = size
   ELSEIF scntr > size
      scntr = 01
   ENDIF
   WCOLOR(color9)
   WPRINT(soldcntr,06,&array[soldcntr])
   WCOLOR(color12)
   WPRINT(scntr,06,&array[scntr])
   CLEAR typeahead
ENDDO
WCLOSE(w_no)
WRELEASE(w_no)
WSELECT(m_wno)
WCOLOR(color9)
WPRINT(01,cols[menu_ptr],cues[menu_ptr])
WCOLOR(color12)
WPRINT( 01, cols[menucntr], cues[menucntr] )
WCOLOR(color9)
code = 28
RETURN .T.
```

- PD_MENU()

```
PROGRAM         AA_PDMNU.PRG
Function(s)     PD_MENU(), PD_OPEN(), NEXT_BOX, PREV_BOX
Purpose         Pull-down menu administrator
Conventions     each menu is an array (filled)
                and has a parallel array of udfs to execute.
Syntax          PD_MENU(cues, sizes[, menu_udf])
Parameters      cues - main menu prompts
                sizes - array of sub-menu sizes
                menu_udf — udf to execute during achoice()
Example         PD_MENU(cues, size)
Assumes         validity of arrays/contents/udfs
Side Effects    crash on bad data
Returns         True
Calls           AFILL(),DRAW_BOX(),L_MENU(),STRINT(),ESC()
                STUFF_RA() - you write this in setup
```

FUNCTION PD_MENU

```
PARAMETERS cues, sizes, menu_udf
PRIVATE choice, is_open, number
choice = 01
IF TYPE("menu_udf") = "U"
   menu_udf = "PD_UDF"
ENDIF
PRIVATE sels[m_size], ;                 && defaults for each pulldown
         wids[m_size]                   && width of each box
AFILL(sels,01)                          && default all sub-menus to 01
i = 01
FOR i = 01 TO m_size                    && auto-declare as many arrays
   n = STRINT(i)                        && as required

DECLARE c&n[sizes[i]], ;                && one for cues
           u&n[sizes[i]], ;             && one for udfs
           l&n[sizes[i]]                && one for legals
NEXT
STUFF_RA()                              && You write this one
is_open = .T.
DO WHILE .T.
   choice = L_MENU( choice, cues )
   IF choice > 0
      PD_OPEN(choice, menu_udf)
```

```
   ELSE
      EXIT  && they pressed escape
   ENDIF
ENDDO
RETURN .T.
```

- PD_OPEN()

FUNCTION PD_OPEN

```
PARAMETERS number, pd_udf
PRIVATE choice, col, right, left, temp_scr1, temp_scr2
str_no = STRINT(number)
carray = "c" + str_no
uarray = "u" + str_no
larray = "l" + str_no
uwidth = wids[number]           && grab the width for this box
choice = sels[number]           && default to last selected
col = cols[number]
ht = sizes[number] + 02         && first item on row 2 + number items
left = 19
right = 04
IF TYPE("pd_udf") != "C"
   pd_udf = .F.
ENDIF
SAVE SCREEN TO temp_scr1

DO WHILE .T.
   SET KEY right TO NEXT_BOX
   SET KEY left TO PREV_BOX
   DRAW_BOX(01,col -1,ht,col+uwidth,13)
   choice = ACHOICE(02, col, ht-1, col+uwidth-1, ;
            &carray, ;          && prompts
            &larray, ;          && legals
            pd_udf, ;           && udf
            sels[number])       && default to
   SET KEY right TO
   SET KEY left TO
   IF choice > 0
      SYSCOLOR(02)              && highlight selected item
      @ ROW(), col SAY &carray[choice]
      SYSCOLOR(01)
      SAVE SCREEN TO temp_scr2
      sels[number] = ROW() - 01 && save the current selection
      is_open = .T.
      udf = &uarray[choice]     && point to the udf
      x = &udf                  && execute the udf
```

```
      RESTORE SCREEN FROM temp_scr2
   ELSE
      EXIT
   ENDIF
ENDDO
RESTORE SCREEN FROM temp_scr1
RETURN ""
```

- NEXT_BOX

PROCEDURE NEXT_BOX

```
sels[number] = ROW() - 01           && save the current selection
KEYBOARD CHR(27) + CHR(04) + CHR(13)&& emulate esc + right + enter
RETURN
```

- PREV_BOX

PROCEDURE PREV_BOX

```
sels[number] = ROW() - 01           && save the current selection
KEYBOARD CHR(27) + CHR(19) + CHR(13) && escape + left + enter
RETURN
```

- PD_UDF()

FUNCTION PD_UDF

```
* default udf for use inside pull-down menus
PARAMETERS mode, curr_sel, relative
PRIVATE x
IF mode = 4
   keystroke = INKEY(0)
   x = 0    && abort selection process
ELSE
   keystroke = LASTKEY()            && continue
   x = 2
ENDIF
IF mode = 3                         && keystroke exception
   DO CASE
      CASE ENTER()                  && make selection, return
```

```
         x = 1
      CASE keystroke = 1              && home key..top of list (^PgUp)
         KEYBOARD CHR(31)
      CASE keystroke = 6              && end key..end of list (^PgDn)
         KEYBOARD CHR(30)
      CASE IS_DATA(keystroke)         && request character search
         x = 3
   ENDCASE
ENDIF
RETURN x
```

• V_MENU()

```
PROGRAM       AA_VMENU.PRG
Function(s)   V_MENU()
Purpose       Generalized vertical menu program, with
              messages
Conventions   typically a Main Menu program
Syntax        V_MENU( choice, array1, array2, array3,
              row, col, clear_scr, header, width )
Parameters    choice - default beginning selection
              array1 - array of menu prompts
              array2 - array of messages,, or .f.
              array3 - array of functions
              header - optional menu header
              row - upper left row
              col - upper left column
              msg_row - row to display messages on
              msg_box - display messages in a box?
              msg_centr - center messages?
              width - menu width (if != len(array1[1]))
              clear_scr - to over-ride default clear
Example       V_MENU(prompts, msgs, udfs)
Assumes       functions named in udfs[] are linked in
Side Effects crashes if the functions are not linked in
Returns       number of prompt selected or 0 if escape
Calls
```

FUNCTION V_MENU

```
PARAMETERS choice, array1, array2, array3, header, ;
            row, col, msg_row, msg_box, msg_centr, ;
            width, clear_scr
SET WRAP ON
PRIVATE choice, b_row, b_col, head, tc1, tc2, ra_len, j_row

IF TYPE("msg_box") = "U"
   msg_box = .F.
ENDIF
IF TYPE("array3") != "A"
   SET MESSAGE TO
ELSE
   IF TYPE("msg_row") != "N"
```

```
      msg_row = IF(msg_box,23,24)
   ENDIF
   IF TYPE("msg_centr") = "U"
      msg_centr = .T.
      SET MESSAGE TO msg_row CENTER
   ELSE
      SET MESSAGE TO msg_row
   ENDIF
ENDIF
IF TYPE("width") != "N"
   width = MIN(24,LONGEST(array1))
ENDIF
IF TYPE("col") != "N"
   col = 29
ENDIF
IF TYPE("row") != "N"
   row = 05
ENDIF
IF TYPE("header") != "C"
   header = "Command Menu"
ENDIF
header = MIDDLE(header, width)
tc1 = col + 1
tc2 = col + 2
ra_len = LEN(array1)
b_row = row + 3 + ra_len
b_col = col + width + 1
j_row = row + 2

DO WHILE .T.
   IF TYPE("clear_scr") = "U"
      CLEAR
   ENDIF
   DRAW_BOX(row, col, b_row, b_col, 03)
   @ j_row, col SAY "C" + REPL("D", width ) + "4"
   SYSCOLOR(02)
   @ row + 1, col + 1 SAY header
   SYSCOLOR(01)
   IF TYPE("array2") = "A"
      IF msg_box
         DRAW_BOX(msg_row - 01, 00, msg_row + 01, 79, 03)
      ENDIF
      FOR i = 1 TO ra_len
         @ j_row + i, tc1 PROMPT  array1[i]  ;
               MESSAGE array2[i]
      NEXT
   ELSE
      FOR i = 1 TO ra_len
         @ j_row + i, tc1 PROMPT array1[i]
      NEXT
```

```
   ENDIF

   MENU to choice

   IF choice = 00
      EXIT
   ELSEIF TYPE("array3") = "A"
      udf = array3[choice]
      x = &udf
   ENDIF

ENDDO

RETURN .T.
```

Chapter 19

Interface Functions

- ASK_FOR — gets input from the user in a pop-up window sized automatically, displaying any message, receiving any data type, checking it against any desired conditions.
- BLINK — displays a message followed by 3 blinking dots, right-justifed, on line 24.
- BASIC_BOX — draws a box for use in BROWSER-based programs.
- CLEAR_GETS — clears pending GETs; a procedure to assign to a key.
- DRAW_BOX — draws every box of every type in every program.
- GEN_PIC — generates a picture statement according to an intelligent system of defaults.
- HEADER — centers the specified string in a box on lines 1 to 3.
- MSG — displays a message right-justified on line 24, with or without waiting, with or without blinking dots afterward, with or without an additional "press any key".
- POP_MSG — pops a message onto the screen, waits for a keystroke, restores the screen. The message may be one or several lines long.
- READ_IT — performs all READs in all programs.
- SEARCH — generalized searching mechanism which handles multiple indexes, turning them into a menu.
- SHADOWBOX — draws a box with a shadow behind it, optionally displaying a header.
- SIGN_OFF — closes the files, displays your logo and says goodnight.
- SIGN_ON — clears the screen, displays your logo.
- WAIT — a procedure which waits for a keystroke (called by some other functions).

• ASK_FOR()

```
PROGRAM        AA_ASK.PRG
Function(s)    ASK_FOR()
Purpose        Prompts the user for data
Conventions    pops up a box containing your msg_str,
               accepts data into memvar using pict_str,
               with optional validation using val_str and
               over-ride of EXACT setting using exact_on
               Restores the screen after the READ.
Syntax         ASK_FOR(msg_str,memvar[,pict_str][,;
                 val_str],[exact_on])
Parameters     msg_str - prompt string to display,
                 3 dots added to it automatically
               memvar - initialized to correct data type
               pict_str - GEN_PIC(memvar) if not passed
                 so it's only necessary for over-ride
               val_str - string containing valid condition
               exact_on - default is OFF or false.
                 returns trim rather than entire memvar
                 pass anything as exact_on to set ON
Example        ASK_FOR("Enter a letter from A to F" ;
                 memvar, "!", "memvar $ "ABCDEF")
Assumes        Calculates size of the box according to the
               length of msg_str, which must be < 80 chars
Side Effects   unpleasant cosmetics if msg_str is too long
               otherwise it behaves in absence of params
Returns        memvar
Calls          PCOUNT(), CENTRE(), MAKE_STR(), DRAW_BOX()
```

```
FUNCTION ASK_FOR

PARAMETERS msg_str, memvar, pict_str, val_str, exact_on
CLEAR GETS
PRIVATE tr, tc, br, bc, add_space, ;
        pos, temp_scr, var_col, msg_col
IF TYPE("exact_on") = "U"           && nothing passed, go default
   exact_on = .F.
ENDIF
msg_str = TRIM(msg_str) + "..."
temp = PCOUNT()
```

```
data = TYPE( "memvar" )
msg_col = CENTRE( msg_str )
var_col = CENTRE( MAKE_STR( memvar ) )
tc = MAX( 0, MIN( var_col, msg_col ) - 03 )
bc = 80 - tc                            && same offset
tr = 05
br = 12

* Instead of doing a case statement in which all the params
* are analyzed, we fill any missing (or incorrectly typed)
* params in with defaults, then execute the GET with a PICTURE
* and a VALID.

IF TYPE("pict_str") != "C"              && nothing passed, go default
   pict_str  = GEN_PIC("memvar")
ENDIF
IF TYPE("val_str") != "C"               && nothing passed, go default
   val_str  = ".T."                     && all is true
ENDIF

temp_scr = SPACE( (br - tr + 1) * (bc - tc + 1) )
temp_scr = SAVESCREEN(tr, tc, br, bc)

SHADOWBOX(tr, tc, br, bc)
@ tr + 2, msg_col SAY msg_str
@ tr + 4, var_col GET memvar PICTURE pict_str ;
         VALID &val_str
READ_IT()

RESTSCREEN(tr, tc, br, bc, temp_scr)

IF !exact_on .AND. TYPE("memvar") = "C"
   memvar = TRIM(memvar)
ENDIF

RETURN memvar
```

• BLINK()

```
PROGRAM       AA_BLINK.PRG
Function(s)   BLINK()
Purpose       display a blinking string in current colors
Conventions   go easy on your users. blinking dots will get
              their attention.
Syntax        BLINK(string[, row][, col])
Parameters    string - to display
              row    - display at row
              col    - display at column
Example       BLINK("Does your head hurt yet?", 10, 12)
Assumes       all params are passed
Side Effects  crash on bad params
Returns       True
Calls         SETCOLOR()
```

```
FUNCTION BLINK

PARAMETERS string, row, col
PRIVATE cc
cc = SETCOLOR()
IF TYPE("row") = "U"
   row = ROW()
ENDIF
IF TYPE("col") = "U"
   col = COL()
ENDIF
SETCOLOR("*" + cc)
@ row, col SAY string
SETCOLOR(cc)
RETURN .T.
```

• BASIC_BOX()

```
PROGRAM         AA_BSBOX.PRG
Function(s)    BASIC_BOX
Purpose        Basic box for DBEDIT() routine
Conventions    call with or without parameters. If no
params
               passed, it defaults to the 03,00,23,79
Syntax          BASIC_BOX(r1,c1,r2,c2)
Parameters     r1 - top row of box - default 03
               c1 - top column of box - default 00
               r2 - bottom row of box - default 23
               c2 - bottom column of box - default 79
Example        BASIC_BOX()
Assumes        A call to DBEDIT() will soon follow
               the box characters are hard-coded
Side Effects   draws the corners to join the heading
separators
Returns        True always
Calls          nothing
```

```
FUNCTION BASIC_BOX

PARAMETERS tr, tc, br, bc
IF TYPE("tr") != "N"
   tr = 03
   tc = 00
   br = 23
   bc = 79
ENDIF
@ tr, tc, br, bc BOX "UM83MT3"
@ tr + 03, tc SAY "FM"            && put the headline corners in
@ tr + 03, bc - 1 SAY "M5"
RETURN .T.
```

• CLEAR_GETS()

```
PROGRAM       AA_CGETS.PRG
Function(s)   CLEAR_GETS
Purpose       Allows CLEAR GETS to be used in a SET KEY proc.
Conventions   Use only if you're attaching special
characteristics
              to cursor movement, e.g. to make up key terminat
              GETs.
Syntax        DO CLEAR_GETS
Parameters    x, y, z - passed automatically to any SET
KEY proc.
              x - procedure name
              y - line number
              z - variable being read, if any
Example       DO CLEAR_GETS
Assumes       Nothing
Side Effects  none
Returns       nothing
Calls         nothing
```

```
PROCEDURE CLEAR_GETS

PARAMETERS x, y, z
CLEAR GETS
RETURN
```

• DRAW_BOX()

```
PROGRAM        AA_DRBOX.PRG
Function(s)    DRAW_BOX()
Purpose        Generalized box routine
Conventions    box types are numbered internally.
               Optional clear-screen parameter.
               Does not check validity of the parameters
Syntax         DRAW_BOX(r1,c1,r2,c2,box_no,clear_it)
Parameters
               r1 - top row
               c1 - top column
               r2 - bottom row
               c2 - bottom column
               box_no - see below. Defaults to 11
               clear_it - any value causes screen to clear first
Example        DRAW_BOX(04,10,16,66,03)
Assumes        valid parameters
Side Effects   could crash with bad parameters
Returns        True always
Calls          SCROLL()
```

```
FUNCTION DRAW_BOX

PARAMETERS Top, Left, Bottom, Right, Border_no, Clear_scr
IF TYPE("Border_no") != "N"
   Border_no = 11
ENDIF
boxchars = "ZD?3YD@3IM;:H:UM83MT3VD7:=DS:\\\[___[\\\^___]"+;
            "[[[[[[[[222222221111111100000000ZD?3MT3        "+;
            "BDB3MT3"
bptr = (box_no - 01) * 08 + 01
box_str = SUBSTR(box_chars, bptr, 08)
IF TYPE("Clear_scr") != "U"          && pass anything to clear screen
   CLEAR
ENDIF
IF Border_no != 0
   SCROLL(Top, left, bottom, right, 0)
   @ Top,left,bottom,right BOX box_str
ENDIF
```

```
RETURN .T.
```

- GEN_PIC()

```
PROGRAM        AA_GNPIC.PRG
Function(s)    GEN_PIC()
Purpose        Intelligent PICTURE generator
Conventions    char fields get special treatment
               < 8 long are capitalized
               "phone" and "city" are looked for if field
               is character. If found, appropriate pictures
               are returned.
               "_no" is searched for (e.g. INVOICE_NO). If
               found, picture returned is "@9"
Syntax         GEN_PIC(field_name)
Parameters     field_name - field to PICTURE
Example        GEN_PIC("H_PHONE") returns "@R (###) 999-9999"
Assumes        field is a valid field
Side Effects can crash on bad data
Returns        appropriate picture string for data passed in
Calls          LTRIM(), STR(), MIN(), MAX()
```

```
FUNCTION GEN_PIC

PARAMETER field_name
PRIVATE pict_str, s, phone, caps
field_name = UPPER(field_name)
phone = "@R (###) 999-9999"         && assumes you'll store as C10
caps  = "@!"
DO CASE
   CASE TYPE(field_name) = "C"      && character field
      DO CASE
         CASE LEN(&field_name) < 10
            pict_str = caps
         CASE "PHONE" $ field_name  && is it a phone field
            pict_str = phone
         CASE "CITY" $ field_name   && is it a city
            pict_str = "!" + REPL("X",LEN(&field_name)-1)
         CASE "_NO" $ field_name    && invoice number etc.
            pict_str = "@9"         && a string resembling a number
         OTHERWISE
            * character field is bounded by window width
            pict_str = "@KS" + LTRIM(STR(MIN(LEN(&field_name), 78)))
      ENDCASE
   CASE TYPE(field_name) = "L"      && logical field
```

```
      pict_str = "Y"
   CASE TYPE(field_name) = "N"      && numeric field
      * convert to character to help format picture string
      str_num = STR(&field_name)
      dec_pos = AT(".", str_num)
      IF dec_pos > 00                   && use "9999.99"
         pict_str = REPLICATE("9", dec_pos - 1) + "." + ;
               REPLICATE("9", LEN(str_num) - dec_pos)
      ELSE
         pict_str = REPLICATE("9", LEN(str_num))
      ENDIF
   OTHERWISE   && no picture
      pict_str = ""
ENDCASE
RETURN pict_str
```

• HEADER()

```
PROGRAM        AA_HEAD.PRG
Function(s)    HEADER()
Purpose        Simple screen header,
               string date at left
               heading centered in reverse video
               time at right
Conventions
Syntax         HEADER(string[,expand_it][,row])
Parameters     string - heading you wish displayed
               expand_it - flag to expand string
               row - start box at row
Example        HEADER("REPORT MENU",.T.,01)
               centers " R E P O R T   M E N U "
               begins box on line 01 rather than default 0
* Assumes      box from 00,00 to 02,79 unless row passed
               in which case the box starts there.
Side Effects none
Returns        True always
Calls          LTRIM()
               EXPAND()
               DRAW_BOX()
               SETCOLOR()
               CENTRE()
```

```
FUNCTION HEADER

PARAMETERS string, expand_it, row
PRIVATE date, cur_color, sp
sp = " "
string = sp + LTRIM(TRIM(string)) + sp

IF TYPE("expand_it") != "U"          && anything will do
   string = EXPAND(string)
ENDIF

IF TYPE("row") != "N"                && default line 0
   row = 00
ENDIF

DRAW_BOX(row, 00, row + 02, 79, 03) && box type 03
```

```
@ row + 01,02 SAY CDOW(DATE()) + ", " + DTOC(DATE())
@ row + 01,69 SAY AMPM(TIME())
cur_color = SETCOLOR("N/W")
@ row + 01,CENTRE(string) SAY string
SETCOLOR(cur_color)
RETURN .T.
```

• MSG()

```
PROGRAM       AA_MSG.PRG
Function(s)   MSG()
Purpose       General message service
Conventions   line 24 is used for these messages
Syntax        MSG(string, wait, blink)
Parameters    string - message to display,
              defaults to "Press any key"
              wait - 0 = no wait, 1 = wait
              blink - add 3 blinking dots to string
Example       MSG("Working",0,.T.)
Assumes       line 24 is the message area, right justified
Side Effects  none
Returns       True always
Calls         SYSCOLOR()
```

```
FUNCTION MSG

PARAMETERS message, number, blinking
PRIVATE temp, row, col, sp, dots
temp = PCOUNT()
ak_msg = " Press any key "
row = 24                               && bottom line of the screen
sp = " "
dots = "..."
IF TYPE("message") != "C"              && press any key + dots
   message = ak_msg
   number = 01
   blinking = .T.
ENDIF
IF TYPE("blinking") = "U"              && default to no dots
   blinking = .F.
ENDIF
IF TYPE("number") != "N"               && default to no wait
   number = 00
ENDIF
message = sp + ALLTRIM( message ) + sp + ;
         IF( number > 0, ". " + ak_msg, "" )
IF blinking
   col = ( 77 - LEN( message ) )       && account for blinking dots
ELSE
   col = ( 80 - LEN( message ) )       && right-justify message
ENDIF
```

```
IF !blinking                            && don't put blinking messages
   SYSCOLOR(02)                         && in reverse video
ENDIF
@ row,col SAY message
SYSCOLOR(01)                            && back to normal
IF blinking
   BLINK(dots, ROW(), COL())
ENDIF
IF number > 00
   DO WAIT
   @ row, col SAY SPACE(LEN(message))
   reply = .T.
ENDIF
RETURN LASTKEY() = 27                   && was escape pressed?
```

• POP_MSG()

```
PROGRAM        AA_PPMSG.PRG
Function(s)    POP_MSG()
Purpose        Pop a message up, wait for a keystroke,
               then restore the screen
Conventions    none
Syntax         POP_MSG(msg[, row][, col])
Parameters     msg - message to display
               row - optional row to start box on
               col - optional col to start box on
Example        POP_MSG("This is a pop-up message")
Assumes        Calculates the size of the window
               according to the number of strings passed.
               "Any key to continue" is displayed
               on the bottom line of the window.
               1 line message : height = 5
               2 line message : height = 7  (counter * 2) + 3
               3 line message : height = 9
               A maximum of 20 lines can be displayed.
               More than 11 causes single-spacing.
               another example of progressive control:
               no pause - pass anything as param 2
               specific location - pass top left row and column
Side Effects   none
Returns        True always
Calls          WAIT, SETCOLOR(), CENTRE(), SAVESCREEN()
               RESTSCREEN(), DRAW_BOX()
```

```
FUNCTION POP_MSG

PARAMETERS message, tlr, tlc
PRIVATE counter, ak_msg, temp_scr, longest, height, width, row,;
      col, m_row, m_col, cur_color, old_color, reverse

temp = PCOUNT()
ak_msg = " Any key to continue "
longest = LEN(ak_msg)                 && Prevent box too small
counter = LEN(message)                && size of first parameter
m_row = ROW()
m_col = COL()
```

```
reverse   = "N/W"                     && black letters on white

IF TYPE("message") = "A"              && array passed?
   FOR i = 1 TO counter               && find its longest element
      longest = MAX(longest, LEN(message[i]))
   NEXT
ELSE
   counter = 1
   longest = MAX(longest, LEN(message))
ENDIF
width     = longest + 6               && add some whitespace
height    = MIN(20, (counter * 2) + 3)
IF temp > 2    && a location was passed
   start_row = tlr
   start_col = tlc
ELSE
   start_row = (22 - height) / 2      && up a little
   start_col = CENTRE(SPACE(width))   && centered
ENDIF
end_row   = start_row + height
end_col   = start_col + width
row       = start_row
col       = start_col + 3
*
* Save just enough screen to conserve memory
temp_scr = SAVESCREEN(start_row, start_col, end_row, end_col)
* draw a box
DRAW_BOX(start_row, start_col, end_row, end_col, 02)
IF TYPE("message") = "A"
   spacing = IF(LEN(message) > 11, 01, 02)
   FOR i = 1 TO counter
         row = row + spacing
         @ row, col SAY message[i]
   NEXT
ELSE
   row = row + 2
   @ row, col SAY message
ENDIF
cur_color = SETCOLOR(reverse)        && grab current value, change
@ end_row, CENTRE(ak_msg) SAY ak_msg
old_color = SETCOLOR(cur_color)      && restore old colors
DO WAIT
RESTSCREEN(start_row, start_col, end_row, end_col, temp_scr)
@ m_row, m_col SAY SPACE(0)          && put the cursor back
RETURN .T.
```

• GET_RANGE()

```
PROGRAM       AA_RANGE.PRG
Function(s)   GET_RANGE()
Purpose       GET upper and lower boundaries of a range
              with optional validation of input
Conventions   any VALIDs can be executed (e.g files open
              etc.)
Syntax        GET_RANGE(msg_str, memvar, pict_str, valstr)
Parameters    rng_str - prompt to display
              memvar - variable used to generate blanks
              pict_str - picture to use in GET
              val_str  - validity check if desired
Example       GET_RANGE( "Enter the report dates", ;
                mDATE, ; && variable pre-declared
                "@D", ; && picture
                "mDATE > DATE()")  && validity check
Assumes       nothing
Side Effects crash if udf is not linked in
Returns       True unless escape is pressed
Calls         CENTRE(), MAKE_STR(), MAX()
```

```
FUNCTION GET_RANGE

PARAMETERS msg_str, memvar, pict_str, val_str, exact_on
PRIVATE tr, tc, br, bc, add_space, pos, temp_scr
CLEAR GETS
temp = PCOUNT()
data = TYPE( "memvar" )
IF TYPE("exact_on") = "U"              && default to trim strings
   exact_on = .F.
ENDIF

mc = CENTRE(msg_str)
vc = CENTRE(MAKE_STR(memvar))
tc = MAX(0, MIN(vc, mc) - 03)          && trap for < 0
bc = 80 - tc   && same offset
tr = 05
br = 12

* SAVESCREEN is a little buggy at this writing...
* temp_scr = SPACE( (br - tr + 1) * (bc - tc + 1) )
temp_scr = SAVESCREEN(tr, tc, br, bc)
```

```
SHADOWBOX(tr, tc, br, bc, 2)
@ tr + 2, mc SAY msg_str

DO CASE
   CASE TYPE("pict_str") = "U"      && nothing but memvar passed
      @ tr + 4, vc GET memvar
   CASE TYPE("val_str") = "U"       && pic passed but no valid
      @ tr + 4, vc GET memvar PICTURE pict_str
   OTHERWISE                        && all params were passed
      @ tr + 4, vc GET memvar PICTURE pict_str VALID &val_str
ENDCASE

READ_IT()

IF TYPE("memvar") = "C" .AND. !exact_on
   memvar = TRIM( memvar )
ENDIF

RESTSCREEN(tr, tc, br, bc, temp_scr)

RETURN memvar
```

• READ_IT()

```
PROGRAM        AA_READT.PRG
Function(s)    READ_IT
Purpose        Sets cursor on, READs, sets cursor off
Conventions    cursor is on only during READs
Syntax         READ_IT()
Parameters     None
Example        READ_IT()
Assumes        at least one pending GET
Side Effects   none
Returns        True if any exit key but escape
Calls          nothing
```

```
FUNCTION READ_IT

SET CURSOR ON
READ
SET CURSOR OFF
RETURN LASTKEY()!=27
```

• SHADOWBOX()

```
PROGRAM      AA SHBOX PRG
Function(s)  SHADOWBOX()
Purpose      Draws boxes with a shadow behind them
Conventions  pass the dimensions of the box you want, not
             the shadow
Syntax       SHADOWBOX( row1, col1, row2, col2, hdr, box_no
Parameters   row1 - top row
             col1 - top column
             row2 - bottom row
             col2 - bottom column
             hdr - string to use as header on box
             box_no - numeric, passed to DRAW_BOX()
Example      SHADOWBOX(08,15,20,65,"Shadow Box",03)
Assumes      nothing
Side Effects bad data may cause crash
Returns      True always
Calls        POP_MSG(), SYSCOLOR(), SETCOLOR(),
             DRAW_BOX(), MIN(), MAX()
```

```
FUNCTION SHADOWBOX

PARAMETERS tr, tc, br, bc, hdr, box_no
IF TYPE("tr") != "N"
   RETURN POP_MSG("No parameters were passed")
ENDIF
IF TYPE("box_no") != "N"
   box_no = 03                         && see DRAW_BOX() for string
ENDIF
IF TYPE("hdr") != "C"
   hdr = ""
ENDIF
tr = MAX( 01, tr )                     && make honest params
tc = MAX( 01, tc )
br = MIN( 22, br )
bc = MIN( 78, bc )
br = IF(!EMPTY(hdr), br + 01, br)      && make room for the header
SYSCOLOR(01)
DRAW_BOX(tr, tc, br, bc, box_no)
IF !EMPTY(hdr)
   SYSCOLOR(02)
   @ tr + 1, tc + 1 SAY MIDDLE( hdr, bc - tc - 1)
```

```
   SYSCOLOR(01)
ENDIF
paint in the black shadow
IF TYPE("monochrome") = "U"
   monochrome = .F.
ENDIF
shadow = IF(monochrome, "1", " ")   && or "0" or "2"
cur_color = SETCOLOR( "W/N" )
@ tr + 1, bc + 1, br + 1, bc + 1 BOX shadow
@ br + 1, tc + 1, br + 1, bc + 1 BOX shadow
SETCOLOR(cur_color)
RETURN .T.
```

• SIGN_OFF()

```
PROGRAM        AA_SINOF.PRG
Function(s)    SIGN_OFF
Purpose        Close all programs with this routine
Conventions    closes files, sets cursor on, quits with
logo
Syntax         SIGN_OFF(exe_name)
Parameters     exe_name - the name of your program
Example        SIGN_OFF("A test program")
Assumes        nothing
Side Effects   none
Returns        True but not actually, since the QUIT is
               inside this function.
Calls          MIDDLE(), DRAW_BOX(), SYSCOLOR()
```

```
FUNCTION SIGN_OFF

PARAMETER exe_name
PRIVATE box_width, thanks, logo_line
IF TYPE("exe_name") = "U"
   exe_name = "Our Software"
   exe_desc = "Professional Clipper Library"
ENDIF

box_width = 39
thanks = MIDDLE( "Thank you for using", box_width )
exe_name = MIDDLE( exe_name, box_width )
exe_desc = MIDDLE( exe_desc, box_width )
logo_line = "Artful Applications    Copyright 1988"

DRAW_BOX( 07, 19, 15, 59, 02, .T. )
@ 08,20 SAY thanks
@ 09,20 SAY REPLICATE( "D", box_width )
@ 11,20 SAY REPLICATE( "D", box_width )
@ 12,20 SAY exe_desc
@ 13,20 SAY REPLICATE( "D", box_width )
@ 14,21 SAY logo_line

SYSCOLOR(02)
@ 10,20 SAY exe_name
SYSCOLOR(01)
CLOSE DATA
```

```
@ 18,00
QUIT
RETURN .T.
```

• SIGN_ON()

```
PROGRAM        AA_SINON.PRG
Function(s)    SIGN_ON()
Purpose        Open all your programs with this routine
Conventions    Expects a program name and a slogan
Syntax         SIGN_ON(exe_name, exe_desc)
Parameters     exe_name - displayed on first line of box
               exe_desc - display on next line of box
Example        SIGN_ON("Sample program", "A test routine")
Assumes        data passed in is valid (strings)
Side Effects   clears screen before display
Returns        True always
Calls          PCOUNT(), MIDDLE(), DRAW_BOX()
```

```
FUNCTION SIGN_ON

PARAMETERS exe_name, exe_desc, boot_msg
PRIVATE temp, box_width, welcome, logo_line, curr_clr
SET CURSOR OFF
temp = PCOUNT()
box_width = 39
welcome = MIDDLE( "Welcome to", box_width )
exe_name = MIDDLE( exe_name, box_width )
exe_desc = MIDDLE( exe_desc, box_width )
logo_line = "Artful Applications    Copyright 1988"

DRAW_BOX( 07, 19, 15, 19 + box_width + 01, 02, .T. )
@ 08,20 SAY welcome
@ 09,20 SAY REPLICATE( "D", box_width )
@ 11,20 SAY REPLICATE( "D", box_width )
@ 12,20 SAY exe_desc
@ 13,20 SAY REPLICATE( "D", box_width )
@ 14,21 SAY logo_line

curr_clr = SETCOLOR()
SYSCOLOR(2)
@ 10,20 SAY exe_name
SETCOLOR(curr_clr)

IF temp > 2
   MSG( boot_msg )
ENDIF
```

```
INKEY(1)
RETURN .T.
```

• SEARCH()

```
Program         AA_SRCH.PRG
Function(s)     SEARCH()
Purpose         Generalized search mechanism
Syntax          SEARCH(keys,cues,pics)
Parameters      keys - string or array of index key(s)
                cues - string or array of key identifiers
                pics - string or array of PICTUREs
                row - optional row to use for display
Example         SEARCH(xkeys, xcues, xpics)
Assumes         xkeys, xcues, and xpics are defined
                in preparation for a call to THE_USUAL()
                this function inherits those definitions
                if called from THE_USUAL().
Side Effects compound indexes with "@R" pictures can
                result in pictures that are too short.
                I'm working on it.
Returns         True only if search succeeds.
Calls           XCOUNT(), XFILL(), ASCAN(), L_MENU(),
   ASK_FOR(), BLANK()
```

```
FUNCTION SEARCH

PARAMETERS keys, cues, pics, row
PRIVATE choice, record_no, temp, result, ht, width, temp_scr, ;
      msg, row, col
temp = PCOUNT()
record_no = RECNO()
choice = 01
result = .T.
msg = "Search for the "
row = 02
col = 02
ht = 00
width = 00
IF TYPE("row") != "N"
   row = 02                              && below THE_USUAL() menu row
ENDIF
IF temp = 00
   k_size = XCOUNT()
   IF k_size  01
      DECLARE keys[k_size], cues[k_size]
      XFILL(keys)
```

```
      XFILL(cues)
   ENDIF
ENDIF
IF TYPE("cues") = "A"              && if array of keys was passed
   choice = ASCAN(keys,INDEXKEY(0))
   ht = LEN(cues) + 02
   width = LEN(cues[01])          && pad element 1 out
   DRAW_BOX(01,col -1, ht, col + width, 13)
   SET KEY left TO PREV_PMT
   SET KEY right TO NEXT_PMT
   choice = ACHOICE(row, col, ht-1, col + width - 1, cues, .T., .T.,
               choice)
   SET KEY left TO
   SET KEY right TO

   IF ESC()
      RESTORE SCREEN FROM temp_scr
      RETURN .F.                  && Out, without changing order
   ENDIF

   msg = msg + cues[choice]
   m_pic = pics
   target = BLANK(&keys)
ELSE
   msg = msg + cues
   m_pic = pics
   target = BLANK(&keys)
ENDIF
SET ORDER TO choice
ASK_FOR(msg, @target, m_pic)
IF !ESC()
   SEEK target
   IF !FOUND()
      POP_MSG("I can't find " + MAKE_STR(target))
      result = .F.
   ELSE
      record_no = RECNO()
   ENDIF
ELSE
   result = .F.
ENDIF
GO record_no
@ row,00
RETURN result
```

```
PROCEDURE PREV_PMT

PARAMETERS x, y, z
```

```
PRIVATE left, esc
left = 19
esc = 27
esc = 27
KEYBOARD CHR(esc) + CHR(left)
RETURN
```

```
PROCEDURE NEXT_PMT

PARAMETERS x, y, z
PRIVATE right, esc
right = 04
esc = 27
KEYBOARD CHR(esc) + CHR(right)
RETURN
```

• WAIT

PROGRAM	AA_WAIT.PRG
Function(s)	PROCEDURE WAIT
Purpose	Simple wait command
Conventions	sets console off, waits, sets console on, returns. It uses a pseudo-wait to avoid SET KEY problems
Syntax	DO WAIT
Parameters	none
Example	DO WAIT
Assumes	nothing
Side Effects	none
Returns	nothing
Calls	nothing

```
PROCEDURE WAIT

SET CONSOLE OFF
INKEY(0)
SET CONSOLE ON
RETURN
```

Chapter 20

String Functions

- ALLTRIM — returns a string shorn of leading and trailing blanks.
- CENTRE — returns the column number at which to begin displaying a string.
- CHK_MARK — displays a check mark in place of true for a logical field.
- CRLF — returns CHR(13)+CHR(10). Useful for multi-line headers in reports.
- ENCODE — encrypts a string.
- EXPAND — double-spaces a string.
- FILLOUT — "fills out" a single-character into a string.
- LANG — a version of FILLOUT, oriented to language.
- LCHAR — returns the last character of a string.
- LPAD — pads a string with leading blanks to the specified length.
- LTOC — turns a logical into a character.
- MIDDLE — centers a string in the specified width, filling it out with blanks on either side.
- MAKE_STR — turns any input into a string.
- PAD — pads out a string with trailing blanks to the specified length.
- PROPER — forces proper case on input string.
- PASSWORD — asks for a password, checks it against legitimate entries.
- SEX — turns M/F into Male/Female.
- SIN — formats input according to Social Insurance Number convention (Canadian).
- SSN — formats input according to Social Security Number convention (American).
- STRINT — returns a trimmed string version of the input number.

• ALLTRIM()

```
PROGRAM AA_ALLTR.PRG
Function(s) ALLTRIM()
Purpose cut strings down to size
Conventions none
Syntax ALLTRIM(string)
Parameters string - object to trim
Example ALLTRIM("  XXXXX   ") returns "XXX"
Assumes string is indeed a string
Side Effects crash on bad data
Returns trimmed string
Calls nothing
```

```
FUNCTION ALLTRIM

PARAMETER string
RETURN LTRIM(TRIM(string))
```

• CENTRE()

```
PROGRAM        AA_TSTRNG.PRG
Function(s)    CENTRE()
Purpose        Display a string centered on the screen
Conventions    24-hour clock
Syntax         CENTRE(string, offset, width)
Parameters     string - object to center
               offset - default 0
               width - default 80
Example        @ 10, CENTRE(msg) SAY msg
Assumes        nothing
Side Effects   none
Returns        column number at which to display
Calls          nothing
```

```
FUNCTION CENTRE

PARAMETERS string, offset, width

temp = PCOUNT()

IF temp < 2
   width  = 80
   offset =  0
ENDIF

RETURN ((width - LEN(string))/2) + offset
```

• CHK_MARK()

```
PROGRAM       AA_CHMRK.PRG
Function(s)   CHK_MARK()
Purpose       transformation of logicals displayed
Conventions   True = a check mark, False = " ".
              test for empty instead of full: avoid
              crashing on non-logicals while also allowing
              interpretation of other data as if logical
              (e.g. full = True, empty = .F.)
Syntax        CHK_MARK(expC/expL)
Parameters    expC/L - expression -- logical
Example       CHK_MARK(Paid).. field paid
Assumes       exp is valid logical or macros to logical
Side Effects  crash on bad data
Returns       CHR(32) or CHR(251)
Calls         nothing
```

```
FUNCTION CHK_MARK

PARAMETER expr
PRIVATE result

IF TYPE("expr") = "C"
   result = &expr
ENDIF

RETURN IF( EMPTY(result), CHR(32), CHR(251) )
```

• CLRF()

```
PROGRAM      AA_CRLF.PRG
Version      1.0
Purpose      Add a carriage return/line feed to a string
Conventions  the string expression passed must be
legitimate
Syntax       CRLF(string)
Parameters   string - the expression to print
Example      ? CRLF(company) + CRLF(address)
Assumes      nothing
Side Effects none
Returns      string + CHR(13) + CHR(10)
Notes        Useful in report forms break headers where you
             want to use several pieces of data in the header
```

```
FUNCTION CRLF

PARAMETER string
RETURN string + CHR(13) + CHR(10)
```

• LANG()

```
PROGRAM        AA_LANG.PRG
Function(s)    LANG()
Purpose        Translate a character into a language
Conventions    add as many languages as you require
               Pad them out to the longest in use
Syntax         LANG(char)
Parameters       char - char which corresponds to a
               language in the CASE statement below
Example        LANG("S") returns "Spanish"
Assumes        char is a character
Side Effects   crashes on bad data
Returns        a string naming the language or a blank if it
               cannot find a match
Calls          nothing
```

```
FUNCTION LANG

PARAMETER char

DO CASE
   CASE char = "F"
      answer = "French  "
   CASE char = "E"
      answer = "English "
   CASE char = "S"
      answer = "Spanish "
   CASE char = "I"
      answer = "Innuit  "
   OTHERWISE
      answer = "        "
ENDCASE

RETURN answer
```

• EXPAND()

```
PROGRAM      AA_EXPAN.PRG
Version      1 .0
Purpose      Expands a string by double-spacing it
Conventions  adds a sp on either end, middle spaces — 3
Syntax       EXPAND(string)
Parameters   string - string to expand
Example      ? EXPAND("HELLO WORLD")
             returns " H E L L O   W O R L D "
Assume       nothing
Side Effects none
Returns      E X P A N D E D   S T R I N G
```

```
FUNCTION EXPAND

PARAMETER string
PRIVATE new_str, char, sp
sp = " "
new_str = sp
string = ALLTRIM(string)

FOR i = 1 TO LEN(string)
   char = SUBSTR(string, i, 1)
   new_str = new_str + IF(char = sp, SPACE(3), char + sp)
NEXT

RETURN new_str + sp
```

• FILL_OUT()

```
PROGRAM         AA_FLOUT.PRG
Function(s)     FILL_OUT()
Purpose         Fills out data entered or displayed, expanding
                a character entered into a string displayed
                beginning at the same location as the GET
                it is validating.
Conventions
Syntax          FILL_OUT(char, string, array, logical )
Parameters
                char - current value (var or fld contents)
                string - list of legal entries
                array - of strings
                logical - indicates read this or translate
Example         DECLARE e_types[04]
                e_types[01] = "Cook    " && fill out strings
                e_types[02] = "Waiter " && to equal length
                e_types[03] = "Bouncer"
                e_types[04] = "Manager"
                emp_code = " "
                @ row, col GET emp_code ;
                VALID FILLOUT(emp_code,"CWBM",e_types,.T.)
Assumes         all parameters are declared and legitimate
Side Effects none known
Returns         True if char $ string
Notes           pad Array elements to the longest's
                length. This will ensure they overwrite
                each other cleanly
                Logical parameter is required because the
                udf relies on cursor location to determine
                where to display the string.
                If a GET is underway, the cursor will be 1
                to its right. If a SAY is underway, the
                cursor will already be in the correct
                location.
```

```
FUNCTION FILL_OUT

PARAMETER char, string, array, reading
```

```
PRIVATE where, col, reply, bell
where = AT( char, string )
col = IF( reading, COL() -1, COL()) && adjust for say/get
bell = CHR(07)
IF where > 0
   string = array[where]
   reply = .T.
ELSE
   ? bell                             && let 'em know of error
   string = SPACE(LEN( array[1]))    && put a blank there
   reply  = .F.
ENDIF

@ ROW(), COL SAY string
RETURN reply
```

• LASTCHAR()

```
PROGRAM       AA_LCHAR.PRG
Function(s)   LASTCHAR()
Purpose       Returns the last character in a string
Conventions
Syntax        LASTCHAR(string)
Parameters    string - assumed to be a string
Example       LASTCHAR("STRING") returns "G"
Assumes       g is a string, does not check data type
Side Effects crashes on bad data
Returns       the last character in
Calls         nothing
```

```
FUNCTION LASTCHAR

PARAMETER string
RETURN SUBSTR( string, LEN( string ) )
```

• LPAD()

```
PROGRAM       AA_LPAD.PRG
Function(s)   LPAD()
Purpose       Pad a string with leading blanks to specified
length
Conventions   right-justify strings, etc.
Syntax        LPAD(string, length)
Parameters    string — object to pad
              length — length to make it
Example       LPAD("This is a string", 30)
Assumes       nothing
Side Effects  trims the string if it's too long
Returns       True
Calls         nothing
```

```
FUNCTION LPAD

PARAMETERS string, n
PRIVATE str_len, whitespace, result
str_len = LEN(string)
IF str_len > n
   result = SUBSTR(string, 1, n)
ELSE
   whitespace = SPACE(n - LEN(string))
   result = whitespace + string
ENDIF
RETURN result
```

• LTOC()

```
PROGRAM        AA_LTOC.PRG
Function(s)    LTOC()
Purpose        Logical to Character translation
Conventions      True  = "True " or "Yes" or checkmark
               False = "False" or "No " or " "    - space
Syntax           LTOC(logical)
Parameters       logical - value to translate
               version - defaults to 0, controls which of the
                       translations is returned
Example        LTOC(.T., 01) returns "Yes"
Side Effects pads the shorter versions out so they
overwrite
               any previous display
Returns        True  = "True " or "Yes" or checkmark
               False = "False" or "No " or " "    - space
Calls          EMPTY()
```

```
FUNCTION LTOC

PARAMETERS logical, version
PRIVATE reply, true
true = !EMPTY(logical)
IF TYPE("version") != "N"
   version = 0
ENDIF
DO CASE
   CASE version = 0
      reply = IF( true, "True ", "False"  )
   CASE version = 1
      reply = IF( true, "Yes", "No " )
   OTHERWISE
      reply = IF( true, CHR(251), " " )
ENDCASE

RETURN reply
```

• MIDDLE()

```
PROGRAM       AA_MIDDL.PRG
Function(s)   MIDDLE()
Purpose       Centers a string inside blanks so the total
length
              is length
Coventions    assumed length of 80
              uneven length favours the left
Syntax        MIDDLE(string,width)
Parameters    string - string to display
              width - total length of centered string
Example       MIDDLE("Sample string", 40)
Assumes       width = 80
Side Effects  none
Returns       string centered in width
Calls         EVEN()
```

```
FUNCTION MIDDLE

PARAMETERS string,number
PRIVATE result
IF !IS_EVEN( number - LEN( string ) )
   string = string + " "
ENDIF

result = SPACE( (number - LEN(string))/2 ) + string + ;
         SPACE( (number - LEN(string))/2 )

RETURN result
```

• MAKE_STR()

```
PROGRAM        AA_MKSTR.PRG
Function(s)    MAKE_STR()
Purpose        Force unknown data type to string
Conventions    a string passed in is simply returned
Syntax         MAKE_STR(data)
Parameters     data - any type of data
Example        MAKE_STR(500*20) returns "1000"
Assumes        data passed in is a valid object
Side Effects   none
Returns        the string equivalent of whatever was passed in
Calls          DTOC()
               STR()
               TYPE()
```

```
FUNCTION MAKE_STR

PARAMETER object
n = TYPE( "object" )
DO CASE
   CASE n = "D"
         answer = DTOC( object )
   CASE n = "N"
      answer = STR( object )
   CASE n = "L"
      answer = IF( object, "True", "False" )
   OTHERWISE
      answer = object                 && character data
ENDCASE

RETURN answer
```

• PAD()

```
PROGRAM        AA_PAD.PRG
Function(s)    PAD()
Purpose        Pad a string with blanks to a desired length
Conventions    data passed must be string, number
               no checks are made internally
Syntax         PAD(msg, width)
Parameters     string - string to pad
               width  - total length desired
Example        PAD("Sample string", 20)
               returns "Sample string" + 8 spaces
Assumes        validity of params, in the correct order
Side Effects   crashes on bad data
Returns        elongated or trimmed string
Calls          TRIM()
               LEN()
               SPACE()
```

```
FUNCTION PAD

PARAMETERS string, length

IF LEN( string ) < length
   string = TRIM( string ) + SPACE( length - LEN( TRIM( string ) ) )
ELSE
   string = LEFT( string, length )
ENDIF

RETURN string
```

• PROFER()

```
PROGRAM        AA_PROPR.PRG
Function(s)    PROPER()
Purpose        Turns a string into Proper case
Conventions    Not infallible. Turns 1st char and all chars
               which follow a space into upper, all else
               lower case
Syntax         PROPER(string)
Parameters     string - item to transform
Example        ? PROPER("This is a sTrInG") ...
               returns "This Is A String"
Assumes        nothing
Side Effects   none
Returns        the string transformed
Calls          UPPER()
               LOWER()
               LEFT()
```

```
FUNCTION PROPER

PARAMETER string1
PRIVATE   string2, char1, char2

* Force the first char up and everything else down
string2 = UPPER(LEFT(string1,1)) + SUBSTR(LOWER(string1),2)

* See if there's anything else to do

DO WHILE .T.
   where = AT(" ",string2)
   IF (where > 0)
      string2 = SUBSTR(string2, 1, where) + ;
                UPPER(SUBSTR(string2,where + 1,1)) + ;
                SUBSTR(string2,where + 2)
   ELSE
      EXIT
   ENDIF
ENDDO

RETURN string2
```

• GET_PSWD()

```
PROGRAM        AA_PSWD.PRG
Function(s)    GET_PSWD()
Purpose        get and validate a user password
Conventions    Fuller's Law: there is either a back door
               a stupid programmer
Syntax         GET_PSWD(key, backdoor)
Parameters     entry - variable to check
               backdoor - if not passed, must be public
               or known
Example        GET_PSWD("Sesame")
Assumes        the data is worth protecting
Side Effects   none
Returns        True if legit entry
Calls          ASK_FOR(), ENCODE()
```

```
FUNCTION GET_PSWD

PARAMETERS m_pass, back_door
PRIVATE pass_word, translate, result

pass_word = SPACE(20)
translate = 0
result = .F.

ASK_FOR("Enter the Password Below", pass_word, "@!")

IF !EMPTY( pass_word )
   translate = ENCODE( pass_word )
   IF translate = m_pass .OR. translate = back_door
      result = .T.
   ELSE
      ?? CHR(7)
      POP_MSG("That is not correct")
   ENDIF
ENDIF

RETURN result
```

• SEX()

```
PROGRAM         AA_SEX.PRG
Function(s)     SEX()
Purpose         Translates "M" or "F" into Male/Female
Conventions     none
Syntax          SEX(char)
Parameters      char - character to translate
Example         ? SEX("M") .... results in "Male  "
Assumes         char can be either a memvar or a field name
Side Effects    none
Returns         "Male  ", "Female" or "      "
Calls           nothing
```

```
FUNCTION SEX

PARAMETER char
PRIVATE reply

DO CASE
   CASE char $ "Ff"
      reply = "Female"
   CASE char $ "Mm"
      reply = "Male  "
   OTHERWISE
      reply = "      "
ENDCASE

RETURN reply
```

• SIN()

```
PROGRAM        AA_SINNO.PRG
Function(s)    SIN()
Purpose        formats Canadian Social Insurance Number
Conventions    store the field as Char 9 and use this udf
               to display it
Syntax         SIN(string)
Parameters     string — 9-character string of numbers
Example        ? SIN("123123123") returns "123 123 123"
Assumes        nothing
Side Effects   none
Returns        string padded appropriately
Calls          SUBSTR()
```

```
FUNCTION SIN

PARAMETER n_string
PRIVATE result

result = SUBSTR(n_string, 1, 3) + " " + ;
         SUBSTR(n_string, 4, 3) + " " + ;
         SUBSTR(n_string, 7)

RETURN result
```

• SSN()

```
Syntax       SSN(n_string)
Returns      Expanded display equivalent of S.S.N.
Notes        606112345 becomes 606-11-2345
```

```
FUNCTION SSN

PARAMETER n_string
PRIVATE result
result = SUBSTR(n_string,1,3) + "-" + ;
         SUBSTR(n_string,4,2) + "-" + ;
         SUBSTR(n_string, 7)

RETURN result
```

• STRINT()

```
PROGRAM       AA_STRINT.PRG
Function(s)   STRINT()
Purpose       Return string of the integer of a number,
              with no leading blanks
Conventions   typically used in macro-expansion
Syntax        STRINT(number)
Parameters    number - number to translate
Example       STRINT(42.1) returns "42"
Assumes       data passed is numeric
Side Effects  no check for valid data, could crash
Returns       string of the int with no leading blanks
Calls         nothing
```

```
FUNCTION STRINT

PARAMETER number
RETURN LTRIM( STR( INT( number ) ) )
```

Chapter 21

System-related Functions

- BELL — rings the bell.
- DOS — opens a DOS window, or runs the program whose name is passed.
- SET_PRN — handles printer control, using a data table to store codes.
- SET_SYS — sets various system flags such as CONFIRM.
- SYSCOLOR — handles all color-control tasks.
- TUBE — draws a show-biz series of boxes on the screen. You might like it for your sign-on.

• BELL()

```
PROGRAM       AA_BELL.PRG
Function(s)   BELL()
Purpose       Ring the bell
Conventions   pass a num to ring the bell more than once
Syntax        BELL([number])
Parameters    number - how many times? default 1
Example       BELL(george)... where george = 56
Assumes       nothing
Side Effects  potential user headaches if abused
Returns       True
Calls         nothing
```

```
FUNCTION BELL

PARAMETER number
PRIVATE i

IF TYPE("number") = "U"
   number = 01
ENDIF

FOR i = 01 TO number
   ?? CHR(7)
NEXT

RETURN .T.
```

• DOS()

```
PROGRAM        AA_DOS.PRG
Function(s)    DOS()
Purpose        DOS window or execute a program
Conventions    no program passed = load command.com
Syntax           DOS([program])
Parameters     program - optional program to execute
Example        DOS(boot)
Assumes        sufficient free memory to load command.com
Side Effects   hang on insufficient memory (bug in S87)
Returns        True
Calls          nothing
```

```
FUNCTION DOS

PARAMETER cmd
PRIVATE cmd, temp_scr

IF TYPE("cmd") = "C"
   cmd = "COMMAND"
ENDIF

SAVE SCREEN TO temp_scr
CLEAR
SET CURSOR ON                          && Be polite, now
RUN &cmd
SET CURSOR OFF
RESTORE SCREEN FROM temp_scr

RETURN .T.
```

- SET_PRN()

```
PROGRAM       AA_SETPR.PRG
Function(s)   SET_PRN(), PRT_MENU(), EDIT_PRN(),
              SEND_CODE(), TEST_PRN()
Purpose       Data-driven printer setup routine
Conventions   assumes a file PRINTER.DBF either in the
              current directory or the root
              (so one file can work with several apps)
Syntax        SET_PRN([file])
Parameters    file - name of printer file
Example       SET_PRN("TOSHIBA")
Assumes       printer file is either in current dir or root
Side Effects  sends selected printer codes to printer
Returns       True if successful
Calls         DUST_1(), POP_MSG(), DB_OPEN()
```

```
FUNCTION SET_PRN

PARAMETER ptr_file
PRIVATE cur_file, cur_rec, ok_dbfs, root_sign, udf, work_area
cur_file = ALIAS()
cur_rec = RECNO()
root_sign = "\"
disp_fld = "Type_style"
udf = "PRT_MENU()"
ok_dbfs = .T.
IF UN_DEF( "ptr_file" )
   ptr_file = "PRINTER"
ENDIF
DO CASE
   CASE DB_OPEN( ptr_file )
      * dummy structure: nothing needs to be done,
      * the CASE executes the function
      * this allows conditional executions without nested IFs.
   CASE DB_OPEN( root_sign + ptr_file )
      *
   OTHERWISE
      POP_MSG( "The printer control file " + ptr_file + ;
            " is missing" )
      RETURN .F.
ENDCASE
BROWSER( .F.,.F.,.F.,.F., udf )
IF !EMPTY( cur_file )
```

```
   SELECT &cur_file
   GO cur_rec
ENDIF
RETURN .T.
```

• PRT_MENU()

```
FUNCTION PRT_MENU

PRIVATE temp_scr
SAVE SCREEN TO temp_scr
@ 04,17 CLEAR TO 12,58
@ 04,17 TO 12,58
@ 06,30 SAY "Printer Options"
@ 10,21 PROMPT " Add "
@ 10,28 PROMPT " Change "
@ 10,38 PROMPT " Delete "
@ 10,49 PROMPT " Send "
MENU TO choice
DO CASE
   CASE choice =1
      EDIT_PRN(1)
   CASE choice =2
      EDIT_PRN(0)
   CASE choice =3
      DUST_1()
   CASE choice =4
      SEND_CODE()
ENDCASE
RETURN choice
```

• SEND_CODE()

```
FUNCTION SEND_CODE

PRIVATE string
DO CASE
   CASE EMPTY( string_1 )
      RETURN POP_MSG( "There are no codes to send" )
   CASE EMPTY( string_2 )
      code = CHR( string_1 )
   CASE EMPTY( string_3 )
      code = CHR( string_1 ) + CHR( string_2 )
   OTHERWISE
```

```
      code = CHR( string_1 ) + CHR( string_2 ) + CHR( string_3 )
ENDCASE
SET CONSOLE OFF
SET PRINT ON
?? code
SET CONSOLE ON
SET PRINT OFF
IF VERIFY( "Send a Test String to the Printer" )
   PRN_TEST()
ENDIF
RETURN .T.
```

- EDIT_PRN()

```
FUNCTION EDIT_PRN

PARAMETER add_a_rec
PRIVATE temp_scr, row, col, l_col, string_1, string_2, string_3
IF !EMPTY(add_a_rec)                    && type is irrelevant
   STORE 0 TO string_1, string_2, string_3
   type_style = SPACE(20)
ELSE
   Type_style = Type_style
   string_1 = string_1
   string_2 = string_2
   string_3 = string_3
ENDIF
SAVE SCREEN TO temp_scr
@ 05,14 CLEAR TO 10,65
@ 05,14 TO 10,65
@ 06,16 SAY "Description of Style    Code 1   Code 2   Code 3"
@ 08,16 GET m->TYPE_STYLE PICTURE "!" + REPL("X",LEN(Type_style)-1)
@ 08,41 GET m->STRING_1 PICTURE "999"
@ 08,50 GET m->STRING_2 PICTURE "999"
@ 08,59 GET m->STRING_3 PICTURE "999"
SET CURSOR ON
READ
SET CURSOR OFF
IF !ESC()
   SELECT PRINTER
   IF !EMPTY( add_a_rec )
      APPEND BLANK
   ENDIF
   REPLACE string_1 WITH m->string_1, string_2 WITH m->string_2, ;
      string_3 WITH m->string_3, Type_style WITH m->Type_style
ENDIF
RESTORE SCREEN FROM temp_scr
```

```
RETURN .T.
```

- ## PRN_TEST()

```
FUNCTION PRN_TEST

numbers  = REPL("1234567890",13)
test_str = "THIS TYPEFACE IS " + TRIM( prn_desc )
occupied = LEN( test_str )
test_str = test_str + SUBSTR( numbers, 1, 80 - occupied )
SET PRINT ON
SET CONSOLE OFF
? test_str
?
? CHR(13) + CHR(10)
SET CONSOLE ON
SET PRINT OFF
RETURN .T.
```

• SET_SYS()

```
PROGRAM        AA_SETSS.PRG
Function(s)    SET_SYS()
Purpose        set system settings via flags in system file
Conventions    allow user to control SOFTSEEK, BELL,
CONFIRM
Syntax         SET_SYS()
Parameters     none
Example        SET_SYS()
Assumes        assumes a system file open and ready for use
Side Effects   alters system SET states
Returns        True
Calls          nothing
```

```
FUNCTION SET_SYS

IF TYPE("Soft_on") = "U"
   soft_on = .F.
ENDIF
IF TYPE("confirm_on") = "U"
   confirm_on = .F.
ENDIF
IF TYPE("bell_on") = "U"
   bell_on = .F.
ENDIF
IF Soft_on
   SET SOFTSEEK ON
ENDIF
IF Confirm_on
   SET CONFIRM ON
ENDIF
IF bell_on
   SET BELL ON
ENDIF

RETURN .T.
```

• SYSCOLOR()

```
PROGRAM        AA_SYCLR.PRG
Function(s)    SYSCOLOR()
Purpose        Central color setter
Conventions    make one or more versions of this to suit
Syntax         SYSCOLOR(number)
Parameters     number - refers to one of your own settings
Example        SYSCOLOR(menu_color)
Assumes        variable monochrome has probably been declared
Side Effects   none
Returns        True
Calls          nothing
```

```
FUNCTION SYSCOLOR

PARAMETER num
IF TYPE("monochrome") = "U"          && color is the future
   monochrome = .F.                  && so assume it but allow
ENDIF                                && for ancient machinery
IF ISCOLOR() .AND. !monochrome
   DO CASE
      CASE num = 01
         clr = "+W/B,+W/R,,,W/B"
      CASE num = 02
         clr = "W+/R,,,,W/B"
      CASE num = 03
         clr = "+GR/N"
      CASE num = 04
         clr = "+W/B,+W/R,,,W/B"
      CASE num = 05
         clr = "+W/B,B/W,,,W/B"
      CASE num = 06
         clr = "GB/W,,,,W/N"
      CASE num = 07
         clr = "+W/GB,,,,GB/N"
      CASE num = 08
         clr = "+GB/W,,,,W/N"
      CASE num = 09
         clr = "N/W,,,,GB/N"
      CASE num = 10
         clr = "B/W"
      CASE num = 11
         clr = ""
```

```
      CASE num = 12
         clr = ""
      CASE num = 13
         clr = "W/N"
   ENDCASE
ELSE
   DO CASE
      CASE num = 01
         clr = ""
      CASE num = 02
         clr = "I"
      CASE num = 03
         clr = "W+"
      CASE num = 04
         clr = "W,,,,W"
      CASE num = 05
         clr = "W,,,,W"
      CASE num = 06
         clr = ""
      CASE num = 07
         clr = ""
      CASE num = 08
         clr = ""
      CASE num = 09
         clr = ""
      CASE num = 10
         clr = "N/W"
   ENDCASE
ENDIF
SET COLOR TO &clr
RETURN 0
```

• TUBE()

```
PROGRAM       AA_TUBE.PRG
Function(s)   TUBE()
Purpose       Show biz
Conventions   explode a box for a logo or something
Syntax        TUBE()
Parameters    none
Example       TUBE()
Assumes       nothing
Side Effects  wakes sleeping users
Returns        True
Calls         nothing
```

```
FUNCTION TUBE

PRIVATE x, y
x = 00
y = 10

FOR x = 00 TO 04
   FOR y = 10 TO 00 STEP -01
      @ y, y TO 24-y, 79-y
   NEXT
   y = 10
NEXT
y = 10

FOR y = 10 TO 00 STEP -01
   @ y, y CLEAR TO 24-y, 79-y
NEXT

RETURN .T.
```

Chapter 22

Time Functions

- SAY_TIME — displays time (cursor off) at specified location.
- TDIFF — difference between two times.
- TIMER — times the execution of another function.
- TNUM — returns a time expressed as a number of seconds.
- TSTRING — turns a number of seconds into a time string.

• SAY_TIME()

```
PROGRAM        AA_STIME.PRG
Function(s)    SAY_TIME()
Purpose        display time at a screen location
Conventions    returns immediately, or waits
Syntax         SAY_TIME(row, col, wait)
Parameters     row - display at row
               col - display at col
               wait - pass anything to force wait
Example        SAY_TIME(24,70,.T.)
Assumes        no restore screen is required
Side Effects   none
Returns        True
Calls          nothing
```

```
FUNCTION SAY_TIME

PARAMETERS row, col, wait
temp = PCOUNT()
IF TYPE("row") != "N"
   row = 24
ENDIF
IF TYPE("col") != "N"
   col = 69
ENDIF

IF TYPE("wait") = "U"
   @ row, col SAY AMPM( TIME() )
ELSE
   x = 00
   DO WHILE x = 00
      @ row, col SAY AMPM( TIME() )
      x = INKEY()
   ENDDO
ENDIF

RETURN .T.
```

• TDIFF()

```
PROGRAM        AA_TDIFF.PRG
Function(s)    TDIFF()
Purpose        return elapsed time either as a string
               or as seconds
Conventions    param 3 indicates your preference
Syntax         TDIFF(time1, time2)
Parameters     time1 - start time
               time2 - stop time
               exp   - any value forces numeric return
Example        ? TDIFF(noon, midnite) returns "12:00:00"
Assumes        times are on same day, except:
               If t2 is less than time1 it assumes midnight
               passed
Side Effects could lead to incorrect result if params in
               wrong order
Returns        a time string or a number of seconds
Calls          nothing
```

```
FUNCTION TDIFF

PARAMETERS time1, time2, in_seconds
PRIVATE ts1, ts2, result
IF TYPE("in_seconds") = "U"
   in_seconds = .F.
ELSE
   in_seconds = .T.
ENDIF
secs_p_day = 86400
ts1 = IN_SECS(time1)
ts2 = IN_SECS(time2)
IF ts2 < ts1
   ts2 = ts2 + secs_p_day
ENDIF
result = ts2 - ts1

RETURN IF(in_seconds, result, TSTRING(result))
```

• TIMER()

```
PROGRAM       AA_TIMER.PRG
Function(s)   TIMER()
Purpose       Times the execution of a function
Conventions   useful in debugging, optimizing
Syntax        TIMER()
Parameters    udf - function you want timed
Example       TIMER(udf)
Assumes       udf is linked in
Side Effects  displays results afterwards
Returns       udf's return value (so execution can proceed)
Calls         your udf and whatever else
```

```
FUNCTION TIMER

PARAMETER udf
PRIVATE start, stop, duration, result
start = TIME()
result = &udf
stop = TIME()
duration = TDIFF(start, stop)
POP_MSG("Elapsed time was: " + duration)

RETURN result
```

• TNUM()

```
PROGRAM       AA_TNUM.PRG
Function(s)   TNUM()
Purpose       turn a time string into a # of seconds
Conventions   valid time string
Syntax        TNUM(time)
Parameters     time - a valid time string
Example       TNUM(TIME())
Assumes       valid time string (24 hour format)
Side Effects  none
Returns       elapsed time in seconds
Calls         nothing
```

```
FUNCTION TNUM

PARAMETER time
PRIVATE result
result = ( VAL(SUBSTR(time, 1, 2)) * 3600 + ;
         VAL(SUBSTR(time, 4, 2)) * 60 + ;
         VAL(SUBSTR(time, 7, 2)) )

RETURN result
```

• TSTRING()

```
PROGRAM        AA_TSTRG.PRG
Function(s)    TSTRING()
Purpose        display number of seconds as a time string
Conventions    seconds  1 day are rounded back to 1 day
Syntax         TSTRING(seconds)
Parameters     seconds - number of seconds to convert
Example        TSTRING(111) returns "01:51:00")
Assumes        seconds > 86400
Side Effects   crash on bad data
Returns        time string equivalent to number of seconds
Calls          MOD(), STRZERO()
```

```
FUNCTION TSTRING

PARAMETER seconds
PRIVATE result

IF seconds > 86400
   seconds = MOD(seconds,86400)
ENDIF

result = STRZERO(INT(MOD(seconds/3600,24)),2, 0 ) +':'+;
         STRZERO(INT(MOD(seconds/60,60)),2,0) +':'+;
         STRZERO(INT(MOD(seconds,60)),2,0)

RETURN result
```

Chapter 23

Keyboard Functions

- Virtually every non-data key that can be mapped is included in this section. These functions are not so much powerful as clarifying — a year from now, you'll know at a glance what your code means.

```
PROGRAM       KEYS.PRG
Purpose       to contain all keyboard UDFs in one source file
Comments      this code is unlikely to be linked into any
              of your programs. Instead just rely on the linke
              to call any of these UDFs out of KEYS.LIB for yo
Syntax        READKEY( )
Returns       Value of last key pressed
Notes         differences between dBASE and Clipper
```

```
FUNCTION READKEY

DO CASE
   CASE PGUP()
      answer = 06 + IF(UPDATED(),256,0)
   CASE PGDN()
      answer = 07 + IF(UPDATED(),256,0)
   CASE LASTKEY() = 27
      answer = 12 + IF(UPDATED(),256,0)
   CASE CTRL_W()
      answer = 14 + IF(UPDATED(),256,0)
   CASE ENTER()
      answer = 15 + IF(UPDATED(),256,0)
   CASE CTRL_PGUP()
      answer = 34 + IF(UPDATED(),256,0)
   CASE CTRL_PGDN()
      answer = 35 + IF(UPDATED(),256,0)
   CASE LASTKEY() = 32               && type past end
      answer = 15 + IF(UPDATED(),256,0)
   OTHERWISE
      answer = 00
ENDCASE                              && entered

RETURN answer
```

KEYPAD KEYS

```
FUNCTION SPACEBAR
RETURN ( LASTKEY() = 32 )

FUNCTION UP
RETURN ( LASTKEY() = 5 )

FUNCTION INS
RETURN ( LASTKEY() = 22 )

FUNCTION HOME
RETURN ( LASTKEY() = 1 )

FUNCTION DEL
RETURN ( LASTKEY() = 07 )

FUNCTION DN
RETURN ( LASTKEY() = 24 )

FUNCTION END
RETURN ( LASTKEY() = 6 )

FUNCTION ENTER
RETURN ( LASTKEY() = 13 )

FUNCTION ESC
RETURN ( LASTKEY() = 27 )
```

```
FUNCTION PGDN
RETURN ( LASTKEY() = 3 )

FUNCTION PGUP
RETURN ( LASTKEY() = 18 )

FUNCTION RT_ARROW
RETURN ( LASTKEY() = 4 )

FUNCTION LT_ARROW
RETURN LASTKEY() = 19 )

FUNCTION CTRL_HOME
RETURN ( LASTKEY() = 29 )

FUNCTION CTRL_END
RETURN ( LASTKEY() = 23 )

FUNCTION CTRL_PGDN
RETURN ( LASTKEY() = 30 )

FUNCTION CTRL_PGUP
RETURN ( LASTKEY() = 31 )

FUNCTION ALT_HOME
RETURN ( LASTKEY() = 430 )

FUNCTION ALT_END
RETURN ( LASTKEY() = 438 )
```

```
FUNCTION ALT_DEL
RETURN ( LASTKEY() = 442 )

FUNCTION ALT_INS
RETURN ( LASTKEY() = 441 )

FUNCTION ALT_UP
RETURN ( LASTKEY() = 431 )

FUNCTION ALT_DN
RETURN ( LASTKEY() = 439 )
```

FUNCTION KEYS

```
FUNCTION F1
RETURN ( LASTKEY() = 28 )

FUNCTION F10
RETURN ( LASTKEY() = -9 )

FUNCTION F2
RETURN ( LASTKEY() = -1 )

FUNCTION F3
RETURN ( LASTKEY() = -2 )

FUNCTION F4
RETURN ( LASTKEY() = -3 )
```

```
FUNCTION F5
RETURN ( LASTKEY() = -4 )

FUNCTION F6
RETURN ( LASTKEY() = -5 )

FUNCTION F7
RETURN ( LASTKEY() = -6 )

FUNCTION F8
RETURN ( LASTKEY() = -7 )

FUNCTION F9
RETURN ( LASTKEY() = -8 )
```

SHIFT F-KEYS

```
FUNCTION SH_F1
RETURN ( LASTKEY() = -10 )

FUNCTION SH_F2
RETURN ( LASTKEY() = -11 )

FUNCTION SH_F10
RETURN ( LASTKEY() = -19 )

FUNCTION SH_F2
RETURN ( LASTKEY() = -11 )
```

```
FUNCTION SH_F3
RETURN ( LASTKEY() = -12 )

FUNCTION SH_F4
RETURN ( LASTKEY() = -13 )

FUNCTION SH_F4
RETURN ( LASTKEY() = -13 )

FUNCTION SH_F5
RETURN ( LASTKEY() = -14 )

FUNCTION SH_F6
RETURN ( LASTKEY() = -15 )

FUNCTION SH_F7
RETURN ( LASTKEY() = -16 )

FUNCTION SH_F8
RETURN ( LASTKEY() = -17 )

FUNCTION SH_F9
RETURN ( LASTKEY() = -18 )
```

CTRL F-KEYS

```
FUNCTION CTRL_F1
RETURN ( LASTKEY() = -20 )
```

```
FUNCTION CTRL_F2
RETURN ( LASTKEY() = -21 )

FUNCTION CTRL_F3
RETURN ( LASTKEY() = -22 )

FUNCTION CTRL_F4
RETURN ( LASTKEY() = -23 )

FUNCTION CTRL_F5
RETURN ( LASTKEY() = -24 )

FUNCTION CTRL_F6
RETURN ( LASTKEY() = -25 )

FUNCTION CTRL_F7
RETURN ( LASTKEY() = -26 )

FUNCTION CTRL_F8
RETURN ( LASTKEY() = -27 )

FUNCTION CTRL_F9
RETURN ( LASTKEY() = -28 )
```

ALT F-KEYS

```
FUNCTION ALT_F1
RETURN ( LASTKEY() = 30 )
```

```
FUNCTION ALT_F2
RETURN ( LASTKEY() = 31 )

FUNCTION ALT_F3
RETURN ( LASTKEY() = 32 )

FUNCTION ALT_F4
RETURN ( LASTKEY() = 33 )

FUNCTION ALT_F5
RETURN ( LASTKEY() = 34 )

FUNCTION ALT_F6
RETURN ( LASTKEY() = 35 )

FUNCTION ALT_F7
RETURN ( LASTKEY() = 36 )

FUNCTION ALT_F8
RETURN ( LASTKEY() = 37 )

FUNCTION ALT_F9
RETURN ( LASTKEY() = 38 )

FUNCTION ALT_F10
RETURN ( LASTKEY() = 39 )
```

ALT ALPHA KEYS

```
FUNCTION ALT_A
RETURN ( LASTKEY() = 286 )

FUNCTION ALT_B
RETURN ( LASTKEY() = 304 )

FUNCTION ALT_D
RETURN ( LASTKEY() = 288 )

FUNCTION ALT_E
RETURN ( LASTKEY() = 274 )

FUNCTION ALT_F
RETURN ( LASTKEY() = 289 )

FUNCTION ALT_G
RETURN ( LASTKEY() = 290 )

FUNCTION ALT_H
RETURN ( LASTKEY() = 291 )

FUNCTION ALT_I
RETURN ( LASTKEY() = 279 )

FUNCTION ALT_J
RETURN ( LASTKEY() = 292 )
```

```
FUNCTION ALT_K
RETURN ( LASTKEY() = 293 )

FUNCTION ALT_L
RETURN ( LASTKEY() = 291 )

FUNCTION ALT_M
RETURN ( LASTKEY() = 306 )

FUNCTION ALT_N
RETURN ( LASTKEY() = 305 )

FUNCTION ALT_O
RETURN ( LASTKEY() = 280 )

FUNCTION ALT_P
RETURN ( LASTKEY() = 281 )

FUNCTION ALT_Q
RETURN ( LASTKEY() = 272 )

FUNCTION ALT_R
RETURN ( LASTKEY() = 275 )

FUNCTION ALT_S
RETURN ( LASTKEY() = 287 )

FUNCTION ALT_T
RETURN ( LASTKEY() = 276 )
```

```
FUNCTION ALT_U
RETURN ( LASTKEY() = 278 )

FUNCTION ALT_V
RETURN ( LASTKEY() = 303 )

FUNCTION ALT_W
RETURN ( LASTKEY() = 273 )

FUNCTION ALT_X
RETURN ( LASTKEY() = 301 )

FUNCTION ALT_Y
RETURN ( LASTKEY() = 277 )

FUNCTION ALT_Z
RETURN ( LASTKEY() = 300 )
```

CTRL ALPHA KEYS

```
FUNCTION CTRL_A
RETURN ( LASTKEY() = 1 )

FUNCTION CTRL_B
RETURN ( LASTKEY() = 2 )

FUNCTION CTRL_C
RETURN ( LASTKEY() = 3 )
```

```
FUNCTION CTRL_D
RETURN ( LASTKEY() = 4 )

FUNCTION CTRL_E
RETURN ( LASTKEY() = 5 )

FUNCTION CTRL_F
RETURN ( LASTKEY() = 6 )

FUNCTION CTRL_G
RETURN ( LASTKEY() = 7 )

FUNCTION CTRL_H
RETURN ( LASTKEY() = 8 )

FUNCTION CTRL_I
RETURN ( LASTKEY() = 9 )

FUNCTION CTRL_J
RETURN ( LASTKEY() = 10 )

FUNCTION CTRL_K
RETURN ( LASTKEY() = 11 )

FUNCTION CTRL_L
RETURN ( LASTKEY() = 12  )

FUNCTION CTRL_M
RETURN ( LASTKEY() = 13  )
```

```
FUNCTION CTRL_N
RETURN ( LASTKEY() = 14 )

FUNCTION CTRL_O
RETURN ( LASTKEY() = 15  )

FUNCTION CTRL_P
RETURN ( LASTKEY() = 16  )

FUNCTION CTRL_Q
RETURN ( LASTKEY() = 17  )

FUNCTION CTRL_R
RETURN ( LASTKEY() = 18  )

FUNCTION CTRL_S
RETURN ( LASTKEY() = 19 )

FUNCTION CTRL_T
RETURN ( LASTKEY() = 20  )

FUNCTION CTRL_U
RETURN ( LASTKEY() = 21 )

FUNCTION CTRL_V
RETURN ( LASTKEY() = 22  )

FUNCTION CTRL_W
RETURN ( LASTKEY() = 23 )
```

```
FUNCTION CTRL_X
RETURN ( LASTKEY() = 24 )

FUNCTION CTRL_Y
RETURN ( LASTKEY() = 25 )

FUNCTION CTRL_Z
RETURN ( LASTKEY() = 26 )
```

RELATIVE KEYS

```
FUNCTION DEL_KEY
RETURN ( LASTKEY() = del_key )

FUNCTION ADD_KEY
RETURN ( LASTKEY() = add_key )

FUNCTION PRN_KEY
RETURN ( LASTKEY() = prn_key )

FUNCTION PRV_KEY
RETURN ( LASTKEY() = prv_key )

FUNCTION QRY_KEY
RETURN ( LASTKEY() = qbe_key )

FUNCTION SEEK_KEY
RETURN ( LASTKEY() = seek_key )
```

```
FUNCTION TOP_KEY
RETURN ( LASTKEY() = top_key )

FUNCTION UPD_KEY
RETURN ( LASTKEY() = upd_key )

FUNCTION ZOOM_KEY
RETURN ( LASTKEY() = zoom_key )

FUNCTION LST_KEY
RETURN ( LASTKEY() = lst_key )

FUNCTION BOT_KEY
RETURN ( LASTKEY() = bot_key )

FUNCTION MEMO_KEY
RETURN ( LASTKEY() = memo_key )
```

Index

B

C

E

F

G

H

K

L

M

N

O

P

Q

R

S

T

U

V

W

X